# BUSINESS PROCESS TRANSFORMATION

# BUSINESS PROCESS TRANSFORMATION

VARUN GROVER
M. LYNNE MARKUS
EDITORS

ADVANCES IN MANAGEMENT
INFORMATION SYSTEMS
VLADIMIR ZWASS SERIES EDITOR

Routledge
Taylor & Francis Group

LONDON AND NEW YORK

First published 2008 by M.E. Sharpe

Published 2015 by Routledge

2 Park Square, Milton Park, Abingdon, Oxon OX14 4RN
711 Third Avenue, New York, NY 10017, USA

*Routledge is an imprint of the Taylor & Francis Group, an informa business*

First issued in paperback 2016

**Library of Congress Cataloging-in-Publication Data**

References to the AMIS papers should be as follows:

Melão, N., and Pidd, M. Business processes: Four perspectives. V. Grover and M. L. Markus, eds., *Business Process Transformation. Advances in Management Information Systems.* Volume 9 (Armonk, NY: M.E. Sharpe, 2008), 41–66.

ISBN  978-0-7656-1191-8  (hbk)
ISBN  978-1-138-67971-9  (pbk)

## ADVANCES IN MANAGEMENT INFORMATION SYSTEMS

AMIS Vol. 1: Richard Y. Wang, Elizabeth M. Pierce,
Stuart E. Madnick, and Craig W. Fisher
*Information Quality*
ISBN  978–0-7656–1133–8

AMIS Vol. 2: Sergio deCesare, Mark Lycett, and
Robert D. Macredie
*Development of Component-Based Information Systems*
ISBN  978–0-7656–1248–9

AMIS Vol. 3: Jerry Fjermestad and Nicholas
C. Romano, Jr.
*Electronic Customer Relationship Management*
ISBN  978–0-7656–1327-1

AMIS Vol. 4: Michael J. Shaw
*E-Commerce and the Digital Economy*
ISBN  978–0-7656–1150-5

AMIS Vol. 5: Ping Zhang and Dennis Galletta
*Human-Computer Interaction and Management
Information Systems: Foundations*
ISBN  978–0-7656–1486–5

AMIS Vol. 6: Dennis Galletta and Ping Zhang
*Human-Computer Interaction and Management
Information Systems: Applications*
ISBN  978–0-7656–1487–2

AMIS Vol. 7: Murugan Anandarajan, Thompson S.H.
Teo, and Claire A. Simmers
*The Internet and Workplace Transformation*
ISBN  978–0-7656–1445–2

AMIS Vol. 8: Suzanne Rivard and Benoit Aubert
*Information Systems Sourcing*
ISBN  978–0-7656–1685–2

AMIS Vol. 9: Varun Grover and M. Lynne Markus
*Business Process Transformation*
ISBN  978–0-7656–1191–8

AMIS Vol. 10: Panos E. Kourouthanassis and George
M. Giaglis
*Pervasive Information Systems*
ISBN  978–0-7656–1689–0

AMIS Vol. 11: Detmar W. Straub, Seymour Goodman,
and Richard Baskerville
*Information Security Policy and Practices*
ISBN  978–0-7656–1718–7

AMIS Vol. 12: Irma Becerra-Fernandez and Dorothy
Leidner
*Knowledge Management: An Evolutionary View*
ISBN  978–0-7656–1637–1

Editor in Chief, Vladimir Zwass (zwass@fdu.edu)

# CONTENTS

## Part IV. Transformation Across a Spectrum of Business Processes

## Part V. Success and Failure in Business Process Transformation

## Part VI. Trends and Challenges in Transforming Business Processes

# SERIES EDITOR'S INTRODUCTION

VLADIMIR ZWASS, EDITOR-IN-CHIEF

Business process is a set of related activities through which an organization accomplishes a specific outcome. Processes are a way of organizing work. The goodness of a process's outcome, and the resources consumed in producing that outcome, can be evaluated, and the process improved or reformed. Organizations may, to a degree, be understood and managed as systems of interrelated processes. Some of the business processes deliver value directly to the external customers, and the effectiveness of such processes determines the very existence of the customers (and, hence, of the firm). Other processes serve the "internal customers," who also work for the firm, and the effectiveness of such processes may be less transparent. All processes use resources, notably, people's time and effort, as well as capital and equipment. The efficiency of this use in the effective delivery of the process outcomes is of importance to the enterprise's bottom line. By transforming business processes toward higher performance levels, we can transform the firm.

This is, of course, not the whole story. The proper identification of processes, the interactions among them, and the process-evaluation criteria are key elements. It is the people who make the processes succeed or fail, and radical process transformations have frequently failed precisely because the "people element" was not treated properly. The implementation of a process change is far from simple. Beyond that, a firm is not a mechanistic system of processes. Organizational learning and continuing innovation, so necessary in the highly competitive business environment of the recent decades, have to be fostered across the process boundaries and in the firm as a whole.

Information is the lifeblood of modern enterprise, in carrying out its own processes, in interacting with the value webs of collaborating firms, and in delivering the products to the customers. Indeed, these products are ever more frequently either information products or have a high information content. The processes deal decreasingly with physical handling, such as machining or transportation of physical products, and increasingly with information and knowledge. Take the "process customer order" as a sample process. The tracking of shipments that have to be delivered within a short time window to a just-in-time customer is ever more valuable as compared to the actual movement of the goods—that is, information. The market knowledge that is necessary to organize a modern marketing campaign and the digitized product knowledge that is necessary to develop a new model of an airliner by relying on electronic prototyping are further examples. Information systems (IS) are, therefore, the crucial enablers of business processes; indeed, major new technologies modify the envelope of the possible in business process design.

As much of organizations' functioning is increasingly seen as systems of business processes, the development of organizations, their seeking of higher performance levels and of competitive advantage, is predicated upon successful business process transformation (BPT). With information technology (IT) as a key resource of the business processes and of their interaction within and across the organizational boundaries, the relationship between IS built around IT and BPT is as intimate as it is complex. This relationship is the subject of this AMIS volume.

Varun Grover and M. Lynne Markus are *the* people to edit the volume. They bring to the table a vast storehouse of experience in action-oriented research and scholarship in BPT. Reading their introductory chapter, where they offer their scholars' travelogues in helping organizations to conceptualize IT-supported BPT and to take full advantage of its possibilities, will be highly instructive. Before you do that, you will have the opportunity to read a substantive introduction by Thomas H. Davenport, who indeed needs no introduction—as he has done more in making BPT effective throughout the world than any other individual. The volume's concept is to bring in new results from the most outstanding authors in the field, and to reflect on their key work in the domain.

The conceptualization and understanding of organizations as systems of business processes is an important advance. It furthers accountability, as business processes have ownership and can be judged by specific criteria in delivering their outputs. It permits the design of business processes to serve as the means of the overall organizational design. It further becomes a means to organizational transformation, both incremental and fundamental, through BPT. Theoretical means can be deployed in this analytical and practical work. These include the coordination theory, discussed and exemplified here by Kevin Crowston, and presented, for example, by Malone et al. (1999), and RPV theory (Christensen et al., 2004). Process-level performance can be analyzed and linked to the economic performance of the firm (Davamanirajan et al., 2006). IT can be deployed to monitor and control the supply-chain processes on the event level (Bodendorf and Zimmermann, 2005). Let me stress once again that the path to positive outcomes is far from simple and direct. It has been determined, for example, that the differentiating effects of IT on such a process as customer service are conditioned on socially complex resources that have to be nourished by a firm: in other words, the human and technological resources have to be combined in a firm-specific manner (Ray et al., 2005).

In the environment of globally spread competition and cooperation, interorganizational processes require particular attention, owing to their complexity, the diversity of human resources and management practices, and the dispersion of ownership. Yet the networks of such processes provide the necessary—and sometimes rapid—access to the capabilities possessed by various firms (Hagel and Brown, 2005). With the proliferation of Web use, active participation of consumers in creating marketable value is gaining in importance. To garner the benefits of this coproduction with consumers and smaller firms, Procter & Gamble has created an innovation process that identifies the potential extramural innovators, connects them with the corporate R&D departments, and develops the innovation into a marketable value (Huston and Sakkab, 2006). The process has clearly defined objectives, inputs, procedures, and outcomes—as well as performance metrics.

Two major developmental directions present themselves in the design and transformation of organizations along the business process lines. By their very nature, processes imply routinized patterns of work and organizational behavior. An important direction of research and practice leads, therefore, to standardization, algorithmization, and, in effect, digitization of many processes. As a result, commodity processes would emerge (Davenport, 2005). They could be supported by reusable software components (Janssen and Wagenaar, 2005). As new standardized IT also emerges, opportunities for rapid configuration of processes, in many cases with mixed corporate ownership, are created. Thus, service-oriented architectures enable the identification of software components (such as Web services) to rapidly configure a process targeted at a specific market opportunity (Cherbakov et al., 2005). The process-oriented approach enabled by such IT helps in the "on-demand" targeting of an opportunity or a problem.

However, as Mary J. Benner and Michael Tushman argue in this volume, organizations need to carefully balance the exploitation of established methods with exploration and innovation. The turbulence of the contemporary business environment requires the combination of routine processes with the experimenting ones. Dual IS that would support such processes have been proposed (Kakola and Koota, 1999). The papers of this AMIS volume will make clear that a successful BPT is a complex enterprise, as it combines the search for organizational efficiency with the sensitivity to nourishing organizational knowledge and innovation.

## REFERENCES

Bodendorf, F., and Zimmermann, R. 2005. Proactive supply-chain event management with agent technology. *International Journal of Electronic Commerce,* 9, 4 (Summer), 57–89.

Cherbakov, L.; Galambos, G.; Harishankar, R.; Kalyana, S.; and Rackham, G. 2005. Impact of service orientation on the business level. *IBM Systems Journal,* 44, 4, 653–668.

Christensen, C.M.; Anthony, S.D.; and Roth, E.A. 2004. *Seeing What's Next: Using the Theories of Innovation to Predict Industrial Change.* Boston: Harvard Business School Press.

Davamanirajan, P.; Kauffman, R.J.; Kriebel, C.H.; and Mukhopadhyay, T. 2006. Systems design, process performance, and economic outcomes in international banking. *Journal of Management Information Systems,* 23, 2 (Fall), 67–92.

Davenport, T.H. 2005. The coming commoditization of processes. *Harvard Business Review,* 83, 6 (June), 101–108.

Hagel, J., III, and Brown, J.S. 2005. *The Only Sustainable Edge: Why Business Strategy Depends on Productive Friction and Dynamic Specialization.* Boston: Harvard Business School Press.

Huston, L., and Sakkab, N. 2006. Connect and develop: Inside Procter & Gamble's new model for innovation. *Harvard Business Review,* 84, 3 (March), 58–66.

Janssen, M., and Wagenaar, R.W. 2005. Business engineering of component-based systems. In S. de Cesare, M. Lycett, and R.D. Macredie (eds.), *Development of Component-Based Information Systems. Advances in Management Information Systems.* Volume 2. Armonk, NY: M.E. Sharpe, pp. 166–186.

Kakola, T.K., and Koota, K.I. 1999. Redesigning computer-supported work processes with dual information systems: The work process benchmarking service. *Journal of Management Information Systems,* 16, 1 (Summer), 87–120.

Malone, T.W.; Crowston, K.G.; Lee, J.; Pentland, B.; Dellarocas, C.; Wyner, G.; Quimby, J.; Osborn, C.S.; Bernstein, A.; Herman, G.; Klein, M.; and O'Donnell, E. 1999. Tools for inventing organizations: Toward a handbook of organizational processes. *Management Science,* 45, 3 (March), 425–443.

Ray, G.; Muhanna, W.A.; and Barney, J.B. 2005. Information technology and the performance of the customer service process: A resource-based analysis. *MIS Quarterly,* 29, 4 (December), 625–652.

# FOREWORD

## Thomas H. Davenport

Business processes have been a focus of the information technology (IT) community since its early history. I once stumbled upon an old Boston newspaper from the 1960s, for example, and looked through the classifieds section at the job advertisements. Two ads noted that the companies that had placed them were looking for candidates who could first redesign processes (actually, they called them "office procedures") before building information systems to support them. I then perused old IT-oriented textbooks from the same period, and they confirmed that the relationship between processes and IT had been a concern of IT professionals from the beginning.

One might imagine, then, that most of the concerns about IT and processes would be largely addressed by now, and that there would be no reason for a book like this one to further elucidate the subject. Fortunately (for those who have already bought this book) or unfortunately (for the world at large), that is not the case. There are still many unresolved issues at the intersection of process and technology, and many organizations continue to find their alignment challenging.

In order to further persuade you of the need for this tome, I will go through a brief history of the process management movement with regard to IT. This overview is much more basic than any of the chapters in the book that follow—they are leading edge, whereas this is background.

### A BRIEF HISTORY OF BUSINESS PROCESS MANAGEMENT FROM AN IT PERSPECTIVE

The idea that work can be viewed as a process, and then improved, is hardly new. It dates at least to Frederick Taylor at the beginning of the twentieth century, and probably before. Taylor and his colleagues developed modern industrial engineering and process improvement, though the techniques were restricted to manual labor and production processes. The "clipboard and stopwatch" techniques were rarely applied to office work and certainly not to the relatively small amount of knowledge work at the time. The Taylorist approaches were widely practiced in the early 1900s, but were largely forgotten by mid-century. Of course, Taylor and his followers had no inkling of IT, and would not even have considered such primitive forms of it as file cabinets and multipart forms, as the process analyses were almost exclusively focused on manufacturing.

The next great addition to process management was created by the combination of Taylorist process improvement and statistical process control. These ideas were advanced by Shewart,

Deming, Juran, and others beginning in the late 1940s and continuing into the early 1980s. Their version of process management involved measuring and limiting process variation, using continuous rather than episodic improvement, and empowering workers to improve their own processes. IT began in the 1960s and 1970s to be used to generate and manage some of the data used in statistical process control, but it was never a primary focus of the discipline.

Japanese firms had both the business need—recovering from war and building global markets—and the discipline to put continuous improvement programs in place. Toyota, in particular, took these approaches and turned them into a distinctive advance in process management. The "Toyota Production System" (TPS) combined statistical process control with continuous learning by decentralized work teams, a "pull" approach to manufacturing that minimized waste and inventory, and treated every small improvement in processes as an experiment to be designed, measured, and learned from. Again, however, sophisticated IT was never a driver of the TPS approach, and it still is not today. Toyota prided itself on the technological simplicity of the TPS, using, for example, paper tags attached to parts on a production line that signified the need to reorder. A somewhat less stringent approach to the TPS is present in the "lean" techniques that many American firms have recently adopted, though these also do not involve IT in any way other than to generate basic data.

The next major variation on business process management (BPM)—and the first to use IT as a major enabler of process change—took place in the 1990s, when many Western firms were facing an economic recession and strong competition from global competitors, particularly Japanese firms. Business process reengineering added to the generic set of process management ideas several new approaches:

- the radical (rather than incremental) redesign and improvement of work;
- attacking broad, cross-functional business processes;
- "stretch" goals of order-of-magnitude improvement; and
- use of IT as an enabler of new ways of working.

Reengineering was also the first process management movement to focus primarily on nonproduction: white-collar processes such as order management and customer service, which were heavily dependent upon IT. It did not emphasize statistical process control or continuous improvement. Many firms in the United States and Europe undertook reengineering projects, but most proved to be overly ambitious and difficult to implement. The IT capabilities that accompanied new process designs were often particularly daunting. Companies embarked upon reengineering because they wanted radical and rapid improvements, but in many cases, they discovered that it would take several years to build or implement all of the new IT applications to support new process designs. Reengineering first degenerated into a more respectable word for head count reductions, and then became substantially less popular.

However, the urge to unite IT and business processes in an integrated fashion did not disappear. In part, because of the difficulties in creating new systems during reengineering projects, many companies turned to enterprise resource planning (ERP) or enterprise systems (ES) in the mid-to-late 1990s, when they were also attempting to address the Y2K issue. Complex ES packages such as those from SAP and Oracle combined substantial IT support for cross-functional business processes and "best-practice" process designs embedded into system configurations. Many firms found it easier to adapt their business processes to their ERP system than to modify the system to suit their idiosyncratic process designs. ERP systems, then, contributed both to firms taking a process orientation and then to the adoption of common processes across industries.

The most recent process management enthusiasm has revolved around "Six Sigma," an approach created at Motorola in the 1980s and popularized by General Electric in the 1990s. In some ways, Six Sigma represents a return to statistical process control; the term *six sigma* means one output defect in six standard deviations of a probability distribution for a particular process output. Six Sigma also typically involves a return to focusing on relatively small work processes and presumes incremental rather than radical improvement. Most frequently, however, Six Sigma improvement techniques are employed on an episodic basis, rather than continuously, and although employees are somewhat empowered to improve their own work, they are generally assisted by experts called "Black Belts." Some firms are beginning to combine Six Sigma with more radical reengineering-like approaches to processes, or with the "lean" techniques derived from the TPS. With none of these variations, however, is there a strong IT orientation.

## THE "MISSING MIDDLE"

One of the key factors preventing process management from becoming sustained and deeply embedded within organizations is the lack of a well-defined "middle" that would connect process management and IT. Process management in organizations is often a key focus at the top of the hierarchy, with senior executives advocating their favorite approaches to process and the benefits they can bring. One might be a devotee of Six Sigma, while another is convinced that reengineering is what is needed. These executives appreciate the benefits of process thinking—cost reduction in particular—but they do not often make informed choices about how one process management approach differs from the others. They certainly do not consider the relationship of IT to process management. Some executives certainly take the time to understand the different types of process interventions and why one might employ them, but it is a distinct minority.

Technologists occupy the other extreme of how organizations address process management. IT may not truly be the bottom of the organization, because IT people are well paid and can easily make it to middle management. But let's call it the bottom for the sake of contrast. IT people are also enthusiastic about process management, but in a different way. They enthuse about BPM technologies, which incorporate such attributes as work flow, decision rule automation, application integration, easier ERP configuration and implementation, and so forth. Their appreciation of process management technologies is largely for their ability to address technical problems rather than for the business benefits they provide.

If we had a middle ground of process management, then the top and the bottom could communicate and relate to each other. But often we do not and often they cannot. Senior executives do not know how technology can advance their process management movements, and IT people do not generally link the BPM tools they fancy with the latest wave of process management benefits. Executives have no idea what BPM technologies can do, and technologists have no notion of how the technologies could support, say, Six Sigma.

There are some who would argue that either the top or the bottom can stretch across the middle. Some would argue that senior executives can get heavily involved in process improvement and management initiatives, but I do not see it happening on a broad scale. They just have too many other responsibilities to delve deeply into process design and execution issues. There are also—and have been for decades—somewhat utopian technologists who argue that BPM technology (or its predecessors such as computer-aided software engineering or object-oriented systems) is going to be so simple and transparent to use that senior executives need only specify their process goals and visions, and a process-oriented IT architecture will be created through automated means. However, I am convinced that this is simply not going to happen, at least not in our lifetimes.

Process management needs a middle—the involvement of middle management, the middle ground between business and IT, the middle between the high-level process objectives and the low-level technical details.

A process management middle would not only connect process-oriented business objectives and the IT that could help accomplish them, but it would also bring a persistence and sustainability to process management. The middle could bring adherence to a long-term process orientation, regardless of the process management technique in vogue at the time. IT would be employed as a tool for sustained process management. The middle could also provide a framework for the various types and generations of BPM software to support.

It is rare to find organizations that have fully aligned process with IT, so it is difficult to know exactly what form that alignment will take. Of course, some elements of a filled-in middle are actually in place in some companies. They include the following:

- *A clear process governance and ownership structure that is linked to IT governance.* Process management will not persist in organizations unless it is clear that it is here to stay within the organizational hierarchy. IBM, for example, has had a clear process ownership structure for over a decade, and it is well integrated with the IT organization and its processes. Cisco Systems gives ownership of all IT application budgets to the owners of each major process. Still, such firms are a distinct (if growing) minority.
- *A process-oriented measurement and information architecture.* Processes will not be a salient aspect of the organizational landscape until we have well-established information about and measures for them and people begin to be evaluated and compensated on those metrics. For example, AT&T Universal Card, which is now owned by Citibank, paid daily bonuses to its workers based on whether process performance targets were achieved. The information from processes should be the core of an organization's information architecture, but it seldom is. Process designs are only one piece of the needed information; a well-filled middle would also incorporate the data and information used by a process, process benchmarks, process performance data, and so forth. A few U.S. organizations (Coors, for example) are beginning to develop this information infrastructure for processes, but it is more likely to be found in European firms.
- *An integrated process management tool kit.* Every process movement has its own tools and techniques, but it is rare to find an organization that integrates multiple types of tools from different movements—including those involving IT. Why not combine quality circles from total quality management, process value analysis from process improvement, IT enablement analysis from reengineering, and defect frequency analysis from Six Sigma? The semiconductor equipment manufacturer Teradyne has such an integrated tool kit, but they're all too unusual.

There are undoubtedly some other attributes of the process management middle, but the ones I have described would be a good start. It is possible, of course, to undertake process management without these attributes, but it will typically be a faddish activity, to be restarted from scratch when the next process movement comes along. That is just what most organizations have been doing, and it is the reason why we have not made the progress that we should have in managing processes as an ongoing aspect of business life and in using IT to support those processes. The chapters in this book illuminate some new and interesting aspects of the process–IT connection, and I suspect that organizations that pursue these leads will be well on the way to filling the missing middle.

# BUSINESS PROCESS TRANSFORMATION

# CHAPTER 1

# CONSOLIDATING KNOWLEDGE ON THE JOURNEY OF BUSINESS PROCESS TRANSFORMATION

M. LYNNE MARKUS AND VARUN GROVER

*Abstract: In this chapter, the authors trace their personal research journeys in business process transformation. Clear learning points are identified through each of the two different paths. One path focused more on theory and empirical work, whereas another was driven by practice and case studies. Despite these differences, the authors observe remarkable consistency in the themes across the two paths, particularly regarding the role of information technology and personnel. However, they also highlight significant gaps in the understanding of process representation, transformation, and alignment with other parts of the organization. The authors consolidate the knowledge from their experiences and describe the approach taken to compile this book. Gaps in knowledge are identified; the chapters in this volume are positioned as partially filling the gaps and providing a foundation for future work in business process transformation.*

*Keywords: Business Process Transformation, Process Research, Reengineering Evolution, Knowledge Gaps*

## INTRODUCTION

Today, processes represent sets of logically related tasks in which resources are deployed to achieve a specific outcome. Historically, work processes were often emergent, sporadic, unplanned, or ambiguous. In the industrial age, people began to develop systematic knowledge about how to organize machines and labor. Much of the latter half of the twentieth century was spent in designing these procedures in order to manage work and its contingencies. Herein lies the genesis of the functional hierarchy. In systems terms, the effort was in honing first-order feedback systems, where inputs, processes, and outputs were put in place and scrutinized to adhere to the requirements of a relatively static environment. Unfortunately, as the environment demanded more in terms of responsiveness and service, the systems proved woefully inadequate. Things came to a head in the early 1990s as various forces—such as highly publicized consulting programs, lack of economic benefits from information technology (IT) investments, cost-cutting pressures due to an economic downturn, and process ideas such as Kaizen and total quality management (TQM)—converged to create the bandwagon effect now called business process transformation (BPT).

Our collective bounded rationality creates problems of management attention. Fads catch attention because they hit a soft spot at the right place and right time. Such was the case for the phenomenon that swept corporations in the early 1990s and used combinations of words such as business, process, redesign, innovation, and, most commonly, reengineering. The mantra was to clean up or blow up "old processes" and put "new processes," better suited for the changing environment, in place. Early books on this topic became phenomenal best sellers. Consultants repackaged old methodologies and printed glossy brochures and charged thousands for their "proprietary" solutions to "fundamental" business problems (Hammer, 1990). Surveys of senior executives indicated that by the mid-1990s, "reengineering" was the number one initiative taken by companies to achieve strategic goals. Academics, both cynics and proponents, jumped on the bandwagon. They wrote treatises on the benefits of radical change or why they had seen it all before. Against this backdrop, business process change initiatives played a dominant role throughout the 1990s as the preeminent managerial intervention to cut cycle time, enhance customer satisfaction, and improve business performance.

Much has changed since then. New waves of initiatives have claimed managerial attention. One was enterprise resource planning (ERP) systems, which promised turnkey IT solutions to tame jungles of functional systems. The Internet offered opportunities for sharing information within and outside the firm. And the management knowledge resources became a new source of competitive advantage. Other managerial fads, magnified by the popular press, include controversial outsourcing practices, the "inevitable" service revolution, and the undeniable importance of innovation in the new economy. These waves of change pushed process reengineering to the background—some experts even prophesized its decline or imminent death.

Of course, process reengineering is not dead. Processes are always with us. We would argue that, if anything, processes and their improvement are more important than ever, because they are the essence of how work gets done. With these waves of change, the notion of business process is being *layered and morphed* with newer and richer concepts. This is exciting stuff! When we think of processes plus ERP systems, we open up provocative issues about the standardization or transfer of "best" business practices and about seamless system interfaces and modernized information architectures. When we think of processes layered with knowledge, we raise issues about how individuals, groups, and organizations can create, reuse, and leverage tacit knowledge and about how firms can cooperate to create new knowledge products. When we think of service processes, we can explore service automation, consumer behavior, and changed information flows between organizations and their customers. Business process outsourcing raises issues of process standards and business networks. Innovation processes focus attention on exploration and discovery instead of exploitation and control. Furthermore, the interactions among these ideas stimulate creative thinking about deep-seated business challenges and opportunities. Whatever it is called today, BPT or any fundamental change in business processes is richly layered with contemporary concepts that are germane to the modern enterprise and demand research attention.

## PATHWAYS TO KNOWLEDGE ABOUT BUSINESS PROCESS TRANSFORMATION

This book is intended to be a repository of cutting-edge research in the field with an emphasis on adding value to research and practice looking forward. Current research in an ongoing tradition usually focuses on knowledge gaps, and the studies we selected for this volume are no exception. They build upon a strong basis of what is already known about the subject and push it into new areas where there is less to stand on.

Consequently, in order to understand the contribution of this book, it is necessary to have a picture of what has come before. The approach we take here is to share with you our own research journeys in the BPT space over a number of years (Bashein et al., 1994; Grover et al., 1993). As we describe our independent knowledge-seeking pathways, we do not mean to belittle the contributions of our numerous collaborators and our interactions (in person and virtual) with many other scholars dealing with similar issues. We also do not mean to imply that our paths have arrived at inevitable and immutable truths. Rather, the paths are our attempts to explain "where we are coming from" in putting together this volume and to highlight the knowledge gaps that book chapters help to fill.

## THE GROVER PATH

A number of my (and colleagues') studies were funded by a grant from the Center for International Business Education and Research (CIBER) and the U.S. Department of Education. Our thinking evolved from conceptual to empirical with more granular examination of models pertaining to process transformation. Below, I trace this evolution by highlighting "learning points" for various project clusters.

Our early exploration of business process reengineering (BPR) was done inductively. In the early 1990s, the primary emphasis was on crystallizing definitions, concepts, and constructs that would form the useful vocabulary for BPR. We reviewed copious cases and anecdotes of organizational initiatives. Our early frameworks induced BPR to be a top-down initiative that required integrated direction from both corporate and IT strategic planning. We also believed that successful BPR needed an innovative organizational environment to support and accept such change. We recognized the adaptive relationship between BPR and IT infrastructure, needed for successful implementation. And we also indicated the importance of the continuous search for process improvement opportunities, facilitated by structural overlays in an innovative environment (Grover et al., 1993; Teng et al., 1994b).

> *Learning Point:* BPR requires an organization-wide integrated approach where strategy, IT, and an innovative environment need to be aligned. Acceptance and continuous assessment of process change are nurtured through an innovative environment.

Our first empirical work examined structural and process risks in BPR, where the former indicates the scope of change from intrafunctional to interorganizational, and the latter, the extent of change, from incremental to radical. We found that the most prevalent projects were either high risk/reward or low risk/reward, with interfunctional projects generating the greatest satisfaction among their participants (Fiedler et al., 1994). In a related study, we found that the tight IT-strategy integration in the firm played a mediating role between the extent of interfunctional and interorganizational BPR and its perceived success. Such a relationship did not hold true for intrafunctional BPR, suggesting more piecemeal approaches involving local IT at this level (Grover et al., 1994). In another study, we examined businesses with low-cost and differentiation strategies and found evidence that firms pursuing greater low-cost orientation engaged in more interfunctional BPR and information systems (IS)–strategy integration strengthened this relationship (Grover, Teng, and Fiedler, 1995).

> *Learning Point:* Cross-functional and cross-organizational projects benefit from an alignment of business strategy with IT. Low-cost-oriented businesses streamline cross-functional processes, and alignment of IT strategy with the cost orientation also helps.

In exploring the specific role of IT in BPR, we proposed a framework that describes processes in terms of their degree of physical coupling and information coupling. Physical coupling of inputs and outputs reflects a serial pattern, where the process consists of a large number of sequential steps performed by different functions. An example of this pattern can often be found in business expense processing that requires many layers of management approvals, auditor evaluation, filing of receipts, and so on. At the other extreme is the parallel pattern, where several functions contribute *directly* to the process outcome without intermediate steps. For example, both the manufacturing function and the advertising function are involved in the process of launching a new product, but the advertising function need not physically possess the product inventory or obtain authorization from the production function in order to advertise the product. Between these two extremes, there can be a mixture of both serial and parallel patterns representing diverse types of physical coupling between inputs and outputs of a process. In addition to, and sometimes instead of, relying on tangible input–output to orchestrate their activities, various functions involved in a process may collaborate with each other through information exchange to make mutual adjustments. The frequency and intensity of information exchange between two functions, termed *information coupling,* can range from none (completely insulated) to extensive (highly collaborative). We illustrate two sets of enablers that can transform processes—IT and organizational. The reduction of physical coupling in process reconfiguration may be enabled through the application of shared computing resources such as databases and imaging. With direct access to shared data and knowledge, various functions can participate in a reengineered process in a parallel fashion. The enhancement of information coupling is primarily enabled by the application of telecommunication technologies, such as a local area network and a variety of office systems products under the rubric of "groupware." Application of these technologies may greatly improve communication and collaboration between different functions involved in a business process. We refer to these IT-enabled process changes as "hard" and "soft" reengineering, respectively. In addition, we argue that complementary organizational enablers, such as cross-functional teams, case managers, and process generalists, provide a powerful means of complementing the IT enablers to successfully institute reengineering (Teng et al., 1994a).

Even though the framework is fairly simple, it opened opportunities for us to study the various paths that organizations could take in implementing hard and soft reengineering. We also recognized the importance of holistic change where changes in process and technology need to be aligned with changes in strategy, structure, incentives, and empowerment. The broader implications of having more parallel-collaborative processes, drawing upon integrated IT repositories, allow broader thinking of an "information age organization" and a process model for BPR as organizational change (Teng et al., 1996).

> *Learning Point:* IT can reduce physical coupling and increase information coupling in processes. These parallel-collaborative processes have implications for structure, management, and people in progressive process-oriented enterprises.

We then turned our attention to theoretically consolidating our understanding of BPR into a theoretical framework for business process change management that defined core concepts in the change environment such as cultural readiness, learning capacity, knowledge capability, IT leveragability, and network relationship balancing. We also differentiated process management from change management and defined the various levels of outcomes achievable from process management efforts (Kettinger and Grover, 1995). An examination of a new product development process in high-technology firms yielded insights into how various functional groups need to collaborate through the various stages of the process (Malhotra et al., 1996).

Importantly, we increasingly recognized the contingent nature of reengineering and its convergence with large-scale change (Grover and Kettinger, 1995). This was reaffirmed through two studies. One was a large-scale empirical study of 105 organizations that undertook reengineering projects. A list of 64 problem areas compiled from literature on implementation and change was evaluated by informed respondents ex post. The results provided us with some fascinating patterns. Change management issues were considered to be very important and tightly tied to success. Problems that were considered low in severity were highly correlated with success. These included human resource issues and problems related to the project such as process delineation, project management, and tactical planning. Curiously, problems that were considered more severe a priori had lower correlations with success. These included issues related to technical competence and management support. This revealed further insight into the causes of reengineering failure with a necessary but not sufficient implication for technological issues, and necessary and sufficient implication for change management issues (Grover, Jeong, and Teng, 1998; Grover, Jeong, Kettinger, and Teng, 1995).

A second study involved three case studies of firms that experienced varying degrees of success with their reengineering. The theoretical framework of business process management described above was assessed by tabulating results across the various dimensions of the framework. The results indicated that the successful project tended to have facilitators across all dimensions of the framework, including the change environment, process management, and change management. The least successful project exhibited inhibitors, primarily in the areas of cultural readiness and change management (Grover and Kettinger, 2000; Guha et al., 1997).

> *Learning Point:* Business reengineering will only be successful if accompanied with the management of change, people, and the project. IT competency is not instrumental for success; however, success requires concurrent changes in a breadth of environmental and managerial facilitators.

In order to add more granularity to these findings, we further explored reengineering projects and the effort expended in seven stages of the project from identification of opportunities to process evaluation. We found that the stages of process transformation, process evaluation, and social design had the strongest relationship with success. Interestingly, greater effort expended in documentation of current processes had the weakest link with success. Also, reinforcing our earlier thinking, firms that engaged in broader changes, including roles, incentives, work flows, IT applications, structure, and so on, had greater success (Teng, Jeong, and Grover, 1998). We also examined the gaps between the attention given to change management, project management, continuous process, strategic planning, and technology management, and the attention that should have been given to these areas. Again, change and project management gaps had the strongest (negative) link with success, whereas technology management had the weakest (Grover, 1999).

> *Learning Point:* Use of consultant-based methodologies to document existing processes does not yield commensurate results. Technology management must be part of a broader change program in order to have an effect.

With the high failure rate of reengineering projects, we also expanded our empirical work to examine "initial conditions" for reengineering. What kind of environment would facilitate fundamental process change? Through a survey of 313 organizations, we determined that firms that have a functional orientation, with minimum IT-based or direct interaction between departments, that view IS as a support function or a utility, and have minimal experience in computing, particularly flexible cooperative computing, have a low readiness for BPR. Such firms would be well advised to increase their readiness for such change before undertaking it (Grover et al., 1999). However, further study reinforces earlier findings that IT is not instrumental for success, but the broader strategic role of IS and organic (innovation facilitating) structures is (Teng, Fiedler, and Grover, 1998).

   *Learning Point:* Organic structures that facilitate innovation and recognition of the broader strategic role of IS are important for both readiness for reengineering and its successful implementation.

   Finally, our research fragmented into areas tied to process change, but with the primary goal of examining the role and impact of IT initiatives. For instance, we examined the importance of process change in realizing productivity value from a variety of different IT (Grover, Teng, Segars, and Fiedler, 1998). We also studied how IT-based market transformations do not always work in the best interest of buyers (Grover and Ramanlal, 1999; Grover and Segars, 1999), processes pertaining to the management of knowledge (Grover and Davenport, 2001), the role of IT in creating process, and knowledge options that could lead to agile responses in a hypercompetitive environment (Sambamurthy et al., 2003), and the role of interorganizational systems on process efficiency (Saeed et al., 2005).

## THE MARKUS PATH

The Markus path runs somewhat parallel to the Grover path in the sense that there are shared themes and conclusions. At the same time, it runs some distance away from the Grover path, because the key driver for the Markus research was practice. Much of my (and colleagues') work related to BPT was funded by industry, and the explicit goals of the work included making actionable recommendations for change.

   The first study, and the only one directed explicitly toward BPR, was funded by the Advanced Practices Council of the Society for Information Management (SIM). The goal was to identify effective organizational change management practices associated with IT-enabled BPR projects. This study was based on the premise, captured in one of Grover's learning points, that organizational change management is central in BPR success.

   For me, the most interesting finding of this work was that IT professionals were often marginalized in BPR projects by their executives, by the external consultants hired by executives to lead the projects, or by both (Bashein et al., 1994). This observation led to an examination of the attitudes and behaviors of IT professionals that contribute to, or detract from, IT professionals' credibility in the eyes of general managers and users. We found that IT professionals often believe their technical expertise gives them all the credibility they need to do their jobs effectively. Business managers, however, tend to attribute both credibility and expertise only to IT professionals with whom they have good working relationships (Bashein and Markus, 1997).

   *Learning Point:* IT professionals have much to contribute to BPT. Sometimes, however, they do not have the credibility they need to make effective contributions. Greater credibility comes not only from technical expertise but also from interpersonal relationships and helping behaviors.

In later work, a colleague and I identified three different role orientations that IT professionals could adopt with respect to major IT-enabled change initiatives such as BPR (Markus and Benjamin, 1996): (1) a technocratic role orientation that centers on the system-building role and the belief that technology drives organizational change, (2) a facilitator role that emphasizes executive involvement and user participation to create buy-in and to elicit valid information about requirements, and (3) a political advocacy role that focuses on coalition building and incentive alignment. None of these roles is appropriate in every situation, and behavioral flexibility—the ability to shift from one orientation to another as circumstances demand—is likely to promote greater personal effectiveness and project success than any one role alone. However, many IT professionals are most comfortable in the technocratic role, and organizational structures and the expectations of colleagues and superiors help to confine IT professionals to the technocratic role.

In a parallel investigation, another colleague and I delved deeper into the conditions that might lead to the exclusion (or even expulsion) of IT professionals from BPR projects (Markus and Robey, 1995). We looked at the literature on other types of organizational staff professionals, such as manufacturing systems engineers and industrial engineers. We found that they, too, were often perceived negatively by business managers, because they sometimes behaved in ways that *hindered* organizational change despite expectations that their role was to *promote* change. We argued that the explanation for this behavior lies in staff professionals' excessively functional (e.g., technocratic) orientation to their roles. Even though BPR is about changing business processes to promote greater cross-functional integration, staff professionals such as IT professionals and human resource specialists often try to approach these efforts by applying their functional expertise in a noncollaborative and unintegrated fashion. This puts them out of step with the goals and values of BPR. The resulting organizational conflicts often hurt the IT professionals politically as much as, or more than, they negatively affect BPR project outcomes.

> *Learning Point:* The notion that cross-functional integration improves business processes also applies to the processes of doing staff work, such as providing IS implementation support or human resources management services. In other words, these processes work best when they are cross-functionally integrated. Staff professionals who fail to work collaboratively with colleagues in other staff specialties can contribute to project failure, and they risk being excluded from major organizational projects because managers perceive them as obstructive.

A conclusion from this work was that BPT calls for new approaches, methodologies, and tools that integrate IS development processes with organizational change management techniques. In a number of studies, several colleagues and I tackled this challenge from a variety of angles. In one project, we actually applied BPR process improvement logic to the system development and implementation process and derived modest recommendations for changes in systems requirements analysis and software design (Markus and Keil, 1994).

I had a chance to develop these ideas further in the context of a "design theory" for emergent knowledge processes (Markus et al., 2002). Design theories comprise a theory about the solution to a particular design problem, plus a theory about how to produce such a solution. Knowledge processes differ from operational and decisional processes in important ways, and emergent processes have even more challenging characteristics. Consequently, we argued, they require a new design theory, which we illustrated with the story of an unusual system designed to support an ad hoc knowledge process about which few professionals care to develop or seek expertise.

In a later paper, I differentiated the type of IT-enabled organizational change management needed in BPT initiatives from simpler "IT projects" and "organizational change programs." I referred to the more challenging initiatives as "technochange" projects—for IT-driven *organizational change* (Markus, 2004). I argued that technochange projects require a different approach, because they involve making near simultaneous and aligned changes in both technology and organization. Existing approaches and methodology do not support the development of combined solutions in which technical and organizational changes are optimally aligned. Thus, new thinking is needed about both how to do BPT and what effectively redesigned systems/processes/organization factors should look like.

User participation or involvement is an important concept both in system development and organizational change. As we try to fuse these two processes for more effective BPT, it becomes useful to review this familiar concept. Doing so led us to develop a new conceptual framework that bridges the gap between IS development and IS implementation (Markus and Mao, 2004). The key is to design participatory processes in a way that will ensure that the system designed has attributes that will facilitate system implementation.

> *Learning Point:* Because successful BPT requires redesigns in which IT, business processes, and other organizational elements are aligned and jointly optimized, new methodologies and tools are needed to bridge gaps between the processes and practices of IS development and organizational change. Although some progress has been made in this direction, much more work needs to be done to create a truly cross-functional approach to the design and implementation of business processes.

As organizations gained more experience with BPR, it became clear that IT was not only a potential enabler of BPR but it was also a potential constraint on successful BPR. Any number of organizations had to abandon or delay their change plans because their IT environments were not flexible enough to support redesigned business processes. As the Y2K problem began to capture managerial attention, managers realized that they would have to overhaul their IT infrastructures. ERP packages with best business practices "built in" promised to solve two problems at once—system modernization and process improvement. Thus, process reengineering took a backseat to ERP package implementation, and my research interests shifted to the ERP systems domain.

With colleagues, I began a stream of research on ERP system implementations, funded by Baan Research—a division of a then-leading ERP vendor—and the Financial Executives Research Foundation. Through this research, we learned that ERP systems solved neither the problem of systems modernization nor that of process improvement easily. However, ERP systems certainly reinforced the idea that the two issues go hand in hand. Many organizations did not want to change their processes to conform to business "best practices." Other organizations could not do so without damage to strategies, business models, or industry practices. They faced the expense and risk of modifying ERP packages, which, in turn, reduced their future flexibility to adopt new software releases. Organizations that decided to change their processes while implementing ERP systems found themselves confronting simultaneously their largest-ever systems projects and their largest-ever organizational change projects (Bashein et al., 1997).

One surprising finding was that, although a major benefit claimed for ERP systems was cross-functional or enterprise-wide integration of business process and systems, organizations often did not achieve that ideal (Markus, Tanis, and van Fenema, 2000). They might have implemented only a single module of an ERP system and integrated it (or not) with their remaining legacy systems. Or they might have implemented different packages in one or several organizational units. They might even have standardized a single ERP package but implemented it differently in each organizational unit. From these observations, we learned that integration lies not in ERP software, but rather in organizational decisions about how to use the software.

> *Learning Point:* The nature and extent of IT-enabled BPT depends, in large part, on organizational decisions about how to deploy enterprise systems.

Organizations that implemented ERP systems encountered many problems (Markus, Petrie, and Axline, 2000; Markus, Axline, Petrie, and Tanis, 2000). From these experiences, we learned that, although much can go wrong during ERP configuration and implementation projects, many problems originate before these projects even start. We used the term *chartering phase* to refer to the decisions executives make (or fail to make) before projects begin—decisions about goals and metrics, schedule, scope, budget, who the project manager will be, and who is responsible for ensuring that the project delivers the desired business results (Markus and Tanis, 2000). Organizations are sometimes able to revisit and fix bad initial chartering decisions, but projects take on lives of their own, which generally inhibits successful rechartering.

> *Learning Point:* The odds of BPT success or failure are often set before projects even begin, during the "project chartering" phase. Savvy project managers owe it to themselves to (politely) challenge the charters they are given, because they will be held responsible if the project fails, regardless of why the failure occurred.

Other projects sponsored by the Financial Executives Research Foundation (Bashein and Markus, 2000) and the SIM Advanced Practices Council (Markus, 2000) allowed my research teams to continue our investigations of "enterprise integration." We learned that organizations were also using technologies and approaches other than ERP systems—including data warehousing, enterprise application integration, services-oriented architectures, and Web services—in their quest for internal business process and systems integration.

In addition, as organizations began to tame their internal integration challenges, they naturally turned (again) to the challenges of integrating systems and business processes with customers, suppliers, and other external partners (Markus et al., 2003). Extra-organizational integration began much earlier with technologies such as electronic data interchange (EDI), but the high cost and technical limitations of those technologies restricted usage to the largest organizations. Cheaper Internet technologies now offer the promise of extending electronic interconnections to many more partners and business processes.

In studies of external integration (several of which are still ongoing, funded by Bentley College, the National Science Foundation, and SIM Advanced Practices Council), it is becoming clear that change management challenges do not end at an organization's doors (Markus, 2007). However, the lack of shared hierarchical authority can make interorganizational change management problems even more challenging to address. Although many organizations try to solve these problems on their own, some organizations in a few industries have collaborated on developing industry-specific IS standards or shared IT infrastructures for business process integration (Markus et al., 2006). Much more remains to be learned about effective strategies and tactics for IT-enabled interorganizational BPT, whether the changes are initiated by single lead organizations or approached collaboratively by groups of organizations.

*Learning Point:* Interorganizational business processes represent a major new frontier for research on BPT. Successful transformation of interorganizational business process may require new integrated tools and methodologies for process analysis and change management, in addition to new systems integration technologies and interorganizational process arrangements.

## GAPS IN KNOWLEDGE ABOUT BUSINESS PROCESS TRANSFORMATION

The learning points from our separate research paths have common themes. Our perspective is admittedly parochial (i.e., based on our own research), but we believe that the consistency in the message across the different paths is interesting. We also believe that it closely parallels the broader research that has been conducted on reengineering and process transformation.

We understand that BPT requires planning and direction, and a facilitating (innovative) environment. Charting decisions need to be negotiated early. IT is important but could be a constraint if it is not flexible. It is one cog in a broad repertoire of changes that need to be made in alignment. IT personnel should not take too much of a functional focus in the conduct of change, should work collaboratively, and should cultivate relationships. IT solutions cannot be imposed by software, but require careful organizational decisions that define how process integration will work in a specific context.

However, the learning points clearly identify gaps in knowledge. We do not understand how earlier concepts of reengineering fit into the modern concepts of transformation. We do not have a fundamental understanding of how processes can be represented or transformed. Our methods and technologies for cultivating broad process changes in alignment with other parts of the organization are embryonic at best. And we lack clearly defined best practices for IT-based process transformation. Further, critical processes today involve knowledge, innovation, and are often in an interorganizational context, and the idiosyncrasies of such processes need to be studied further.

This book attempts to address these knowledge gaps. Tom Davenport's foreword sets the stage for our entire volume by arguing the need to fill the gap in process management between executive management that promotes new process initiatives such as Six Sigma and technologists who understand new technologies such as work flow management but not the business imperatives and benefits. For the chapters, we wanted work that reflected the *best thinking* in the knowledge gaps. We extensively scanned the literature base on BPT, and through numerous iterations identified articles and authors that could potentially be included in this volume. We sought authors who were on the cutting edge of thinking in important areas of BPT where knowledge was sparse. The selected authors were approached and asked to expand and refine their earlier work, based on our desire to create a milestone of knowledge in BPT that can set the tempo for future research. Some of the chapters in this volume are completely original, whereas others have their origins in previously published papers; all have been modified and updated to reflect the authors' most recent learning. The chapters went through one or more rounds of refereeing and refinement.

In Figure 1.1, we present a map of key concepts in the knowledge space, and we flag the key knowledge gaps with circled letters. Table 1.1, described below, shows how the chapters of our book link to and address the knowledge gaps.

The two chapters in Part I deal with knowledge gaps involving two fundamental concepts of BPT—reengineering and process. Gap A involves the concept of BPR. Today, the term has fallen into disuse. Our search of the literature revealed almost no recent research in which that term was used. Yet, as we scoured the literature, we identified dozens of studies that were essentially about

Figure 1.1 **Maps and Gaps of the BPT Knowledge Space**

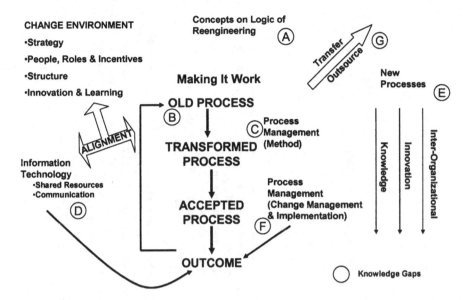

the transformation of business processes, even though those words were never used. Where did the term go and why? What replaced it and why? This knowledge gap is addressed in Chapter 2, "Whatever Happened to Business Process Reengineering? The Rise, Fall, and Possible Revival of Business Process Reengineering from the Organizing Vision Perspective" by Ping Wang. Gap B concerns our basic understanding of the concept of process itself. Many approaches to representing business processes derive, as the reengineering label implies, from engineering-oriented disciplines such as industrial engineering and IS. Do these approaches capture the essence of business processes? Are there other, fundamentally different, perspectives on business processes? And, if so, what do these perspectives reveal? These questions are tackled in Chapter 3, "Business Processes: Four Perspectives," by Nuno Melão and Michael Pidd.

Part II of the book focuses on techniques for the analysis and redesign of business processes. This section's two chapters both address knowledge Gap C, which concerns the most effective methods of process management. One set of questions related to Gap C concerns the fundamental building blocks of business processes, by which processes can be compared and contrasted in a generalizable way. In Chapter 4, Kevin Crowston addresses these issues through a discussion of coordination theory and its application to "The Bug Fixing Process in Proprietary and Free/Libre Open Source Software: A Coordination Theory Analysis." Mark E. Nissen grapples with the challenge of applying basic heuristics of process redesign by automating this knowledge in Chapter 5, "Transforming Business Process Transformation with Diagnostic Knowledge-Based Tools."

The two chapters in Part III of the book address knowledge Gap D about the role of IT in organizational change. Chapter 6, "Breaking the Functional Mind-Set: The Role of Information Technology," by Ann Majchrzak, helps to explain why IT alone does not produce the benefits expected from process change. In Chapter 7, "ERP-Enabled Business Process Reengineering: Implications from Texas Instruments," Joseph Sarkis and R.P. Sundarraj deal with the integration of process and technology.

Part IV has three chapters directed at knowledge Gap E. Chapter 8, "Redesigning IT-Enabled Customer Support Processes for Dynamic Environments," by Omar A. El Sawy, describes a knowl-

Table 1.1

**How This Book Addresses the BPT Knowledge Gaps**

| Gap Label (Figure 1.1) | Knowledge Gap | Addressing Gap | Central Questions Posed | Major Concept(s) Employed |
|---|---|---|---|---|
| | There is a process management gap between executives who initiate process transformation efforts and technologists who deploy enabling technologies. | Foreword, *Tom Davenport* | | |

Part I. Tracing Business Processes and Transformation

| Gap Label (Figure 1.1) | Knowledge Gap | Addressing Gap | Central Questions Posed | Major Concept(s) Employed |
|---|---|---|---|---|
| A | There are a number of BPR concepts that have been proposed with compelling logic for reengineering, but the term seems to have disappeared. | 2. Whatever Happened to BPR? The Rise, Fall, and Possible Revival of Business Process Reengineering from the Organizing Vision Perspective, *Ping Wang* | Where did BPR go? How the concepts of BPR get morphed with other organizing visions and where are we going with process concepts? (Knowledge, innovation, and interorganizational focus?) | Organizing visions |
| B | Much has been written about the representation of business processes, but many of these are adapted from other fields (such as industrial engineering or information systems). | 3. Business Processes: Four Perspectives, *Nuno Melão and Michael Pidd* | Are there fundamental perspectives on business processes? Can these be contrasted and complemented to get a more robust understanding of processes and consequently their process of transformation? | Deterministic machines, complex dynamic systems, interacting feedback loops and social constructs |

## Part II. Fundamental Approaches to the Analysis and Redesign of Business Processes

| | Chapter | Description | Question | Theme |
|---|---|---|---|---|
| C | 4. The Bug Fixing Process in Proprietary and Free/Libre Open Source Software: A Coordination Theory Analysis, *Kevin Crowston* | Although there has been significant focus on the "what" and "how" of business process transformation, there does not seem to be consistency across the variety of methodologies proposed. | Is there any fundamental thinking (the "why") behind process methodologies? Can processes be compared and contrasted across contexts on some fundamental basis? If so, can we develop tools that can diagnose and treat these processes in a way that is generalizable? | Coordination theory: dependencies and mechanisms |
| C | 5. Transforming Business Process Transformation with Diagnostic Knowledge-Based Tools, *Mark E. Nissen* | Most process analysis tools have graphical representations that put most of the onus on users to diagnose problems and propose solutions. The analytical methods used are unsystematic. | Can documented knowledge and heuristics be used effectively to reduce that burden? How can this knowledge be incorporated in order to facilitate practical benefits? | Process pathologies and interventions using knowledge-based tools |

## Part III. The Role of Information Technology in Organizational Change

| | Chapter | Description | Question | Theme |
|---|---|---|---|---|
| D | 6. Breaking the Functional Mind-Set: The Role of Information Technology, *Ann Majchrzak* | In theory, the role of IT in process transformation is clear, but, in practice, IT does not seem to have the purported benefits. | What needs to be considered so that IT can play a major demonstrable role in enabling successful process change? | Collective sense of responsibility |
| D | 7. ERP-Enabled BPR: Implications from Texas Instruments, *Joseph Sarkis and R.P. Sundarraj* | ERP systems with their focus on integrated solutions and best process practices are often discussed in conjunction with process change. | Is it important for ERP-type systems to be integrated with large-scale process transformation endeavors? If so, how should this integration be managed? | Alignment of process and technology |

*(continues)*

Table 1.1 (continued)

| Gap Label (Figure 1.1) | Addressing Gap | Knowledge Gap | Central Questions Posed | Major Concept(s) Employed |
|---|---|---|---|---|
| Part IV. Transformation Across a Spectrum of Business Processes | | | | |
| E | 8. Redesigning IT-Enabled Customer Support Processes for Dynamic Environments, *Omar A. El Sawy* | Work flow analysis usually takes a static efficiency–oriented focus. Little consideration has been given to learning, knowledge capture, and outcomes as part of the work flow, especially in environments that rapidly change. | How can business process transformation cope with dynamic environments that demand the need to sense and respond? Are there ways in which concepts of learning and agility can be brought together in innovative way to create IT-enabled knowledge-creating processes that facilitate rapid responsiveness to customer needs? | Customer support through adaptive learning |
| E | 9. Transforming the New Product Development Process: Leveraging and Managing Knowledge, *Anne P Massey, Mitzi M. Montoya-Weiss, and Tony M. O'Driscoll* | Most illustrations of process transformation involve primary processes, often operational, that have fairly well-defined inputs, participants, and performance-based outputs. | How can ad hoc knowledge processes that lack structure and involve a variety of disparate people be transformed? Can IT support the creative interactions required for such processes? In doing so, can knowledge be effectively captured and used? | Knowledge-intensive fuzzy front end of new product development |
| E | 10. Business Network Redesign Methodologies in Action, *Rainer Alt* | Cross-functional processes have been the primary focus of research, while most of the current action is at the interorganizational and industry network level. | Can business process transformation approaches be applied at the interorganizational level? Are integrative contemporary Web-based technologies such as portals useful in creating greater visibility across networks of customers and suppliers, thereby facilitating superior processes? | Business network redesign using process portals |

## Part V. Success and Failure in Business Process Transformation

| | | | | |
|---|---|---|---|---|
| F | Some have estimated that around 70 percent of large-scale process change initiatives fail, and yet we have piecemeal understanding of what it takes to succeed. | 11. Successful Business Process Transformation at J.D. Edwards, *Dursun Delen and Nikunj Dalal* | Are there best practices that should be considered when large-scale process and IT initiatives are undertaken? | Best practices |
| F | Success stories are often analyzed even though failure rates are high. More obvious lessons from success are published, while the hidden lessons from failure might also provide rich insights. | 12. A Case Study of BPR Failure, *Suprateek Sarker and Allen S. Lee* | What goes wrong when major process transformations fail? Are these problems apparent or hidden in politics and personal agendas? Are there general lessons to be learned from past failures that can help anticipate and mitigate such problems? | Critical problems and lessons |

## Part VI. Trends and Challenges in Transforming Business Processes

| | | | | |
|---|---|---|---|---|
| G | The incidence of business process outsourcing is increasing, but research is sparse and the governance of these arrangements remains a challenge. | 13. Transforming Human Resource Processes Through Outsourcing: Enterprise Partnership at BAE Systems, *Leslie P. Willcocks, Mary Lacity, and David Feeny* | Are there partnership models that can facilitate contradictory objectives of improving services and reducing costs? Are there lessons from successful models that can guide future business process outsourcing relationships? | Enterprise partnership |
| G | While there is significant research on innovation diffusion and software reuse, very little is known about the ability to transfer knowledge from successful process transformation projects to other parts of the enterprise. | 14. Problems in the Transfer of Reengineering Efforts: An Illustrative Case, *Sue Newell, Linda Edelman, Harry Scarbrough, Jacky Swan, and Mike Bresnen* | In order to achieve broader success of process transformation, why can't successful efforts be transferred to other parts of the enterprise? Is there something about the original context that makes transfer of best practices difficult? How can any barriers to transfer be alleviated so that knowledge gained can be reused for broader impact in the future? | Relational knowledge in process context |

*(continues)*

Table 1.1 (continued)

| Gap Label (Figure 1.1) | Knowledge Gap | Addressing Gap | Central Questions Posed | Major Concept(s) Employed |
|---|---|---|---|---|
| F | Business process transformation has its origins in the search for greater efficiency. Whether it is possible to improve efficiency without sacrificing innovation is a fundamental unanswered question. | 15. Process Management, Technological Innovation, and Organizational Adaptation, *Mary J. Benner and Michael Tushman* | Do major process change initiatives focus too much on achieving cost reduction and efficiencies? If so, are organizations losing the critical ability to undertake the major innovation, so critical to compete in the global economy? How can organizations prevent this from occurring? | Exploratory and exploitative innovations |

edge creating process and its broader implications for process management. Anne P. Massey, Mitzi M. Montoya-Weiss, and Tony M. O'Driscoll, in Chapter 9, "Transforming the New Product Development Process: Leveraging and Managing Knowledge," deal with the tricky problem of designing processes for innovation and creativity. In Chapter 10, "Business Network Redesign Methodologies in Action," Rainer Alt focuses on design methods at the interorganizational (network) level. All of these chapters emphasize contemporary IT in creating value through transformation.

The two chapters in Part V address knowledge Gap F. These chapters focus on identifying best practices in BPT implementation through studying success and failure. Chapter 11, "Successful Business Process Transformation at J.D. Edwards," by Dursun Delen and Nikunj Dalal, examines generalizable implications from a successful case, and Suprateek Sarker and Allen S. Lee study lessons learned through a failed BPT in Chapter 12, "A Case Study of BPR Failure."

In the final Part VI, two chapters address knowledge Gap G, concerning the transfer and outsourcing of process management. In Chapter 13, "Transforming Human Resource Processes Through Outsourcing: Enterprise Partnership at BAE Systems," Leslie P. Willcocks, Mary Lacity, and David Feeny examine innovative partnership models that can guide business process outsourcing relationships. Sue Newell, Linda Edelman, Harry Scarbrough, Jacky Swan, and Mike Bresnen, in Chapter 14, "Problems in the Transfer of Reengineering Efforts: An Illustrative Case," examine what it takes to transfer successful BPT to other organizations. Finally, in Chapter 15, "Process Management, Technological Innovation, and Organizational Adaptation," Mary J. Benner and Michael Tushman provide some provocative closing thoughts and caveats regarding BPT initiatives by questioning whether, even if done well, they inhibit innovativeness and what we should do about it.

In putting together these chapters, we were looking for them to have one of three key attributes—fundamental thinking, innovative directions, and implications from deep practice. Fundamental thinking involves concepts and conceptualization that form the building blocks of future work and withstand the test of time. Innovative directions involve ideas that are at the bleeding edge, still new and unrefined but worthy of greater research attention. And deep practice involves descriptions of situations that can be well contextualized and have something meaningful to say. We hope that you enjoy the book as much as we did in putting it together.

## REFERENCES

Bashein, B.J., and Markus, M.L. 1997. A credibility equation for IT specialists. *Sloan Management Review,* 38, 4 (Summer), 35–44.
———. 2000. *Data Warehouses: More Than Just Mining.* Morristown, NJ: Financial Executives Research Foundation.
Bashein, B.J.; Markus, M.L.; and Finley, J.B. 1997. *Safety Nets: Secrets of Effective Information Technology Controls.* Morristown, NJ: Financial Executives Research Foundation.
Bashein, B.J.; Markus, M.L.; and Riley, P. 1994. Preconditions for BPR success, and how to prevent failure. *Information Systems Management,* 11, 2 (Spring), 7–13.
Fiedler, K.D.; Grover, V.; and Teng, J.T.C. 1994. Information technology–enabled change: The risks and rewards of business process redesign and automation. *Journal of Information Technology,* 9, 267–275.
Grover, V. 1999. From business reengineering to business process change management: A longitudinal study of trends and practices. *IEEE Transactions on Engineering Management,* 46, 1, 36–46.
Grover, V., and Davenport, T.H. 2001. General perspectives on knowledge management: Fostering a research agenda. *Journal of Management Information Systems,* 18, 1 (Summer), 5–23.
Grover, V., and Kettinger, W.R. 1995. *Business Process Change: Concepts, Methods and Technologies.* Harrisburg, PA: Idea Group.
———. 2000. *Process Think: Winning Perspectives for Business Change in the Information Age.* Harrisburg, PA: Idea Group.

Grover, V., and Ramanlal, P. 1999. Six myths of information and markets: Information technology networks, electronic commerce, and the battle for consumer surplus. *MIS Quarterly,* 23, 4, 455–485.

Grover, V., and Segars, A.H. 1999. Electronic commerce and market transformation. *International Journal of Electronic Commerce,* 3, 4, 3–10.

Grover, V.; Fiedler, K.D.; and Teng, J.T.C. 1999. The role of organizational and information technology antecedents in reengineering initiation behavior. *Decision Sciences,* 30, 3, 749–782.

Grover, V.; Jeong, S.R.; and Teng, J.T.C. 1998. Survey of reengineering challenges. *Information Systems Management,* 15, 2, 53–59.

Grover, V.; Teng, J.T.C.; and Fiedler, K.D. 1993. Business process re-design: An integrated planning framework. *OMEGA: The International Journal of Management Science,* 21, 4, 433–447.

———. 1994. Exploring the success of information technology enabled business process reengineering. *IEEE Transactions on Engineering Management,* 41, 3, 276–284.

———. 1995. An empirical study of information technology enabled business process redesign and corporate competitive strategy. *European Journal of Information Systems,* 4, 17–30.

Grover, V.; Jeong, S.R.; Kettinger, W.J.; and Teng, J.T.C. 1995. The implementation of business process engineering. *Journal of Management Information Systems,* 12, 1, 109–144.

Grover, V.; Teng, J.T.C.; Segars, A.H.; and Fiedler, K.D. 1998. The influence of information technology diffusion and business process change on perceived productivity: The IS executive's perspective. *Information & Management,* 34, 141–159.

Guha, S.; Grover, V.; Kettinger, W.J.; and Teng, J.T.C. 1997. Exploring an antecedent model of business process change and organizational performance. *Journal of Management Information Systems,* 14, 1 (Summer), 119–155.

Hammer, M. 1990. Reengineering work: Don't automate, obliterate. *Harvard Business Review,* 68, 4 (July–August), 104–112.

Kettinger, W., and Grover, V. 1995. Toward a theory of business process change. *Journal of Management Information Systems,* 12, 1 (Summer), 9–30.

Malhotra, M.K.; Grover, V.; and Desilvio, M. 1996. Reengineering the new product development process: A framework for innovation and flexibility in high technology firms. *OMEGA,* 24, 4, 425–441.

Markus, M.L. 2000. Paradigm shifts—E-business and business/systems integration. *Communications of the AIS,* 4, 10 (November). Available at http://cais.aisnet.org (accessed June 7, 2007).

Markus, M.L. 2004. Technochange management: Using IT to drive organizational change. *Journal of Information Technology,* 19, 1 (March), 4–20.

———. 2007. Building successful interorganizational systems: IT and change management. In C.-S. Chen, J. Filipe, I. Seruca, and J. Cordeiro (eds.), *Enterprise Information Systems,* VII. Dordrect: Springer, forthcoming.

Markus, M.L., and Benjamin, R.I. 1996. Change agentry—The next IS frontier. *MIS Quarterly,* 20, 4 (December), 385–407.

Markus, M.L., and Keil, M. 1994. If we build it they will come: Designing information systems that users want to use. *Sloan Management Review,* 35, 4 (Summer), 11–25.

Markus, M.L., and Mao, J.Y. 2004. Participation in development and implementation: Updating a tired, old concept for today's IS contexts. *Journal of the AIS,* 5, 11–12 (November). Available at http://jais.aisnet.org (accessed June 7, 2007).

Markus, M.L., and Robey, D. 1995. Business process reengineering and the role of the information systems professional. In V. Grover and W. Kettinger (eds.), *Business Process Reengineering: A Strategic Approach.* Middletown, PA: Idea Group, pp. 569–589.

Markus, M.L., and Tanis, C. 2000. The enterprise systems experience—From adoption to success. In R.W. Zmud (ed.), *Framing the Domains of IT Research: Glimpsing the Future Through the Past.* Cincinnati, OH: Pinnaflex Educational Resources, pp. 173–207.

Markus, M.L.; Majchrzak, A.; and Gasser, L. 2002. A design theory for systems that support emergent knowledge processes. *MIS Quarterly,* 26, 3 (September), 179–213.

Markus, M.L.; Petrie, D.; and Axline, S. 2000. Bucking the trends: What the future may hold for ERP packages. *Information Systems Frontiers,* 2, 2 (September) 181–193.

Markus, M.L.; Tanis, C.; and van Fenema, P.C. 2000. Multisite ERP implementations. *Communications of the ACM,* 43, 3 (April), 42–46.

Markus, M.L.; Axline, S.; Edberg, D.; and Petrie, D. 2003. The future of enterprise integration: Strategic and technical issues in systems integration. In J.N. Luftman (ed.), *Competing in the Information Age: Align in the Sand,* 2d ed. Oxford: Oxford University Press, pp. 252–287.

Markus, M.L.; Axline, A.; Petrie, D.; and Tanis, C. 2000. Learning from adopters' experiences with ERP—Successes and problems. *Journal of Information Technology,* 15, 4 (December), 245–265.

Markus, M.L.; Steinfield, C.W.; Wigand, R.T.; and Minton, G. 2006. Industry-wide IS standardization as collective action: The case of the U.S. residential mortgage industry. *MIS Quarterly,* 30, 2 (June), 439–465.

Saeed, K.; Malhotra, M.; and Grover V. 2005. Examining the impact of inter-organizational systems on process efficiency and sourcing leverage in buyer–supplier dyads. *Decision Sciences,* 36, 3, 365–396.

Sambamurthy, V.; Bharadwaj, A.; and Grover, V. 2003. Strategic agility through digital options: Reconceptualization the role of IT in contemporary firms. *MIS Quarterly,* 27, 2, 237–265.

Teng, J.T.C.; Fiedler, K.D.; and Grover, V. 1998. An exploratory study of the influence of the IS function and the organizational context on business process reengineering project initiatives. *OMEGA: The International Journal of Management Science,* 26, 6, 679–698.

Teng, J.T.C.; Grover, V.; and Fiedler, K.D. 1994a. From business process reengineering to organizational transformation: Charting a strategic path for the information age. *California Management Review,* 36, 3, 9–31.

———. 1994b. Planning for information technology and business process reengineering. *Long Range Planning,* 27, 1, 95–106.

———. 1996. Developing strategic perspectives on business process reengineering: From process reconfiguration to organizational change. *OMEGA: The International Journal of Management Science,* 24, 3, 271–294.

Teng, J.T.C.; Jeong, S.R.; and Grover, V. 1998. Profile of successful reengineering projects. *Communications of the ACM,* 41, 6, 96–102.

# PART I

# TRACING BUSINESS PROCESSES AND TRANSFORMATION

# PART I

## TRACING BUSINESS PROCESS AND TRANSFORMATION

# CHAPTER 2

# WHATEVER HAPPENED TO BUSINESS PROCESS REENGINEERING?

## The Rise, Fall, and Possible Revival of Business Process Reengineering from the Organizing Vision Perspective

PING WANG

*Abstract:* *The abundance of innovative concepts in the business world and their differentiated influence on business practices make one wonder what shapes these concepts. Taking the perspective that a concept evolves as an organizing vision for applying an innovation in firms, this chapter addresses one aspect of the evolution: how does the popularity of one concept influence that of the other? Studying the discourse on business process reengineering (BPR) in the past 15 years, I found that the popularity of BPR, at different points in time, was associated with the popularity of four other concepts: total quality management (TQM), enterprise resource planning (ERP), knowledge management, and e-business. The intrinsically related contents of these concepts not only explained their correlated popularity but also revealed a moving frontier of BPR. Historically, TQM served as a comparative vision for understanding BPR, and ERP offered a means to do reengineering. More recently, as traditional focal processes such as order fulfillment and software development have already been reengineered, knowledge management and e-business have helped shift the focus to knowledge-intensive and interorganizational processes. The chapter ends with a call for more research into the process by which innovative concepts emerge and business knowledge spreads.*

*Keywords:* *Discourse, Organizing Vision, Popularity, Total Quality Management, Enterprise Resource Planning, Knowledge Management, E-Business, Business Process Reengineering*

## INTRODUCTION

Today's business world changes fast. So does the discourse—what is said and written—about business. Management scholars have recently shown increasing research interest in discourse (e.g., Boje et al., 2004; Wynn et al., 2002) not only because discourse reflects or embodies the dynamic business reality but also because discourse *constructs* the very reality (Phillips and Hardy, 2002). For instance, long aware that discourse matters, knowledge entrepreneurs such as consultants and industry pundits produce and disseminate discourse promoting an innovation (i.e., a new technique or technology) in order to prompt and extend the adoption of the innovation by firms or consumers (Abrahamson and Fairchild, 1999). In doing so, through their ongoing conversations and multiple readings of the innovation across time and place, these actors create and sustain a collective concept

(Tillquist, 2000) that describes, for example, what the innovation is, why firms should adopt it, and how to implement and benefit from it. It is through such a concept, termed an *organizing vision* by Swanson and Ramiller (1997), that discourse shapes the diffusion of innovations.

As a concept for applying an innovation in organizations, each organizing vision characterizes one type of innovation, such as quality circles, data warehouses, and customer relationship management (CRM). In the context of information technology (IT) innovations, a vision plays three functions in diffusing an innovation (Swanson and Ramiller, 1997). First, the vision addresses the uncertainties shrouding the innovation by providing an interpretation of the innovation. Second, the vision legitimates the innovation by developing the underlying rationale for it. Third, the vision helps mobilize entrepreneurial and market forces that emerge to support the material production, adoption, and utilization of the innovation. To the extent that an organizing vision successfully serves these functions, the innovation may come to be widely adopted. Considering the influential role an organizing vision plays in an innovation's diffusion, one may ask what shapes the vision itself. For instance, why do some visions become highly popular and generate voluminous discourse and others do not?

The scant empirical research on organizing visions has focused on the characteristics of particular visions. For example, Ramiller and Swanson (2003) related a vision's interpretability, plausibility, importance, and discontinuity to the ascendant and descendant stages in the vision's career. However, no vision arises in isolation. Little is known about the relationship among organizing visions. When two visions are related somehow, will one vision's popularity influence that of the other? If so, how? In this chapter, by reviewing the evolution of the organizing vision for business process reengineering (BPR) for the past 15 years, I found that the popularity of the BPR vision, at various points in time, was associated with the popularity of four other visions related to BPR—total quality management (TQM), enterprise resource planning (ERP), knowledge management (KM), and e-business. As the chapter will show, the intrinsically related contents of these visions not only explained their correlated popularity but also revealed a moving frontier for BPR. The chapter will end with a call for more research into the process by which innovative concepts emerge and business knowledge spreads.

## MULTIDIMENSIONAL RELATIONSHIP AMONG ORGANIZING VISIONS

How might the organizing visions of innovations be related? Most conspicuously, *technological commonality* among innovations affects the relationship between their visions. For example, both CRM and business intelligence utilize data mining technology. Thus, their visions are intrinsically related, and it is common to read about one with reference to the other. Innovations such as job enrichment and quality circles that do not share apparent technical components may still be related in discourse because they share people's *attention*—focused mental engagement on particular ideas (Davenport and Beck, 2001).

Attention is multidimensional and so is the relationship among organizing visions. First, when an innovation is perceived to solve the same problem as are other innovations, its organizing vision may come to "overlap, blend, or clash with other organizing visions" in the same *problem domain* (Swanson and Ramiller, 1997, p. 469). For example, despite their differences, EDI (electronic data interchange) and XML (extensible markup language) have both been purported to transfer business transactional data across organizations. Hence, in discourse, the two innovations are often compared and their visions related. Similarly, in the domain of techniques for "managing employees," the collapse of the job enrichment vision was suspected to have released much attention needed for the rise of the quality circles (QC) vision (Abrahamson and Fairchild, 1999). Second, several innovations may require the attention from the same *group of people* in an organization. A case in point is that both computer-aided software engineering (CASE) and object-oriented programming (OOP) require the attention of software developers. Third, different innovations may address the same *business process or function*. For example, the adoption of an integrated CRM package may help the customer service departments meet the standardization requirement of the TQM programs in some organizations. Hence, it is not surprising to see the discourses for CRM and TQM intertwined, at least in those organizations. Although other dimensions than the three mentioned above (problem domain, group of people, and business process or function) may exist, this chapter does not aim to catalog all possible dimensions along which organizing visions may be related.

Current thinking suggests that, however related the visions are, their popularity is *negatively* correlated. That is, when vision A is related to vision B, one vision will become more popular and the other will become less so. The reason is that A and B share attention, the amount of which is finite and limited for a given problem domain (Swanson and Ramiller, 1997) or multidimensional "niche" (Whittaker and Levin, 1975). In other words, organizing visions are competing with each other for attention. When they encounter each other, more discourse is needed for "separating the visions, integrating them, or abandoning one in favor of another" (Swanson and Ramiller, 1997, p. 469). The validity of this argument depends on the assumption that visions A and B exclusively occupy the same multidimensional space (i.e., A and B perfectly overlap with each other in all dimensions, but neither overlaps with any other vision). In reality, perfect substitute visions may be hard to find. More common are visions that are related in some aspects and unrelated in others. In that situation, little is known about how the popularity of one vision influences that of another. This chapter examines how four visions related to BPR (TQM, ERP, KM, and e-business) influenced the popularity of BPR.

## THE BPR VISION

In the early to mid-1980s, Michael Hammer, an MIT computer science professor-turned business consultant, became disenchanted with office automation (OA). He realized that using computers to automate outdated business activities would never address a company's performance deficiencies. Declaring that "OA has no future" (Hammer, 1984), he began to search for a more compelling consulting practice. With the consulting firm Index Group, Hammer participated in a multifirm research program to understand new ways to improve work flows with IT. Based on the positive outcomes firms such as Ford, Hewlett-Packard, IBM Credit, and Mutual Benefit Life had obtained from their work flow redesign projects, Hammer coined the term *business process reengineering* in 1987, aiming to shift managers' attention from improving individual functions incrementally to redesigning value-creating business processes. Index immediately selected BPR to label this new practice over "business process transformation," which sounded too "touchy-feely" (Kleiner, 2000, p. 29). Meanwhile, Thomas Davenport, Hammer's collaborator at Index, proposed an article on BPR to the *Harvard Business Review,* which, however, rejected his proposal. At this stage it was uncertain whether BPR would become the "next big thing."

### The Rise

The economic recession in the early 1990s gave the nascent BPR vision a boost. In July 1990, readers of the *Harvard Business Review,* many of whom were struggling with sagging corporate performances, saw an article entitled "Reengineering Work: Don't Automate, Obliterate," in which Hammer urged managers to strive for a "dramatic level of improvement" and to "use information technology not to automate an existing process but to enable a new one" (Hammer, 1990, p. 108). At about the same time, Davenport and James Short published an article in the *Sloan Management Review* that provided detailed guidance for redesigning business processes with IT (Davenport and Short, 1990). The initial vision for BPR, introduced in these two prominent management journals, was quickly picked up first by IT-related periodicals and then by outlets with broader audiences. In 1993, Davenport's book, *Process Innovation: Reengineering Work Through Information Technology,* was published. Almost concurrently, Hammer and James Champy released *Reengineering the Corporation: A Manifesto for Business Revolution.* In this best-selling book, the authors define reengineering as "the fundamental rethinking and radical redesign of business processes to achieve dramatic improvements in critical, contemporary measures of performance, such as cost, quality, service, and speed" (Hammer and Champy, 1993, p. 33). With this definition, Hammer and Champy stressed a number of principles for BPR. First, by "fundamental rethinking," they encouraged discontinuous thinking, that is, identifying and abandoning old rules and assumptions underlying existing business processes. Second, by "radical redesign," they asked managers to discard existing structures and procedures and design new processes with "a clean sheet of paper" (Hammer and Champy, 1993, p. 49). Third, by "dramatic improvement," they differentiated BPR from marginal or incremental improvements, which often characterized the objectives of TQM programs. Fourth, by "business processes," they accentuated the "process orientation" where tasks performed by specialists should be brought back together into business processes that deliver value to the customer. Last, they acknowledged the enabling role of IT for BPR.

From these pioneering articles and books, the BPR discourse grew exponentially in the form of more articles, books, conferences, and workshops. Figure 2.1 shows that the number of articles about BPR in ABI/Inform Global,[1] a database of nearly 1,800 worldwide business periodicals, took a dramatic leap in 1993 and 1994, reaching the peak in 1995, when the BPR vision turned into a $51 billion consulting industry. In 1993, the management consulting firm Bain and Company began surveying firms worldwide regarding their use of various management tools.[2] Figure 2.1 also shows that 66 percent of the respondents taking Bain's survey said that they were using some form of reengineering in 1993. Like the discourse, the usage reached its full ascendancy (78 percent) in 1995. Another survey conducted by CSC Index[3] in 1994 found that firms most frequently reengineered their customer service, order fulfillment, and manufacturing processes. Despite these impressive figures, BPR's popularity did not last long.

**The Fall**

In a November 1995 *Fast Company* article, describing the fall of those corporate exemplars of BPR, Davenport wrote "reengineering isn't dead; it is effectively over" (Davenport, 1995, p. 70). Bain's annual management tools survey (see Figure 2.1) saw the usage of BPR drop for the first time in 1996, and it continued to drop for the next five years. With regard to the benefits of financial results, market share, growth, and competitive stance, the survey showed that BPR's scores were below average, whereas BPR had topped the same benefit categories just two years before. This change mirrored BPR's rapidly waning popularity in the corporate world. "A series of studies in the early 1990s established that 70 percent or more of reengineering initiatives had actually made things worse" (Kleiner, 2000, p. 28). Amid the "confusion, delays, resentment, and screwups" (Kleiner, 2000, p. 28), middle managers led a fierce backlash against BPR, because they were then vulnerable to the downsizing attributed to reengineering. Unwilling to take all of the blame

Figure 2.1 **Business Process Reengineering Discourse and Usage**

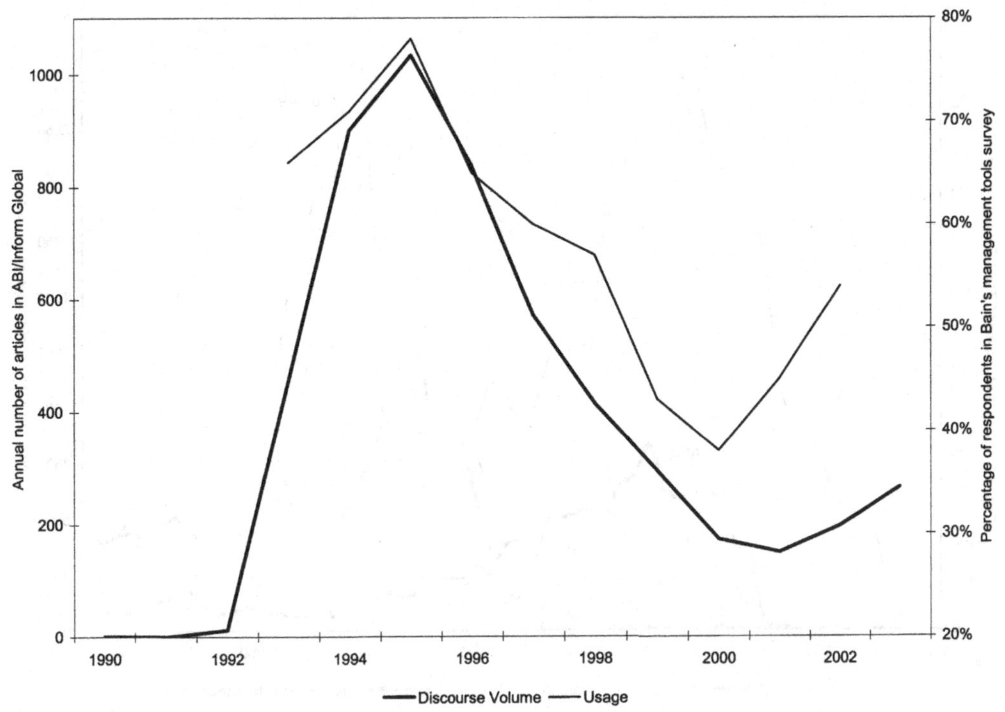

heaped on BPR, reengineering gurus apologized for forgetting about people. "I wasn't smart enough about that," Hammer told the *Wall Street Journal* in November 1996. "I was reflecting my engineering background and was insufficiently appreciative of the human dimension. I've learned that's critical" (White, 1996, p. A1). Similarly, Davenport wrote: "The rock that reengineering has foundered on is simple: people. Reengineering treated the people inside companies as if they were just so many bits and bytes, interchangeable parts to be reengineered. But no one wants to 'be reengineered'" (1995, p. 70). The term *reengineering* suddenly became an expletive in addition to a fad. Major consulting firms that had made fortunes from reengineering practices dropped the BPR label. Some found new labels ("organizational agility" at CSC Index); others (e.g., Ernst & Young and Andersen Consulting) terminated their reengineering practice and embarked on KM and ERP implementations. Accordingly, as shown in Figure 2.1, BPR discourse declined in the late 1990s nearly as quickly as it had risen.

**Signs of Revival?**

BPR did not go away with the old millennium, however. Both BPR usage reported by Bain's annual management tools survey and BPR discourse volume measured by the number of articles in ABI/Inform rose again in 2000 and 2001 (see Figure 2.1). In March 2000 when the Internet bubble burst, *CIO Magazine* published a special report, entitled "Reengineering Redux," including a roundtable discussion by Hammer and "a stellar panel of CIOs and business executives." The introduction of the report claimed, "[n]ow the headlong rush to e-business is bringing us

Figure 2.2 **Discourse on Business Process Reengineering and Related Innovations**

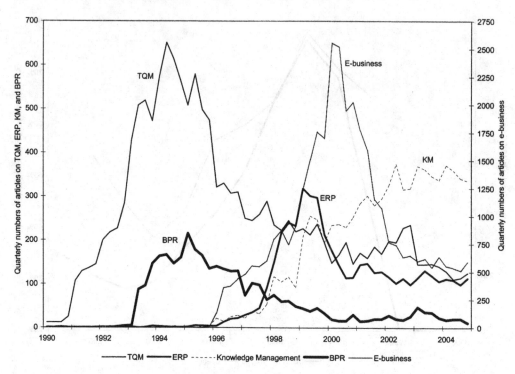

back to the reengineering bowl for another dip" (2000, p. 143). A month later, Hammer's former collaborator Champy ended his search for "a better label." In a *Computerworld* column, also entitled "Reengineering Redux," Champy wrote that "so-called business-to-business digital marketplaces will succeed only if they offer re-engineered processes to sellers and buyers. . . . The New Economy won't work without re-engineering" (2000, p. 47). By 2002, Bain's survey of 708 global executives found that 54 percent of their firms had reengineering initiatives, suggesting a likely revival for BPR.

As this short history suggests, the rise, fall, and possible revival of BPR overlapped with the rise and fall of several other visions. I have chosen to look at four of them in more detail. First, TQM is "a set of systematic activities carried out by the entire organization to effectively and efficiently achieve company objectives so as to provide products and services with a level of quality that satisfies customers, at the appropriate time and price."[4] Second, ERP represents a class of IT that integrates an organization's diverse business functions into one system. Third, KM, however diversely defined, represents organizational endeavors to stimulate learning and to benefit from knowledge. Last, e-business enables suppliers, distributors, and customers to conduct business electronically. Figure 2.2 portrays the popularity of these four visions and BPR in ABI/Inform. The next section describes how I analyzed the relationships among the visions.

## DATA AND THEIR ANALYSIS

The primary data source for this chapter is archived written discourse—articles published in periodicals indexed by ABI/Inform. Discourse researchers count the number of articles on particular

Table 2.1

**Top 20 Periodicals that Published Articles on BPR**

|   | Periodical | BPR Article Count |
|---|---|---|
| 1 | *Computerworld* | 239 |
| 2 | *InformationWeek* | 112 |
| 3 | *CIO* | 89 |
| 4 | *Industry Week* | 80 |
| 5 | *Industrial Engineer* | 74 |
| 6 | *Computing Canada* | 64 |
| 7 | *Quality Progress* | 61 |
| 8 | *Chemical Week* | 60 |
| 9 | *CRN* | 59 |
| 10 | *InfoWorld* | 57 |
| 11 | *Manufacturing Systems–MSI* | 55 |
| 11 | *Strategic Finance* | 55 |
| 13 | *National Underwriter* | 54 |
| 14 | *Government Executive* | 53 |
| 15 | *Progressive Grocer* | 52 |
| 16 | *Executive Excellence* | 50 |
| 17 | *Datamation* | 49 |
| 18 | *Journal of Organizational Excellence* | 47 |
| 19 | *Management Services* | 46 |
| 20 | *Best's Review* | 43 |

topics to trace changes in the popularity of those topics (Kabanoff and Abrahamson, 1997). Likewise, I measured the popularity of the BPR vision by counting the number of articles whose titles, abstracts, or subjects included the phrase *business process reengineering* for each periodical for each quarter from 1990, when the first article about BPR appeared in ABI, to the last quarter of 2004. Among the 5,511 articles identified, ABI did not record the quarters in which 671 articles were published, and thus I dropped those articles and focused on the remaining 4,840 articles, published by 647 periodicals. The articles were unevenly distributed across those periodicals. Table 2.1 shows the top 20 periodicals that published nearly 30 percent of the BPR articles. Interestingly, the three major IT periodicals—*Computerworld, InformationWeek,* and *CIO Magazine*—are the top three publishers of articles on BPR, suggesting a strong IT flavor in the BPR discourse. In contrast, 535 periodicals published fewer than 10 articles in the 15 years. The 122 periodicals that each published 10 or more BPR articles were retained for further analysis. Observations for each periodical began with the first quarter when the article count was not zero and ended in the last quarter of 2004.

For the volume of discourses carrying other visions related to BPR (i.e., TQM, ERP, KM, and e-business), I counted articles on each vision in the entire ABI/Inform Global database for each quarter in the same period, with the caveat that these four visions are illustrative rather than comprehensive. I also assumed that each periodical's decisions about whether and how much to publish about BPR in each quarter was shaped by the total volume of discourses about related visions, not by the volume published by any particular periodical.

Table 2.2 lists operational definitions of all variables. The dependent variable (Variable 1) is the BPR article count $y_{jq}$ for each periodical $j$ each quarter $q$. To partial out the effect of periodical-specific factors on the outcome, I included four control variables (Variables 2–5, denoted as $x_{kjq}$ for the $k$th variable for each periodical $j$ each quarter $q$): each periodical's age, authorship, and

Table 2.2

## Summary Statistics and Bivariate Correlations

| Variable | Mean | Standard Deviation | 1 | 2 | 3 | 4 |
|---|---|---|---|---|---|---|
| 1 Quarterly number of articles on BPR per periodical | 0.63 | 1.45 | | | | |
| 2 Age of periodical in years | 43.05 | 30.23 | -0.06*** | | | |
| 3 Academic periodical (0,1) | 0.25 | 0.44 | -0.07*** | -0.19*** | | |
| 4 Frequency of publication per year | 16.64 | 15.00 | 0.13*** | 0.25*** | -0.29*** | |
| 5 U.S.-based periodical (0,1) | 0.76 | 0.42 | 0.05*** | 0.17*** | -0.33*** | 0.15*** |
| 6 Quarter | 38.01 | 13.09 | -0.34*** | 0.09*** | 0.02 | -0.01 |
| 7 Quarterly percentage change of S&P 500 index | 2.30 | 6.84 | 0.08*** | -0.03 | 0.00 | 0.00 |
| 8 Quarterly number of articles on TQM in ABI | 277.14 | 148.68 | 0.36*** | -0.07*** | -0.03* | 0.02 |
| 9 Quarterly number of articles on ERP in ABI | 102.39 | 87.71 | -0.27*** | 0.04** | 0.02 | -0.01 |
| 10 Quarterly number of articles on knowledge management in ABI | 167.81 | 140.97 | -0.32*** | 0.09*** | 0.02 | -0.01 |
| 11 Quarterly number of articles on e-business in ABI | 772.55 | 684.84 | -0.27*** | 0.04** | 0.02 | -0.01 |

| Variable | 5 | 6 | 7 | 8 | 9 | 10 |
|---|---|---|---|---|---|---|
| 6 Quarter | -0.04** | | | | | |
| 7 Quarterly change of S&P 500 index | 0.01 | -0.25*** | | | | |
| 8 Quarterly number of articles on TQM in ABI | 0.03* | -0.75*** | 0.14*** | | | |
| 9 Quarterly number of articles on ERP in ABI | -0.03* | -0.51*** | -0.09*** | -0.62*** | | |
| 10 Quarterly number of articles on knowledge management in ABI | -0.03* | 0.76*** | -0.35*** | -0.79*** | 0.54*** | |
| 11 Quarterly number of articles on e-business in ABI | -0.03 | 0.47*** | -0.24*** | -0.64*** | 0.69*** | 0.51*** |

*Notes:* $N = 5,389$. * $p < 0.05$; ** $p < 0.01$; *** $p < 0.001$.

readership (academic or nonacademic), publication frequency, and headquarters location (U.S.- or non-U.S.-based). These data came from *Ulrich's Periodicals Directory* reported annually by R.R. Bowker. To exclude the potential influence of time, a linear time trend (Variable 6, updated each quarter) was included as a control variable. Moreover, Cyert and March (1992) argued that "performance gaps" between aspirations and achievement motivate managers to increase their search for innovations that may help narrow the gaps. At an aggregate level, firm performance thus may drive the volume of discussions about certain innovations. To account for that possibility, I included another control variable (Variable 7)—the quarterly change of the Standard & Poor's 500 index—as a proxy for aggregate performance. Variables 8–11 in Table 2.2 are the independent variables. Each independent variable $x_{kjq}$ measures the $k$th factor for each periodical $j$ each quarter $q$. In order to make inference about causality, the dependent variable (BPR article count) was lagged one quarter behind all independent and control variables.

Because the dependent variable is the quarterly BPR article count, count data regression was used. In particular, I used negative binomial regression,[5] a general form of count data regression, in order to test the statistical significance of the covariates' influence. Essentially, the expected number of articles on BPR published by each periodical each quarter can be modeled as a function of the popularity of related visions and control factors:

$$\mu_{jq} = \exp[\beta_0 + \beta_1 x_{1j(q-1)} + \beta_2 x_{2j(q-1)} + \dots + \beta_m x_{mj(q-1)}],$$

where $\mu_{jq}$ is the expected value of $y_{jq}$ (i.e., $\mu_{jq} = E[y_{jq}|x_{1j(q-1)}, x_{2j(q-1)}, \dots, x_{mj(q-1)}]$) and $\beta$s are parameters to be estimated. To estimate coefficients in the model, I used Stata® because of its straightforward procedure for negative binomial regression.[6]

## RESULTS

Between July 1990 and December 2004, the 122 periodicals published 3,401 articles on BPR in ABI/Inform. Table 2.2 displays the summary statistics for the 11 variables and their pairwise correlations. On average, each periodical published 0.63 articles on BPR each quarter. The average age for the periodicals was 43.05 years. A quarter of the periodicals were academic journals; three-quarters were based in the United States. Ranging from weekly to quarterly, the periodicals published 16.64 times a year. In the same period, about 773 articles on e-business were published in each quarter on average, making e-business the vision with the largest discourse among the four. All correlations between the dependent variable and other variables are significant. The correlations between several pairs of independent and control variables are relatively high but give no indication of serious multicollinearity problems.

Reflecting the distinctly larger volume of the e-business discourse, a different axis was used in Figure 2.2. The figure indicates that, despite the different life cycles of the five visions, some phases of their life cycles may have been correlated at different times. For example, in the early 1990s, the upswing phase of the BPR discourse largely paralleled with the rise of the TQM discourse with some delay. The downswing phase of the BPR vision in the second half of the 1990s concurred with the rise of discourses on ERP, e-business, and KM.

Table 2.3 presents the results from negative binomial regression analysis. Model 1 is a full model including all 10 covariates. The interaction terms between independent variables and time (measured in quarters) were then added (Model 2).[7] Both models utilized the entire data set of the 15-year data. All the interaction terms are significant (Model 2), meaning the strength of associations depended on time. Therefore, I broke the 15-year period into three five-year subperiods

Table 2.3

# Results of Negative Binomial Regressions on BPR Article Count

| | 1990–2004 | | | | 1990–1994 | | 1995–1999 | | 2000–2004 | |
| | Model 1 | | Model 2 | | Model 3 | | Model 4 | | Model 5 | |
| Variable | Coefficient | Standard Error | Coefficient | Standard Error | Coefficient | Standard Error | Coefficient | Standard Error | Coefficient | Standard Error |
|---|---|---|---|---|---|---|---|---|---|---|
| **Control Variable** | | | | | | | | | | |
| Age | −0.01* | (0.00) | −0.01* | (0.00) | 0.00 | (0.00) | 0.00 | (0.00) | −0.02*** | (0.00) |
| Academic | −0.12 | (0.13) | −0.11 | (0.13) | −0.50** | (0.19) | −0.13 | (0.12) | 0.28 | (0.21) |
| Frequency | 0.02** | (0.01) | 0.02** | (0.01) | 0.02* | (0.01) | 0.01* | (0.01) | 0.02** | (0.01) |
| US | 0.05 | (0.13) | 0.06 | (0.13) | 0.14 | (0.19) | 0.10 | (0.13) | 0.04 | (0.20) |
| Quarter | −0.03** | (0.01) | −0.03** | (0.01) | 0.15** | (0.06) | −0.12** | (0.04) | 0.02 | (0.06) |
| S&P 500 Change | 0.02*** | (0.00) | 0.02*** | (0.00) | 0.05* | (0.02) | 0.03** | (0.01) | 0.04** | (0.01) |
| **Independent Variable** | | | | | | | | | | |
| TQM | 0.66** | (0.23) | 0.34** | (0.11) | 2.00** | (0.70) | 0.39 | (0.50) | 0.95 | (0.80) |
| TQM × Quarter | | | −0.02** | (0.01) | | | | | | |
| ERP | −0.09 | (0.07) | −0.08 | (0.06) | −0.05* | (0.02) | 0.04** | (0.01) | 0.21 | (0.51) |
| ERP × Quarter | | | 0.01*** | (0.00) | | | | | | |
| KM | 0.02 | (0.02) | 0.01 | (0.00) | 0.07 | (0.04) | 0.06 | (0.06) | 1.45* | (0.68) |
| KM × Quarter | | | 0.02** | (0.01) | | | | | | |
| E-business | 0.02 | (0.02) | 0.01 | (0.01) | 0.16 | (0.12) | 0.02 | (0.06) | 2.85** | (0.89) |
| E-business × Quarter | | | 0.02** | (0.01) | | | | | | |
| N | 5,389 | | 5,389 | | 593 | | 2,390 | | 2,406 | |
| Wald χ² (degrees of freedom) | 422.84 (10) | | 416.57 (14) | | 38.17 (10) | | 175.18 (10) | | 36.22 (10) | |
| Probability > χ² | 0.000 | | 0.000 | | 0.000 | | 0.000 | | 0.000 | |

*$p < 0.05$; ** $p < 0.01$; *** $p < 0.001$.

(1990–94, 1995–99, and 2000–4) that represented the rise, fall, and likely revival of BPR, respectively. Accordingly, I performed the same regression analysis on data for each five-year subperiod in Models 3, 4, and 5. Analogous to the $F$-test in ordinary least squares (OLS) linear regression, the Wald chi-square tests show that all models are significant improvements from the unrestricted models of simple means.

Among the six control variables, publication frequency was significantly positively associated with the BPR article count in all models. Similarly, the effect of S&P 500 index change was significant and positive in all models, confirming the "performance gap" theory. Being headquartered in the United States did not matter at all to how many BPR articles each periodical published. Interestingly, the academic or scholarly nature of a periodical had a significant negative effect on the number of BPR articles the periodical published between 1990 and 1994, indicating that academic periodicals published fewer articles about BPR than their practitioner counterparts did in each quarter in those years, ceteris paribus. However, the academic effect disappeared after 1995.

Among the independent variables, only the TQM article count had a significant (positive) effect on the dependent variable over the 15 years (Model 1). However, the significant and negative coefficient for the interaction between TQM and time in Model 2 suggests that TQM's positive effect significantly decreased over time, as confirmed by the nonsignificant effect of TQM after 1995 in Models 4 and 5. Although article counts on the other visions (ERP, KM, and e-business) had no effects on the dependent variable (Model 1), their interactions with time were all significant and positive. Model 3 suggests that ERP and BPR went in opposite directions in terms of article count before 1995. However, that relationship was reversed in the next five years (Model 4). The effects of KM and e-business discourses on the dependent variable were similar. They were not significant in the first 10 years, but were significant and positive in the new millennium.

In sum, the regression results suggest that the effects of related visions on the BPR vision were different at different times. Between 1990 and 1994, the rise of BPR discourse was positively associated with the rise of TQM discourse, but negatively associated with ERP discourse. The fall of BPR discourse in the second half of the 1990s was positively associated with ERP discourse. After 2000, BPR's seeming resurgence was associated positively with discourses on e-business and KM.

## DISCUSSION

The above discourse analysis has established that the popularity of BPR and that of the other four visions was linked at various times. The linkage, as I discuss below, can be interpreted by the intrinsic relationship among these visions in terms of their substance.

### Total Quality Management

The U.S. Naval Air Systems Command coined the term *total quality management* to describe its Japanese-style management approach to quality improvement in the early 1980s. However, the quality movement was initiated as early as the 1940s. BPR inherited a number of principles from TQM. First, rejecting the traditional formulation of quality control that only examined the characteristics of the end products, TQM incorporates quality diagnosis and correction in the entire production process that often cuts across a number of functions. BPR applies this process orientation to redesigning not only production processes but also other processes such as order fulfillment and customer services. Second, like TQM, BPR espouses the customer-centric view. Just as "quality is what customers say it is," business processes must deliver what customers value.

Third, both TQM and BPR emphasize measuring results, and, thus, the rigorous techniques for quality measurement have been employed to evaluate BPR outcomes in terms of quality as well as cost, profit, and speed.

Besides inheriting the TQM legacies mentioned above, BPR contrasts strikingly with TQM in other aspects. Foremost, TQM programs seek to improve existing processes, and contemporary quality management emphasizes continuous improvements that are often incremental. BPR, as formulated by Hammer and Champy, seeks radical improvements and "breakthroughs, not by enhancing existing processes, but by discarding them and replacing them with entirely new ones" (1993, p. 49). Such radicalness makes TQM's bottom-up, employee-empowerment approach inapplicable to BPR programs, which often follow a top-down route. This dissimilarity has been attributed to cultural differences. Hammer and Champy wrote, "Reengineering isn't another idea imported from Japan. . . . Reengineering capitalizes on the same characteristics that have tradition-ally made Americans such great business innovators: individualism, self-reliance, a willingness to accept risk, and a propensity for change" (1993, pp. 2–3).

Both the similarities and differences between TQM and BPR, I suspect, explain the positive correlation between their discourses, especially in the early 1990s. Later on, TQM gradually lost its popularity and was increasingly called quality management in the United States. Today, TQM has arguably been folded into standardization initiatives such as Six Sigma and ISO 9000. The nonsignificant coefficients for TQM in Models 4 and 5 indicate that the BPR discourse has parted with that of TQM.

## Enterprise Resource Planning

In April 1990, IT research firm Gartner Group introduced ERP as the next generation of MRP II (manufacturing resource planning). The heart of an ERP system is a central database that collects data from and feeds data into the system's individual application components (called modules), supporting diverse business functions and processes such as finance, manufacturing, logistics, human resources, and so on. When new information is entered or updated in one module, other related modules in the system are automatically updated.

Apparent in the ERP vision is the cross-functional process orientation, consistent with the BPR vision. Radically new business processes coming out of the redesign sessions need redesigned and reimplemented information systems. However, most manufacturing firms did not have the capabili-ties to develop new IT anymore, partly because they had downsized their software development workforce, which had not been considered a "core competency." The call of new business processes for new enabling IT made many firms shift from building to buying IT, especially packaged busi-ness software, throughout the 1990s (Swanson, 2003). In 1992, market leader SAP introduced a client/server–based ERP suite that quickly conquered the European and the U.S. markets. Major ERP vendors (SAP, Oracle, PeopleSoft, Baan, and J.D. Edwards) enjoyed dramatic growth in the mid-to-late 1990s. By the end of 1998, more than 60 percent of the Fortune 1000 companies had implemented ERP core applications (Stein, 1999). With expanding functionalities and new inter-faces added, ERP packages quickly spread from large companies to mid-sized companies, from European and U.S. markets to Asia Pacific and Latin America, from manufacturing and logistics companies to other vertical industries such as wholesale, health care, banking, and insurance.

However, a tension existed between the business processes packaged in the ERP systems and those written on that "clean sheet of paper" in the BPR programs. ERP packages were notoriously difficult to customize to match the processes either previously existing in the firms or desired by reengineering managers. Therefore, when ERP systems were introduced to companies, managers found that their first priority was to change their existing business processes to fit with the "best practices" prepackaged in the ERP systems. Possibly, they shifted their attention originally allocated to BPR to the business process change posed by ERP, leading to a significant negative correlation between the discourses on ERP and BPR (Model 3). Nonetheless, the "best practices" embedded in ERP were newer and significantly different from the existing processes in many firms. Gradually, ERP became a means to do BPR, as more and more firms adopted ERP systems with specific embedded processes that they would like to obtain (Davenport, 2000). In this way, the relationship between ERP and BPR became increasingly complementary—a proposition confirmed by both the positive coefficient for the interaction between ERP and time in Model 2 and the positive coefficient for ERP in Model 4, suggesting that the ERP and BPR visions became supportive of each other in the late 1990s.

**Knowledge Management**

The concept of KM emerged in the 1980s and remained largely unknown until the late 1990s, when KM became popular in discourse (Figure 2.2) and practice. In 2001, market research firm IDC reported that worldwide spending on KM services was $3.7 billion. Most of the money was paid for KM consulting, succeeding BPR as a new "advisory practice" in major consultancies. The succession struck Brown and Duguid as particularly interesting as they observed: "As reengineering stumbled, reengineering consultants themselves began to be downsized. They probably needed little sympathy, for many moved swiftly across the hall to the suites reserved for the next fashion, 'knowledge management'" (2000, p. 93). KM and BPR are related not only because they both were likely advised by the same consultants but also because KM has extended the BPR vision.

Despite the numerous definitions for KM and the still heated debate on whether knowledge can actually be "managed," it is generally accepted that KM has at least two broad "tracks"—information management and practice management (Prusak, 2001; Sveiby, 1999). Both are subtly related to BPR. On one hand, information management focuses on how information is created, processed, stored, retrieved, and used with the help of IT. In the business context, information flows in every process, and managing information is thus an essential part of managing business processes. As mentioned earlier, BPR programs were initially concentrated on processes in customer services, order fulfillment, and manufacturing, where processes can be relatively clearly defined, outcomes accurately measured, and thus information management relatively straightforward. As BPR has advanced into more "knowledge-intensive" processes such as sales, marketing, research and development, and management, where knowledge workers are autonomous, knowledge work invisible, and work flow nonlinear, reengineering these processes thus requires a more sophisticated form of information management, or KM. For example, when it comes to reengineering photocopier repair processes, a product manual, however improved, that ignores the unique context in which each copier works may not be so helpful to service technicians as is a "knowledge base" composed of tips extracted from "war stories" told by technicians (Bobrow and Whalen, 2002).

On the other hand, reengineering knowledge-intensive processes also requires practice management, the other track of KM. Practice, the way in which work gets done (Brown and Duguid, 2001), is often different from the process described formally in manuals, training programs, organizational charts, and job descriptions (Brown and Duguid, 1991). Some scholars attribute this difference to different levels of abstraction, whereas others maintain that practices are always situated in particular contexts and thus should not be codified into processes and applied to other contexts (Brown and Duguid, 2000). According to the latter, the sensible way to "manage" practice is to facilitate or support people in getting their work done. A notable example of such practice management is to foster access to and membership of "communities of practice" (Brown and Duguid, 1991; Lave and Wenger, 1991). Therefore, reengineering processes entails careful attention to the practices that make the processes. Together, information management and practice management made KM a driver for BPR, as the significant association between the BPR and KM discourses in 2000–4 corroborated (Model 5 in Table 2.3).

### E-Business

The commercialization of the Internet technology and spread of the World Wide Web in the 1990s made it possible for firms to engage in e-business. The implications of e-business for business processes became clear and important. Fahey et al. wrote:

> [E-business] provides the electronic means to enable connections among and between processes to take place in fundamentally new ways and at such speeds that it literally opens up the ability to radically reconfigure each core operating process, to create new subprocesses within each core operation process, and to enable new modes of integration across the operating processes. (2001, p. 895)

The core processes, as Fahey et al. argued, include processes that directly buttress and enable developing, producing, and delivering products and services valuable to the customers (e.g., product development, customer services, and supply-chain management). Many of the processes in the traditional "brick-and-mortar" firms were inadequate to the demands of e-business (Kleiner, 2000). The fall of the first crop of "dot-com" ventures suggested that a slick Web storefront without seamless and efficient business processes would not work. Ventures that had reengineered their internal processes (whether by implementing ERP or not) in the 1990s found themselves facing another round of process reengineering in the new millennium. This time, the focus was on the interenterprise processes linking suppliers, producers, distributors, and customers in an "e-business value web." Linkages that did not exist had to be built. Disparate processes needed to be standardized. Rigid processes, typically packaged in ERP systems, were to be relaxed. In this sense, e-business might have created new hope for BPR's possible revival, a conjecture supported by the finding that the volume of e-business discourse had significant correlation with that of the BPR discourse in 2000–4 (Model 5 in Table 2.3).

To summarize, Table 2.4 encapsulates my interpretation of the relationships between BPR and the four other visions around the three questions the BPR vision is supposed to answer: *What* is BPR? *Why* do it? And *how* to do it? For instance, discourse that compared BPR with TQM helped clarify the similarities and differences between the two visions, making it relatively easy to *interpret* what is BPR. Further, regarding why firms should do BPR, newer visions such as KM and e-business provided new *rationales* and *motivations* much needed for BPR's possible revival. Moreover, the techniques, methods, and technologies underlying other visions equipped reengineers with the necessary *know-how* to carry out the BPR vision in practice.

### CONCLUSION

The 15-year evolution of BPR indicated that the popularity of the four organizing visions (TQM, ERP, KM, and e-business) I chose to study were *positively* associated, with the exception of ERP in 1990–94, with the popularity of BPR at different times. The association, as interpreted above, was rooted in the inherently related substance of the visions. Historically, TQM served as a compara-

Table 2.4

## Interpretation of the Relationships Between BPR and Other Visions

|  | What Is BPR? | Why Do BPR? | How To Do BPR? |
|---|---|---|---|
| Total Quality Management | + The similar principles (e.g., process orientation, customer-centric view, and emphasis on measurement) and the different principles (e.g., incremental versus radical improvements, bottom-up versus top-down, Japanese versus American) help compare the TQM and BPR visions clearly. | + TQM and BPR share the objective to improve quality in the production process. | + Rigorous quality control and evaluation methods can be applied to assessing the outcomes from reengineering programs. |
| Enterprise Resource Planning |  |  | – Tension exists between the processes designed or redesigned in BPR programs and processes prepackaged in ERP systems.<br>+ ERP systems enable cross-functional business processes. Implementing ERP systems is therefore an opportunity to integrate previously siloed business activities and functions into reengineered processes. |
| Knowledge Management |  | + KM and BPR share the objective to improve knowledge-intensive processes such as product development (R&D), marketing, and management. | + KM methods such as information management and practice management are useful in reengineering knowledge-intensive processes. |
| E-business |  | + For firms to conduct business electronically with suppliers, partners, and customers, internal and interenterprise business processes must be created and redesigned to meet the new requirements. | + A variety of e-business technologies (e.g., XML and Web services) enable the reengineered e-business processes. |

*Notes:* + is positive implication on the relationship between the vision and the **BPR** vision; – is negative implication on the relationship between the vision and the **BPR** vision.

tive vision for understanding BPR, and ERP offered a means to do reengineering. More recently, as traditional focal processes such as order fulfillment and software development have already been reengineered, KM and e-business have helped shift the focus to knowledge-intensive and interorganizational processes. The trend is clear: as some business processes are reengineered, commoditized, standardized, and outsourced (Davenport, 2005), other processes will become the new, interesting frontier of reengineering, and transforming those processes early on will bring competitive advantage before the even newer frontier emerges.

Essentially, this chapter addresses a knowledge-intensive, interorganizational process not yet well understood—namely, the process of creating and popularizing grand concepts (or organizing visions) for business innovations. It is knowledge intensive because each organizing vision contains knowledge about the innovation's purpose, function, and outcome. The process is also interorganizational because various organizations contribute and synthesize knowledge in discourse that goes beyond organizational boundaries. As a case study of BPR, this chapter shows that the extent to which BPR was popular depended on the popularity of other related visions at different times. At this point, we do not know, for example, how much of the relationship among visions and timing is subject to human agency and how the visions are related in a dynamic, multidimensional network. Apparently, we have just begun this line of inquiry into the process by which innovative concepts are created and business knowledge diffuses. An understanding of the process can help us improve, or perhaps even *reengineer,* it.

## ACKNOWLEDGMENTS

The author is grateful to the editors of this volume and Burt Swanson for their helpful comments. The study was supported, in part, by the Information Systems Research Program at UCLA Anderson School of Management.

## NOTES

1. All articles were counted if their titles, abstracts, or subjects include the phrase *business process reengineering.*
2. See www.bain.com/management_tools/home.asp (accessed on June 15, 2007).
3. Computer Services Corporation acquired Index in 1988.
4. JUSE (Union of Japanese Scientists and Engineers), a spearhead organization for quality management, provided this definition.
5. The most commonly used count models are Poisson and negative binomial. Poisson is the special case of negative binomial when the conditional variance equals the conditional mean. In this study, the variance of the dependent variable far exceeds its mean (i.e., the data are overdispersed), as shown in Table 2.2, so negative binomial is more appropriate than Poisson. For technical details, see Cameron and Trivedi (1998).
6. The BPR article counts are assumed independent across periodicals, but not necessarily for each periodical. Therefore, I used the cluster option of Stata's nbreg procedure (Stata Corporation, 2001) to correct the estimated standard errors, accounting for the lack of independence across observations for each periodical.
7. In Model 2, the counts on the related visions were logarithm transformed and then centered around the means.

## REFERENCES

Abrahamson, E., and Fairchild, G. 1999. Management fashion: Lifecycles, triggers, and collective learning processes. *Administrative Science Quarterly,* 44, 4, 708–740.

Bobrow, D.G., and Whalen, J. 2002. Community knowledge sharing in practice: The Eureka story. *Reflections: The SOL Journal on Knowledge, Learning, and Change,* 4, 2, 47–59.

Boje, D.M.; Oswick, C.; and Ford, J.D. 2004. Language and organization: The doing of discourse. *Academy of Management Review,* 29, 4, 571–577.

Brown, J.S., and Duguid, P. 1991. Organizational learning and communities-of-practice: Toward a unified view of working, learning, and innovation. *Organization Science,* 2, 1, 40–57.

———. 2000. *The Social Life of Information.* Boston: Harvard Business School Press.

———. 2001. Knowledge and organization: A social-practice perspective. *Organization Science,* 12, 2, 198–213.

Cameron, A.C., and Trivedi, P.K. 1998. *Regression Analysis of Count Data.* Cambridge: Cambridge University Press.

Champy, J. 2000. Re-engineering redux. *Computerworld,* 34, 17 (April 24), 47.

Cyert, R.M., and March, J.G. 1992. *A Behavioral Theory of the Firm,* 2d ed. Cambridge, MA: Blackwell Business.

Davenport, T.H. 1993. *Process Innovation: Reengineering Work Through Information Technology.* Boston: Harvard Business School Press.

———. 1995. The fad that forgot people. *Fast Company,* 1, 70–74.

———. 2000. *Mission Critical: Realizing the Promise of Enterprise Systems.* Boston: Harvard Business School Press.

———. 2005. The coming commoditization of processes. *Harvard Business Review,* 83, 6, 101–108.

Davenport, T.H., and Beck, J.C. 2001. *The Attention Economy: Understanding the New Currency of Business.* Boston: Harvard Business School Press.

Davenport, T.H., and Short, J.E. 1990. The new industrial engineering: Information technology and business process redesign. *Sloan Management Review,* 31, 4, 11–27.

Fahey, L.; Srivastava, R.; Sharon, J.S.; and Smith, D.E. 2001. Linking e-business and operating processes: The role of knowledge management. *IBM Systems Journal,* 40, 4, 889–907.

Hammer, M. 1984. In focus: The OA mirage. *Datamation,* 30, 2, 36–38.

———. 1990. Reengineering work: Don't automate, obliterate. *Harvard Business Review,* 68, 4, 104–112.

———. 2000. Reengineering redux. *CIO,* 13, 10 (March 1), 143.

Hammer, M., and Champy, J. 1993. *Reengineering the Corporation: A Manifesto for Business Revolution.* New York: HarperBusiness.

Kabanoff, B., and Abrahamson, E. 1997. OB meets the information superhighway. In C.L. Cooper and S.E. Jackson (eds.), *Creating Tomorrow's Organizations: A Handbook for Future Research in Organizational Behavior.* New York: John Wiley & Sons, pp. 453–474.

Kleiner, A. 2000. Revisiting reengineering. *Strategy+Business,* 20, 27–31.

Lave, J., and Wenger, E. 1991. *Situated Learning: Legitimate Peripheral Participation.* Cambridge: Cambridge University Press.

Phillips, N., and Hardy, C. 2002. *Discourse Analysis: Investigating Processes of Social Construction.* Thousand Oaks, CA: Sage.

Prusak, L. 2001. Where did knowledge management come from? *IBM Systems Journal,* 40, 4, 1002–1007.

Ramiller, N.C., and Swanson, E.B. 2003. Organizing visions for information technology and the information systems executive response. *Journal of Management Information Systems,* 20, 1, 13–50.

Stata Corporation. 2001. nbreg-negative binomial regression. In *Stata Reference Manual Release 7.* College Station, TX: Stata Press, 2001, pp. 383–392.

Stein, T. 1999. Big strides for ERP. *InformationWeek,* 715, 67–68.

Sveiby, K.-E. 1999. Designing business strategy in the knowledge era. In R. Ruggles and D. Holtshouse (eds.), *The Knowledge Advantage: 14 Visionaries Define Marketplace Success in the New Economy.* Dover, NH: Capstone Publishing, pp. 177–190.

Swanson, E.B. 2003. Innovating with packaged business software: Towards an assessment. In G. Shanks, P. Seddon, and L.P. Willcocks (eds.), *Second-Wave Enterprise Resource Planning Systems.* Cambridge: Cambridge University Press, pp. 56–73.

Swanson, E.B., and Ramiller, N.C. 1997. The organizing vision in information systems innovation. *Organization Science,* 8, 5, 458–474.

Tillquist, J. 2000. Institutional bridging: How conceptions of IT-enabled change shape the planning process. *Journal of Management Information Systems,* 17, 2, 115–152.

White, J.B. 1996. Next big thing. *Wall Street Journal* (November 26), A1.

Whittaker, R.H., and Levin, S.A. 1975. *Niche: Theory and Application.* Stroudsburg, PA: Downden, Hutchinson & Ross.

Wynn, E.H.; Whitley, E.A.; Myers, M.D.; and DeGross, J.I. 2002. *Global and Organizational Discourse About Information Technology.* Boston: Kluwer Academic.

# CHAPTER 3

# BUSINESS PROCESSES

## Four Perspectives

### NUNO MELÃO AND MICHAEL PIDD

*Abstract:* As organizations strive to do things faster, cheaper, and better, it is increasingly important to redesign and improve business processes so as to meet customer needs efficiently and effectively. Although there is widespread literature on business process transformation, there is little discussion of the nature of business processes. This is surely important if transformation is to be successful. This chapter provides a conceptual framework to support a thorough exploration of the nature of business processes. The framework uses four viewpoints to group different notions of business processes, each highlighting certain aspects while placing less emphasis on others. The viewpoints provide the basis for a discussion of the strengths and limitations of different modeling approaches used in the transformation of business processes. We conclude that business processes are multifaceted, and, therefore, successful transformation may require the combination of both soft and hard modeling approaches.

*Keywords:* Business Processes, Business Process Transformation, Business Process Reengineering, Business Process Management, Business Process Modeling, Conceptual Framework

## INTRODUCTION

There can be little doubt that today's business world is very competitive. Globalization means that companies that were not in direct competition now find themselves competing for the same market. Even small businesses operate internationally via the Internet and, like large businesses, have customers who are increasingly demanding. All of this produces a volatile business environment in which managers must respond better, faster, and quicker. Recognizing this, many companies have made significant attempts to improve their business processes. These efforts come in many forms and guises, including, for example, quality improvement programs (e.g., ISO 9001:2000, Six Sigma), business process reengineering (BPR) programs, enterprise information systems (IS) programs (e.g., enterprise resource planning), and, more recently, e-business programs. Another approach, business process modeling (BPM), has been proposed to support the transformation of business processes, based on the construction of models for the exploration of alternative scenarios and designs before their implementation.

Surprisingly, perhaps, little attention has been given to the important task of understanding the nature of business processes. Instead, most advocates of process improvement take the nature of a business process as a given and then proceed to suggest how these processes should be improved. According to Hammer and Champy's (1993) observations, around 70 percent of the BPR projects fail. Even though this estimate is dated, it is clear that many process improvement projects are far from successful. Of course, there are many reasons for this, and we would argue that failure to understand the nature of business processes plays a major part. With few exceptions (Armistead and Roland, 1996; Garvin, 1998; Smith and Fingar, 2003), most of the existing literature provides only superficial accounts on the nature of business processes. Although the BPM community has produced considerable research in recent times, most of it is restricted to studying a given approach or to discussing different approaches from a given perspective. The implication is that the debate of the BPM field as a whole has been neglected, and we may be missing an important part of the puzzle of how to transform business processes.

To fill this gap, we propose an integrated, multidisciplinary framework that helps to clarify the nature of business processes, with implications for how they might be modeled. We argue that different views of business processes can be organized around four perspectives. After discussing the assumptions behind each of these perspectives, the implications for modeling are outlined, and the underlying approaches, including their strengths and weaknesses, are identified. We hope this framework will enable both researchers and practitioners to conduct their work more successfully, possibly leading to enhanced theoretical and practical developments.

## FROM REENGINEERING TO PROCESS MANAGEMENT

Interest in streamlining business processes is not new. Its origins can be found in the scientific management movement in the early years of the past century. However, with the emergence of BPR in the early 1990s, interest has grown. BPR was first described in North America by Davenport and Short (1990) and Hammer (1990). It quickly became popular with management consultancies (e.g., CSC Index) and best-selling books (Davenport, 1993; Hammer and Champy, 1993). The rhetoric convinced many organizations that dramatic breakthroughs in performance could only be achieved by moving away from "functional hierarchy" toward a process-based paradigm using the power of information technology (IT). BPR became a panacea for many organizations around the world.

### Some Paradoxes of Business Process Reengineering

Despite its popularity, BPR has many internal contradictions (Jones, 1994; 1995), which have led to much confusion. From its early days, different management consultants used BPR as a way to sell their proprietary methods (Grover and Malhotra, 1997). Inevitably, this led to confusion and disagreements. Responding to the claims made for BPR and the resulting confusion, the academic community criticized the powerful rhetoric and vested interests of many consultancies for having no sound theoretical basis. Earl and Khan (1994) questioned whether there was anything new in BPR. Mumford (1994) asked similar questions, although focusing on the similarities between BPR and socio-technical design. Deakins and Makgill (1997) argued that the original literature of BPR was essentially anecdotal, lacking serious and rigorous research to support its recommendations and assertions.

More recent literature strongly suggests that the radical approach to change is being softened by the lessons gleaned from successes and failures in the course of implementations. Perhaps the best example is Davenport and Stoddard (1994), who reported on a field study and challenge some of the central tenets of reengineering as "myths." Their distinctive insight triggered others to critically analyze the BPR phenomenon (Burke and Peppard, 1995; Grover and Kettinger, 1995, 2000). Recent trends in technology and management thinking, such as the Internet and e-business, further shaped developments in BPR (El Sawy, 2001; Harmon et al., 2001). We summarize the issues as follows:

1. *Radical versus incremental redesign.* Hammer and Champy presented BPR as "the radical redesign of business processes for dramatic improvement" (1993, p. 32). However, more recent empirical research (Jarvenpaa and Stoddard, 1998; Stoddard and Jarvenpaa, 1995) supports the view that, although the radical approach works well in some organizations, others, perhaps more conservative, prefer a more incremental view. For example, Cock and Hipkin (1997) compared the incremental approach of total quality management (TQM) with the radical view espoused in early BPR. Even Hammer (1996; 2001) recognized his original mistake in asserting that the key word of the reengineering concept was "radical." This word, he admitted, was responsible for the bandwagon effect and excitement among managers. He now asserts that the most important word in the definition is "process."

2. *Clean-slate versus existing process.* Given their emphasis on radical thinking, it is perhaps unsurprising that Hammer and Champy insisted that "disregarding all existing structures and procedures" (1993, p. 33) was essential to BPR—presumably, based on a view that a new world requires new ways of working. However, Stoddard and Jarvenpaa (1995) asserted that such clean-slate change is rarely found. Indeed, Teng et al. (1998) reported that considerable effort is spent on analyzing existing processes in many BPR projects.

3. *Intra- versus interorganizational processes.* The original notion of BPR focused on the redesign of cross-functional business processes. For example, Davenport (1998) discussed organizations' use of enterprise resource planning for that purpose. However, globalization, networked organizations, and supply-chain management alongside advances in technology led various authors (El Sawy, 2001; Kalakota and Robinson, 2003) and BPR originators (Champy, 2002; Hammer, 2001) to make a case for redesigning business processes that span multiple organizations in a value chain. An empirical study illustrating this point is El Sawy et al. (1999).

4. *IT led versus IT enabled.* Both Davenport and Short (1990) and Hammer (1990) stressed the centrality of IT in BPR. Emerging research and case evidence (Broadbent et al., 1999; Guha et al., 1997) support another perspective—IT is an "enabler" and a "creator of opportunities." After the 2000 dot-com crash, Carr (2003) suggested a secondary, more humble, role for IT in business strategy.

5. *Mechanistic versus holistic.* The original BPR literature is heavily dominated by a hard systems approach and by machine metaphors of organization. But several authors call for a more holistic and softer approach in order to take into account strategic and people issues. For instance, Earl et al. (1995) reported on field studies that demonstrated the danger of a mechanistic approach. In the context of operations management, Silver (2004) argued for a more holistic approach so as to improve (rather than to optimize) business processes. Galliers and Baker (1995) argued that soft organizational research, which assumes that the world is problematic rather than given, provides one possible way of approaching BPR.

6. *Dramatic versus modest.* Hammer and Champy claimed that BPR involved "dramatic improvements in critical, contemporary measures of performance" (1993, p. 32). Yet empirical investigation (Bashein et al., 1994; Grover and Kettinger, 2000) reveals that BPR initiatives often deliver less than they promise.

7. *Top down versus bottom up.* Hammer and Champy insisted that BPR "never, ever happens from bottom up" (1993, p. 207). Nevertheless, several studies found that the participation, commitment, ownership, and initiative from the front line were vital for many successful BPR programs. For instance, Willcocks and Smith (1995) explored some of the human dimensions of such change. Dennis et al. (2003) and Hengst and de Vreede (2004) showed how groupware and modeling can be used to support the participation of middle management and other stakeholders.

8. *Inspiration versus methodology.* Hammer (1990) and Hammer and Champy (1993) argued that BPR depends largely on imagination, creativity, and experience. As with many movements, such an inspirational orientation may work well for the pioneers. However, others may need more systematic approaches. This is reflected in the variety of different methodologies, techniques, and tools that are available to support BPR (Kettinger et al., 1997).

9. *Operational versus knowledge processes.* BPR originally focused on the redesign of operational processes. However, as knowledge plays an increasingly important role in creating and sustaining competitive advantages, several authors (Davenport et al., 1996; El Sawy, 2001; see also El Sawy, this volume, pp. 157–183) stressed the need to streamline knowledge processes, such as product development, marketing, and customer-facing processes, and so on. For instance, El Sawy and Bowles (1997) discussed how a knowledge management system was used to enable the redesign of a customer support process.

## Reengineering Business Process Reengineering

In light of these developments, it could be argued that the original concept of BPR is being reengineered to take a broader perspective. Davenport (1996), one of the pioneers of BPR, claimed that reengineering has a negative connotation in the United States, often being associated with restructuring, layoffs, and failed change programs. However, recent times have seen many attempts at a rebirth of BPR, although not using the *reengineering* term. For example, Hammer and Champy (2001) revised their original best-selling book to bring it more up to date with the electronic economy. Hammer (2001) abandoned the original radical tone in favor of a more process-centric approach both within and, more important, between organizations. Similarly, Champy (2002), stressed the need to redesign interorganizational processes. Hammer (2002) related his views on process management with the quality improvement approach Six Sigma. In turn, Davenport et al. (2003) stated that although the original BPR focused on redesigning back-office processes, the next phase of BPR should focus on redesigning knowledge processes. More recently, Hammer (2004) used the term *operational innovation* rather than *reengineering*.

Although the use of the term *reengineering* may be dying, the focus on business processes remains important. In fact, the emergence of the electronic economy, as Porter (2001) pointed out, further amplifies the need for efficient, effective, and flexible business processes. Processes are a natural way to describe how work is done within and between organizations so as to create value for internal or external customers. This usually implies a distinction between different types of processes based on value-chain concepts such as the following (Earl and Khan, 1994):

- core processes, which have external customers and which include the primary activities of the value chain;
- support processes, which have internal customers and concern secondary activities in the value chain;

Figure 3.1 **From Reengineering to Process Management and Business Process Modeling**

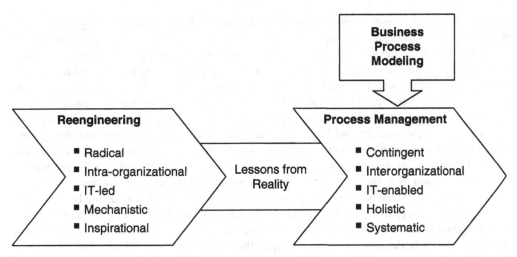

*Source:* Adapted from Melão and Pidd (2000). Reprinted with permission of Blackwell Publishing.

- management processes, which manage core and support processes; and
- interorganizational processes, which cross organizational boundaries into suppliers, partners, and customers.

It therefore seems reasonable to suggest that the first generation of reengineering—which presented BPR as a radical, intra-organizational, IT-led, mechanistic, and inspirational approach—is evolving into second-generation process management. Process management views BPR as a contingent, interorganizational, IT-enabled, holistic, and systematic approach (Figure 3.1). This evolution results mainly from the recognition of an overemphasis on reductionist and mechanistic aspects, where crucial issues such as people and strategic issues are simply ignored. It also results from technological advances such as the Internet, which have enabled organizations to conduct their business with customers, suppliers, and partners in novel ways.

A process management perspective, as espoused lately by BPR pioneers such as Davenport et al. (2003) and Hammer (2001; 2002; 2004), as well as by their critics (Becker et al., 2003; El Sawy, 2001; Grover and Kettinger, 2000; Kalakota and Robinson, 2003; Peppard, 1996; Silver, 2004; Smith and Fingar, 2003), is a continuum of approaches to process transformation. It focuses on business processes and includes radical (reengineering) and incremental (continuous improvement) perspectives, both of which should be customized to the problem and context under consideration. To support their improvement, the development of process modeling approaches and tools is an important item in the new research agenda.

## UNDERSTANDING BUSINESS PROCESS MODELING

Reports of research on BPM can be classified in various ways. Here, it is done under three headings—reports of practice, attempts to develop theoretical positions, and discussions of the nature of business processes. Doing so highlights the importance of suitable and inclusive definitions of what might constitute a business process.

**Reports of Practice**

The first group of research reports examined BPM as an activity by matching the typical process stages against the tools and techniques commonly used by practitioners. Kettinger et al. (1997) surveyed 25 methodologies, 72 techniques, and 102 tools for supporting business process change programs. From this, they constructed a generic methodology, matching its stages with the available techniques and tools. This led to a conceptual framework for tool and technique selection, based on the characteristics of the project. El Sawy (2001) proposed a five-stage methodology for transforming intra- and interorganizational processes, in which the modeling stage is supported by software tools, simulation, and RosettaNet standards. These studies confirm that practitioner methodologies share many common features, despite the differences in philosophical orientation toward IT, scale of change, and people issues. Most consultancies have their own proprietary methodologies and tools and stress a well-defined sequence of stages and activities.

A second group of research reports discussed existing techniques for modeling business processes. Giaglis (2001) provided an overview of several BPM and IS modeling techniques, based on a framework for technique evaluation and selection using the characteristics of the project. Kamath et al. (2003) discussed diverse techniques that can be used to model business processes to be executed by enterprise IS. From a practitioner perspective, Melão and Pidd (2003) surveyed the use of modeling and simulation techniques among potential BPM users. Gunasekaran and Kobu (2002) reviewed various modeling techniques used in BPR from a production perspective and suggested guidelines for choosing them given the areas to be reengineered. Similarly, Aguilar-Savén (2004) discussed and compared a number of techniques for modeling business processes, including flowcharts, data flow diagrams, role activity diagrams, role interaction diagrams, Gantt charts, IDEF (Integrated DEFinition), object-oriented methods, work flow, Petri nets, and simulation.

A third group of research reports investigated the use of software tools. Classe (1994), for example, usefully reviewed 19 tools to support process improvement and redesign including static, dynamic, computer-assisted software engineering (CASE), and work flow. Im et al. (1999) discussed the role of software tools in BPR projects based on survey data received from practitioners. Perhaps the most extensive survey to date is by Hommes (2005), who listed over 350 BPM tools.

Taken together, studies of BPM techniques and tools suggest that a contingent approach best describes current practice, the contingent aspects being factors such as the goals of the project, scale, and scope of change; the opportunity for IT support; culture; and so on. It should also be noted that, although advanced modeling can sometimes be important, often simple word processors and spreadsheets are adequate for a BPM exercise. If more formal BPM techniques and tools are employed, this would not only provide technical rigor and test the effects of alternative designs but also support communication and participation.

Although many different approaches and methodologies are in use, few have been specifically designed to cope with the demands of modeling business processes. Instead, practitioners adapted techniques and tools from manufacturing, industrial engineering, IS, the quality movement, or human resource management and applied them to BPM. Although this may sometimes be adequate, it is important to consider the nature of business processes. Childe et al. (1996) reported a fieldwork exploration of BPR experiences, in which they found that UK companies in general had an adequate understanding of the business process concept and that further research should instead be directed toward other areas. We are less sanguine about this issue and argue that a better understanding of the nature and features of business processes is crucial if modeling is to be more effective.

**Theoretical Views of Business Process Modeling**

Surprisingly, there are fewer theoretical papers on BPM than there are from advocates of particular methodologies and approaches. There are even fewer theoretical papers that examine BPM from an integrated perspective. An early exception is Curtis et al. (1992), who reviewed several modeling approaches and suggested a conceptual framework for process modeling in the context of software engineering. This framework places business processes in four positions: functional, representing the activities being performed with relevant flows; behavioral, representing when and how the activities are performed; organizational, representing where and by whom the activities are executed and what physical communication mechanisms and storage are used; and informational, representing entities flowing through the process, their structure, and relationships.

From a multidisciplinary point of view, Ackermann et al. (1999) developed a framework for process transformation that integrates strategy, IS, operations management, and statistical modeling. In a similar vein, Scholz-Reiter et al. (1999) reviewed state-of-the-art issues on BPM. Hommes and Reijswoud (2000) derived a framework with eight properties for evaluating the quality of BPM techniques. Lin et al. (2002) extended Curtis et al.'s framework with two additional perspectives—verification/validation and modeling procedure.

These apart, there are few significant attempts to develop theoretical and integrative positions on approaches to BPM, possibly because the development of BPM has been driven by practitioners rather than by academics. Although increasingly involved in researching BPM, academics generally focus their efforts on a given approach or respond and report on developments in practice. As Warboys et al. pointed out: "process modeling today still, to an extent, lacks such a theoretical grounding. A great deal of practical work has been carried out with mixed results, but an essential cohesion is absent" (1999, p. 31). In this chapter, we propose a theoretical framework that provides a cohesive discussion of the different streams of thought of BPM, including both soft and hard approaches.

**Business Processes: The Core of Business Process Modeling**

Without suitable definitions of business processes, it is hard to develop suitable approaches, whether theoretical or practical, to BPM. It would, however, seem that providing suitable definitions is more difficult than might appear to be the case. Most of the literature simply quotes (or adapts) the vague definitions put forward by reengineering pioneers—that is, a business process is a set of related activities that are of value to a customer.

Moreover, most attempts to take this debate a step further have a rather mechanistic feel. For example, Armistead and Rowland (1996) dedicated four chapters of their BPR book to business processes, but their strong operations management bias, with its mechanistic emphasis, is apparent. Similarly, Kock and McQueen (1996) reported an empirical study of 15 business processes in three companies but chose to stress structural features and information flows, using ideas from industrial engineering and systems analysis and design. Both studies argued that a business process is best viewed as a transformation of inputs from suppliers into outputs to customers and that this transformation can be hierarchically decomposed into subprocesses and activities. Although such views are not without value, they underemphasize the human side of business processes.

Moving away from such views, Ould (1995) argued that real-world processes are messier than the input–transformation–output view might suggest and that the "neat and tidy" hierarchy hides as much as it reveals. Instead, he argued that business processes are best viewed as networks in which a number of roles collaborate and interact to achieve a business goal. This still has a less-than-human feel, but it is a step in the right direction. Going further, Dietz (2001) emphasized people's roles and relationships and add a new dimension—a business process is seen as a set of closed loops of commitments.

Adopting a managerial perspective, Garvin (1998) discussed three types of organizational processes—work (business) processes, behavioral processes, and change processes. He argued that behavioral processes (i.e., decision-making processes, communication processes, and organizational learning processes) shape the way business processes are performed, determining their success or failure. Therefore, any successful attempt to improve business processes should explicitly tackle these rather implicit and intangible processes.

Given this diversity of views, what are the implications for business processes? A useful way to understand business processes is to regard them as multifaceted. Each perspective on business process is based on a set of assumptions about, for example, the nature of organizational life, and these assumptions in turn affect approaches to BPM. Each worldview thus acts as a filter that allows us to see certain things but to miss others. Therefore, in the next section, we propose a framework of four viewpoints so as to shed light on the multifaceted nature of business processes and to figure out how they might be modeled.

## FOUR PERSPECTIVES ON BUSINESS PROCESSES

The four perspectives presented here view business processes as deterministic machines, complex dynamic systems, interacting feedback loops, and social constructs. We first explain the theoretical background of our conceptual framework. We next discuss the underlying assumptions of each perspective and tease out their modeling implications and weaknesses.

### Background

This section organizes views of business process around four themes, each with a different emphasis and each illustrating important features of business processes. Two of these views are similar to metaphors found in Morgan (1997), whereas the other two are not really metaphors, but viewpoints. Morgan's metaphors have been widely employed in fields close to BPM. For instance, Peppard and Preece (1995) applied them to BPR, Pidd (1995) to operational research/management science (OR/MS), and Walsham (1991) to IS. It seems obvious that views and understandings of organizations are important when discussing BPM, as organizations provide the arena for business processes.

Our conceptual framework does not attempt to match each author's definition of business processes with a single perspective. Even one person's views can be multifaceted. Instead, it provides a useful way of organizing different points of views about business processes and allows a discussion of the assumptions underlying BPM's main streams. Thus, a richer and wider picture is likely to occur. As with Morgan's metaphors of organization, each viewpoint sheds light on some elements while obscuring others, and each has strengths and limitations. However, when considered together, they produce a set of complementary, yet competing, perspectives from which the nature of business process emerges.

### Business Processes as Deterministic Machines

The first view regards a business process as a fixed sequence of well-defined activities or tasks performed by "human machines" that convert inputs into outputs in order to accomplish clear objectives (Figure 3.2). Not surprisingly, this standpoint is close to Morgan's bureaucratic machine

Figure 3.2 **Business Processes as Deterministic Machines**

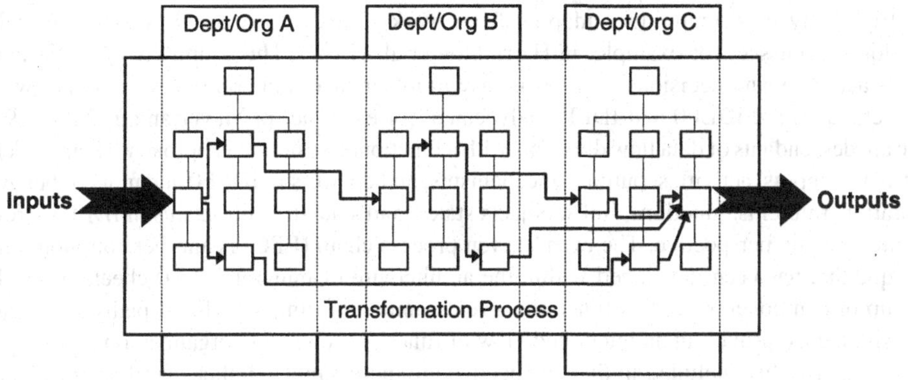

*Source:* Adapted from Melão and Pidd (2000). Reprinted with permission of Blackwell Publishing.

metaphor, and it assumes that the nature of a business process is unquestioned and its design is analogous to a technical engineering activity.

This view emphasizes structure (tasks, activities, and areas of responsibility), procedures (constraints and rules of the work to be performed), and goals (nature of the output to be obtained) of the business process being designed. The main criterion of good process design is efficiency in the use of money, resources, and time, subject to the constraint of satisfying customers' needs. IT plays an important role in this perspective—automating, coordinating, and supporting the reengineered process. This accords well with many structured processes found in stable manufacturing-type environments (e.g., order fulfillment and fast-food processes), and with many bureaucratic, paper-based processes found in some service environments (e.g., credit application and back-office processes).

The notion that a business process is a deterministic machine can be traced to Taylor's scientific management, in which manufacturing processes were made more efficient by an analytical approach. This divided manufacturing processes into well-defined tasks to be performed by interchangeable people. Each task was to be organized optimally by a manager who would instruct and train the worker in the best way to do the task. This would lead to an efficient overall manufacturing process.

In this vein, Davenport and Short defined a business process as "a set of logically related tasks performed to achieve a defined business outcome" (1990, p. 12). Clearly, this notion, along with their "new industrial engineering" metaphor, is symptomatic of a mechanistic view. Hammer and Champy (1993) gave a similar definition, although highlighting customer orientation and cross-functional activity. This is also the view of Armistead and Rowland (1996) and Kock and McQueen (1996), who focused on the structural and operational features of business processes. Early criticisms, which argued that BPR is the use of industrial engineering techniques applied to office and service environments, were therefore inevitable.

*Static Business Process Modeling*

As far as BPM is concerned, the view of a business process as a deterministic machine corresponds to the body of work underlying much of the hard and static approaches to BPM. In this, the stress is on mapping and documenting the flow of items, the activities, their logical dependency, and the resources needed. In recent times, many techniques from operations management, operational research, and IS have been "repackaged" to a BPM context.

A frequently used technique, adapted from work study, is process flow charting and its extensions, discussed, for example, in Harrington et al. (1997). The simplicity of its basic elements—activities and decisions—makes it easy to understand and communicate. Other widely used techniques are IDEF0 and IDEF3, advocated, for example, in Mayer and deWitte (1999). These are descendants of data flow diagrams with a functional, structured approach. Their modeling constructs—inputs, activities, outputs, mechanisms, and controls in IDEF0 and units of behavior, elaboration, referents, junctions, links, objects states, and state–transition arcs in IDEF3—reveal their mechanistic perspective. The event-driven process chain (EPC) is another commonly used technique that has been developed within the architecture of integrated IS (Scheer, 2000). It is made up of components such as functions, events, units, information, flows, paths, connectors, and assignments, providing an integrated view of functions, data, and organization.

Some approaches included in this perspective are more subtle. Rather than focusing on procedures and data, Ould (2005) proposed the Riva approach, which uses a more process-oriented technique called role activity diagrams (RAD). RAD allows a business process to be modeled diagrammatically through roles, goals, activities, interactions, and business rules. Unlike flow charts, IDEF, and EPC, RAD techniques are more appropriate for modeling business processes that involve the cooperation of several entities and less appropriate for modeling complex routings.

Other approaches are more ambitious. The business process modeling notation (BPMN), for instance, was developed in an attempt to standardize the process diagramming techniques (BPMI. org, 2004). Its modeling constructs—events, activities, gateways, sequence and message flows, associations, pools, lanes, data objects, groups, and annotations—derive from flow charting, but unlike these, they support the modeling of both intra- and interorganizational processes. Furthermore, they can be translated into a language for execution purposes. It is still unclear whether this notation will accomplish its goals, as its success is largely dependent on practitioner acceptance. Other relevant modeling standardization efforts at the level of interorganizational processes are the Supply-Chain Operations Reference Model (Supply Chain Council, 2005) and the RosettaNet Partner Interface Process (RosettaNet, 2005).

*Difficulties with a Mechanistic View*

Although these approaches have different strengths and limitations, we argue that the mechanistic view has two major drawbacks. First, by assuming that business processes can only be designed in rational and technical terms, it neglects human and organizational issues. Empirical evidence (Davenport, 1998; Markus and Keil, 1994; Markus et al., 2000; Sarker and Lee, 2002; Willcocks and Smith, 1995) strongly suggests that IT-driven BPR projects and a lack of attention to social-political and organizational issues are major reasons so many BPR projects fail. This does not mean that technical and rational issues can be ignored. Rather, it means that they should not be overemphasized at the cost of the mismanagement of human and organizational issues. The original view of the BPR pioneers that business processes should be designed efficiently, even at the expense of the human factor, may explain the stress of the mechanistic view in the literature. Writing on this same theme, Morgan stated that "by placing primary emphasis on the design of technical 'business systems' as the key to change, the majority of reengineering programs mobilized all kinds of social, cultural and political resistance that undermined their effectiveness" (1997, pp. 38–39).

The second criticism of this mechanistic view is that business processes are assumed static. Static models are simplified representations of business processes at a particular point in time. As such, they ignore dynamic behavior, which may change over time due to resource competition, interactions, or other sources of uncertainty. This does not mean that static models are pointless. In fact, static models are useful in understanding and representing the structural features of business processes and can be a valuable means of communication. However, business processes often display complex interactions that can only be understood by unfolding behavior through time.

**Business Processes as Complex Dynamic Systems**

Rather than viewing a business process as an assembly of interchangeable components, this second viewpoint focuses on the complex, dynamic, and interactive features of business processes. The basic idea is close to Morgan's metaphors of organism and flux and transformation, in which an open system adapts to a changing environment in order to survive. The mechanistic view focuses exclusively on structure and static objects, whereas this view emphasizes interaction and dynamic behavior.

Viewed in these open systems terms, a business process can have inputs, transformation, outputs, and boundaries (Figure 3.3). A business process can then be defined as a set of subsystems—people, tasks, structure, technology, and so on—that interact with each other (internal relationships) and with their environment (external relationships) in order to fulfill some objective(s). Each subsystem can be seen as a system, which can be hierarchically decomposed into further levels of detail. This, in turn, implies the definition of interfaces between subsystems so that they are able to communicate with each other. The view of a business process as a system, for example, is illustrated by Earl and Khan, who said that the "interdependent, interactive, boundary-crossing, super-ordinate goal conceptualization of process is essentially a systems view" (1994, p. 24).

The mechanistic perspective ignored important issues such as interactions with the external environment, but this viewpoint pays much more attention to this. Therefore, effectiveness (e.g., quality and service level) is likely to be a major design criterion rather than solely efficiency. Another characteristic of this point of view is holism, stressing the behavior of a business process as a whole rather than its parts. For example, Hammer argued that a sensible view of a business process "transcends individual activities. It concentrates instead on how activities fit together to produce the best outcome" (2001, p. 63). The use of multiskilled and autonomous workers/teams to deal with a business process in a holistic way illustrate particularly well how this holistic thinking can be put into practice.

This viewpoint matches well with many IT-enabled business processes. Writing in the context of business process management systems, Smith and Fingar expressed a systems view in writing that a business process is "the complete and dynamically coordinated set of collaborative and transactional activities that deliver value to customers" (2003, p. 47). This view is also portrayed in the notion of business processes emerging from Web services (Kalakota and Robinson, 2003), which they see as sets of dynamically integrated activities, crossing multiple applications, departments, and organizations that deliver services to employees, customers, suppliers, partners, and other players.

*Discrete Event Business Process Simulation*

Business processes are dynamic because of the interaction of their internal components and because of the interaction of the process with its environment. Discrete event simulation (Pidd,

Figure 3.3 **Business Processes as Complex Dynamic Systems**

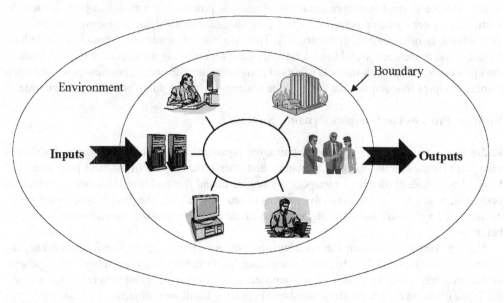

*Source:* Adapted from Melão and Pidd (2000). Reprinted with permission of Blackwell Publishing.

2004) provides a suitable way to model this dynamic behavior in terms of entities (e.g., items and resources) and discrete events (e.g., begin task and end task). The simulation model can then be used to conduct "what-if" experiments, avoiding the need for building or disrupting the real-world business process (Laguna and Marklund, 2004; Melão, 2001). Modular, parsimonious construction (Pidd, 2003) may usefully be employed by a modeler who needs to understand complex business processes. Other, more complex approaches, such as Petri nets (Dalal et al., 2004), or more emerging approaches, such as agent-based simulation (Strader et al., 1999), could also be applied under this stream.

Various authors have proposed discrete event simulation approaches to model business processes. Nidumolu et al. (1998) suggested discrete event systems specification (DEVS)/scheme, a generic simulation environment based on Lisp. Here, a business process is seen as a complex dynamic system that can be decomposed into a set of relatively independent subsystems. DEVS captures the structure of a business process through two generic modeling abstractions—atomic and coupled models. Vreede et al. (2003) reported on a custom Arena template of process modeling abstractions. This template was developed to support a problem-solving approach known as *dynamic modeling,* which combines groupware, participative design, and simulation modeling to analyze and improve business processes. In particular, they saw a business process as a network of interacting objects that display dynamic behavior and thus proposed the following modeling abstractions—message, product, person, actor, repository, link, tasks, and decisions. While DEVS seems best suited for complex and highly tuned simulations, dynamic modeling seems best suited for a high-level, and possibly fast, modeling exercise because it is based on a visual interactive modeling system.

Also in the context of BPM, Melão and Pidd (2006) proposed an improvement over existing business process simulation approaches. They described an extendable library of modeling components called BPSim++ that is simultaneously easy to use by business users and flexible so as to address new application areas or complex human behavior. BPSim++ bridges this compromise via a two-layered, component-based architecture. The top layer provides a visual, user-friendly environment in which the user can build models by composition from a repository of tailored components to a business process setting. These components were derived from a comparison of business and manufacturing processes. For model-building purposes, a business process is a network of interconnected activity components through which items flow. The second layer provides a programming framework from which the skilled user can modify the behavior of existing components and develop new components from other existing components or entirely from scratch.

*Difficulties with a Complex Dynamic Systems View*

If the complex dynamic system viewpoint is taken to an extreme, it also has weaknesses. First, it may lead to the neglect of the social-political dimension of a business process, since there is an implied belief that a business process can only be approached in logical and rational terms. The human aspect is only regarded as relevant as a resource for executing tasks; that is, the humanity of process participants is ignored. In this sense, this perspective is much like the previous one—the nature of the business process and of its actors is taken for granted. Better process designs are, in this view, based on an understanding of the logic of complex interactions with a view to meeting the objectives set for the process in question.

The second problem is that such approaches obviously have a cost. The time and skills required to build dynamic computer models of simple systems may not add any value over simple flowcharts or spreadsheets. Third, it ignores the feedback loops that may determine the behavior of many real-world business processes. Nevertheless, this viewpoint reminds us that different subsystems of a business process interact to produce complex dynamic behavior.

## Business Processes as Interacting Feedback Loops

This third perspective extends the complex dynamic system viewpoint by highlighting the information feedback structure of business processes. Both stress the complex, interactive, and dynamic features of business processes using systems thinking principles. However, the complex dynamic system viewpoint focuses on business processes with no intrinsic control (i.e., open loop systems), whereas this perspective claims that business processes are closed loops with intrinsic control. This standpoint is thus an attempt to understand the dynamic behavior of a business process not in terms of individual components but, rather, in terms of interactions between internal structure and policies.

The concept of a business process as a network of interacting feedback loops is shown in Figure 3.4. This depicts a business process as flows (rates) of resources (physical or nonphysical) from outside its boundaries through a sequence of stocks (levels) representing accumulations (e.g., materials) or transformations (e.g., raw material to finished product). The flows are regulated by policies (decisions) that represent explicit statements of actions to be taken in order to achieve a desired result (Pidd, 2003). These actions are taken based on information, and this is where the notion of information feedback loop comes into play.

Although the pioneers of BPR did not explicitly acknowledge the need to understand information feedback loops, it is widely recognized that a well-designed business process should include a control mechanism (Powell et al., 2001). For example, Smith and Fingar (2003) argued that the business process management life cycle includes eight distinct activities, one of which is monitoring

Figure 3.4 **Business Processes as Interacting Feedback Loops**

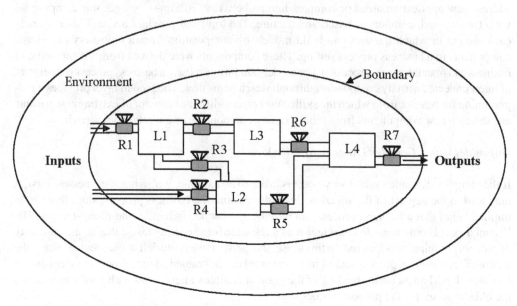

*Source:* Adapted from Melão and Pidd (2000). Reprinted with permission of Blackwell Publishing.

and control. However, there remains some dispute as to how to embed such monitoring and control activity within business processes. The use of system dynamics concepts discussed by Sterman (2000) and Vennix (1996) may offer one way to investigate how this could be achieved.

*System Dynamics*

Within the BPM field, the view of a business process as interacting feedback loops is supported by system dynamics modelers. A discrete event simulation is concerned with modeling discrete state changes and individual entities, whereas a system dynamics model of a business process operates at a more aggregated level of abstraction in which flow rates are modeled as continuous variables. System dynamics models can be used in two ways (Pidd, 2003; Vennix, 1996; Wolstenholme, 1990). First, they can be used in a qualitative mode, in which the structural features of the process are made explicit through diagrams (e.g., causal loop and flow diagrams). These, in turn, may become a basis for debate about process behavior. For example, if a process were to be organized along particular lines, then such qualitative models can provide insight into their potential stability. Second, system dynamics can be applied in a quantitative mode by transforming the diagrams into a set of equations so that a simulation of the process can be conducted. This allows a modeler to provide quantitative estimates of system effects.

Surprisingly, there are few reports of the application of system dynamics modeling in a BPM context. The few research studies conducted in this area have been primarily concerned with justifying the use of systems dynamics in a BPM context and illustrating the potential of its different uses, but going little further. This suggests two things. The first is that the BPM community may not be entirely convinced of the value of systems dynamics models. The second is that this area remains relatively unexplored and thus presents rich opportunities for further research. For example, van

Ackere et al. (1993) discussed the difficulties in controlling the behavior of logistical processes due to commonly occurring feedback and delay structures using the classic "beer game." They then showed the value of continuous simulation in redesigning the structure of business processes in terms of decision processes, physical processes, and information channels. More recently, Dutta (2001) suggested system dynamics simulation to investigate several business issues of network service provision processes.

Wolstenholme and Stevenson (1994) took a rather similar line but showed the value of both qualitative and quantitative system dynamics in mitigating the misperceptions of feedback loop structure using the Ithink system dynamics software. A more critical line is followed by Davies (1996), who showed the relevance of both qualitative and quantitative system dynamics to the BPM field. He concluded by asserting that "challenges for the future development of business dynamics centre on ease of use, integration with other methods, and education" (Davies, 1996, p. 241) in order to challenge some of the skepticism about system dynamics. From a different angle, Powell et al. (2001) used system dynamics models in an attempt to ascertain design guidelines for measuring and controlling typical business processes. We would argue, however, that the application of system dynamics to BPM is limited by the difficulty of deriving generic implications of different internal structures for organizational design.

*Difficulties with a Feedback Loop View*

As with the previous perspectives, the view of a business process as interacting positive and negative feedback loops has its limitations. First, when this perspective is taken to an extreme there is the risk of considering the human factor as only an instrument to be controlled or as an instrument exercising control. System dynamics methods can be used in a sensitive, interpretive mode, but the method carries no such guarantees. Indeed, it could be argued that its roots in control theory and the apparent ease with which models may be constructed could encourage an unthinking dehumanization of BPM.

Second, as Lane commented, "there is still too much belief and too little evidence" (1995, p. 617). Also taking a critical stance, Davies wrote, "system dynamics is easy to know but impossible to apply" (1996, p. 241). That is, system dynamics approaches are easy to understand at a superficial level, but may be difficult to use properly. Coyle (2000) and Wolstenholme (1999) suggested that system dynamics methods are best used when both qualitative and quantitative modes are mixed in a balanced way, providing the means not only to elicit different views, to foster learning, and to generate commitment, but also to add rigor to the modeling exercise. As far as BPM is concerned, this may well be a sensible way to proceed, if time and quantitative data are not critical constraints.

Perhaps these comments suggest that researchers might profitably devote some of their efforts into engaged research. An example is Nandhakumar and Jones (1997), who attempt to use system dynamics methods in real-world BPM as action research.

**Business Processes as Social Constructs**

Instead of seeing a business process as a predictable machine or as a dynamic organism pursuing clear objectives, this fourth perspective emphasizes business processes as made and enacted by people with different values, expectations, and (possibly, hidden) agendas. This implies that business processes need not exist in the objective and concrete sense as in the previous perspectives. Rather, they are abstractions, meanings, and judgments that people put on the real world, which result from a process of subjective construction of the minds of people. The focus here is on subjective and human aspects of the business process.

In this point, a business process can be defined in terms of different perceptions constructed by various individuals and groups as a result of different frames of interpretation. These frames, shaped by beliefs, values, expectations, and previous experience, act as filters enabling people to perceive some things but ignore others. For example, a production manager may regard an order fulfillment process as a way to ensure that the products are manufactured on time, while a marketing manager may regard it as a way to satisfy a customer's needs.

The existence of multiple (and often conflicting) views about what is going on, and about how the process is being and should be carried out, means that a different view of change is required. It implies that changes should result from a process of negotiation of conflicting interests, difficult as this may be. The view of a business process as a social construct is well suited with strategic, knowledge-intensive, and less tangible processes in which human activity is the major driver, such as health- and social-care processes, research processes, strategic planning processes, and so on. This view comes across quite strongly, for example, in Tinaikar et al. (1995), who called for a more humanistic social constructionist perspective in an attempt to encourage the adoption of an alternative conceptualization of business process.

*Soft Business Process Modeling*

It should be no surprise that this view of business processes as social constructs is closely linked to a "soft" strand of thinking about BPM. Unlike the previous viewpoints, soft models are sense-making interpretive devices developed to generate debate and learning about how the process is and should be carried out. It should be noted that the technical view is not entirely ignored. Indeed, techniques may be called in this perspective if the organizational context requires it.

Several authors suggested the application of Checkland's (1981) soft systems methodology (SSM) to provide a more balanced approach to modeling business processes. For example, Galliers (1994) observed that little attention has been given to exploring the role of soft modeling in dealing with process issues and then goes on to outline an SSM-based approach to undertake IS strategy/process change studies. Taking a more practitioner perspective, Patching (1995) showed how SSM provides a high-level, process-based language to approach business process change from a holistic point of view. Similarly, Chan and Choi (1997) illustrated how SSM can be used to provide methodological support and an analytical framework as well as to deal with ill-defined situations in a business process setting.

In these studies, SSM is used to represent a business process as a would-be purposeful human activity system consisting of a set of logically interconnected activities through which actors convert inputs into outputs for customers. In addition, the business process operates under certain environmental constraints, and monitoring and control are executed by process owners. Moreover, the purposeful activity of the business process can be seen from different angles (Figure 3.5).

Soft BPM also relates to the humanistic view advocated by Mumford (2003) in which a business process is seen as a set of interacting socio-technical systems. The objective is an integration of both social and technical needs through a participative approach. Unlike SSM, socio-technical design places little stress on the cultural and political environment. Another approach that could be employed under this perspective is cognitive mapping (Eden, 1988; Eden and Ackermann, 2001). For instance, Kwahk and Kim (1999) proposed a two-phase cognitive modeling approach so as to help to identify organizational conflicts and to help generate commitment to transform business processes. Here, a business process is a set of cause–effect relationships as perceived by different organizational members. This approach recognizes that conflicting interests may cause

Figure 3.5 **Business Processes as Social Constructs**

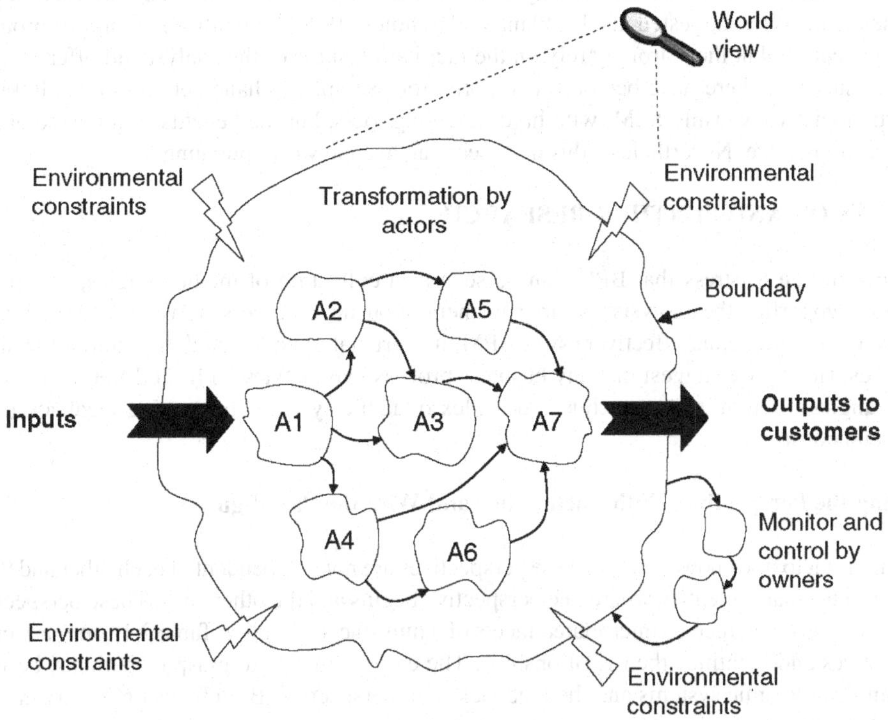

*Source:* Adapted from Melão and Pidd (2000). Reprinted with permission of Blackwell Publishing.

resistance to change from participants and, unlike SSM and socio-technical design, offers advice on how to resolve them.

Also with foundations on social construction is the goal–exception–dependency framework suggested by Katzenstein and Lerch (2000). This framework aims to map the social and psychological context underneath business processes. Here, a business process is seen as a network of dependencies between individuals who play different organizational roles and those who may have conflicting goals. As with cognitive mapping, this framework focuses on the constructions made by individuals, but it is more process oriented, as it goes beyond simple cause–effect relationships. Dietz (2001) proposed an alternative methodology for modeling business processes called dynamic essential modeling of organization (DEMO), based on the language-action paradigm (Habermas, 1984; Winograd and Flores, 1987). Unlike previous approaches, DEMO focuses on activities performed by people who engage in conversations. Thus, a business process is a social system made of a network of commitments between actors involving three different steps—order, execution, and result. DEMO includes several diagramming techniques that capture such networks of commitments.

*Difficulties with a Social Construction View*

The social constructionist viewpoint, when considered as the sole basis for modeling business processes, may also have difficulties. First, the stress on "cultural feasibility" may impede the attainment of more efficient and radical designs. Second, this perspective alone is unable to provide an objective, quantitative assessment of business process changes. Finally, although it recognizes the political environment, it offers no way of dealing with it other than the need to conduct several analyses of the type suggested in Checkland and Scholes (1990). Cognitive mapping approaches are an exception, but they strongly rely on the facilitation skills of the analyst and offer no guarantee of success. There have been a few reports, for example, Lehaney et al. (1999), linking a constructionist view, using SSM, with hard modeling tools, but the benefits of doing so are not yet clear in practice. Nevertheless, this does seem an avenue worth pursuing.

## DISCUSSION AND FURTHER RESEARCH

We have chosen to stress that BPM can be seen as a collection of methodologies, techniques, and tools supporting the analysis and improvement of business processes. We have argued that to achieve greater modeling effectiveness in BPM, it is crucial to understand the nature of business processes. Hence, we suggest that any business process may be viewed from different and competing angles—deterministic machines, complex dynamic systems, interacting feedback loops, and social constructs.

### Relating the Perspectives With Each Other and With the Paradigms

It is important to note, however, that these perspectives are not independent of each other and that it is difficult to clearly identify where one perspective begins and the other ends. These perspectives are perhaps best regarded as interrelated facets of a multifaceted reality. Table 3.1 summarizes the perspectives and identifies their relationships. The easiest linkage to grasp is, perhaps, between the complex dynamic systems and the feedback loop perspective. Both focus on the organic and dynamic features of business processes. However, the latter view extends the former in an attempt to consider information feedback structure. Both perspectives in turn are related to the mechanistic view, as they all tend to overlook social considerations if taken to extremes.

On the other hand, the links with the social construction view are more difficult to perceive because it explicitly attempts to consider what other perspectives missed—the human nature of business processes. However, it is still possible to establish relationships with the complex dynamic systems and the feedback loop perspectives in the domain of SSM. All have in common systems ideas, although they are used in different ways. In the complex dynamic systems perspective, systems ideas are used to represent real-world business processes, whereas in the social construction view, systems thinking is applied as an intellectual device to reason about peoples' perspectives. In the feedback loop view, the use of systems ideas is not so obvious because it can be used in both a positivistic and an interpretive way.

As mentioned earlier, each perspective has strengths, but also limitations when taken to extremes. When combined, however, as with metaphors, they provide a range of complementary ideas from which one can better consider the nature of business processes. This observation and the known problems of practical BPM lead us to state that business processes have a mixed and apparently conflicting nature. They have technical and social, tangible and intangible, objective and subjective, quantitative and qualitative dimensions. Supporting this view, Grover et al. (1995) reported on a large-scale survey of the implementation of BPR, in which they found that business processes are best seen as dynamic socio-technical systems. Sarker and Lee (2002) provided evidence of the dangers associated with exclusive technocentric or sociocentric approaches. They argued, instead, that the successful implementation of business process transformation relies on a balanced consideration to both social and technical issues. In the broader field of IS, Checkland

Table 3.1

## Summary of the Perspectives and Their Relationships

| | Deterministic Machines | Dynamic Complex Systems | Interacting Feedback Loops | Social Constructs |
|---|---|---|---|---|
| Focus | Structural and operational features | Dynamic and complex behavior | Feedback control mechanisms | Human aspects |
| Strengths | Emphasizes rational and efficient designs | Highlights the value of understanding dynamic behavior | Stresses the role played by feedback loop structure | Stresses the need to tackle social-cultural issues |
| Weaknesses | Neglects human issues; ignores dynamic behavior | Neglects human issues; ignores feedback control | Can be mechanistic | Cannot provide objective and quantitative assessments |
| Paradigm | Positivism | Positivism | Positivism, phenomenology | Phenomenology |
| Ontology | Processes are objective and "out there" | Processes are objective and "out there" | Depends on the paradigm chosen | Processes are subjective and socially constructed |
| Epistemology | Modeler is independent | Modeler is independent | Depends on the paradigm chosen | Modeler is involved |
| Modeling | Static modeling | Discrete event simulation | System dynamics | Soft modeling |
| Relationships | | Disregard social issues | | |
| | | Dynamic behavior of business processes | | |
| | | Systems thinking | | |

and Holwell (1998) argued that real organizations have a mixed nature as social units that rationally pursue well-defined objectives and as (changing) social constructs in which individuals or subgroups have different interests and agendas.

Table 3.1 also shows that each perspective is based on different philosophical assumptions about the nature of business processes and the relationship between the modeler and the business process being modeled. For example, the roots of the mechanistic view in hard, technical systems lead to an ontology in which the nature of the business process is objectively given, external, and composed of a number of discrete and tangible things. Epistemologically, the role of the modeler is to independently abstract the real-world business process so as to propose a cost-effective design that meets given objectives. Similarly, in the complex dynamic systems perspective, there is an implicit belief that business processes are "out there" and consist of external interacting entities. The role of the modeler is to understand, external to the real-world business process, the complex set of interactions by mimicking its dynamic behavior in order to propose a design alternative that meets the objectives of effectiveness and efficiency.

Unlike the other perspectives, the social construction view regards the nature of business processes as problematic, subjective, and nonmaterial. The modeler, more a facilitator than a technical expert, cannot appreciate real-world business processes neutrally and needs to work with the perceptions and meanings of the people involved in the process. The ontological and epistemological positions of the feedback loop viewpoint are more difficult to discern because of its hybrid nature. However, there may be a heavier inclination toward the positivistic stance due to its roots in control theory. Finally, it must be pointed out that the philosophical stances suggested here should not be regarded as rigid. For example, there is no reason why the dynamic complex systems perspective should not be applied in an interpretive way, uncommon though this may be.

**Implications for Practice**

What are the practical implications of these four perspectives on business processes and BPM? One practical problem with contingent frameworks is that what seems beguilingly simple on paper turns out to be rather difficult in practice, and a framework based on these four perspectives is no exception. Nevertheless, it would be wrong to regard it as useless, because it may be difficult at this stage to prescribe how it might be used by practitioners. There is a parallel with the approach to problem structuring in management science suggested in Pidd (2003), using the ideas of Goffman (1974) and Schön (1982). Problem structuring is an attempt to define the issues to be tackled in the modeling process. Pidd suggests that problems should be viewed as social constructs that, "like beauty, . . . are defined in the eyes of the beholder" (2003, p. 63). Problem structuring, thus, is a process in which different frames are applied and various "problems" are named, so as to provide a handle for their resolution. Thus, problem structuring is a process of exploration in which multiple perspectives are useful, and it may be that the same ideas apply in the early stages of business process investigation. It is unlikely that many management science practitioners will gladly delve into the detail of Goffman's sociology. Nevertheless, it provides useful insights that can be used to guide thoughtful practice.

Perhaps the same is true of the four perspectives presented here? Few BPM and IS professionals will bother to delve into the detailed assumptions that underlie the development of the perspectives. Nevertheless, the multifaceted view does provide useful insights for practice. For example, if a BPM project focuses on the analysis and improvement of technical, well-defined processes, then the techniques and tools underlying the mechanistic perspective may well be appropriate. If the business process being analyzed displays unpredictable, complex interactions, then discrete event simulation techniques may be suitable. A business process with a feedback loop structure would seem to call for systems dynamic approaches. On the other hand, if the focus is on problematic human processes, then the methodologies under the social construction umbrella would seem to deliver a useful contribution.

To aid practitioners further in selecting the methodologies, tools, and techniques appropriate to the process under study, this chapter also discussed the strengths and limitations of different BPM approaches. In general, static approaches are useful for understanding and communicating the structure of business process, but they lack a time dimension and, if used in isolation, ignore social-political issues. Discrete event simulation approaches are invaluable for understanding complex process interactions, yet they are resource consuming and, used blindly, may neglect social-political considerations. System dynamics approaches are helpful for modeling business processes with feedback loop structure; however, they may be rather mechanistic. Soft approaches are useful for addressing social-cultural issues, but they lack the ability to provide an objective, quantitative assessment of business process changes.

In addition, the results of this study stress the importance of pluralistic and multidisciplinary modeling approaches. Willcocks and Smith (1995) suggested that many process improvement programs end in failure because the methodologies adopted are partial in their approach. Commenting on the reengineering fiasco, Davenport and Perez-Guardado (1999) argued that process change programs are better approached from different fronts in a multifaceted way and illustrate this using an ecology metaphor. Hence, IS professionals can use these viewpoints to construct more powerful modeling approaches. By thinking about alternative views on business processes and using different BPM approaches, the modeler should be in a better position to capture the richness and complexity of the situation, avoiding the limitations of partial analysis.

Thus, any practical methodology should include provisions for more than one viewpoint. For example, the complex dynamic systems view could be strengthened by the social construction view, with simulation to provide a quantitative assessment of process changes and with SSM to ensure social and cultural feasibility. Ackermann et al. (1999), Warboys et al. (1999), Wastell et al. (1994), and Wood et al. (1995) proposed a number of approaches aiming to link hard and soft modeling tools. Although their pertinence to a business process context needs to be established, these examples provide evidence of interest in such a methodology.

## CONCLUDING REMARKS

Throughout this chapter, we have argued that the business process transformation literature has sparse and inconsistent discussions about the nature of business processes. This is perplexing given that understanding the nature of business processes is essential for their transformation. We proposed a four-viewpoint framework to enable the examination of the nature of business processes and the discussion of the multifarious modeling approaches used to transform them. Our conclusion is that business processes have a multifaceted nature and, consequently, many business process transformation projects would be better off if they incorporated pluralistic and multidisciplinary approaches.

This chapter contributes to the IS literature in three fundamental ways. First, it provides a lucid discussion of the evolution of BPR into process management. In particular, we have discussed how BPR evolved from a radical, intra-organizational, IT-led, mechanistic, and inspirational approach to a contingent, interorganizational, IT-enabled, holistic, and systematic approach. Second, it draws the attention of the IS community to the fact that business processes are characterized by a multitude of aspects and that any successful transformation effort needs to consider all of those aspects.

62    MELÃO AND PIDD

Finally, the conceptual framework clarifies the nature of business processes as well as brings cohesion to what is currently a fragmented field. It extends the conceptual framework of Curtis et al. (1992) by giving a place to soft modeling and by considering BPM from a holistic and multidisciplinary perspective. It brings together a wide and diverse literature including OR/MS, IS/IT, software engineering, operations management, industrial engineering, and organizational research. An interesting avenue for further research is to extend and fully develop the practical aspects of this framework.

## ACKNOWLEDGMENT

This is a revised and updated version of an article previously published as N. Melão and M. Pidd, A conceptual framework for understanding business processes and business process modelling. *Information Systems Journal,* 10 (2000), 105–129. Portions of previous material reprinted with permission of Blackwell Publishing.

## REFERENCES

Ackermann, F.; Walls, L.; Meer, R.; and Borman, M. 1999. Taking a strategic view of BPR to develop a multidisciplinary framework. *Journal of the Operational Research Society,* 50, 195–204.

Aguilar-Savén, R. 2004. Business process modelling: A review and framework. *International Journal of Production Economics,* 90, 129–149.

Armistead, C., and Rowland, P. (eds.). 1996. *Managing Business Processes: BPR and Beyond.* Chichester, UK: John Wiley & Sons.

Bashein, B.; Markus, M.; and Riley, P. 1994. Preconditions for BPR success and how to prevent failures. *Information Systems Management,* 11 (Spring), 7–13.

Becker, J.; Kugeler, M.; and Rosemann, M. (eds.). 2003. *Process Management: A Guide for the Design of Business Processes.* Berlin: Springer-Verlag.

BPMI.org. 2004. Business process modeling notation (BPMN), version 1.0. Needham, MA, May 3, http://www.bpmi.org/downloads/BPML1.0.zip.

Broadbent, M.; Weill, P.; and Clair, D. 1999. The implications of information technology infrastructure for business process redesign. *MIS Quarterly,* 23, 2, 159–182.

Burke, G., and Peppard, J. (eds.). 1995. *Examining Business Process Re-engineering: Current Perspectives and Research Directions.* London: Kogan Page.

Carr, N. 2003. IT doesn't matter. *Harvard Business Review,* 81, 5, 41–49.

Champy, J. 2002. *X-Engineering the Corporation: Reinventing Your Business in the Digital Age.* New York: Warner Books.

Chan, S., and Choi, C. 1997. A conceptual and analytical framework for business process re-engineering. *International Journal of Production Economics,* 50, 211–223.

Checkland, P. 1981. *Systems Thinking, Systems Practice.* Chichester, UK: John Wiley & Sons.

Checkland, P., and Holwell, S. 1998. *Information, Systems and Information Systems: Making Sense of the Field.* Chichester, UK: John Wiley & Sons.

Checkland, P., and Scholes, J. 1990. *Soft Systems Methodology in Action.* Chichester, UK: John Wiley & Sons.

Childe, S.; Maull, R.; and Mills, B. 1996. UK experiences in business process re-engineering. The ESRC Business Processes Resource Centre, University of Warwick, Coventry.

Classe, A. 1994. *Software Tools for Re-engineering.* London: Business Intelligence.

Cock, D., and Hipkin, I. 1997. TQM and BPR: Beyond the beyond myth. *Journal of Management Studies,* 34, 5, 659–675.

Coyle, G. 2000. Qualitative and quantitative modelling in system dynamics: Some research questions. *System Dynamics,* 16, 3 (Fall), 225–244.

Curtis, B.; Marc, K.; and Over, J. 1992. Process modeling. *Communications of the ACM,* 35, 9, 75–90.

Dalal, N.; Kamath, M.; Kolarik, W.; and Sivaraman, E. 2004. Toward an integrated framework for modeling enterprise processes. *Communications of the ACM,* 47, 3, 83–87.

Davenport, T. 1993. *Process Innovation.* Boston: Harvard Business School Press.

———. 1996. Why re-engineering failed: The fad that forgot people. *Fast Company,* 1, 1, 70–74.

———. 1998. Putting the enterprise into the enterprise system. *Harvard Business Review,* 76, 4 (July–August), 121–131.

Davenport, T., and Perez-Guardado, M. 1999. Process ecology: A new metaphor for reengineering-oriented change. In J. Elzinga, T. Gulledge, and L. Chung-Yee (eds.), *Business Process Engineering: Advancing the State of the Art.* Norwell, MA: Kluwer Academic, pp. 25–41.

Davenport, T., and Short, J. 1990. The new industrial engineering: Information technology and business process redesign. *Sloan Management Review,* 31, 4, 11–27.

Davenport, T., and Stoddard, D. 1994. Re-engineering: Business change of mythic proportions? *MIS Quarterly,* 18, 2, 121–127.

Davenport, T.; Jarvenpaa, S.; and Beers, M. 1996. Improving knowledge work processes. *Sloan Management Review,* 37, 4, 53–65.

Davenport, T.; Prusak, L.; and Wilson, H. 2003. *What's the Big Idea? Creating and Capitalizing on the Best New Management Thinking.* Boston: Harvard Business School Press.

Davies, M. 1996. Business dynamics: Business process re-engineering and systems dynamics. In C. Armistead and P. Rowland (eds.), *Managing Business Processes: BPR and Beyond.* Chichester, UK: John Wiley & Sons, pp. 215–242.

Deakins, E., and Makgill, H. 1997. What killed BPR? Some evidence from the literature. *Business Process Management Journal,* 3, 1, 81–107.

Dennis, A.; Carte, T.; and Kelly, G. 2003. Breaking the rules: Success and failure in groupware-supported business process reengineering. *Decision Support Systems,* 36, 1, 31–47.

Dietz, J. 2001. DEMO: Towards a discipline of organization engineering. *European Journal of Operational Research,* 128, 351–363.

Dutta, A. 2001. Business planning for network services: A systems thinking approach. *Information Systems Research,* 12, 3, 260–283.

Earl, M., and Khan, B. 1994. How new is business process redesign? *European Management Journal,* 12, 1, 20–30.

Earl, M.; Sampler, J.; and Short, J. 1995. Strategies for business process re-engineering: Evidence from field studies. *Journal of Management Information Systems,* 12, 1 (Summer), 31–56.

Eden, C. 1988. Cognitive mapping. *European Journal of Operational Research,* 36, 1–13.

Eden, C., and Ackermann, F. 2001. SODA—The principles. In J. Rosenhead and J. Mingers (eds.), *Rational Analysis for a Problematic World Revisited.* Chichester, UK: John Wiley & Sons, pp. 43–60.

El Sawy, O. 2001. *Redesigning Enterprise Processes for e-Business.* Boston: McGraw-Hill.

———. 2008. Redesigning IT-enabled customer support processes for dynamic environments. In V. Grover and M.L. Markus (eds.), *Business Process Transformation. Advances in Management Information Systems.* Volume 9. Armonk, NY: M.E. Sharpe, pp. 157–183.

El Sawy, O., and Bowles, G. 1997. Redesigning the customer support process for the electronic economy: Insights from Storage Dimensions. *MIS Quarterly,* 21, 4, 457–483.

El Sawy, O.; Malhotra, A.; Gosain, S.; and Young, K. 1999. IT-intensive value innovation in the electronic economy: Insights from Marshall Industries. *MIS Quarterly,* 23, 3, 305–335.

Galliers, R. 1994. Information systems, operational research and business re-engineering. *International Transactions in Operational Research,* 1, 2, 159–167.

Galliers, R., and Baker, B. 1995. An approach to business process re-engineering: The contribution of socio-technical and soft OR concepts. *Infor,* 33, 4, 263–277.

Garvin, D. 1998. The processes of organization and management. *Sloan Management Review,* 39, 4, 33–50.

Giaglis, G. 2001. A taxonomy of business process modelling and information systems modelling techniques. *International Journal of Flexible Manufacturing Systems,* 13, 209–228.

Goffman, E. 1974. *Frame Analysis.* Harmondsworth, UK: Penguin Books.

Grover, V., and Kettinger, W. (eds.). 1995. *Business Process Change: Re-engineering Concepts, Methods and Technologies.* Harrisburg, PA: Idea Group.

———. 2000. *Process Think: Winning Perspectives for Business Change in the Information Age.* Harrisburg, PA: Idea Group.

Grover, V., and Malhotra, M. 1997. Business process re-engineering: A tutorial on the concept, evolution, method, technology and application. *Journal of Operations Management,* 15, 193–213.

Grover, V.; Jeong, S.; Kettinger, W.; and Teng, J. 1995. The implementation of business process re-engineering. *Journal of Management Information Systems*, 12, 1 (Summer), 109–144.

Guha, S.; Grover, V.; Kettinger, W.; and Teng, J. 1997. Business process change and organizational performance: Exploring an antecedent model. *Journal of Management Information Systems*, 14, 1 (Summer), 119–154.

Gunasekaran, A., and Kobu, B. 2002. Modeling and analysis of business process reengineering. *International Journal of Production Research*, 40, 11, 2521–2546.

Habermas, J. 1984. *The Theory of Communicative Action.* Boston: Beacon Press.

Hammer, M. 1990. Re-engineering work: Don't automate, obliterate. *Harvard Business Review*, 90, 4 (July–August), 104–112.

———. 1996. *Beyond Re-engineering.* London: Harper Collins.

———. 2001. *The Agenda: What Every Business Must Do to Dominate the Decade.* London: Random House.

———. 2002. Process management and the future of Six Sigma. *Sloan Management Review*, 43, 2, 26–32.

———. 2004. Deep change: How operational innovation can transform your company. *Harvard Business Review*, 82, 4 (April), 84–93.

Hammer, M., and Champy, J. 1993. *Re-engineering the Corporation: A Manifesto for Business Revolution.* New York: Harper Business.

———. 2001. *Re-engineering the Corporation: A Manifesto for Business Revolution,* rev. ed. New York: Harper Business.

Harmon, P.; Rosen, M.; and Guttman, M. 2001. *Developing E-Business Systems and Architectures: A Manager's Guide.* San Francisco: Morgan Kaufmann.

Harrington, H.; Esseling, E.; and Nimwegen, H. 1997. *Business Process Improvement Workbook.* New York: McGraw-Hill.

Hengst, M., and de Vreede, G. 2004. Collaborative business engineering: A decade of lessons from the field. *Journal of Management Information Systems*, 20, 4 (Spring), 85–113.

Hommes, B. 2005. Overview of business process modelling tools. Available at http://www.isa.its.tudelft. nl/~hommes/tools.html (accessed on June 21, 2005).

Hommes, B., and Reijswoud, V. 2000. Assessing the quality of business process modeling techniques. In R.H. Sprague Jr. (ed.), *Proceedings of the 33rd Annual Hawaii International Conference on System Sciences.* Los Alamitos, CA: IEEE Computer Society. Available at http://doi.ieeecomputersociety.org/10.1109/ HICSS.2000.926591.

Im, I.; El Sawy, O.; and Hars, A. 1999. Competence and impact of tools for BPR. *Information & Management*, 36, 301–311.

Jarvenpaa, S., and Stoddard, D. 1998. Business process redesign: Radical and evolutionary change. *Journal of Business Research*, 41, 1, 15–27.

Jones, M. 1994. Don't emancipate, exaggerate: Rhetoric, reality and reengineering. In R. Baskerville, S. Smithson, O. Ngwenyama, and J. DeGross (eds.), *Transforming Organisations with Information Technology.* Amsterdam: Elsevier Science, pp. 357–378.

———. 1995. The contradictions of business process re-engineering. In G. Burke and J. Peppard (eds.), *Examining Business Process Re-engineering: Current Perspectives and Research Directions.* London: Kogan Page, pp. 43–59.

Kalakota, R., and Robinson, M. 2003. *Services Blueprint: Roadmap for Execution.* Boston: Addison-Wesley.

Kamath, M.; Dalal, N.; Chaugule, A.; Sivaraman, E.; and Kolarik, W. 2003. A review of enterprise process modeling techniques. In V. Prabhu, S. Kumara, and M. Kamath (eds.), *Scalable Enterprise Systems: An Introduction to Recent Advances.* Boston: Kluwer Academic, pp. 1–32.

Katzenstein, G., and Lerch, F. 2000. Beneath the surface of organizational processes: A social representation framework for business process redesign. *ACM Transactions on Information Systems*, 18, 4, 383–422.

Kettinger, W.; Teng, J.; and Guha, S. 1997. Business process change: A study of methodologies, techniques, and tools. *MIS Quarterly*, 21, 1, 55–80.

Kock, N., and McQueen, R. 1996. Product flow, breadth and complexity of business processes. *Business Process Management Journal*, 2, 2, 8–22.

Kwahk, K., and Kim, Y. 1999. Supporting business process redesign using cognitive maps. *Decision Support Systems*, 25, 155–178.

Laguna, M., and Marklund, J. 2004. *Business Process Modeling, Simulation and Design.* Upper Saddle River, NJ: Prentice Hall.

Lane, D. 1995. On the resurgence of management simulations and games. *Journal of the Operational Research Society,* 46, 604–625.

Lehaney, B.; Clark, S.; and Paul, R. 1999. A case of an intervention in an outpatients department. *Journal of the Operational Research Society,* 50, 877–891.

Lin, F.; Yang, M.; and Pai, Y. 2002. A generic structure for business process modelling. *Business Process Management Journal,* 8, 1, 19–41.

Markus, M., and Keil, M. 1994. If we build it they will come: Designing information systems that users want to use. *Sloan Management Review,* 35, 4, 11–25.

Markus, M.; Axline, S.; Petrie, D.; and Tanis, C. 2000. Learning from adopters' experiences with ERP—Successes and problems. *Journal of Information Technology,* 15, 4, 245–265.

Mayer, R., and deWitte, P. 1999, Delivering results: Evolving BPR from art to science. In J. Elzinga, T. Gulledge, and L. Chung-Yee (eds.), *Business Process Engineering: Advancing the State of the Art.* Norwell, MA: Kluwer Academic Publishers, pp. 83–130.

Melão, N. 2001. Improving the effectiveness of business process modelling and simulation. Ph.D. dissertation, Lancaster University.

Melão, N., and Pidd, M. 2000. A conceptual framework for understanding business processes and business process modelling. *Information Systems Journal,* 10, 105–129.

———. 2003. Use of business process simulation: A survey of practitioners. *Journal of the Operational Research Society,* 54, 2–10.

———. 2006. Using component technology to develop a simulation library for business process modelling. *European Journal of Operational Research,* 172, 1, 163–178.

Morgan, G. 1997. *Images of Organization,* 2d ed. Thousand Oaks, CA: Sage.

Mumford, E. 1994. New treatments or old remedies: Is business process re-engineering really socio-technical design? *Journal of Strategic Information Systems,* 3, 313–326.

———. 2003. *Redesigning Human Systems.* Hershey, PA: Idea Group.

Nandhakumar, J., and Jones, M. 1997. Too close for comfort? Distance and engagement in interpretive information systems research. *Information Systems Journal,* 7, 109–131.

Nidumolu, S.; Menon, N.; and Zeigler, B. 1998. Object-oriented business process modeling and simulation: A discrete event system specification framework. *Simulation Practice and Theory,* 6, 533–571.

Ould, M. 1995. *Business Processes: Modelling and Analysis for Re-engineering and Improvement.* Chichester, UK: John Wiley & Sons.

———. 2005. *Business Process Management: A Rigorous Approach.* Swindon: British Computer Society.

Patching, D. 1995. Business process re-engineering: Don't scare the horses. *Management Services,* 39, 4, 8–11.

Peppard, J. 1996. Broadening visions of business process re-engineering. *Omega,* 24, 3, 255–270.

Peppard, J., and Preece, I. 1995. The content, context, and process of business process re-engineering. In G. Burke and J. Peppard (eds.), *Examining Business Process Re-engineering: Current Perspectives and Research Directions.* London: Kogan Page, pp. 157–185.

Pidd, M. 1995. Pictures from an exhibition: Images of OR/MS. *European Journal of Operational Research,* 81, 479–488.

———. 2003. *Tools for Thinking: Modelling in Management Science,* 2d ed. Chichester, UK: John Wiley.

———. 2004. *Computer Simulation in Management Science,* 5th ed. Chichester, UK: John Wiley.

Porter, M. 2001. Strategy and the Internet. *Harvard Business Review,* 79, 3 (March), 63–78.

Powell, S.; Schwaninger, M.; and Trimble, C. 2001. Measurement and control of business processes. *System Dynamics,* 17 (Spring), 63–91.

RosettaNet. 2005. RosettaNet home: "Standards." Dayton, OH. Available at http://portal.rosettanet.org/cms/sites/RosettaNet/Standards/index.html (accessed on June 21, 2005).

Sarker, S., and Lee, A. 2002. Using a positivistic case research methodology to test three competing theories-in-use of business process redesign. *Journal of the AIS,* 2, 1–72.

Scheer, A. 2000. *Aris: Business Process Modeling,* 3d ed. Berlin: Springer-Verlag.

Scholz-Reiter, B.; Stahlmann, H.; and Nethe, A. (eds.). 1999. *Process Modelling.* Berlin: Springer-Verlag.

Schön, D. 1982. *The Reflective Practitioner: How Professionals Think in Action.* New York, Basic Books.

Silver, E. 2004. Process management instead of operations management! *Manufacturing & Service Operations Management,* 6, 4, 273–279.

Smith, H., and Fingar, P. 2003. *Business Process Management: The Third Wave.* Tampa: Meghan-Kiffer Press.

Sterman, J. 2000. *Business Dynamics: Systems Thinking and Modeling for a Complex World.* Boston: McGraw-Hill.

Stoddard, D., and Jarvenpaa, S. 1995. Business process redesign: Tactics for managing radical change. *Journal of Management Information Systems,* 12, 1 (Summer), 81–107.

Strader, S.; Lin, F.; and Shaw, M. 1999. Business-to-business electronic commerce and convergent assembly supply chain management. *Journal of Information Technology,* 14, 4 (December), 361–374.

Supply Chain Council. 2005. SCOR model. Washington. Available at http://www.supply-chain.org/cs/root/scor_tools_resources/scor_model/scor_model (accessed on June 21, 2005).

Teng, J.; Jeong, S.; and Grover, V. 1998. Profiling successful reengineering projects. *Communications of the ACM,* 41, 6, 96–102.

Tinaikar, R.; Hartman, A.; and Nath, R. 1995. Rethinking business process re-engineering: A social constructionist view. In G. Burke and J. Peppard (eds.), *Examining Business Process Re-engineering: Current Perspectives and Research Directions.* London: Kogan Page, pp. 107–116.

van Ackere, A.; Larsen, E.; and Morecroft, J. 1993. Systems thinking and business process redesign: An application to the beer game. *European Management Journal,* 11, 4, 412–423.

Vennix, J. 1996. *Group Model Building: Facilitating Team Learning Using System Dynamics.* Chichester, UK: John Wiley & Sons.

Vreede, G. de; Verbraeck, A.; and Eijck, D. 2003. Integrating the conceptualization and simulation of business processes: A modelling method and Arena template. *Simulation,* 79, 43–55.

Walsham, G. 1991. Organisational metaphors and information systems research. *European Journal of Information Systems,* 1, 2, 83–94.

Warboys, B.; Kawalek, P.; Robertson, I.; and Greenwood, M. 1999. *Business Information Systems: A Process Approach.* London: McGraw-Hill.

Wastell, D.; White, P.; and Kawalek, P. 1994. A methodology for business process redesign: Experiences and issues. *Journal of Strategic Information Systems,* 3, 1, 23–40.

Willcocks, L., and Smith, G. 1995. IT-enabled business process re-engineering: Organizational and human resource dimensions. *Journal of Strategic Information Systems,* 4, 3, 279–301.

Winograd, T., and Flores, F. 1987. *Understanding Computers and Cognition.* Reading, MA: Addison-Wesley.

Wolstenholme, E. 1990. *System Enquiry: A System Dynamics Approach.* Chichester, UK: John Wiley & Sons.

———. 1999. Qualitative vs. quantitative modelling: The evolving balance. *Journal of the Operational Research Society,* 50, 4, 422–428.

Wolstenholme, E., and Stevenson, R. 1994. Systems thinking and systems modeling—New perspectives on business strategy and process design. *Management Services,* 38, 9, 22–25.

Wood, J.; Vidgen, R.; Wood-Harper, A.; and Rose, J. 1995. Business process redesign: Radical change or reactionary tinkering? In G. Burke and J. Peppard (eds.), *Examining Business Process Re-engineering: Current Perspectives and Research Directions.* London: Kogan Page, pp. 245–261.

# PART II

# FUNDAMENTAL APPROACHES TO THE ANALYSIS AND REDESIGN OF BUSINESS PROCESSES

CHAPTER 4

# THE BUG FIXING PROCESS IN PROPRIETARY AND FREE/LIBRE OPEN SOURCE SOFTWARE

## A Coordination Theory Analysis

KEVIN CROWSTON

*Abstract:* To support business process transformation, we must first be able to represent business processes in a way that allows us to compare and contrast them or to design new ones. This chapter uses coordination theory to analyze the bug fixing processes in the proprietary operating system development group of a large minicomputer manufacturer and for the Free/Libre Open Source Software Linux operating system kernel. Three approaches to identifying dependencies and coordination mechanisms are presented. Mechanisms analyzed include those for task assignment, resource sharing, and managing dependencies between modules of source code. The proprietary development organization assigned problem reports to engineers based on the module that appeared to be in error, because engineers only worked on particular modules. Alternative task assignment mechanisms include assignment to engineers based on workload or voluntary assignment, as in Linux. In the proprietary process, modules of source code were not shared but, rather, were "owned" by one engineer, thus reducing the need for coordination. In Linux, where multiple developers can work on the same modules, alternative resource sharing mechanisms have been developed to manage source code. Finally, the proprietary developers managed dependencies between modules informally, relying on their personal knowledge of which other engineers used their code. The Linux process allows developers to change code in multiple modules, but emphasizes modularity to reduce the need to do so. By helping in the identification of dependencies in the bug fixing processes, drawing upon coordination theory streamlines bug fixing activities of a large mini-computer manufacturer and for the Free/Libre Open Source Software Linux operating system kernel.

*Keywords:* Free/Libre Open Source Software, Software Maintenance, Coordination Theory, Linux, Bug Fixing

## INTRODUCTION

To support business process transformation, we must first be able to represent business processes in a way that allows us to compare and contrast them or to design new ones (Malone et al., 1999). Consider the software problem (bug) fixing process, a process that I will use as a source for examples in this chapter. Customers having problems with a piece of software (a bug) report the problems to its developers, who (they hope) eventually provide some kind of solution (a bug fix). In this chapter, I compare the bug fixing processes for a proprietary minicomputer operating system and for the Free/Libre Open Source Software (FLOSS)[1] Linux kernel project. The company I studied had an elaborate process to receive problem reports, filter out duplicates of known problems, identify which modules of the system are apparently at fault for novel problems, and route the reports to the software engineers responsible for those modules. Along the way, an engineer might develop a work-around (i.e., a way to avoid the problem); the responsible software engineer might develop a change to the code of part of the system (i.e., a patch) to fix it. The patch would then be sent to other groups who test it, integrate it into the total system, and, eventually, send it to the customers who originally had the problem. (A more detailed description of this process appears below.) The Linux bug fixing process (which has evolved over time) has a similar but different set of steps. The description and comparison of these processes raise several questions that are key for business process transformation: Why is the process structured this way, with finely divided responsibility for different parts of the process? In what ways are the two processes (proprietary and FLOSS) similar or different and what are the implications of these similarities and differences? And, more simply, how else could software development organizations approach problem fixing?

In the remainder of this chapter, I present one approach to answering these questions. In the next section I briefly review coordination theory and show how it can guide the analysis and transformation of a process. The bulk of the chapter presents a detailed example. The following sections describe the case sites—the software development division of a minicomputer manufacturer and the Linux kernel project—and the data collection and analysis methods. The analysis section presents the dependencies and coordination mechanisms identified in the cases. The chapter concludes by briefly evaluating the coordination theory approach and discussing its application in other settings.

## THEORY: A COORDINATION THEORY APPROACH TO BUSINESS PROCESSES

I use coordination theory as an approach to analyzing processes and for understanding their diversity. If we examine many companies, we will observe a wide variety of approaches to the software bug fixing process. For example, in other companies (and other parts of the company I studied), when a problem report arrives, it is simply assigned to the next free engineer. If we examine many processes, we will see a similar range of possibilities. Individuals (or firms) may be either generalists who perform a wide variety of tasks or specialists who perform only a few. Activities may be assigned to actors within a single organization, as with bug fixing; other assignments may take place in a market, as with auditing, consulting, and an increasingly wide variety of services; and, finally, assignments may be given to others in a network of corporations.

Despite this diversity, when we systematically compare processes, patterns emerge. Organizations that perform the same task often perform essentially the same basic activities. For example, organizations that fix software bugs must diagnose the bug, write code for a fix, and integrate the change with the rest of the system. More broadly, many engineering change processes have activities similar to those for software.

Although these general activities are often the same, the processes differ in important details: how these large abstract tasks are decomposed into activities, who performs particular activities, and how the activities are assigned. In other words, processes differ in how they are coordinated. However, even with coordination, there are common patterns: similar problems arise and are managed similarly. For example, nearly every organization must assign activities to specific actors, and task assignment mechanisms can be grouped into a few broadly similar categories. Such mechanisms are the subject matter of coordination theory.

## Coordination Theory

To analyze these patterns of coordination, I use the framework developed by Malone and Crowston, who define coordination as "managing dependencies between activities" (1994, p. 90). They define coordination theory as the still developing body of "theories about how coordination can occur in diverse kinds of systems" (1994, p. 87). Malone and Crowston analyze group action in terms of *actors* performing *interdependent activities* to achieve *goals*. These activities may also require or create *resources* of various types (defined broadly as anything necessary for, or the product of, an activity, including raw materials, tools, information, and the effort of actors).

For example, in the case of software bug fixing, *activities* include diagnosing the bug, writing code for a fix, and integrating it with the rest of the system, as mentioned above. *Actors* include the customers and various employees of the software company. In some cases, it may be useful to analyze a group of individuals as a collective actor (Abell, 1987). For example, to simplify the analysis of coordination within a particular subunit, the other subunits with which it interacts might all be represented as collective actors. The *goal* of software bug fixing appears to be eliminating problems in the system, but alternative goals—such as appearing responsive to customer requests—could also be analyzed. In taking this approach, we adopt Dennett's (1987) intentional stance: as there is no completely reliable way to determine someone's goals (or if they have goals at all), we, as observers, can only impute goals to the actors and analyze how well the process accomplishes these goals. Finally, *resources* include the problem reports, information about known problems, computer time, software patches, source code, and so on.

It should be noted that in developing this framework, Malone and Crowston describe coordination mechanisms as relying on other necessary group functions, such as decision making, communications, and development of shared understandings and collective sense making (Britton et al., 2000; Crowston and Kammerer, 1998). To develop a complete model of some process would involve modeling all of these aspects: coordination, decision making, and communications. In practice, our analyses have tended to focus on the coordination aspects, bracketing the other phenomena.

According to coordination theory, actors in organizations face *coordination problems* that arise from dependencies that constrain how tasks can be performed. These dependencies may be inherent in the structure of the problem (e.g., components of a system may interact with each other, constraining the kinds of changes that can be made to a single component without interfering with the functioning of others) or they may result from decomposition of the goal into activities or the assignment of activities to actors and resources (e.g., two engineers working on the same component face constraints on the kind of changes they can make without interfering with each other).

To overcome these coordination problems, actors must perform additional activities, which Malone and Crowston (1994) call *coordination mechanisms*. For example, a software engineer planning to change one module in a computer system must first check if the changes will affect other modules and then arrange for any necessary changes to modules that will be affected; two engineers working on the same module must each be careful not to overwrite the other's changes. Coordination mechanisms may be specific to a particular setting, such as a code management system to control changes to software, or general, such as hierarchical or market mechanisms to manage assignment of activities to actors or other resources.

The first key claim of coordination theory is that dependencies and the mechanisms for managing them are general—that is, a particular dependency and a mechanism to manage it will be found in a variety of organizational settings. For example, a common coordination problem is that a particular activity may require specialized skills, thus constraining which actors can work on it; this dependency between an activity and an actor arises in some form in nearly every organization. Coordination theory thus suggests identifying and studying common dependencies and their related coordination mechanisms across a wide variety of organizational settings.

The second claim is that there are often several coordination mechanisms that could be used to manage a dependency, as the task assignment example illustrates. Possible mechanisms to manage the dependency between an activity and an actor include manager selection of a subordinate, first-come-first-served allocation, and various kinds of markets. Again, coordination theory suggests that these mechanisms may be useful in a wide variety of organizational settings. Organizations with similar activities to achieve similar goals will have to manage the same dependencies, but may choose different coordination mechanisms, thus resulting in different processes.

Finally, the previous two claims taken together imply that, given an organization performing some task, one way to generate alternative processes is to first identify the particular dependencies and coordination problems faced by that organization and then consider what alternative coordination mechanisms could be used to manage them.

To summarize, according to coordination theory, the activities in a process can be separated into those that are necessary to achieve the goal of the process (e.g., that directly contribute to the output of the process) and those that serve primarily to manage various dependencies between activities and resources. This conceptual separation is useful because it focuses attention on the coordination mechanisms, which are believed to be a particularly variable part of a process, thus suggesting an approach to redesigning processes. Furthermore, coordination mechanisms are primarily information processing activities and therefore, good candidates for support from information technology.

The aim of coordination theory is not new: defining processes and attempting to improve performance have been constant goals of business process transformation. The focus on dependencies is also a recurring theme. Even the idea of substitute mechanisms has been suggested; for example, Lawler (1989) argues that the functions of an organization's hierarchy, many of which are ways of coordinating lower-level actions, can be accomplished in other ways, such as work design, information systems, or new patterns of information distribution. However, coordination theory makes many of these earlier notions more precise by decomposing tasks and resources. For example, the classic distinction among sequential, interdependent, and network processes of organizing can be decomposed into particular dependencies managed by particular mechanisms. In this view, a network (Powell, 1990), for example, is not a property of a collection of organizations per se, but rather a restriction on which actor is chosen to work on a particular task (i.e., how a task–actor dependency is managed). In a hierarchy, a task is assigned to an actor chosen from within the organization, such as based on specialization or managerial decision; in a market, from the set of suppliers active in the market, such as by bidding; and in a network, from the appropriate member of the network.

## A Typology of Coordination Mechanisms

As a guide to such analyses, Crowston (1991a; 2003) presents a typology of dependencies and associated coordination mechanisms. The typology of dependencies and examples of associated coordination mechanisms are shown in Table 4.1.

Table 4.1

## A Typology of Dependencies and Associated Coordination Mechanisms

**Task Uses Resource**
1. Determine needs
2. Identify resources
   - ads
   - prepared list
   - only one resource
3. Collect information on resources
   - by bidding
   - manager knows
4. Pick best
5. Do assignment
   - mark resource in use
6. Manage flow dependencies from acquiring resource to using resource

**Task Requires Multiple Resources Simultaneously**
1. Preassign resources to simplify coordination problem
2. Manage dependency on the fly
   - avoid or detect and resolve deadlock
   - detect and resolve starvation

**Sharing: Multiple Tasks Use the Same Resource**
- Ensure same version of sharable resources
   - destroy obsolete versions
   - copy master prior to use
   - check versions prior to use
   - detect and fix problems after the fact
- Schedule use of nonshareable but reusable resources
   1. check for conflict before using and then mark the resource as "in use"
   2. manage flow of resource from one task to another
- Allocate nonreusable resources
   - divide the resource among the tasks
   - abandon one task
   - get more resources

**Flow: One Task Uses a Resource Created by Another**
1. Usability (i.e., the right thing)
   - user adapts to resource as created
   - creator gets information from user to tailor resource
   - third party sets standard, followed by both producer and consumer
2. Prerequisite (i.e., at the right time)
   - producer produces first
     - follow plan
     - monitor usage
       - wait to be asked
       - standard reorder points
       - when out
       - just-in-time
   - consumer waits until produced
     - monitor
     - be notified
3. Accessibility (i.e., in the right place)
   - physical goods
     - truck
   - information
     - on paper
     - verbally
     - by computer

*(continues)*

Table 4.1 *(continued)*

**Common Output: Multiple Tasks Create the Same Output**
1. Detect **common output**
   - database of known problems
2. Manage **common outputs**
   - effects overlap or are the same
     - eliminate one task (manage shared resource)
     - merge tasks take advantage of synergy
   - effects are incompatible
     - abandon one
     - do not try to achieve them at the same time

**Composition of Tasks**
- Choose tasks to achieve a given **goal** (a planning problem)

**Composition of Resources**
- Trace **dependencies** between resources to determine if a coordination problem exists

*Source:* Crowston (2003).
*Notes:* Dependencies are shown in boldface. Numbered items are components of the coordination mechanism for managing the given dependency. Bulleted items are alternative mechanisms or components of the mechanism for the given dependency.

The main dimension of the typology involves the types of objects involved in the dependency. To simplify the typology, we compress the elements of Malone and Crowston's (1994) framework into two groups—tasks (which includes goals and activities) and resources used or created by tasks (which here includes the effort of the actors). Logically, there are three kinds of dependencies between tasks and resources—those between two tasks, those between two resources, and those between a task and a resource. (As a further simplification, dependencies between more than two elements are decomposed into dependencies between pairs of elements.)

Some aspects of this typology are more developed than others; for example, task–task dependencies have been analyzed in some detail, whereas the others have not. Specifically, task–task dependencies have been further distinguished by considering what kinds of resources are shared by the two tasks (e.g., shareable or reusable resources), how these resources are used (as an input or as an output of the task), and whether the required uses conflict with each other (e.g., two different uses of a non-reusable resource).

For each dependency, a brief description of an associated coordination mechanism is given. For example, to manage a task–resource dependency, the typology notes that it is necessary to first identify required and available resources, then to choose a particular resource, and, finally, to assign the resource. Managing a prerequisite dependency (a task–task dependency) requires ordering the tasks, ensuring that the output of the first is usable by the second, and managing the transfer of the resource from the first to the second. These activities can be performed in many different ways. For example, a manager with a task to assign might know of the available resources or might have to spend time hunting them down. Usability might be managed reactively by testing the resource and returning problems or proactively by involving the user in the production of the resource.

## RESEARCH SETTING AND DATA COLLECTION

Coordination theory is intended to analyze organizations in a way that facilitates redesign. The question is, does this approach work; that is, can we find dependencies and coordination mechanisms in a real process? Does this analysis help explain commonly used alternative processes or suggest novel ones? I undertook two case analyses to answer these questions, in a setting where the precise processes for decomposing and completing tasks were observable. In the remainder of this chapter, I present the application of coordination theory to a particular process, thus grounding the claims of coordination theory within a carefully specified organizational domain. In this section, I provide an overview of the research setting, the data collection, and data analysis approaches.

## Data Collection

### Proprietary Software

The proprietary software organization in this example was the minicomputer division of a large corporation. In 1989, when the study started, the entire corporation had sales of approximately $10 billion and roughly 100,000 employees. The computer division produced several lines of minicomputers and workstations and developed system software for these computers. The group in this study was responsible for the development of the kernel of a proprietary operating system, a total of about 1 million lines of code in a high-level language.

The analysis of the proprietary software development process presented here was based on 16 interviews with 12 individuals, including six software engineers, two support group managers, three support group members, and one marketing engineer. The interviews were carried out during six trips to the company's engineering headquarters; most were one to two hours long. A former member of the software development group assisted in the data collection and analysis.

As discussed above, coordination mechanisms are primarily information processing activities. Therefore, this study adopted the information processing view of organizations, which focuses on how organizations process information (Galbraith, 1977; March and Simon, 1958; Tushman and Nadler, 1978). The goal of the data collection was to uncover, in March and Simon's (1958) terms, the programs used by the individuals in the group. March and Simon suggest three ways to uncover these programs: (1) interviewing individuals, (2) examining documents that describe standard operating procedures, and (3) observing individuals. I relied most heavily on interviews. As March and Simon point out, "most programs are stored in the minds of the employees who carry them out, or in the minds of their superiors, subordinates or associates. For many purposes, the simplest and most accurate way to discover what a person does is to ask him" (1958, p. 142).

I started the data collection by identifying different kinds of actors in the group. This identification was done with the aid of a few key informants and refined as the study progressed. When available, formal documentation of the process was used as a starting point. For example, a number of individuals designed and coded parts of the operating system, all working in roughly the same way and using the same kinds of information; each was an example of a "software engineer actor." However, response center or marketing engineers used different information, which they processed differently; therefore, they were analyzed separately.

Interview subjects were identified by the key informants, based on their job responsibilities; there was no evidence, however, that their reports were atypical. I then interviewed each subject to identify the type of information received by each kind of actor and the way each type was handled. Data were collected by asking subjects: (1) what kinds of information they received, (2) from whom they received it, (3) how they received it (e.g., from telephone calls, memos, or computer systems), (4) how they processed the different kinds of information, and (5) to whom they sent messages as a result. When possible, these questions were grounded by asking interviewees to talk about items they had received that day.

I also collected examples of documents that were created and exchanged as part of the process or that described standard procedures or individual jobs. Not surprisingly, the process as performed often differed from the formally documented process. For example, there was a formal method for tracking which engineers used which interfaces, but, in practice, most engineers seemed to rely on their memories. It was this informal process (as well as the formal process surrounding it) that I sought to document.

The initial product of these studies was a model of the change process (presented in more detail below) that described the actors involved, which steps each performed, and the information they exchanged. It should be noted that data were collected for only one group because my contact at this company worked in that group. My impression from interviews with individuals who had worked in or who interacted with other groups was that processes were similar in other software development units; however, I have no direct information about other groups.

Relying on interviews for data can introduce some biases. First, people do not always say what they really think. Some interviews were conducted in the presence of another employee of the company, so interviewees may have been tempted to say what they thought they should say (the "company line"), what they thought I wanted to hear, or what would make them or the company look best. Second, individuals sometimes may not know the answer or may be mistaken.

To control for interview bias, I cross-checked reported data with other informants. I also used the modeling process as a check on the data, applying the negative case study method (Kidder, 1981). In this method, researchers switch between data collection and model development, using predictions or implications of the model to guide the search for disconfirming evidence. When such data cannot be found, the model is refined to agree with all available data.

*Linux*

As a comparison to the proprietary software company, I examined the bug fixing processes for the kernel of the Linux operating system. Linux is a FLOSS Unix-like operating system. The original release was created by Linus Torvalds in 1991, but it has since grown with the contributions of literally thousands of developers (Moon and Sproull, 2000) and is now a full-featured and widely used system. The most recent release, 2.6 in 2004, is reported to have more than 4 million lines of code (Wheeler, 2005). A unique feature of Linux is the dual version approach to development, in which even-numbered versions (2.2, 2.4, 2.6, etc.) are intended to be stable for end users and odd-numbered versions (2.1, 2.3, 2.5, etc.) are for development and may therefore be unstable.

FLOSS development differs greatly from proprietary development in that it is not owned by a single organization. Developers contribute from around the world, meet face-to-face infrequently if at all, and coordinate their activity primarily by means of computer-mediated communications (CMC) (Raymond, 1998; Wayner, 2000). These teams depend on processes that span traditional boundaries of place and ownership. The research literature on software development and on distributed work emphasizes the difficulties of distributed software development, but the case of FLOSS development presents an intriguing counterexample. What is perhaps most surprising about the FLOSS process is that it appears to eschew traditional project coordination mechanisms such as formal planning, system-level design, schedules, and defined development processes (Herbsleb and Grinter, 1999). As well, many (though by no means all) programmers contribute to projects as volunteers, without working for a common organization or being paid. Characterized by a globally distributed developer force and a rapid and reliable software development process, effective FLOSS development teams somehow profit from the advantages and overcome the challenges of distributed work (Alho and Sulonen, 1998).

My analysis of the Linux bug change process is based primarily on published descriptions of the process (e.g., Moon and Sproull, 2000). These analyses have been extended by analysis of Linux kernel bug tracking logs. It is important to note that the Linux process has changed over time, with a particularly significant change for the 2.6 version (Larson, 2004). Therefore, I will discuss the process as it appeared at different points in time. For ease of reference, I will refer to these as the original and current change processes, respectively.

**The Bug Fixing Processes**

In this subsection, I briefly describe the bug fixing processes as implemented in the proprietary and Linux development processes.

*The Proprietary Bug Fixing Process*

The proprietary software organization stated the following goals for the change process:

- ensure that all critical program parameters are documented—customer commitments, cross-functional dependencies;
- ensure that a proposed change is reviewed by all affected software development units/functions and formally approved or rejected;
- ensure that document status is made available to all users—stable (revision number and date), changes being considered, approved/rejected/withdrawn; and
- ensure changes are made quickly and efficiently.

In addition, the change process had two larger goals: maintain the quality of the software and minimize the cost of changes. To maintain quality, the process ensured that changes were made by someone who understands the module, that changes were fully tested, and that the module and its documentation were kept in agreement. To reduce the cost of changes, the change process required that changes be made only to fix a problem or add an authorized enhancement. As one manager put it, the "formal change control process is there to prevent changes."

The activities performed for a typical change in the proprietary process are summarized in the flowchart shown in Figure 4.1. Although no particular bug is necessarily treated in exactly this way, these activities were described as typical by my interviewees. Roles in bug fixing included customer, marketing engineer, engineering manager, software engineers, and quality assurance. Actors involved in the process are listed at the top of the column of activities they perform. (To save space, the flow continues from the bottom right of the chart to the top left; the activities on the right follow rather than overlap those on the left.)

The software maintenance process started when a problem was encountered. When a customer called the customer support center with a problem, the call handler tried to solve it using manuals, product descriptions, and the database of known problems. If the problem appeared to be a bug that was not already in the database, a new problem report was entered. Many problems were found during the development process by the testing group, who entered problem reports directly. (Note that the response center was treated as a collective actor. As a result, internal center activities are omitted from the flowchart of the process.)

A marketing engineer periodically reviewed new entries in the database. Marketing engineers reviewed problem reports for completeness and attempted to replicate the problem. The marketing engineer might decide that the problem was really a request for an enhancement, which was

Figure 4.1 **Flowchart of Proprietary Software Bug Fixing Process**

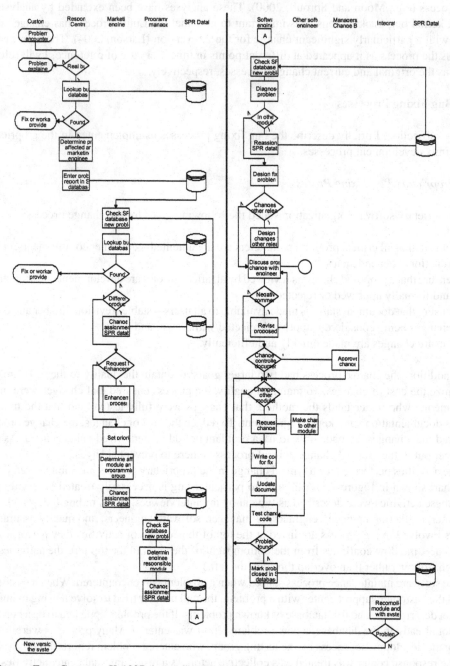

*Source:* From Crowston, K. 1997. A coordination theory approach to organizational process design. *Organization Science,* 8, 157–175. Copyright © 1997, the Institute for Operations Research and the Management Sciences, 7240 Parkway Drive, Suite 310, Hanover, MD 21076. Reprinted with permission.

*Note:* The flow continues from the bottom right of the chart to the top left; the activities on the right follow rather than overlap those on the left.

handled by a separate process. If the bug was genuine, the marketing engineer determined the location of the problem and assigned the problem report to the software development unit responsible for that module.

A coordinator in the development unit next assigned the problem report to the appropriate software engineer, who investigated the problem. If the problem turned out to be entirely in another module, then the engineer passed the request to the engineer responsible for the other module. If the problem was internal to a single module, the engineer just fixed the module. If the problem required changes to multiple modules, the engineer discussed the changes with the owners of the affected modules (as well as other interested engineers) and arranged for them to modify their modules appropriately. All changes required the approval of management. Changes to interfaces intended for general use required as well a design review and approval from a change review board.

When the engineer was satisfied with the change and it had been approved, he or she submitted the new code to the testing and integration group. The integration group then recompiled the changed code and relinked the system. The kernel was then tested; any bugs found were reported to the appropriate engineers, potentially starting another pass through the process. Customers were periodically sent the most recent release of the system. In a few cases, they received a patch for a single particularly important or relevant change.

*The Original Linux Bug Fixing Process*

We next consider the original bug fixing process for the Linux kernel. The goals of the Linux change management process are not explicitly stated but can be inferred from the descriptions of the process. During development for kernels 2.4 and earlier, the concern seemed to be adding code to improve the kernel while maintaining the quality of the system. Unlike the proprietary process, the FLOSS process does not necessarily distinguish between new features and bug fixes; it also does not attempt to control what is added beyond ensuring that the code is of good quality (though adding code that might impact the stability of even-numbered kernels, such as a significant new feature, is discouraged). Since developers are also users, the fact that code has been developed is generally justification enough for at least considering its inclusion, though there is no guarantee that a new piece of code will ever be incorporated in an official release.

As with the proprietary process, the original Linux kernel bug fixing process started with bug reports posted to a mailing list for kernel developers for a particular subsystem. Appendix 4.1 shows an example e-mailed bug report for the kernel along with follow-up messages and an eventual fix (note that to save space, the source code listings that were contained in the messages have been redacted). The kernel developer list gets thousands of such messages per month. Based on the report, a developer might have tried to characterize the bug or develop a fix. The decision to work on a fix depended on the interest and ability of the individual. The work done is in turn sent to the kernel mailing list. Because multiple developers are working on the system in parallel, it is necessary for a new piece of code to be provided in a form that can quickly be integrated with the existing source code and any other new code that may have been created in the meantime (that is, another goal of the change process is to incorporate changes from multiple developers). The most common way to distribute new code is as a "patch," that is, a set of changes to the current files. Patch tools can integrate multiple patches and identify conflicting ones, that is, patches that make overlapping changes to the same lines of code.

Once a patch is developed and posted to the list, other users can provide feedback, such as on the coding style, design approach, or experiences using the patch. Kernel testing depends heavily on peer review (indeed, Glance, 2004, goes as far as to claim that no testing is done). If users encounter problems with the patch, then they provide feedback on the list, thus restarting the bug fixing process.

Linus Torvalds coordinates the overall maintenance of the kernel. If user experiences with a patch were positive, Torvalds might incorporate it into his kernel source code tree, often rewriting it in the process. Torvalds's acceptance of a patch was (and still is) the only way into an official Linux release. As Moon and Sproull note:

> there is no confusion about who has decision authority in this project. Torvalds manages and announces all releases—all 569 of them to date. He acts as a filter on all patches and new features—rejecting, accepting, or revising as he chooses. He can single-handedly decide to redo something completely if he wishes. (2000)

Torvalds has stated that he is more likely to accept patches from the small number of developers he knows and trusts, so patch writers often send their patches to the maintainers for a particular module and count on them evaluating and forwarding it to Torvalds. Several other developers maintain their own copies of the source with different policies about which patches they accept, and companies (and end users) that use Linux can also maintain their own trees with their own selection of patches.

*The Current Linux Bug Fixing Process*

With the more recent versions of the kernel, the bug fixing process has changed to be less centered on Torvalds and to make more use of information and communications technology (ICT) support; specifically, the Bugzilla[2] bug tracker and a source code control system. Again, we can infer some of the goals of the new bug changing process by noting the problems the new process is said to fix. Larson notes that, with the original process, "nobody really knew which changes were in, whether they were merged properly, or what new things to expect in the upcoming release," while the new processes "ensure that patches aren't forgotten" and give developers the "ability to always be working with the latest copy of the code" and "to update as soon as a feature or bug fix they need goes into the kernel" (2004). We infer then that the current process is intended to keep track of bug reports and patches and to ensure the latter are widely available.

Rather than posting bug reports to the mailing list, in the current process, bug reports can be posted on a bug tracking system (Larson, 2004). Use of the Bugzilla system provides a single source for all bug reports and enables tracking the status of each—fixed or not. However, not all developers use the system, as will be discussed below.

Linux kernel sources, which were originally maintained by Torvalds, are now kept in a source code control system; at first BitKeeper (Larson, 2004) and now a new system called Git[3] (Shankland, 2005). Both systems allow patches (in particular, patches spanning multiple files) to be easily tracked and included or dropped in a release so different developers can more easily create patches that can be brought together into a final release. Torvalds is quoted as saying that use of the BitKeeper sped up development by a factor of two (LeClaire, 2005). Because some developers objected to using BitKeeper, which is proprietary software, kernel sources can be obtained in a variety of other ways and patches may still be posted to the mailing list. Git similarly allows easier maintenance of a set of patches, but it is not yet clear how its use will affect kernel development.

Finally, the testing process for the current release is somewhat more systematic (Larson, 2004). For example, the Linux Test Project (http://ltp.sourceforge.net/) has developed test suites for the kernel. Automated systems exist that allow a developer to provide a patch for the kernel and have the tests run automatically using the patched code. The system can also pull the current release of the kernel from the source code control system and run the regression tests on it. Official releases are still made by Torvalds.

## ANALYSIS APPROACH

In this section, we describe a coordination theory analysis for the processes such as the ones described above by identifying the dependencies and coordination mechanisms in place. Three heuristics have been developed to identify dependencies and coordination mechanisms in different ways (Crowston and Osborn, 2003). First, we can examine activities in the current process, identify those that seem to be part of some coordination mechanism, and then determine what dependencies they manage. Second, we can list the activities and resources involved in the process, consider what dependencies are possible between them, and then determine how these dependencies are being managed. Finally, we can look for problems with the process that hint at unmanaged coordination problems and identify the underlying dependencies. In this section, we describe each heuristic and give examples of the dependencies and coordination mechanisms identified with this approach. In the following section, we will systematically present the integrated results of the analysis.

### Looking for Coordination Mechanisms

Taking the first approach, many of the activities in the bug fixing process appear to be instances of the coordination mechanisms discussed earlier. To illustrate this approach, Table 4.2 lists in detail the activities performed in the proprietary bug fixing process. The dependency the activity manages, if any, is listed in the third column.

For example, one of the first things the customer service center staff and marketing engineers in the proprietary firm do upon receiving a problem report is check if it duplicates a known problem listed in the change database. In the typology, *detect common output* is listed as a coordination mechanism for managing a dependency between two tasks that have duplicate outcomes. The organization can avoid doing the same work twice by looking for the common output in a database of known problems and reusing the result of one of the tasks (as happened in this example). Linux developers similarly mark bugs in Bugzilla as duplicates.

*Task assignment* is a coordination mechanism for managing the dependency between a task and an actor by finding the appropriate actor to perform the task. Such coordination mechanisms are performed repeatedly in this process: customers assign tasks to the customer service center, the customer service center assigns novel tasks to the marketing engineers, marketing engineers assign tasks to the software engineers, and software engineers assign tasks to each other.

### Looking for Dependencies

The second approach to identifying coordination mechanisms is to list the tasks and resources involved in the process and then consider what dependencies are possible between them. It may be that some of the activities in a process are coordination mechanisms for managing those dependencies. As mentioned above, tasks necessary to respond to problem reports include noticing there is a problem, finding a work-around, reproducing and diagnosing the problem, designing a fix, writing new code, and recompiling the system with the new code. These activities are shown in boldface in Table 4.2. Resources include the problem reports, the efforts of a number of specialized actors, and the actual code.

Table 4.2

## Activities and Coordination Mechanisms in the Proprietary Bug Fixing Process

| Actor | Activity | Dependency managed between |
|---|---|---|
| Customer | **find a problem while using system** | |
| | report problem to response center | problem fixing task and capable actor |
| Response Center | look for bug in database of known bugs; if found, return fix to customer and stop | problem fixing task and duplicate tasks |
| | **attempt to resolve problem** | |
| | refer hardware problems to field engineers | problem fixing task and capable actor |
| | if problem is novel, determine affected product and forward bug report to marketing engineer | problem fixing task and capable actor |
| Marketing Engineer | look for bug in database of known bugs; if found, return fix to customer | problem fixing task and duplicate tasks |
| | request additional information if necessary | usability of problem report by next activity |
| | attempt to reproduce problem | usability of problem report by next activity |
| | **attempt to find work-around** | |
| | set priority for problem | problem fixing task and actor's time |
| | if the report is actually a request for an enhancement, then treat it differently | |
| | determine affected module | |
| | if unable to diagnose, forward to SWAT team | |
| | if bug is in another product, forward to appropriate product manager | |
| | forward bug report to manager of group responsible for module | task and resources required by tasks |
| | problem fixing task and capable actor | |
| Programming Manager or Designate | determine engineer responsible for module and forward bug report to that engineer | problem fixing task and capable actor |

| | | |
|---|---|---|
| Software Engineer | pick the report with the highest priority, or the oldest, or the one you want to work on next | problem fixing task and actor's time |
| | **diagnose the problem** | |
| | if the problem is in another module, forward it to the engineer for that module | problem fixing task and capable actor |
| | **design a fix for the bug** | |
| | check if change is needed in other releases and make the change as needed | problem fixing task and capable actor |
| | send the proposed fix to affected engineers for their comments; if the comments are negative, then revise the bug and repeat the process | two modules |
| | if the change requires changes to a controlled document, then send the proposed change to the various managers and the change review board for their approval | management of usability task and capable actor |
| Managers | approve the change | usability of fix by next activity |
| Software Engineer | **write the code for the fix** | |
| | determine what changes are needed to other modules | task and subtasks needed to accomplish it |
| | if necessary, ask the engineers responsible for the other modules to make any necessary changes | problem fixing task and capable actor |
| | test the proposed fix | usability of fix by next activity |
| | send the changed modules to the integration manager | task and capable actor |
| | release the patch to be sent to the customer | transfer to customer |
| Integration | check that the change has been approved | usability of fix by integration activity |
| | **recompile the module and link it with the rest of the system** | |
| | test the entire system | usability of entire system by next activity |
| | release the new software | transport to customers |

*Source:* From Crowston, K. 1997. A coordination theory approach to organizational process design. *Organization Science*, 8, 157–175. Copyright © 1997, the Institute for Operations Research and the Management Sciences, 7240 Parkway Drive, Suite 310, Hanover, MD 21076. Reprinted with permission.
*Note:* Activities in boldface are those logically necessary to respond to problem reports.

*Task–Task Dependencies*

Dependencies between tasks can be identified by looking for resources used by more than one task. For example, many tasks create some output, such as a bug report, a diagnosis, or new code, which is used as input by some other task, thus creating a *prerequisite dependency* between the two. Malone and Crowston (1994) note that such dependencies often impose usability and transfer constraints. Some steps in the process appear to manage such constraints. For example, testing that a new module works correctly addresses the usability constraint between creating code and relinking and using the system; releasing the new system addresses the transfer constraint between the development organization and the final user of the system.

If there are two problems in the same module, then both bug fixing tasks need the same code, thus creating a *shared resource dependency*. In the proprietary development process, this dependency is managed by assigning modules of code to individual programmers and then assigning all problems in these modules to that programmer. This arrangement is often called "code ownership," because each module of the system has a single owner who performs all tasks that modify that module. Such an arrangement allows the owner of the code to control all changes made to the code, simplifying the coordination of multiple changes.

*Task–Resource Dependencies*

The second category of dependencies is those between tasks and resources, which are managed by some kind of task or resource assignment. These coordination mechanisms were identified and discussed above, such as the assignment of bugs to developers by marketing engineers.

*Resource–Resource Dependencies*

Finally, there are dependencies between modules owned by different engineers—that is, resource–resource dependencies that constrain what changes can be made. A module depends on another if the first makes use of services provided by the second. For example, the process management code may call routines that are part of the file system; therefore, the process management code depends on the file system code. Such dependencies must be noticed or identified before they can be managed by arranging for coordinated changes. Interactions between different parts of a software system are not always obvious, because they are not limited to direct physical connections.

**Looking for Coordination Problems**

A final approach for identifying dependencies is to look for problems in the process that suggest unmanaged dependencies. For example, the proprietary developers occasionally found at system integration or during testing that a change made to one module was incompatible with others, despite the efforts to detect and avoid interactions described in the previous section. These problems occur because some dependency between the module being changed and other modules was not detected and managed.

In the case of Linux, the original process had the problem that patches would get dropped due to Torvalds being overloaded with submissions. The bug fixing process could be quite frustrating for a developer if a patch was not accepted, because it was hard to know if the decision was based on the quality of the code or because Torvalds was simply too busy to handle the submission. In case it was the latter, individuals would often repost patches. As Larson notes, "bugs were often missed, forgotten, or ignored unless the person reporting the bug was incredibly persistent" (2004). As developer Rob Landley succinctly put it, "Linus doesn't scale" (Barr, 2002).

To summarize, there are three heuristics that can be used to identify dependencies and coordination mechanisms in a process. The first approach is to match activities performed against known coordination mechanisms, such as searching for duplicate tasks or task assignment. The second approach is to identify possible dependencies between activities and resources and then search for activities that manage these. In the example, we identified prerequisite, shared resource, and resource–resource dependencies that were managed. The final approach is to look for problems that suggest unmanaged or incompletely managed dependencies. The coordination mechanisms identified are both generic, such as task assignments, and specific, such as code sharing systems.

## RESULTS: DEPENDENCIES AND COORDINATION MECHANISMS IN SOFTWARE BUG FIXING

In this section, we discuss the dependencies and coordination mechanisms found in the bug fixing process using the analysis techniques presented above. We will then discuss differences between the FLOSS and proprietary processes as well as additional alternatives suggested by the analysis. Following the typology of dependencies in Table 4.1, we consider task–task, task–resource, and resource–resource dependencies in turn. Table 4.3 presents a summary of this comparison.

### Task–Task

Task–task dependencies include shared output, shared resource, and flow dependencies.

### Duplicate (Shared Output)

The first type of dependency is a common output dependency, meaning that two tasks create the same output. Avoiding *duplicate tasks* is difficult if there are numerous workers who could be working on the same task. For example, the same bug may be reported by many users; in a software development company, managers of the development group would prefer not to waste resources diagnosing and solving the same problem repeatedly.

In the proprietary bug fixing process, this dependency is managed by the marketing engineers, who search the databases for each bug report to identify possible existing solutions or duplicate reports. In the original Linux process, this dependency was managed by allowing users to see all bugs as they were reported or to search the mailing list, thus hopefully avoiding duplicates. However, it seems unlikely that average users are able to keep up with the volume of messages or to identify matching reports. Instead, the burden would fall on the developers to identify when a user report was a duplicate. In the current process, users are encouraged to search the Bugzilla database for duplicate problem reports before filing a new one. Nevertheless, there is no guarantee that users will search or that they will find a duplicate even if it exists, so duplicate bugs are reported and have to be identified and marked as such by developers.

### Shared Resource

The second type of task–task dependency is a shared resource dependency, which arises when multiple processes need the same resources. For example, multiple bug fixes may have to be made to the same module of code. As mentioned above, one approach to dealing with these dependen-

Table 4.3

**Comparison of Coordination Problems and Mechanisms in Proprietary and FLOSS Bug Fixing Processes**

| Dependency | Example coordination problem | Proprietary process | Original Linux process | Current Linux process |
|---|---|---|---|---|
| Task–Task | | | | |
| Shared output | Duplicate bug report. | Marketing engineers search databases for each bug report to identify possible existing solutions or duplicate reports. | Users can see bugs as they are reported or search mailing list for duplicates. Developers identify when a user report is a duplicate. | Users search Bugzilla database for duplicate problem reports. Developers identify when a user report is a duplicate. |
| Shared resource | Two bugs to be fixed in same module of code. | Single developer handles all changes and resulting dependencies. | Torvalds commits all patches to official source. | Patch control system for managing patches. |
| Flow—usability | Bug reports from users may not be usable by developers. Patches must be tested to ensure suitability for release. | Marketing engineers correspond with users to refine bug reports. Manager approves patches. Testing group tests patches. | Developers might post follow-up messages to a report requesting details. Peer testing. | Developers might post follow-up messages to a report requesting details. Combination of peer and formal testing. |
| Task–Resource | Bug report must be worked on by appropriate engineer. | Multistage assignment process to route bug report to responsible engineer based on specialization. | Developers self-assign to bug reports. | Developers self-assign to bug reports. |
| Resource–Resource | Changes in one source code module may require changes in other modules. | Tracking of use of interfaces by subscription to documentation. Informal checks by developers. | Modular design to reduce dependencies. Informal checks by developers. | Modular design to reduce dependencies. Informal checks by developers. |

cies is to have a single person handle all of the changes and the resulting dependencies. This approach does not eliminate the dependencies, but does allow a single user to see and thus manage all of them. In the original Linux process, Torvalds essentially performed this role, because he maintained the kernel source code. In the post-2.4 Linux process, the use of a source code control system helps to manage multiple changes to various files by facilitating integration of changes made by multiple developers and providing notification of conflicts when developers check code back into the system.

*Flow*

The third type of task–task dependency is a flow dependency, which arises when one task creates a resource that another task requires as an input. In general, a flow dependency implies the need for three different kinds of coordination mechanisms to manage transfer of the resource, ordering of the tasks, and usability, but we will focus on the third, because usability is the most significant issue in the processes studied. Usability means that there must be some mechanism in place to ensure that the output of the first task is usable by the second task. At the highest level, the entire bug fixing process might be viewed as a mechanism to ensure usability for the users of the software being developed, thus managing a flow dependency from developers to users.

Within the bug fixing process, several activities ensure that the output of one task is usable by another. An interesting usability constraint, common to both cases, is that bug reports from the general public are often not detailed enough to be useful for developers (Glance, 2004). The low quality of bug reports discourages developers from relying on the system, thus further decreasing the quality of the bug reports. In response, some developers may take on the role of filtering or improving reports. In the proprietary process, marketing engineers check that problem reports are detailed enough to be used by the engineers fixing the bugs. In the Linux process, developers might post follow-up messages to a report (either on the e-mail list or in the Bugzilla database) requesting additional information.

Similarly, bug fixes need to be tested to check that they correctly fix the problem and do not introduce new problems, so testing is a way to check that output of bug fixing is suitable for use. Testing was done through a rather formal process for the proprietary system, and by a combination of individual and peer review for the Linux process.

In the proprietary process, managers must approve changes before they can be implemented. In Linux, module managers and Torvalds play a similar role. Such approvals provide a check on the quality of the change, either directly, if the manager notices problems, or indirectly, if engineers are more careful with changes they have to show their managers. There are other possible interpretations of this approval process: managers might use the information to allocate resources among different projects, to track how engineers spend their time, or even to demonstrate their political power. However, if approvals are a quality check, other mechanisms might be appropriate (in this and any other process). For example, if approvals are time-consuming yet likely, it may be more effective to continue the change process without waiting for approval. Most changes will be implemented more quickly; the few that are rejected will require additional rework, but the overall cost might be lower. Alternatively, managerial reviews could be eliminated altogether in favor of more intensive testing and tracking of test results. Interestingly, Linux allows developers to take this approach, because anyone can maintain a kernel source tree that includes the patches they want to test or use, approved or not.

**Task–Resource**

The next type of dependencies I consider are dependencies between tasks and the resources they need. The primary resources in the bug fixing process are the modules of code and the time and effort of developers.

*Task Assignment*

In the analysis, we noted numerous places where actors perform part of a task assignment process. For example, customers give problem reports to the service center, which in turn, assigns the problems to product engineers, who then assign them to software engineers. In addition, software engineers may assign reports or subtasks to each other. The typology points out that a key problem in task assignment is choosing the actor to whom to assign a task. For the proprietary process, the choice is made based on specialization. Specialization allows engineers to develop expertise in a few modules, which is particularly important when the engineers are also developing new versions of the system. Furthermore, because modules are assigned to engineers, the code sharing problem discussed above is minimized. However, there are also disadvantages. First, diagnosing the location of a problem can be difficult, because symptoms can appear to be in one module as a result of problems somewhere else. In the best case, an error message will clearly identify the problem; otherwise, the problem will be assigned to the most likely area and perhaps transferred later. In any event, making the assignment correctly requires a fair amount of work and experience for the assigner, as is evidenced by the multiple layers involved in making the assignment. A second problem is load balancing; one engineer might have many problems to work on, whereas others have none.

An alternative basis for choosing engineers was found in a new support group that was set up in the proprietary company during our study. Support engineers were not specialized by module but were instead organized around change ownership—that is, an engineer assigned a particular problem report makes changes to any affected modules. As a result, task assignment can be done based on workload rather than specialization. In this case, a manager can make the assignment by tracking the status of individual engineers, or engineers can assign work to themselves whenever they finish a task. Many processes could be similarly redesigned to use generalists rather than specialists. For example, in a customer service process, the person who answers the phone could be enabled to resolve any problem rather than having to refer the problem to a specialist.

With change ownership, multiple engineers may have to work on the same module, thus creating a new shared resource dependency. This problem illustrates an important point: coordination mechanisms are themselves activities, and using a different kind of coordination mechanism to manage one dependency may create new dependencies that must, in turn, be managed. In this case, to manage these new task dependencies, the company implemented a source control system to maintain a copy of all source files. When engineers want to modify a file, they check it out of the system, preventing other programmers from modifying it (by contrast, the Linux source code control system does not lock files, thus permitting parallel development). When the modification is complete, the module is checked back in and the system records the changes made.

Interestingly, the Linux process does not rely on explicit assignment but instead relies on developers to assign themselves to tasks. With the Bugzilla system, depending on the module with the bug, bugs start off assigned to the default maintainer; however, default maintainers may not be the ones who actually fix the bug. This approach makes the assignment process similar to the market approach suggested by Crowston (1997). In a market form of task assignment, a description

Figure 4.2 **BitKeeper Contributions Versus Number of Developers**

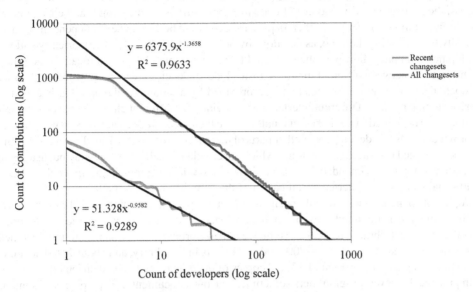

Count of Linux Kernel BitKeeper contributions

*Source:* http://linux.bkbits.net:8080/linux-2.4/stats?nav=index.html.

*Notes:* Changes per developer follow a power law distribution: a small number of developers contribute many changes, while many developers contribute only a few. Black lines are fitted power law trend lines.

of each task is sent to all available agents. Each evaluates the task and, if interested in working on it, submits a bid, saying how long it would take, how much it would cost, or even what they would charge to do it. The task is then assigned to the best bidder, thus using information supplied by the agents as the basis for picking who should work on the task. However, the Linux process differs in that there is often no explicit assignment of the task; rather, each developer chooses autonomously whether to work on a bug.

The self-selection process results in two significant differences from the commercial process. First, there is an uneven distribution of tasks per developer, as shown in the plot of the number of change sets contributed to BitKeeper versus the number of developers in Figure 4.2. This figure shows that a few developers contribute many patches, while most developers contribute only a few, something that would likely be undesirable in most companies. A second problem is that multiple developers may choose to work on the same code modules at the same time. Rather than preventing such conflicting uses, the source code control system used for Linux identifies and often resolves any problems created by the parallel uses as they are found (a process sometimes called "optimistic concurrency control").

The use of a market-like task assignment mechanism in the Linux process is consistent with predictions of the effect of the more extensive use of ICT. ICT makes it easier to gather information about available tasks and resources and to distribute the decision about which resources to use for a particular task. At a macro level, Malone et al. (1987) suggest that decreased coordination costs favor more extensive use of markets, which usually have lower costs but require more coordination activities, over vertical integration, which makes the opposite trade-off.

## Resource–Resource

The final type of dependency in the typology is resource–resource dependencies. In the bug fixing process, these arise because modules of code may be interrelated, meaning that a change in one module can require changes in another. In principle, it should be easy to detect dependencies automatically by examining the code, as was done by Schach et al. (2002). In the proprietary software development company, however, there seemed to be no reliable mechanical means to determine the interactions between different modules. Instead, dependencies are tracked by manually tracking documents. The set of routines and data provided by a module make up what is called the interface to that module. Different interfaces are provided for different classes of users. Customer interfaces are described in published manuals and are therefore rarely changed. Service interfaces are provided for use by developers of other parts of the system software and are described in formal documents, called external specifications, which are circulated within the company but usually not to customers. Interfaces intended for use within only a single development group are described in an informally circulated internal specification, if they are documented at all.

Copies of manuals and external specifications are kept in a documentation library; internal specifications are maintained only by their developer. Programmers who request a document from the document library are tracked so they can be informed of any changes to the document. At the time of my study, there were 800–900 documents in the library, and about 1,000 document requestors being tracked. A total of 15,000 copies of documents had been distributed.

In practice, however, programmers sometimes borrow a document or copy pieces of someone else's code and therefore do not realize that they should inform the developer that they are using the interface. Because the documentation subscriber lists are not reliable, the software engineer planning a change identifies the other affected engineers based mostly on their knowledge of the system's interactions and what other developers are doing.

Some coordination problems can be traced to the reliance on a heuristic mechanism to locate dependencies. In particular, because there is less informal communication between divisions, the mechanism does not work very well for dependencies between modules developed in different divisions. For example, in the organization studied, a word processing program once became the source of mysterious system crashes. It turned out that the word processor's developers had used a low-level system call that had been changed between releases of the operating system. However, because the word processor was developed in another unit from the operating system, the programmers of the two modules did not communicate. Thus, the developers of the word processor did not know they should avoid the system call nor did the developer of the system call know the word processor developers were using it. In other words, the usual social mechanism for managing the dependencies between modules failed, leading to the problems.

In the Linux environment, it is not clear how dependencies between modules are handled. A key goal of most FLOSS development efforts is to reduce the number of intermodule linkages because they make it harder for developers to understand and work with the code (Reis and Fortes, 2002). Still, there are reports that the degree of linkage in the Linux kernel is increasing, raising concerns about maintainability (Schach et al., 2002). Understanding the nature of dependencies between modules and their management should be a fruitful area for future research on FLOSS development.

For *sharing information resources,* communications and database technologies may automate the necessary coordination mechanisms. For example, coordination is necessary if multiple tasks use common information stored on paper (a shared resource dependency). It may therefore be desirable to have a single individual handle all of the data to simplify the coordination. For example, a paper-based conference room schedule is usually kept in one central location because of the possibility of conflicting reservations and the prohibitive cost of updating copies every time a reservation is made. Data such as customer accounts or credit information are often handled similarly, resulting in specialization of actors based on their access to information. Database and communications systems enable multiple workers to access and make changes to data. By empowering workers and reducing the need for specialization, ICT can change the basis for assigning tasks. For example, if all workers are equally capable of performing a task, then tasks can be assigned on criteria such as workload or the customer involved, rather than on availability of data or specialization. Such a change was made to the Citibank letter of credit process when a group of specialists, each performing a single step of the process, were replaced by generalists who handle the entire process for particular customers (Matteis, 1979).

## CONCLUSION

To conclude, I consider the implications of a coordination theory approach for process transformation, discuss limitations of the approach, and present ideas for future research.

### Implications of Coordination Analysis for Process Transformation

Engineering change provides a microcosm of coordination problems and mechanisms to solve them. Successful implementation of a change requires management of numerous dependencies among tasks and resources. A variety of mechanisms are used to manage these dependencies. For example, the possibility of duplicate tasks may be ignored or may be investigated before engineers attempt to solve the problem. Dependencies between tasks and the resources needed to perform them are managed by a variety of task assignment mechanisms, such as managerial decision making based on expertise or workload; those between modules of the system, by technological coordination mechanisms, such as source control systems. The choice of coordination mechanisms to manage these dependencies results in a variety of possible business processes, some already known (such as change ownership) and some novel (such as voluntaristic selection of work by developers). The relative desirability of mechanisms is likely to be affected by the use of ICT. For example, the use of a computer system such as Bugzilla makes it easier to find existing solutions to a problem. Such a system could reduce both duplicate effort and coordination costs.

The software change process has interesting parallels in other industries. Despite differences in the products, other engineering change processes studied by this author (Crowston, 1991b) had similar goals, activities, coordination problems, and mechanisms. Further afield, there are parallels between diagnosing software bugs to assign them to engineers and diagnosing patients to assign them to medical specialists. An analysis similar to the one presented here might reveal interesting alternatives in the medical diagnosis domain as well.

### Limitations of Coordination Theory Analysis

Of course, our analysis has several limitations. Coordination theory, like all theories, is a simplification of the complexity of real processes in order to highlight possibilities for transformation. The single example presented here demonstrates the potential of this approach. A coordination theory analysis can identify important dependencies or coordination problems that must be addressed in some way for a process to be successful. However, the suggestions of the analysis need to be tempered by consideration of omitted factors. The technique focuses on how tasks are performed, rather than how employees are motivated to perform, come to understand their jobs, or develop shared cultures. For example, a lower mechanism cost does not mean that that mechanism is always better or should be implemented. As mentioned above, market-like task assignment mechanisms may have certain cost benefits and are also susceptible to agency problems that must be addressed if they are to succeed. Rather than dictating what must be done, the analysis suggests possibilities for transformation that an informed manager can consider and modify to fit the particulars of the organization.

Put another way, coordination theory does not make strong predictions about what should happen to any single organization that implements a new communication system, although it does suggest what will happen in aggregate (Malone et al., 1987). Rather than the specific accuracy of its predictions, therefore, an appropriate test for the theory is its utility for organization designers. Coordination theory is a success if those attempting to understand or redesign a process find it useful to consider how various dependencies are managed and the implications of alternative mechanisms. As an example, we have used these techniques to compile a handbook of business processes at a variety of levels and in different domains (Malone et al., 1999; Malone et al., 2003). Coordination theory makes the handbook feasible by providing a framework for describing more precisely how processes are similar and where they differ. Managers or consultants interested in redesigning a process can consult the handbook to identify likely alternatives and to investigate the advantages or disadvantages of each. A further advantage of this approach is its ability to suggest new processes by navigating through the dual hierarchies, abstraction, and composition. As well, the work reviewed above on modelling techniques shows that coordination can be incorporated into many modeling techniques.

## Future Research

A process transformation agenda suggests several additional projects for future research. First, development of the process handbook and general use of a coordination theory analysis require more rigorous methods for recording processes and identifying dependencies in organizations. There are already many techniques for data collection that are relevant, but none focus explicitly on identifying dependencies. Researchers affiliated with the handbook project have proposed an approach that relies on basic techniques of ethnographic interviewing and observation to collect data and activity lists to identify dependencies and coordination mechanisms (Crowston and Osborn, 2003).

A second question is how to classify different coordination processes. The initial approach to this problem was to list coordination processes by the dependencies they address. Goethals et al. (2005) extend the analysis given here, whereas Malone et al. (1999) take this approach further by proposing a hierarchy of coordination processes from general to specific. Other authors have proposed different organizations. For example, Etcheverry et al. (2001a; 2001b) propose a catalog of coordination patterns. A pattern is defined as "a solution to a problem in a given context" (Etchevarry et al., 2001a, p. 159), so the catalog is organized by coordination contexts. More work could be done to bring together and organize the mechanisms that have been studied.

A third question is about the generality of coordination mechanisms. Most of the work applying the typology of coordination mechanisms has assumed rather than tested the generality of the mechanisms. Nevertheless, the list of mechanisms does seem to have been useful in a variety of settings.

A final question is how to analyze specific coordination practices, e.g., resource allocation. Malone and Crowston ask, "Can we characterize an entire 'design space' for solutions to this problem and analyze the major factors that would favor one solution over another in specific situations?" (1994, p. 110). Most applications of coordination theory are not very explicit about evaluation or factors that make particular coordination mechanisms more or less desirable. There has been some work addressing specific metrics for coordination. For example, Frozza and Alvares (2002) offer a list of criteria for comparing mechanisms—predictivity, adaptability, action control, communication mode, conflicts, information exchange, agents, applications, advantages, and disadvantages. Albino et al. develop the notion of coordination load, "a quantitative index that measures the effort required to properly coordinate a given process" (2002, p. 10), based on an analysis of the workflow in the process. The goal of this index is to allow a comparison of alternative coordination modes. Nevertheless, it is clear that we are far from characterizing the design space for any of the identified dependencies or coordination mechanisms.

Even in its current stage of development though, coordination theory seems to provide a much needed underpinning for the study and design of new business processes. The result of these efforts will be a coordination theory–based set of tools for analysts and designers, thus enabling business process transformation.

## APPENDIX 4.1. EXAMPLE OF E-MAIL BUG REPORT AND PATCH IN THE LINUX KERNEL

(*Source:* From http://lkml.org/lkml/2003/5/28/204)

Subject   2.4 bug: fifo-write causes diskwrites to read-only fs !
From      R
Date      Wed May 28 2003-13:02:20 EST

Hi all,

It turns out that Linux is updating inode timestamps of fifos (named pipes) that are written to while residing on a read-only filesystem. It is not only updating in-ram info, but it will issue *physical* writes to the read-only fs on the disk !

I use a CompactFlash in an embedded application with a read-only root-fs on it. There are several processes that communicate with each other via fifos. This bug in Linux causes frequent writes to my CF and will shorten it's lifetime enormously . .

I've posted a report on the "mysterious writes" before: (http://www.ussg.iu.edu/hypermail/Linux/kernel/0303.2/1753.html) (incorrectly) linking it to a possible bug in O_SYNC. Nothing came out of it.

But now I've completely tracked down the bug (logging all diskaccesses and seeing it undoubtly write in disksectors containing time-stamp info of fifo's). Looking back it would have been easier to prove that something is wrong: the modified time-stamps survive power-cycles. This is not supposed to happen on a read-only fs.

I've tried reading the kernel source to find where the bug lives, But I'm not too familiar with it. Anyone out there who can pin it down ?
greetings, R

Sysinfo:
---------
- various 2.4 kernels including RH-2.4.20–13.9, but also straight 2.4(ac) ones.
- CompactFlash (= IDE disk)
- Geode GX1 CPU (i586 compatible)

---

Date     Wed, 28 May 2003 15:17:38 -0400 (EDT)
From     D
Subject  Re: 2.4 bug: fifo-write causes diskwrites to read-only fs !

How does it 'know' it's a R/O file-system? Have you mounted it R/O, mounted it noatime, or just taken whatever you get when you boot from a ramdisk?

FYI, I created a FIFO with mkfifo, remounted the file-system R/O, executed 'cat' with it's input coming from the FIFO, and then waited for a few minutes. I then wrote to the FIFO. The atime di heers, D

---

Subject  Re: 2.4 bug: fifo-write causes diskwrites to read-only fs !
Date     Wed, 28 May 2003 21:34:17 +0200
From     R

Hi D,

The kernel has the "ro" commandline-parameter. There is no remount after the system boots. "touch /bla" gives a read-only fs error.

> FYI, I created a FIFO with mkfifo, remounted the file-system
> R/O, executed 'cat' with it's input coming from the FIFO, and
> then waited for a few minutes. I then wrote to the FIFO.
> The atime did not change with 2.4.20.

Just did the same here (on my workstation). And the times *did* change . . More precisely: the "modification" & "change" were updated, the "access" time remained unchanged.

RH9, kernel-2.4.20–13.9

greetings, R

---

Date     Wed, 28 May 2003 16:22:47 -0400 (EDT)
From     D
Subject  Re: 2.4 bug: fifo-write causes diskwrites to read-only fs !

Okay. I can now verify the problem. There are two problems as this script will show:

Script started on Wed May 28 16:10:13 2003

```
# cat xxx.c
#include <stdio.h>
. . . test program listing omitted . . .
# gcc -02 -o xxx -Wall xxx.c
# ./xxx
atime = 3ed51750
mtime = 3ed517c5
ctime = 3ed517c5
. . . test program output omitted . . .

# >/alt/foo
bash: /alt/foo: Read-only file system
# exit
exit
Script done on Wed May 28 16:11:12 2003
```

As you can clearly see, access time (atime) is not changed. However, both ctime and mtime are both changed with every FIFO access. Since this FIFO is provably on a R/O file system, nothing should change.

Now, somebody will probably claim that this is the correct POSIX defined behavior <sigh> so you might have to make some work-around like use a pipe or socket instead of the FIFO??

Cheers, D

---

Subject  Re: 2.4 bug: fifo-write causes diskwrites to read-only fs !
Date     Wed, 28 May 2003 22:52:30 +0200
From     R

Hi D,

Yeah !, I'm no longer alone . . :-)

Note that the fact that you see the times changing in the fs while it is mounted doesn't imply a problem in itself: serial and tty device nodes get their time-stamps updated too on a read-only fs when they are written. But these changes are in ram only: when you reboot you get the old values back.

But with FIFOs the changes *do* get written out to the read-only fs !

Hmm, wonder what happens if you try it on a real read-only medium like a CDR. Maybe kernel errors/panic . .

> Now, somebody will probably claim that this is the correct
> POSIX defined behavior <sigh> so you might have to make some
> work-around like use a pipe or socket instead of the FIFO??

Seems very stupid to me if POSIX specifies this. I don't have the POSIX spec, but maybe it specifies what "read-only" is supposed to mean somewhere too . .

But let's wait & see . . :-)

greetings, R

---

Subject   Re: 2.4 bug: fifo-write causes diskwrites to read-only fs !
From      S
Date      Fri May 30 2003-08:27:17 EST

Hi,

On Wed, May 28, 2003 at 10:52:30PM +0200, R wrote:

> I don't have the POSIX spec, but maybe it specifies what "read-only"
> is supposed to mean somewhere too . .

SingleUnix says:

http://www.opengroup.org/onlinepubs/007904975/basedefs/xbd_chap04.html#tag_04_07

"Marks for update, and updates themselves, are not done for files on read-only file systems"

So we're wrong here. Patch below fixes it for me for 2.4.

Cheers, S

```
--- Linux-2.4-odirect/fs/inode.c.=K0004=.orig
+++ Linux-2.4-odirect/fs/inode.c
@@ -1194,6 +1194,24 @@ void update_atime (struct inode *inode)
mark_inode_dirty_sync (inode);
} /* End Function update_atime */

+/**
+ * update_mctime-update the mtime and ctime
+ * @inode: inode accessed
+ *
+ * Update the modified and changed times on an inode for writes to special
+ * files such as fifos. No change is forced if the timestamps are already
+ * up-to-date or if the filesystem is readonly.
+ */
+
+void update_mctime (struct inode *inode)
+{
+ if (inode->i_mtime == CURRENT_TIME && inode->i_ctime == CURRENT_TIME)
+ return;
```

```
+ if ( IS_RDONLY (inode) ) return;
+ inode->i_ctime = inode->i_mtime = CURRENT_TIME;
+ mark_inode_dirty (inode);
+} /* End Function update_mctime */
+

/*
* Quota functions that want to walk the inode lists. .
--- Linux-2.4-odirect/fs/pipe.c.=K0004=.orig
+++ Linux-2.4-odirect/fs/pipe.c
@@ -230,8 +230,7 @@ pipe_write(struct file *filp, const char
/* Signal readers asynchronously that there is more data. */
wake_up_interruptible(PIPE_WAIT(*inode));

- inode->i_ctime = inode->i_mtime = CURRENT_TIME;
- mark_inode_dirty(inode);
+ update_mctime(inode);

out:
up(PIPE_SEM(*inode));
--- Linux-2.4-odirect/include/Linux/fs.h.=K0004=.orig
+++ Linux-2.4-odirect/include/Linux/fs.h
@@ -201,6 +201,7 @@ extern int leases_enable, dir_notify_ena
#include <asm/byteorder.h>

extern void update_atime (struct inode *);
+extern void update_mctime (struct inode *);
#define UPDATE_ATIME(inode) update_atime (inode)

extern void buffer_init(unsigned long);
```

---

## ACKNOWLEDGMENTS

This is a revised and updated version of an article previously published as K. Crowston, A co-ordination theory approach to organizational process design, *Organization Science,* 8, 2 (1997), 157–175. Portions of previous text reprinted with permission of INFORMS, 7240 Parkway Drive, Suite 310, Hanover, MD 21076.

## NOTES

1. FLOSS is a broad term used to embrace software that is developed and released under some sort of free or open source license. The free software and the open source movements are distinct and have different philosophies but mostly common practices. The licenses they use allow users to obtain and distribute the software's original source, to redistribute the software, and to publish modified versions as source code and in executable form. While the open source movement views these freedoms pragmatically (as supporting a development methodology), the Free Software movement regards them as human rights, a meaning captured by the French/Spanish word "libre" and by the saying "think of free speech, not free beer." (See http://www.

gnu.org/philosophy/ and http://opensource.org/ for more details.) This paper focuses on development practices, which we expect to be largely shared across the virtual teams in both movements. However, in recognition of these two communities, we use the acronym FLOSS, standing for Free/Libre and Open Source Software, rather than the more common OSS.

2. Bugzilla was originally developed for the Mozilla project, but is now widely used by FLOSS developers.

3. BitKeeper is a proprietary source code control system whose developers provided a free license to Linux developers. Torvalds began using BitKeeper in 2002. After a dispute, the license was revoked in April 2005, after which Torvalds developed his own system, named Git, specialized for Linux kernel sources (Shankland, 2005).

# REFERENCES

Abell, P. 1987. *The Syntax of Social Life: The Theory and Method of Comparative Narratives.* New York: Clarendon Press.

Albino, V.; Pontrandolfo, P.; and Scozzi, B. 2002. Analysis of information flows to enhance the coordination of production processes. *International Journal of Production Economics,* 75, 7–9.

Alho, K., and Sulonen, R. 1998. Supporting virtual software projects on the Web. Paper presented at the Workshop on Coordinating Distributed Software Development Projects, 7th International Workshop on Enabling Technologies: Infrastructure for Collaborative Enterprises (WETICE '98), Palo Alto, CA, June 17–19.

Barr, J. 2002. Linus tries to make himself scale. *LinuxWorld.com,* February 11. Available at http://linux.sys-con.com/read/32722.htm (accessed on March 20, 2005).

Britton, L.C.; Wright, M.; and Ball, D.F. 2000. The use of co-ordination theory to improve service quality in executive search. *Service Industries Journal,* 20, 4, 85–102.

Crowston, K. 1991a. Modelling coordination in organizations. In M. Masuch and G. Massimo (eds.), *Artificial Intelligence in Organization and Management Theory.* Amsterdam: Elsevier.

———. 1991b. Towards a coordination cookbook: Recipes for multi-agent action. Ph.D. dissertation, MIT Sloan School of Management, Cambridge, MA.

———. 1997. A coordination theory approach to organizational process design. *Organization Science,* 8, 2, 157–175.

———. 2003. A taxonomy of organizational dependencies and coordination mechanisms. In T.W. Malone, K. Crowston, and G. Herman (eds.), *The Process Handbook.* Cambridge, MA: MIT Press, pp. 85–108.

Crowston, K., and Kammerer, E. 1998. Coordination and collective mind in software requirements development. *IBM Systems Journal,* 37, 2, 227–245.

Crowston, K., and Osborn, C.S. 2003. A coordination theory approach to process description and redesign. In T.W. Malone, K. Crowston, and G. Herman (eds.), *Organizing Business Knowledge: The MIT Process Handbook.* Cambridge, MA: MIT Press, pp. 335–370.

Dennett, D.C. 1987. *The Intentional Stance.* Cambridge, MA: MIT Press.

Etcheverry, P.; Lopisteguy, P.; and Dagorret, P. 2001a. Pattern-based guidelines for coordination engineering. *Database and Expert Systems Applications,* 2113, 155–164.

———. 2001b. Specifying contexts for coordination patterns. In V. Akman, P. Bouquet, R.H. Thomason, and R.A. Young (eds.), *Modeling and Using Context: Third International and Interdisciplinary Conference, CONTEXT, 2001,* Dundee, UK. *Lecture Notes in Artificial Intelligence, Volume 2116.* Berlin: Springer, pp. 437–440.

Frozza, R., and Alvares, L.O. 2002. Criteria for the analysis of coordination in multi-agent applications. In F. Arbab and C. Talcott (eds.), *Proceedings of the 5th International Conference on Coordination Models and Languages,* York, UK. *Lecture Notes in Computer Science.* Berlin: Springer, pp. 158–165.

Galbraith, J.R. 1977. *Organization Design.* Reading, MA: Addison-Wesley.

Glance, D.G. 2004. Release criteria for the Linux kernel. *First Monday,* 9, 4.

Goethals, F.; De Backer, M.; Lemahieu, W.; Snoeck, M.; and Vandenbulcke, J. 2005. Identifying dependencies in business processes. Paper presented at the Communication and Coordination in Business Processes (LAP-CCBP) Workshop, Kiruna, Sweden, June 22.

Herbsleb, J.D., and Grinter, R.E. 1999. Splitting the organization and integrating the code: Conway's law revisited. In *Proceedings of the International Conference on Software Engineering (ICSE '99).* Los Angeles, CA: ACM Press, pp. 85–95.

Kidder, L.H. 1981. *Research Methods in Social Relations,* 4th ed. New York: Holt, Rinehart and Winston.

Larson, P. 2004. Kernel comparison: Improvements in kernel development from 2.4 to 2.6. Available at http://www.ibm.com/developerworks/linux/library/l-dev26/ (accessed on March 19, 2005).

Lawler, E.E., III. 1989. Substitutes for hierarchy. *Organizational Dynamics,* 163, 3, 39–45.

LeClaire, J. 2005. Torvalds adopts new programming management system. *www.LinuxInsider.com,* April 22. Available at http://www.macnewsworld.com/story/42548.html (accessed on July 25, 2005).

Malone, T.W., and Crowston, K. 1994. The interdisciplinary study of coordination. *Computing Surveys,* 26, 1, 87–119.

Malone, T.W.; Crowston, K.; and Herman, G. (eds.). 2003. *Organizing Business Knowledge: The MIT Process Handbook.* Cambridge, MA: MIT Press.

Malone, T.W.; Yates, J.; and Benjamin, R.I. 1987. Electronic markets and electronic hierarchies. *Communications of the ACM,* 30, 484–497.

Malone, T.W.; Crowston, K.; Lee, J.; Pentland, B.; Dellarocas, C.; Wyner, G.; Quimby, J.; Osborn, C.; Bernstein, A.; Herman, G.; Klein, M.; and O'Donnell, E. 1999. Tools for inventing organizations: Toward a handbook of organizational processes. *Management Science,* 43, 3, 425–443.

March, J.G., and Simon, H.A. 1958. *Organizations.* New York: John Wiley and Sons.

Matteis, R.J. 1979. The new back office focuses on customer service. *Harvard Business Review,* 57, 146–159.

Moon, J.Y., and Sproull, L. 2000. Essence of distributed work: The case of Linux kernel. *First Monday,* 5, 11.

Powell, W.W. 1990. Neither market nor hierarchy: Network forms of organization. *Research in Organizational Behavior,* 12, 295–336.

Raymond, E.S. 1998. The cathedral and the bazaar. *First Monday,* 3, 3.

Reis, C.R., and Fortes, R.P.d.M. 2002. An overview of the software engineering process and tools in the Mozilla project. Available at http://opensource.MIT.edu/papers/reismozilla.pdf (accessed on March 1, 2005).

Schach, S.R.; Jin, B.; Wright, D.R.; Heller, G.Z.; and Offutt, A.J. 2003. Maintainability of the Linux kernel. *IEE Proceedings—Software,* 149, 1, 18–23.

Shankland, S. 2005. Torvalds unveils new Linux control system. *CNET News.com,* April 20. Available at http://news.com.com/2100-7344_3-5678651.html (accessed on July 25, 2005).

Tushman, M., and Nadler, D. 1978. Information processing as an integrating concept in organization design. *Academy of Management Review,* 3, 613–624.

Wayner, P. 2000. *Free for All.* New York: HarperCollins.

Wheeler, D.A. 2005. Linux kernel 2.6: It's worth more! Available at http://www.dwheeler.com/essays/linux-kernel-cost.html (accessed on March 18, 2005).

# CHAPTER 5

# TRANSFORMING BUSINESS PROCESS TRANSFORMATION WITH DIAGNOSTIC KNOWLEDGE-BASED TOOLS

## MARK E. NISSEN

*Abstract: Business process transformation remains a vital element of competitive power. Building on more than a decade of experience with radical change, organizations continue to transform their business processes in pursuit of competitive advantage. Despite such experience, however, our techniques and tools for process analysis have advanced only negligibly over this period. Process analysis today reflects the same kinds of unsystematic methods linked over a decade ago to precarious reengineering failure rates. The research described in this chapter addresses such problems with process transformation by focusing on process transformation itself; that is, we focus on transforming the process of business process transformation (i.e., process meta-transformation). Targeting explicitly the unsystematic analytical methods that persist in terms of business process transformation today, we integrate and illustrate the use and utility of two diagnostic knowledge-based tools for process analysis. Such knowledge-based tools address directly the knowledge required for effective transformational analysis. This pushes the state of the art in terms of business process transformation and reveals opportunities for immediate practical application. We illustrate the use and utility of this approach through an example of process analysis and transformation in the field. The chapter closes with key conclusions, suggestions for practical application, and topics for continued research along the lines of this investigation.*

*Keywords: Artificial Intelligence, Business Process Reengineering, Change Management, Knowledge-Based Systems, Process Analysis, Transformation*

## INTRODUCTION

Business process reengineering (BPR) arose as a phenomenon in the early 1990s—with great fanfare and hyperbole—offering a compelling, new approach to competitive advantage (see seminal articles by Davenport and Short, 1990, and Hammer, 1990). Central to this phenomenon and approach was the transformational scope and rapid pace of change prescribed for business processes (Stoddard and Jarvenpaa, 1995). In many cases, business processes were transformed into completely different entities, reflecting order of magnitude performance improvements (e.g., see Davenport, 1993; Hammer and Champy, 1993). Performance improvements of this magnitude provided bases for competitive advantage. The BPR phenomenon became pervasive in part as a result.

Fifteen years later, the term *reengineering* finds its way into the academic literature and management press only occasionally. The last vestiges of BPR as a strategic corporate objective faded along with the 1990s. The short, "second wave" of reengineering (Caron et al., 1994)—in which BPR assumed a broader role in the enterprise, even redefining business scope (Venkatraman, 1994)—crested, broke, and then subsided. Reengineering in the mid-1990s shifted from an analytical focus on process redesign and transformation to dogmatic concentration on downsizing and cost reduction. Failures stemming from process transformations gone awry (see Davenport and Stoddard, 1994) grew larger and more common.

This author's personal and professional experience during the times of reengineering frenzy revealed widespread, radical process change taking place with negligible analysis of current conditions or design alternatives. Transformation for the sake of transformation became rampant. So long as costs were cut, redesign decisions seemed to be well justified. It is no wonder that many in the management press proclaimed BPR as "dead" (see, e.g., Harari, 1996) during this period.

Notwithstanding such reengineering frenzy and the associated failures, however, Nissen (1998) argued that opportunities for performance improvement had not been exhausted and that needs for process redesign had not diminished. Rather, the same kinds of hypercompetitive pressures (D'Aveni, 1994), global operations, and intensive customer demands that existed in the early 1990s continued to represent compelling forces for change.

Today, with a persistent and pervasive focus on knowledge management, organizations continue to change their business processes in pursuit of competitive advantage (Davenport et al., 1998). New information technologies (e.g., "intelligent" software agents) continue to present novel capabilities and opportunities for performance improvement. Even the U.S. military, viewed by many as impervious to process innovation, has embraced transformational change (Office of Force Transformation, 2004). Rather than "dying," the kind of radical process transformation associated with BPR has been integrated deeply into the everyday activities and lexicons of organizations today. One needs to look no further than current offshoring, telecommuting, and enterprise resource planning trends to see business process transformation proliferating still across public- and private-sector institutions.

Unfortunately, some of the same, systemic problems that plagued reengineering efforts in the 1990s continue to afflict transformation efforts in the current decade. In particular, our techniques and tools for process analysis have advanced only negligibly over this period. Despite steady advances in the development of sophisticated, graphical tools for process representation (see Curtis et al., 1992), corresponding *analysis* (e.g., diagnosing process pathologies, recommending appropriate managerial transformations, evaluating comparative performance of alternate designs) reflects the same kinds of unsystematic methods (e.g., trial and error, imitation, blank sheet of paper) linked over a decade ago to reengineering failure rates of 50 percent and higher (e.g., see Caron et al., 1994; Davenport and Stoddard, 1994).

The research described in this chapter addresses such problems with process transformation by focusing on process transformation itself; that is, we focus on transforming the process of business process transformation. Targeting explicitly the unsystematic analytical methods that persist in terms of business process transformation today, here we integrate and illustrate the use and utility of two diagnostic knowledge-based tools for process analysis. Qualitatively distinct from graphical tools for process representation and like tools that thrust all analytical burden on the user—and, hence, depend fundamentally upon the user's preexisting knowledge of and experience with process transformation—such knowledge-based tools directly address the knowledge required for effective transformational analysis. This pushes the state of the art in terms of business process transformation and reveals opportunities for immediate practical application.

The balance of this chapter follows with a background review of the two diagnostic knowledge-based tools examined through this research. Integration of these tools to transform the process of process transformation (i.e., process meta-transformation) follows. We then illustrate the use and utility of this approach through an example of process analysis and transformation in the field. The chapter closes with key conclusions, suggestions for practical application, and topics for continued research along the lines of this investigation.

## BACKGROUND

In this section we provide background review of the two diagnostic knowledge-based tools examined through our research—KOPeR and OrgCon. Each tool is discussed in turn.

## KOPeR

KOPeR (pronounced "cope-er") stands for knowledge-based organizational process redesign. As implied by the name, it is a knowledge-based system that supports analysis of business processes. As an analytical tool, KOPeR employs measurement-driven inference to automatically diagnose process pathologies and to recommend appropriate transformational interventions. KOPeR has been described in considerable detail elsewhere over the years (e.g., Nissen, 1996; 1997; 1998; 1999; 2000; 2001). Here we provide a high-level summary.

Drawing principally from Nissen (1998), the process of process transformation can be viewed in terms of a spiral as depicted in Figure 5.1. The spiral path represents a common notation for evolutionary processes (see Boehm, 1988, for discussion pertaining to software engineering). Step one is to identify a target process for transformation. Next, a model is constructed to represent the baseline (i.e., "as is") configuration of this process. Configuration measurements then drive the diagnosis of process pathologies. The diagnostic results are used in turn to match the appropriate transformational interventions available to "treat" pathologies that are detected. This sequence of analytical activities leads systematically to the generation of one or more new designs. Most experts argue that various alternatives should be tested through some mechanism (especially simulation) prior to selection of a preferred choice for implementation. Notice from the figure that the three key analytical activities—measure configuration, diagnose pathologies, and match transformations—are performed manually at present. These three steps are targeted specifically for automation by KOPeR and are described briefly here.

### Measure Configuration

Process measurement represents the first analytical activity addressed by KOPeR. Our techniques for process measurement draw from two classic, diagnostic rule-based systems called SOPHIE (see Brown et al., 1982) and MYCIN (see Shortliffe, 1976). SOPHIE uses system measurements to drive automated diagnosis of faults in electronic circuits. MYCIN similarly employs blood-cell counts to diagnose bacterial infections in people. KOPeR counts nodes, edges, and attributes in graph-based representations of business processes to diagnose pathologies. A set of example process measures is presented in Table 5.1 along with their corresponding graph-based definitions. Details pertaining to the definition, operationalization, and use of these measures are described in detail by Nissen (1996). The key is that once a business process has been represented using graph-based notation (e.g., nodes representing process activities, edges delineating sequencing,

Figure 5.1 **Process Transformation Process**

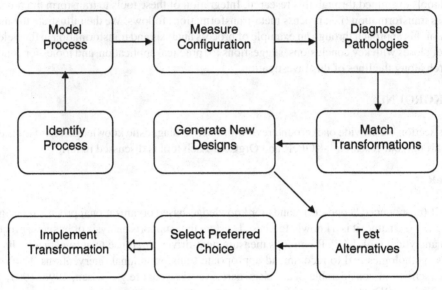

*Source:* Adapted from Nissen (1998).

Table 5.1

**KOPeR Process Measures**

| Dimension | Measure | Definition |
|---|---|---|
| Process | Process length | Number of nodes in the longest path |
| | Process breadth | Number of distinct paths |
| | Process depth | Number of process levels |
| | Process size | Number of nodes in process model |
| | Process feedback | Number of cycles in graph |
| | Parallelism | Process size divided by length |
| Information Technology (IT) | IT support | Number of IT-support attributes |
| | IT communication | Number of IT-communication attributes |
| | IT automation | Number of IT-automation attributes |
| Organizational | Organizations | Number of unique agent organization attributes |
| | Organizational roles | Number of unique agent role attributes |
| | Value chains | Number of unique activity value-chain attributes |
| | Handoffs | Number of interrole edges |

*Source:* Adapted from Nissen (1998).

attributes describing activities), KOPeR can count, analyze, and compare automatically the nodes, edges, and attributes to make diagnostic inferences about process pathologies.

For instance, Figure 5.2 presents a simple, linear process comprised of four sequential steps (i.e., labeled "A," "B", "C", and "D"). Using the graph-based definitions summarized in Table 5.1, one can see the process is four steps long (i.e., length = 4), has one path through it (i.e., breadth = 1), and is represented at a single hierarchical level (i.e., depth = 1). Process size (4) accounts for

Figure 5.2 **Example of Process Measurements**

**Process Graph**

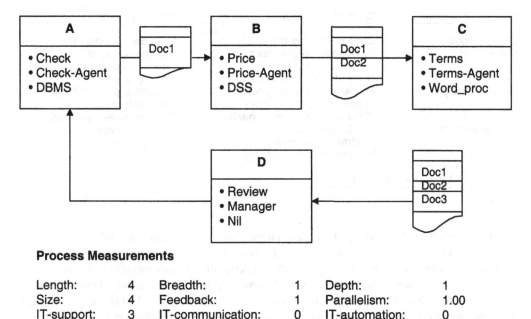

**Process Measurements**

| Length: | 4 | Breadth: | 1 | Depth: | 1 |
|---|---|---|---|---|---|
| Size: | 4 | Feedback: | 1 | Parallelism: | 1.00 |
| IT-support: | 3 | IT-communication: | 0 | IT-automation: | 0 |

*Source:* Adapted from Nissen (1998).

the four activities, and the one feedback loop between D and A is counted (feedback = 1). The IT measurements are taken from corresponding attributes listed under each process step in the model (e.g., the "DBMS," "DSS" and "word_proc" each count toward the IT-support value of 3). Other graph-based models can be measured accordingly.

*Diagnose Pathologies*

Pathology diagnosis represents the second analytical activity addressed by KOPeR. To develop a measurement-driven diagnostic capability, we introduce a taxonomy of process pathologies to be used for classification of problems and shortcomings. The taxonomy is constructed from the BPR literature. Classes and instances of pathologies are synthesized from the various process problems and shortcomings noted in expert reengineering methodologies (e.g., Andrews and Stalick, 1994; Davenport, 1993; Hammer and Champy, 1993; Harrington, 1991; Johansson et al., 1993) in addition to the problematic conditions described in many redesign cases (e.g., Goldstein, 1986; King and Konsynski, 1990; Stoddard and Meadows, 1992; Talebzadeh et al., 1995). The class-level taxonomy of process pathologies is presented in Table 5.2 along with a sample instance from each of the ten classes.

Process measures from above are used to detect pathologies set forth in this taxonomy. For example, the listed class "problematic process structure" refers to problems stemming from the layout of process configurations. The corresponding sample instance "sequential process flows" is

Table 5.2

**Taxonomy of Process Pathologies**

| Process Dimension | Class of Pathology | Pathology Instance |
|---|---|---|
| Organizational | Centralized authority | Long decision chains |
| Management | Bureaucratic organization | Job specialization |
| | Inhibitive leadership | Directive supervision |
| | Underutilized human potential | Training emphasis |
| Process Configuration | Problematic process structure | Sequential process flows |
| | Fragmented process flows | Process friction |
| | "Checking" approach to quality | Review-intensive process |
| IT Management | IT infrastructure | Manual process |
| | Centralized information | Central database architecture |
| | Deficient core competency | Low IT expertise |

*Source:* Adapted from Nissen (1998).

noted widely in the reengineering literature as problematic (e.g., see Hammer and Champy, 1993, p. 54), particularly with the associated implications in terms of cycle time for a process. Notice from above, the measure *parallelism* can be used to detect this process pathology; that is, a (low) parallelism measurement quantifies the extent to which a process structure is laid out in terms of sequential work flows. Other diagnostic inferences follow accordingly. The key is graph-based measurements from above employed autonomously by KOPeR to diagnose process pathologies through class-level matching called *heuristic classification.* This technique helps obviate the analytical intractability and computational complexity associated with search in the kinds of large design spaces associated with business processes in practice.

For instance, referring back to Figure 5.2, we noted above that the parallelism measurement (1.00) reflects a sequential process. Indeed, from the definition in Table 5.1, such unit value represents a theoretical minimum for the corresponding graph-based measure *parallelism:* a process cannot have measured parallelism lower than unity. KOPeR infers that a process measured with unit parallelism suffers from the pathology "sequential process flows," an instance of the class "problematic process structure." This example is representative of the measurement-driven diagnostic approach employed by KOPeR. Inference based on other measures and pathologies is performed in a similar manner.

*Match Transformations*

Transformation matching represents the third analytical activity addressed by KOPeR. To develop a measurement-driven matching capability, we introduce a taxonomy of redesign transformations to be used for matching with pathologies. As above, this taxonomy is also constructed by drawing from the BPR literature. Classes and instances of transformational interventions are synthesized from the various enabling technologies, organizational changes, work flow modifications, and like approaches noted in the expert reengineering methodologies and BPR cases. The class-level taxonomy of transformational interventions is presented in Table 5.3 along with a sample instance from each of the seven classes. Process pathologies diagnosed from above are used to recommend transformational interventions set forth in this taxonomy.

Table 5.3

**Taxonomy of Transformational Interventions**

| Nature of Transformation | Transformation Class | Transformation Instance |
|---|---|---|
| Organizational Structure | Organizational design<br>Interorganizational alliance | Case manager<br>Supplier-managed inventory |
| Human Resource<br>Management | Human resource compensation<br>Management and culture | Team-based compensation<br>Employee stock ownership |
| Work Flow Structure | Workflow reconfiguration | Process delinearization |
| Information Management | Information technology<br>Information availability | Shared database system<br>Informate agents |

*Source:* Adapted from Nissen (1998).

For instance, referring to Figure 5.2, we noted above that the unit parallelism measurement drives inference to diagnose the pathology "sequential process flows." Using rule-based inference, KOPeR can match this pathology with an appropriate transformation. An example rule follows. The relevant diagnostic measurement is noted next to this rule for reference.

IF *pathology* = "sequential process flows"          (parallelism = 1.00)
THEN *transformational intervention* = "delinearization"

*Transformation in the Field and Laboratory*

Nissen (1998) explained how KOPeR has been used in "industrial strength" contexts to guide and support business process transformation. Such use demonstrates the operational capability and performance of KOPeR. It also illustrates the practical use and utility of this knowledge-based system. Both automation effects (e.g., decreasing the time required to perform analytical activities required for transformation) and knowledge effects (e.g., increasing analytical consistency and completeness, enhancing formalization, and distribution of transformation knowledge) are reported in the associated studies.

KOPeR has also been used in the laboratory (Nissen, 2001) to assess the relative efficacy of process transformations generated by people using this tool versus those generated by people without it. Used in a decision-support role, KOPeR helps novices outperform their peers when analyzing business processes for transformation. Further, in laboratory tests of head-to-head analytical performance—that is, analysis accomplished autonomously by KOPeR compared with analysis of unaided human subjects—KOPeR generates a higher quantity of transformational interventions than human subjects, and such interventions have a greater impact than those generated by people.

**OrgCon**

OrgCon stands for organization consultant (Burton and Obel, 2004). In this section, we draw from Nissen (2005) to summarize the key background information. OrgCon is a knowledge-based system that employs automated inference based on academic scholarship. This system's knowledge base is supported by a huge formalization and integration of the contingency theory literature. Most such formalization is made in terms of research propositions, expressed via if–then rules.

For instance, one proposition reads: "If environmental complexity is *simple,* and environmental change is *static,* then the organizational structure should be *functional*" (Burton and Obel, 1998, p. 19). Here, the symbols "simple" and "static" represent inputs to the system, and the symbol "functional" represents the output. This formalizes one chunk of contingency theory (e.g., see Duncan, 1979). We can express this chunk in rule form.

> IF *environmental complexity* = "simple"
> AND *environmental change* = "static"
> THEN *organizational structure* = "functional"

Other, similar chunks from Duncan's theoretical articulation are formalized similarly in terms of rules. Then theoretical chunks from other authors (e.g., Mintzberg, 1979; Perrow, 1967; Thompson, 1967) are formalized into additional rules, and so forth, until a substantial segment of the contingency theory literature is captured in the knowledge base.

Clearly, all authors from the organization studies literature do not agree with one another. Hence, many theoretical chunks are mutually inconsistent. OrgCon uses the approach *certainty factors* to integrate such diverse and possibly conflicting theoretical chunks. This approach assigns confidence values to various propositions in the knowledge base, values that are combined algorithmically to determine a composite level of confidence in a particular chunk. For instance, if two authors with propositions in the system agree with one another but a third one disagrees, one might expect to see a certainty factor of 0.67 (i.e., two-thirds) associated with the proposition. This represents a long-standing and effective approach to knowledge integration in knowledge-based systems.

*System Inputs*

Operationally, OrgCon takes as input description of an organization in terms of six dimensions (i.e., management and leadership style, organizational climate, size, environment, technology, and strategy). The system asks a number of questions to gather inputs in each area. In the area concerning management style, questions pertain to organizational characteristics such as top management involvement in data gathering and interpretation; top management control over decision making; top management preferences in terms of proactivity, risk aversion, and control; middle management control over budgets, rewards, hiring, and unit evaluation; and others. In the area concerning organization climate, questions pertain to characteristics such as interpersonal trust, sharing, and openness; intra-organizational conflict, disagreement, and friction; employee morale, confidence, and enthusiasm; resistance to change; leader credibility; and others. Inputs such as these involve judgment and interpretation on the part of the person answering OrgCon's questions.

Size and ownership questions are more objective than are those above. For instance, size is measured principally by the number of employees, the age of the organization is selected from among multiple descriptive categories (e.g., new, mature), and the organization's establishment as a public or private enterprise is input. These represent factual questions. Questions pertaining to technology are similar but require some additional judgment. For instance, the user must determine whether the primary outputs are products or services; whether the technology involves mass production, automation, specialized customization, or some other type; how routine (e.g., analyzable, with few exceptions) the technology is; how divisible (e.g., involving decomposable tasks) the work is; the extent of information systems use; and others.

Arguably, questions pertaining to the organizational environment and strategy fall somewhere in between those above in terms of judgment required to answer them. In the area concerning environment, questions pertain to characteristics such as environmental complexity, uncertainty, equivocality, hostility, and others. In the area concerning strategy, questions pertain to characteristics such as capital requirements, product and process innovation, concern for quality, relative price level, and others.

## System Outputs

OrgCon uses inputs gathered through such questions and answers to drive a matching process with its myriad propositional rules and confidence factors. Through the analytical lens of contingency theory, it uses evaluation criteria (e.g., effectiveness, efficiency, viability) to assess the organization's fit in terms of these inputs as well as an overall assessment of appropriateness in terms of organizational mission and environment. In a natural language format, it associates user inputs with theory through a series of classifications. For instance, it may characterize an organization as "small" or "large" based on the number of employees and the nature of their professionalism. Such classifications are rooted in organization theory. As another instance, it may characterize an organization as having an "internal process climate" or "developmental climate" based on the user's answers provided to questions about organizational climate. As above, such classifications are rooted in organization theory. Theory-rooted classifications in the other areas are provided as well in similar fashion.

Where potential misfits are diagnosed, OrgCon also provides relatively fine-grained, contextualized recommendations for improving fit through different organizational design alternatives. For instance, it may classify the organization as pursuing a "Defender" strategy but recommend that an alternate strategy such as "Analyzer" appears to be more appropriate (see Miles and Snow, 1978). As another instance, it may recommend restructuring a "machine bureaucracy" along the lines of an alternate organizational form as "functional configuration." And it may suggest other structural changes such as decreasing the degree of differentiation, formalization, and centralization. Where multiple recommendations are suggested by the system rules and automated inference, it will list each recommendation separately, along with the corresponding certainty factor as an estimate of relative confidence, and explain the characteristics and implications of each. This section on diagnosed misfits and recommendations can be empty or very long, depending upon how well the organizational design appears to be appropriate for its mission and environment.

## Transformation in the Field and Laboratory

OrgCon is being used today to help the U.S. military reconceptualize its approach to organizing through what it calls "command and control" (Nissen, 2005). This reflects a shift in military focus from the kinds of large, clear, monolithic threats faced during the cold war era to asymmetric, illusive, loosely coupled threats associated with global terror today. Using OrgCon, researchers today are diagnosing misfits in terms of organization structure, inducing requirements for organizational redesign, and delineating transformations for large-scale organizational change. OrgCon is also being used in the laboratory. Developed principally from academic theory, OrgCon researchers continually focus on validating its rule-based propositions and conclusions (Baligh et al., 1996). Such validation involves computational analysis and laboratory experimentation as well as fieldwork.

## PROCESS META-TRANSFORMATION

As suggested above, the term *process meta-transformation* refers to transforming the process of process transformation. We use knowledge-based systems to transform the manner in which we analyze processes for transformation. Specifically, we look to diagnostic knowledge-based systems to enhance and systematize our transformational analysis of business processes. Knowledge-based systems offer excellent advantages in terms of formalizing expert knowledge of how to analyze business processes for transformation. Once captured through rules or other inferential mechanisms, and once formalized via computer, such expert knowledge can be widely distributed and applied even by novices at performance levels approaching those of human transformation experts.

Further, with stable rule bases, the inferential reasoning of knowledge-based systems is reliable: the same system inputs generate consistently the same system outputs. Stable rule bases also increase the interpersonal reliability of diverse analysts who examine business processes with transformational intent: again, the same system inputs generate consistently the same system outputs. Moreover, once developed and validated, knowledge-based systems perform their analytical reasoning quickly: order of magnitude cycle time reductions are reported for transformational analysis through the use of knowledge-based systems (e.g., see Nissen, 1998; 2001). By inserting diagnostic knowledge-based systems into the front-end, analytical phase of the transformation process, we seek to transform the transformation process itself. In the next section, we first examine similarities and differences between the KOPeR and OrgCon systems. We then address system-process integration and develop several research propositions to articulate the putative benefits and practical implications envisioned through this research.

## SYSTEM SIMILARITIES AND DIFFERENCES

The two diagnostic knowledge-based systems described above—KOPeR and OrgCon—share similarities and have differences that affect their potential in terms of process meta-transformation. In terms of similarities, both systems are rule-based and focus on diagnosis, and both systems support analytical activities required for business process transformation. Inputs to both systems include descriptions of organizations as they exist (i.e., "as is" processes), and outputs from both systems include diagnosed problems and recommended transformations. Both systems draw their knowledge principally from the academic literature: reengineering in the case of KOPeR and contingency theory in the case of OrgCon.

In terms of differences, KOPeR requires as input a graph-based representation of business processes, whereas OrgCon requires answers to stylized, natural language questions. KOPeR focuses principally on the work flows and technologies associated with business processes, whereas OrgCon focuses on organizational structure and strategy. KOPeR includes some bias toward recommending radical process transformations, whereas OrgCon is biased more toward recommending conventional organizational forms and strategies. KOPeR performs its inference at the class level, which leads to relatively high-level transformational recommendations, whereas OrgCon performs its inference at the instance level, which leads to detailed recommendations.

Both KOPeR and OrgCon offer potential to support transformational analysis. Drawing from the similarities and differences summarized above, for instance, KOPeR could be used to analyze an organization's business processes and technologies and OrgCon could be used to analyze an organization's structure and strategy. In this manner, the two knowledge-based systems appear to be complementary. KOPeR can offer limited advice regarding organizational structure (e.g., using case managers and case teams, delegation, and empowerment), but it is not nearly as detailed or extensive as OrgCon's advice. And KOPeR does not address organizational strategy at all. In complementary fashion, OrgCon can offer limited advice regarding process technologies (e.g., for communication, barriers to market entry), but it is not as fine-grained or process focused as KOPeR's advice. To summarize, these two knowledge-based systems overlap a bit in their diagnostic foci, but they are largely complementary, addressing different aspects of business processes being analyzed for transformation.

## System–Process Integration

Here, we briefly discuss the issue of system–system integration before addressing our primary focus on process transformation.

### System–System Integration

The two diagnostic knowledge-based systems described above were developed independently, at different times, by different researchers, to address different problem domains, with no expectation of system integration. In our effort to use both complementary systems for transformational analysis, we must consider not only how to integrate these two systems with one another but also how to integrate them into the transformation process. At this point, we defer the first step to future research; that is, we leave the two knowledge-based systems as separate, stand-alone entities, using KOPeR as one independent, diagnostic system and OrgCon as another. Where their diagnostics and recommendations overlap, manual effort is required at present to reconcile any conflicts and to integrate complementary advice.

This manual approach is expedient for our present purposes, but it neglects an opportunity for system integration. Both KOPeR and OrgCon are rule-based systems that follow similar input–processing–output schemata. We can now envision a single combined-user interface that asks for input both in terms of graph-based process representations and in terms of answers to stylized natural language questions. But with further research, we may be able to design an *integrated* interface, which perhaps captures and converts some currently graphical input in natural language form, and which perhaps captures and converts some currently natural language input in graphical form. We may also integrate the two systems' knowledge bases and overlay their respective mechanisms for rule-based inference. Clearly, a single integrated output report in terms of recommendations can be envisioned as well. However, at this point, we must leave such system–system integration for future research.

### Process Transformation

Alternatively, we can address system–process integration here. The key requirement is to integrate both the KOPeR and OrgCon systems into a process of process transformation. We return to the process transformation process delineated in Figure 5.1. Recall the three analytical steps of such process that are addressed through this research: measure configuration, diagnose pathologies, and match transformations. We repeat these analytical steps in Figure 5.3, listing some additional elements and relations to reflect incorporation of our two knowledge-based systems. In a straightforward manner, we insert two parallel steps for process modeling: (1) create a graphical model and (2) create a stylized model. The graphical model provides input to KOPeR in the same format as described above. Such a graphical model is used by KOPeR to obtain measurements of a represented business process, which in turn, drive KOPeR's diagnostic inference. In parallel, the

Figure 5.3 **Transformed Process of Transformational Analysis**

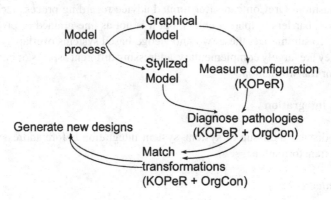

stylized natural language model provides input to OrgCon in the same format as described above. Such a stylized model is used by OrgCon directly (i.e., skipping the measurement step associated with KOPeR) to diagnose business process pathologies.

Note that we show two arrows in Figure 5.3 linking to the step *match transformations.* This depicts the parallel use of KOPeR and OrgCon in this process; that is, KOPeR and OrgCon run independently and use their respective knowledge bases to match transformational interventions based on pathologies diagnosed in the preceding step. Notice the units of analysis differ but are complementary: KOPeR analyzes the *process,* whereas OrgCon analyzes the *organization.* Clearly, the organization provides context and structure for the process, and the process provides action and performance for the organization. Alternatively, we show two arrows converging together at the subsequent step *generate new designs.* This depicts the integration and synthesis of outputs from the two knowledge-based systems. At present, such integration and synthesis must take place manually.

Several research propositions stem directly from our discussion above pertaining to the two diagnostic knowledge-based systems. Specifically, several putative benefits of integrating such systems into our transformation process can be proposed. For instance, recall from above the combination of automation and knowledge effects noted to result from KOPeR implementation in the laboratory and field. We propose, at minimum, that our transformation of the transformation process will enjoy similar benefits. More formally, three propositions follow.

P1. *Integrating diagnostic knowledge-based systems into the process transformation process will decrease the time required to perform analytical activities required for transformation.*

P2. *Integrating diagnostic knowledge-based systems into the process transformation process will increase analytical consistency and completeness of transformational analysis.*

P3. *Integrating diagnostic knowledge-based systems into the process transformation process will enhance formalization and distribution of transformation knowledge.*

Proposition 1 addresses the automation effect of using knowledge-based systems for transformational analysis: such analysis can be accomplished quickly. Indeed, results from KOPeR use suggest order of magnitude reduction in analysis time may derive from integration of our diagnostic knowledge-based systems. Propositions 2 and 3 address the knowledge effects of using diagnostic systems for transformational analysis. In the former case, such analysis can reflect greater interpersonal reliability, as the knowledge-based systems reduce analytical variation from one user-analyst to the next. Such analysis can also reflect more thorough transformational analysis, as the substantial transformation knowledge formalized into the systems' rule bases is made available to even relatively ignorant user-analysts. In the latter case, the capability for performing transformational analysis well (e.g., quickly, with analytical consistency and completeness) can be broadly distributed through an organization, as myriad copies of the same knowledge-based systems can be used simultaneously. A logical next step for research would be to seek to operationalize these propositions and subject them to formal testing.

## PRACTICAL APPLICATION

In this section, we employ our transformed transformation process in the field to illustrate its use and utility. Specifically, we augment analysis of the justification and analysis (J&A) process, as reported by Nissen (1998), to integrate analytical support from *both* the KOPeR and OrgCon diagnostic knowledge-based systems. J&A represents an important operational process performed in a public-sector enterprise. Analysis of this real-world organization and process demonstrates the practical application of our research approach. Our review of the literature suggests that this is the first time a business process has been analyzed by both the KOPeR and OrgCon tools. As the first published report of such an integrated analysis, this chapter makes a contribution through illustration of process meta-transformation in application. We use the transformation process steps delineated in Figure 5.3 to organize this discussion.

### Step 1: Model the Process

The J&A process is involved with all sole-source or "other than full and open competition" procurements in the government. This process is not large, but it is complex and has been identified by senior procurement officials as particularly important and dysfunctional. The process is described in considerable detail elsewhere (see especially Nissen, 1996). Following our transformed transformation process, this first step includes two parts: (1) develop a graphical model for KOPeR input, and (2) develop a stylized natural language model for OrgCon input. We address each part in turn.

### *Develop a Graphical Model*

Figure 5.4 presents a high-level, graphical model of the J&A process. It is composed of five activities: (1) Customer assistance ("Customer assist"), (2) J&A documentation ("J&A doc"), (3) Contract Specialist Assignment ("CS assign"), (4) Approvals, and (5) Filing ("File"). The three circle icons represent atomic activities. The two squares represent decomposable activities including one or more sublevels of activities. To avoid complicating this discussion unnecessarily, we show only the level-1 process in Figure 5.4. But note that the Approvals activity (i.e., represented as a square icon) is three levels deep; that is, Figure 5.4 shows only the first of three levels comprising the Approvals activity. When measuring the J&A process, all levels (i.e., shown here and hidden) are included in the KOPeR graph-based counts.

### *Develop a Stylized Model*

Table 5.4 summarizes a selected set of OrgCon model inputs used to describe the J&A organization. The OrgCon system requires roughly 60 separate inputs in the form of answers to questions.

Figure 5.4 **J&A Process Model—Level 1**

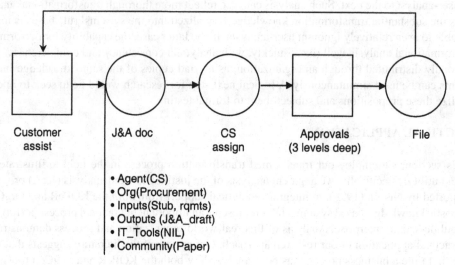

|   |   |   |   |   |
|---|---|---|---|---|
| Customer assist | J&A doc | CS assign | Approvals (3 levels deep) | File |

• Agent(CS)
• Org(Procurement)
• Inputs(Stub, rqmts)
• Outputs (J&A_draft)
• IT_Tools(NIL)
• Community(Paper)

*Source:* Adapted from Nissen (1998).

Here we present only the few key inputs that drive our transformational analysis. For instance, the system will ask, "What is the major activity of the organization?" The user-analyst selects the best response from a list of multiple choices (e.g., production, *service,* retail). As another instance, the system will ask, "What kind of technology does the organization have?" As above, the user-analyst selects the best response from a list of multiple choices (e.g., standard and high-volume, highly automated, *specialized and customer oriented*). Answers to these two questions are reflected in the first row of the table: specialized customer-oriented service. The other table entries reflect similar question–answer pairs.

**Step 2: Diagnose Pathologies**

As above, our two knowledge-based systems take separate paths to diagnose pathologies. The KOPeR system obtains measurements from the graph-based process model and uses such measurements to drive diagnostic inference. The OrgCon system skips the measurement step and applies inferential techniques directly to the stylized model. We address each path in turn.

*Obtain Process Measurements*

We note above how KOPeR obtains process measurements and uses them to drive diagnostic inference. Table 5.5 summarizes the key J&A process measurements and corresponding diagnoses. These measurements reflect the full three-level J&A model (i.e., which extends beyond the level-1 representation presented in Figure 5.4). The parallelism measurement (1.00) reflects the linear layout of the process and signals sequential process flows. The three "IT fractions" reflect negligible information technology (IT) employed in the organization and signal a manual (0.03), paper-based (0.00), labor-intensive (0.00) process. Notice the measured values for *parallelism,* *IT-communication fraction,* and *IT-automation fraction* reflect theoretical extrema for such mea-

Table 5.4

**Selected OrgCon Model Inputs**

**J&A Characterization**
Specialized customer-oriented service
Routine work and highly divisible work processes
Low product and process innovation
No advanced information systems
Complex environment
Medium uncertainty and equivocality
Management is risk averse, reactive, and control oriented
Low level of trust and morale
High level of conflict and resistance to change

Table 5.5

**J&A Process Measurements and Diagnoses**

| Graph-based Measure | Value | KOPeR Diagnosis |
| --- | --- | --- |
| Parallelism | 1.00* | Sequential process flows |
| IT-support fraction | 0.03 | Manual process |
| IT-communication fraction | 0.00* | Paper-based process |
| IT-automation fraction | 0.00* | Labor-intensive process |
| Feedback fraction | 0.35 | Review-intensive process |
| Organizational roles | 7.00 | Job specialization |
| Handoff fraction | 0.58 | Process friction |

*Source:* Adapted from Nissen (1996).
* Denotes theoretical extremum.

sures; that is, the measured values are as low as they can be. The feedback fraction (0.35) reflects numerous quality review steps (especially within the Approvals activity) and signals a review-intensive process. The organizational roles measurement (7) reflects substantial horizontal differentiation and signals considerable job specialization. Finally, the handoff fraction (0.58) reflects disjointed work activities that pass from one department to another within the organization and signals considerable process friction.

*Diagnose Organizational Misfits*

OrgCon uses the term *fit* to characterize coherence between an organizational design and its mission–environmental context. The term *misfit* pertains to problems with fit that are diagnosed by the system. Table 5.6 summarizes the key J&A misfits diagnosed by OrgCon and includes the corresponding transformations.

The first misfit diagnosed by OrgCon involves its basic IT. Due to the organization's functional structure and management's predilection for micro-involvement, the rudimentary information systems found in the current J&A organization are deemed inadequate. Note that this OrgCon diagnosis is consistent with the IT-related diagnoses made by KOPeR above. KOPeR provides some additional detail, however, identifying three different classes of IT (i.e., support, communication, automation) in its diagnostic analysis.

Table 5.6

**J&A Diagnosed Organizational Misfits and Transformations**

| Misfit | Transformation |
|---|---|
| Basic IT | Top management needs an excellent information system to monitor the environment. |
| Medium differentiation and centralization | Low horizontal and vertical differentiation, along with high centralization, are more appropriate for the Defender strategy, routine technology, and management preference for micro-involvement. |
| Routine technology | Nonroutine technology is important for the organization to adapt to changes inherent in an unpredictable and uncertain environment. |
| Low innovation | New product and process innovation are important for the organization to adapt to changes inherent in an unpredictable and uncertain environment. |
| Defender strategy | An Analyzer strategy is more appropriate for a complex environment. |

The second misfit summarized in Table 5.6 involves the organization structural elements *differentiation* and *centralization*. Differentiation has two relevant components here. Horizontal differentiation refers to job breadth, and vertical differentiation refers to hierarchical levels in the organization. Centralization refers to patterns of information flows and decision making. The current J&A organization is characterized by "medium" levels for all three of these structural factors. But given its current Defender strategy, and management's preference for micro-involvement, low differentiation would be more appropriate, as would high centralization. Note the KOPeR diagnosis in terms of job specialization (i.e., horizontal differentiation) is consistent with the OrgCon analysis, as is the KOPeR detection of a review-intensive process (i.e., managerial micro-involvement).

The third misfit summarized in the table involves the routine technology noted for the J&A organization. Recall from above that *routine technology* refers to work problems that are analyzable and that generate few exceptions. Routine technology is appropriate for stable and predictable environments but problematic for environments that change in unpredictable ways. The fourth misfit of low innovation follows as problematic in the current J&A organizational environment. Innovation, like nonroutine technology, is important for the organization to adapt to changes inherent in an unpredictable and uncertain environment. The fifth misfit identifies a problem with the J&A organization's Defender strategy. The Analyzer strategy calls for an organization to seek out actively new opportunities in an uncertain, complex environment, whereas the Defender strategy depends upon efficiencies in a stable environment. KOPeR has no capability to diagnose pathologies along these lines.

**Step 3: Match Transformations**

As above, our two knowledge-based systems take separate paths to match transformations. We first address the KOPeR transformations and then look toward integration of OrgCon recommendations.

Table 5.7

**J&A Process Transformations**

| Diagnosis | Recommendation | Alternative |
|---|---|---|
| Sequential process flows + review-intensive process | Delinearize (approvals) | 1. Concurrent reviews |
| Sequential process flows + review-intensive process | Delinearize (approvals) | **2. Joint reviews** |
| Manual process + paper-based process + process friction | Shared database + e-mail | 3. E-document infrastructure |
| Manual process + paper-based process + process friction + labor-intensive process | Work flow management system | **4. Contracts work flow system** |
| Job specialization + process friction | Case manager | 5. J&A case team |
| Job specialization | Empowerment (3) | 6–8. CS and KO job enlargement |

*Source:* Adapted from Nissen (1996).
*Note:* Boldface denotes "preferred" redesign alternative.

*KOPeR Transformations*

The KOPeR tool uses diagnoses summarized in Table 5.5 to generate the set of business process transformations presented in Table 5.7. The first column of the table summarizes the diagnosed pathologies associated with each recommended transformation in the second column. Here, KOPeR is combining multiple, individual diagnoses to form sets. For instance, the first such set includes the two pathologies *sequential process flows* and *review-intensive process*. The corresponding transformation is to delinearize the approvals process (i.e., where many reviews and much management micro-involvement take place).

Notice the first and second rows include this same set of diagnosed pathologies and recommended transformations. In the third column, two different management alternatives are presented to implement this transformation. In the first, the alternative suggests conducting each of several management reviews in parallel, as opposed to the current serial-review setup. In the second, the alternative suggests conducting all reviews in a single meeting, as opposed to multiple, independent meetings. Notice this second alternative is shown in boldface. This indicates the corresponding transformation is identified as preferable by J&A management. Preference was determined during a series of process-redesign management reviews and based on management's predisposition toward alternatives that were beneficial, feasible, and implementable in the current organization.

The next two recommended transformations are more technology focused than the two above, stemming from KOPeR's diagnoses of IT limitations in the J&A organization. One transformation calls for shared databases and e-mail to help transform the current paper-based work flows. The corresponding management alternative is appropriately labeled "E-document infrastructure." The other transformation calls for more sophisticated work flow management systems. The corresponding management alternative labeled "Contracts work flow system" signals that such systems should be tailored specifically to the J&A organization and process environment (i.e., to support work flows associated with managing contracts). Note that this latter management alternative is shown in boldface to signal it as a preferred transformation.

The final two recommended transformations focus on people and organizational structure. The case manager calls for increased job breadth (i.e., decreased horizontal differentiation) and the elimination of functional departments. The management alternative labeled "J&A case team" reflects that a cross-functional team of people would be formed to work together on each J&A work item, from start to finish. The empowerment transformation calls for increased delegation from management (i.e., less micro-involvement) to allocate more decision rights in the operational core of the organization. This is specifically represented by the management alternative labeled "CS and KO job enlargement." Through such transformation, the contract specialist (CS) and contracting officer (KO) would become authorized to make more high-level decisions than is the case in the baseline organization.

*OrgCon Integration*

As noted above, Table 5.6 lists recommended transformations corresponding to each misfit diagnosed through analysis, and we briefly explained how each such transformation applies to the situation. Here, we look to integrate this set of OrgCon recommendations with those outlined above for the KOPeR analysis. To begin, OrgCon's call for excellent information systems to help top management is subsumed, at least in part, by KOPeR's call for an e-document infrastructure. Although the two transformations address somewhat different pathologies—paperwork in the case of KOPeR and management monitoring in the case of OrgCon—the IT-based approaches are similar. Instead of labeling the management alternative either "E-document infrastructure" or "Contracts work flow system" as in Table 5.7, we could expand the scope a bit and call it instead "Enhanced IT infrastructure." Such an enhanced infrastructure would address horizontal flows of J&A work as well as vertical flows of information. Given that J&A management has already expressed a preference for the work flow system, this proposed enhancement could be viewed more as an expansion of scope than as a separate alternative.

Next, we examine the second OrgCon transformation listed in Table 5.6, which calls for lesser differentiation and greater centralization to match the J&A organization's Defender strategy. Here, the former call is consistent with the KOPeR case manager transformation. Indeed, the case manager/team approach represents a path to effect the kind of reduced differentiation prescribed by OrgCon. However, OrgCon's call for increased centralization is antithetical to KOPeR's call for empowerment. We find the two systems' recommended transformations appear to be irreconcilable. Management would be forced to choose between them. Neither KOPeR nor OrgCon possess the inferential capability to resolve the issue.

Another conflict between the two systems' recommended transformations becomes apparent in terms of OrgCon's calls for nonroutine technology and increased innovation. The implementation of work flow systems implicitly assumes a relatively stable environment and relatively routine technology with stable work processes. IT automation and support along the lines of work flow systems cannot accommodate work processes that exhibit high degrees of variability and incur frequent, unpredictable exceptions. Likewise, such systems cannot adapt well to process or product innovation. As above, at least in terms of the work flow management alternative recommended by KOPeR, these two OrgCon prescriptions appear to be antithetical as well. And, as above, management would be forced to choose between them. The same holds for the OrgCon recommendation to adopt an Analyzer strategy. Looking for new opportunities is inconsistent with the kind of stability and predictability required generally for work flow systems success.

To summarize, some recommended transformations (e.g., IT-based work flow and information flow systems, increased job breadth) are consistent between the KOPeR and OrgCon inferential outputs. We continue to see some rationale for integrating the KOPeR and OrgCon systems. And we observe some predicted degrees of complementarity between the diagnostic tools. Alternatively, other recommended transformations (e.g., empowerment versus centralization; work flow systems versus nonroutine technology, innovation, and an analyzer strategy) conflict with one another. Such conflicts may represent differences in the knowledge bases of the two systems, differences that would have to be addressed via certainty factors or through further research to identify additional factors able to resolve irreconcilable recommendations.

Nonetheless, we illustrate here how the two diagnostic knowledge-based systems can be integrated and used to transform the process of business process transformation. And we demonstrate how such a transformed transformation process can be applied to analyze operational organizations in the field. This provides the basis for substantial contribution and practical application. And it elucidates an exciting agenda for continued research along these lines.

## CONCLUSION

Business process transformation remains a vital element of competitive power. Building on more than a decade of experience with radical change, organizations continue to transform their business processes in pursuit of competitive advantage. Despite such experience, however, our techniques and tools for process analysis have advanced only negligibly over this period. Indeed, process analysis today reflects the same kinds of unsystematic methods linked over a decade ago to precarious reengineering failure rates. The research described in this chapter addresses such problems with process transformation by focusing on process transformation itself; that is, we focus on transforming the process of business process transformation (i.e., process meta-transformation). Targeting explicitly the unsystematic analytical methods that persist in terms of business process transformation today, we integrate and illustrate here the use and utility of two diagnostic knowledge-based tools for process analysis. Such knowledge-based tools directly address the knowledge required for effective transformational analysis. This pushes the state of the art in terms of business process transformation and reveals opportunities for immediate practical application.

We illustrate the use and utility of this approach through an example of process analysis and transformation in the field. Incorporating both the KOPeR and OrgCon systems into our transformation process, we identify a number of process pathologies, and we recommend several corresponding transformational interventions, generating a diverse set of management alternatives for consideration. We find that several KOPeR recommendations are consistent with and complementary to those generated by OrgCon. But we also find several others that appear to be antithetical. At present, we have no automated means for reconciling conflicting recommendations. This signals the need for continued computational research to integrate these two diagnostic knowledge-based systems.

Other promising research stems from our integration of knowledge-based systems into the transformation process. For instance, drawing from prior research, we develop multiple propositions pertaining to performance and other putative benefits of using knowledge-based systems for process meta-transformation. Such propositions can be operationalized to develop testable hypotheses and to guide corresponding empirical research. Results from such empirical work can, in turn, inform further computational research as well as guide the process of process transformation in practice. Of course, field studies of practical implementation of KOPeR, OrgCon, and possibly other diagnostic knowledge-based systems into process transformation in practice could provide a wealth of rich data for analysis and interpretation. Business process transformation does not appear to be going away. As a process, business process transformation stands to gain as much from process transformation as do planning, decision making, operating, and other kinds of business processes. Why not use techniques of process transformation to make process transformation as efficient and effective as we can? Using diagnostic knowledge-based systems for transformation analysis represents a large step in this direction. Of course, many subsequent steps also need to be taken. We encourage other researchers to join us in our journey.

## REFERENCES

Andrews, D.C., and Stalick, S.K. 1994. *Business Re-engineering: The Survival Guide.* New York: Yourdon Press Computing Series.

Baligh, H.H.; Burton, R.M.; and Obel, B. 1996. Organizational consultant: Creating a useable theory for organizational design. *Management Science,* 42, 12, 1648–1662.

Boehm, B. 1988. A spiral model of software development and enhancement. *Computer, 21,* 5, 61–72.

Brown, J.S.; Burton, R.R.; and de Kleer, J. 1982. Pedagogical, natural language and knowledge engineering techniques in SOPHIE I, II and III. In D. Sleeman and J.S. Brown (eds.), *Intelligent Tutoring Systems.* London, UK: Academic Press, pp. 227–282.

Burton, R.M., and Obel, B. 1998. *Strategic Organizational Diagnosis and Design: Developing Theory for Application,* 2d ed. Boston, MA: Kluwer.

———. 2004. *Strategic Organizational Diagnosis and Design: Developing Theory for Application,* 3d ed. Boston, MA: Kluwer.

Caron, J.R.; Jarvenpaa, S.L.; and Stoddard, D.B. 1994. Business re-engineering at CIGNA Corporation: Experiences and lessons learned from the first five years. *MIS Quarterly,* 18, 3 (September), 233–250.

Curtis, B.; Kellner, M.I.; and Over, J. 1992. Process modeling. *Communications of the ACM,* 35, 9 (September), 75–90.

D'Aveni, R.A. 1994. *Hypercompetition: Managing the Dynamics of Strategic Maneuvering.* New York: Free Press.

Davenport, T.H. 1993. *Process Innovation: Re-engineering Work Through Information Technology.* Boston: Harvard Business School Press.

Davenport, T.H., and Short, J.E. 1990. The new industrial engineering: Information technology and business process redesign. *Sloan Management Review,* 31, 4 (Summer), 11–27.

Davenport, T.H., and Stoddard, D.B. 1994. Re-engineering: Business change of mythic proportions? *MIS Quarterly,* 18, 2, 121–127.

Davenport, T.H.; De Long, D.W.; and Beers, M.C. 1998. Successful knowledge management projects. *Sloan Management Review* (Winter), 43–57.

Duncan, R.B. 1979. What is the right organization structure? *Organizational Dynamics* (Winter), 59–79.

Goldstein, D.K. 1986. Hallmark cards. Harvard Business School Case No. 9-186-044, Boston, July.

Hammer, M. 1990. Re-engineering work: Don't automate, obliterate. *Harvard Business Review,* 68, 4 (July–August), 104–112.

Hammer, M., and Champy J. 1993. *Re-engineering the Corporation: A Manifesto for Business Revolution.* New York: Harper Business School Press.

Harari, O. 1996. Why did re-engineering die? *Management Review,* 85, 6 (June), 49–52.

Harrington, H.J. 1991. *Business Process Improvement: The Breakthrough Strategy for Total Quality, Productivity, and Competitiveness.* New York: McGraw-Hill.

Johansson, H.J.; McHugh, P.; Pendlebury, A.J.; and Wheeler, W.A., III. 1993. *Business Process Re-engineering: Breakpoint Strategies for Market Dominance.* Chichester, UK: Wiley.

King, J.L., and Konsynski, B. 1990. Singapore Tradenet: A tale of one city. Harvard Business School Case No. 9-191-009, Boston.

Miles, R.E., and Snow, C.C. 1978. *Organizational Strategy, Structure and Processes.* New York: McGraw-Hill.

Mintzberg, H. 1979. *The Structuring of Organizations.* Englewood Cliffs, NJ: Prentice Hall.

Nissen, M.E. 1996. Knowledge-based organizational process redesign: Using process flow measures to transform procurement. Ph.D. dissertation, University of Southern California, Los Angeles.

————. 1997. Re-engineering support through measurement-driven inference. *International Journal of Intelligent Systems in Accounting, Finance and Management,* 6, 2, 109–120.

————. 1998. Redesigning re-engineering through measurement-driven inference. *MIS Quarterly* 22, 4, 509–534.

————. 1999. Knowledge-based knowledge management in the re-engineering domain. *Decision Support Systems,* 27, Special Issue, 47–65.

————. 2000. An intelligent tool for process redesign: Manufacturing supply chain applications. *International Journal of Flexible Manufacturing Systems,* 12, 4, Special Issue, 321–339.

————. 2000–1. An experiment to assess the performance of a redesign knowledge system. *Journal of Management Information Systems,* 17, 3 (Winter), 25–44.

————. 2005. A computational approach to diagnosing misfits, inducing requirements, and delineating transformations for edge organizations. *Proceedings of the 10th International Command and Control Research and Technology Symposium.* Washington, DC: Command and Control Research Program. Available at www.dodccrp.org:80/events/10th_ICCRTS/CD/foreword.htm (accessed October 26, 2007).

Office of Force Transformation. 2004. U.S. Department of Defense. Available at http://www.oft.osd.mil:80/ (accessed October 26, 2007).

Perrow, C. 1967. A framework for comparative analysis of organizations. *American Sociological Review,* 32, 194–208.

Shortliffe, E.H. 1976. *Computer-Based Medical Consultations: MYCIN.* New York: Elsevier.

Stoddard, D.B., and Jarvenpaa, S.L. 1995. Business process redesign: Tactics for managing radical change. *Journal of Information Management Systems,* 12, 1, 81–107.

Stoddard, D.B., and Meadows, C.J. 1992. Capital Holding Corporation—Re-engineering the direct response group. Harvard Business School Case No. 9-192-001, Boston.

Talebzadeh, H.; Mandutianu, S; and Winner, C.F. 1995. Countrywide Loan—Underwriting expert system. *AI Magazine,* 16, 1, 51–64.

Thompson, J.D. 1967. *Organizations in Action: Social Science Bases in Administrative Theory.* New York: McGraw-Hill.

Venkatraman, N. 1994. IT-enabled business transformation: From automation to business scope redefinition. *Sloan Management Review,* 35, 2 (Winter), 73–87.

# PART III

# THE ROLE OF INFORMATION TECHNOLOGY IN ORGANIZATIONAL CHANGE

CHAPTER 6

# BREAKING THE FUNCTIONAL MIND-SET

## The Role of Information Technology

### ANN MAJCHRZAK

*Abstract: Process-based organizations are those designed to include the entire set of functions needed to complete an entire process. Process-based organizations tend to only be efficient when managers instill a collective sense of responsibility. Information systems can help support this collective sense of responsibility when designed according to five requirements: (1) provide real-time training and knowledge about both immediate tasks and the complete process, (2) provide and maintain a transactive memory of who knows what in the group, (3) provide real-time monitoring of performance and decision-making support, (4) provide a virtual work space to allow people to see each other's work, and (5) simplify coordination of work.*

*Keywords: Process-Based Organizations, Information Systems, Organizational Culture, Organizational Structure*

In 1996, I coauthored an article in the *Harvard Business Review* describing results of a study of the problems encountered when functional mind-sets are left intact as a functional organization is transformed to a process-based organization (Majchrzak and Wang, 1996). In that article, we briefly mentioned the role of information technology in breaking the functional mind-set. It has been almost a decade since that article was published, and the results seem to speak to issues as current today as they were then. My intention in this chapter is to focus on the role of information technology in breaking the functional mind-set. The chapter first reviews the results from that original study, discusses the currency of these results, and then describes how information technology made a difference in those organizations that succeeded a decade ago in breaking the functional mind-set. The chapter ends with a section on ways in which information technology can play that role today.

## THE 1996 STUDY

A traditional functionally based manufacturing organization even today is subdivided into many different departments. The manufacturing department is responsible only for the actual assembly or production of the product. Other departments are responsible for creating the manufacturing schedule (e.g., scheduling department), inventory movement (e.g., materials handling department), purchasing parts (e.g., purchasing department), quality inspection of incoming and outgoing

125

parts (e.g., quality control department), customer feedback (e.g., marketing department), process improvements (e.g., manufacturing engineering department), product improvements (engineering design department), setting up and repairing the machines (e.g., machine maintenance department), and worker recruitment and training (e.g., human resource department).

In the 1990s, business process reengineering experts questioned whether this functionally oriented structure was the most efficient. Functional units create white spaces on the organization chart (Rummler and Brache, 1995) that need to be managed. Buffers and inventory build up as parts flow between departments, adding processing time. Quality is often harmed when information is misunderstood or miscommunicated as it travels across departments. Finally, because each department has its own priorities, the needs of the department may suboptimize the needs of the complete process, as when a purchasing agent may continue to buy parts efficiently, not realizing that the manufacturing process could be improved so that those parts are no longer needed.

More than many other sectors (e.g., retail, hospitality, oil and gas, transportation, government), the manufacturing sector responded to the call of business process reengineering experts to move to process-based organizations. Some were aided by the advent of flexible manufacturing cells, a set of hardware and software that allows for automated machine setup for different processes and parts, automated material handling, automated inspection systems, and a layout that did not tie people to individual machines but instead allowed them to work as a team observing and correcting the manufacturing flow. Others were motivated by a need to improve their competitiveness, believing that the coordination benefits of a process-based organization would reduce costs by speeding up throughput times, reducing inventory, and reducing rework. Finally, others were motivated by the needs of a workforce that was increasingly unhappy with the routine of narrowly defined jobs.

For a variety of reasons, then, many manufacturing organizations in the United States did exactly what Hammer and Champy (1993) recommended: they reorganized so that their manufacturing departments were responsible for the complete order fulfillment process. Instead of having a separate department (e.g., material handling department) move materials into place to be manufactured, workers in the department would obtain the materials. Instead of submitting requests to a different department for process improvements, the workers would turn to process improvement experts reporting to the same supervisor to make the improvements. Instead of waiting to receive reports on customer feedback from the marketing department, employees in the department would contact customers to get their feedback. Instead of sending manufactured materials to a quality control department to be inspected, inspections would be done by the manufacturing employees. In the automotive manufacturing sector, Volvo and Saturn pioneered such organizations. The hope was that with such reorganization, the manufacturing organization would be more efficient, leading to lower manufacturing costs and increased competitiveness. Figure 6.1 graphically depicts the difference between functional manufacturing departments and departments responsible for the complete order fulfillment process.

The 1996 study was initially intended to test the assumption that process-based manufacturing organizations were more efficient than functionally based organizations. To do this required a way to measure efficiency objectively and comparably across a large sample of manufacturing organizations. Consequently, manufacturing organizations needed to be identified that produced the same product so that efficiency metrics were comparable. Manufacturers of printed circuit boards were selected because a population of over 100 different manufacturers of printed circuit boards had manufacturing facilities in the United States. Also, a measure of efficiency needed to be derived that reliably measured differences in manufacturing efficiency across the printed circuit board manufacturers. Cycle time (also called throughput time) was selected because it could be objectively obtained. Throughput time is defined as the total time from order to delivery.

Figure 6.1 **Functional Versus Process-Complete Departments**

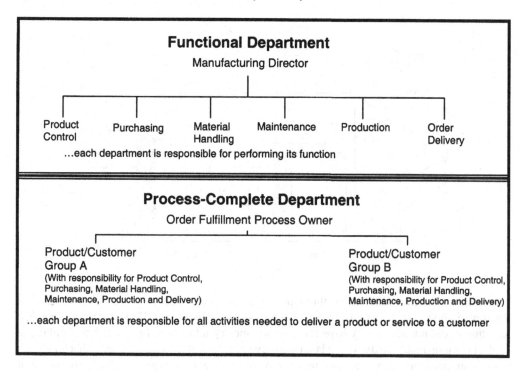

Throughput time includes times for operation, setup, queuing, transportation between work sites, inspection, testing, and rework. As such, throughput time measures efficiency of the manufacturing flow, with lower times indicative of a more efficient operation. To enhance reliability, throughput time was obtained by having trained observers visit the facility, identify the three products that accounted for the highest percentage of the manufacturing department's output during the most recent six-month period, and obtain actual observed times for operation, setup, queuing, transportation, testing, and rework for each product. Throughput time for the plant was calculated as the total of the time for each product, averaged across the three products, weighted by the percentage of output attributed to each product.

Out of 100 manufacturers contacted, 86 agreed to participate. The high participation rate was probably due to the study's sponsorship as a benchmarking study by the National Center for Manufacturing Sciences, a nationally known consortium of U.S. manufacturing organizations. Each company's manufacturing vice president was asked to identify a manufacturing department he or she thought was the one with the best practices in their company. We limited departmental size to no more than 300 workers to ensure similarly sized departments. We did not specifically ask the vice presidents to nominate process or functionally organized departments.

Once a department was nominated, trained observers were sent to each department to spend three days each to collect data on throughput times, organizational structure, as well as a host of variables expected to affect throughput times (Majchrzak, 1997). Of the 86 departments, 31 could be classified as responsible for the entire order fulfillment process with the remaining 55 departments classified as functionally organized.

Figure 6.2 **Cycle Times for Functional Versus Process-Complete Departments**

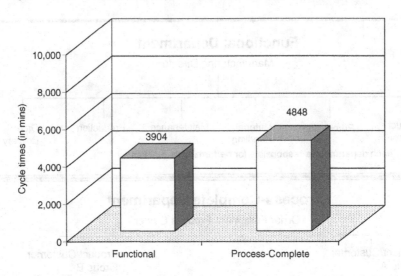

A simple *t*-test of the difference in throughput times between process and functionally organized departments did not yield a significant difference, as shown in Figure 6.2. That is, process-organized departments did not necessarily have faster cycle times than functional departments. Looking at the data in more detail, we discovered that the only process-organized departments that had faster throughput times were those that had taken steps to foster what we called "a collective sense of responsibility." Five ways to develop this collective responsibility were identified.

The first way, broader jobs, described departments in which jobs were designed with a relatively broad range of duties. The observers had a list of 25 tasks that departmental employees could perform. The list included scheduling, quality inspection, process improvements, material handling, and so on. For each job title in the department, the observer checked off which tasks were performed by the employee with that job title. The numbers of tasks were then averaged across the job titles. As shown in Figure 6.3, which focuses just on the 31 process-organized manufacturing departments, process-organized departments in which employees had more tasks per job title had the fastest throughput times. More important, those process-based departments with more tasks per job title had faster throughput times on average than the functionally organized departments with a comparable number of tasks per job title, while those process-based departments with fewer tasks per job title (i.e., narrow jobs) had *worse* throughput times than functionally organized departments with a comparable number of tasks per job title. Thus, introducing a process-based organization without broader jobs was worse than leaving the functional organization alone. Moreover, adding broadly defined jobs to a process-based organization leads to faster throughput than adding broadly defined jobs to a functional organization.

The second way to achieve a collective sense of responsibility was by assigning multiple people to the same job title. For example, in one 61-person department, instead of the 10–13 job titles traditionally observed in most manufacturing departments, there were only five job titles: 29 employees were "operators," 25 were "operators or inspectors," two were "maintenance technicians," and two were "quality controllers," all reporting to a single "supervisor." Having fewer job titles meant that more people were responsible for the same activities, allowing for overlapping job knowledge and responsibility. For example, operators were responsible for all machines rather

Figure 6.3 **Cycle Times for Departments Varying in Number of Job Titles**

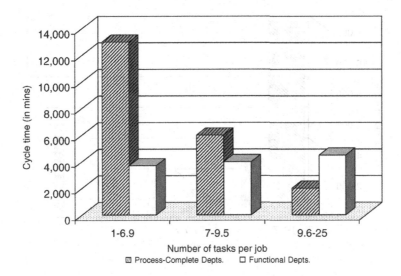

*Source:* Adapted from Majchrzak and Wang (1996). Used with permission of *Harvard Business Review.*

than for a single machine; if a machine went down, it was every operator's responsibility to get it functioning again. As shown in Figure 6.4 (again representing just the 31 process-organized manufacturing departments), process-organized departments with fewer job titles had the fastest throughput times. More important, process-based departments with fewer job titles had faster throughput times on average than functionally organized departments with a comparable number of job titles, while process-based departments with more job titles had worse throughput times than functionally organized departments with a comparable number of job titles. Thus, again, introducing a process-based organization without mechanisms for collective responsibility (in this case, fewer job titles) was worse than leaving the functional organization alone. Moreover, consolidating job titles in a process-based organization provided more value (in terms of lower throughput times) than consolidating job titles in a functionally based organization.

The third way to achieve collective responsibility was by basing rewards on unit performance. Observers asked employees (not supervisors) whether they received bonuses, raises, or nonfinancial recognition, whether these incentives were based on meeting department-wide (versus individual) targets, and whether the employees knew how the department was doing at any point in time with respect to the targets. Just looking at the 31 process-organized manufacturing departments (see Figure 6.5), those with visibly monitored unit-wide performance-based rewards had faster throughput times than those with individual-based rewards, no rewards, or performance-based rewards that were not visibly monitored so employees could act on them. Moreover, those process-based departments with unit-wide performance-based rewards had substantially faster throughput times than functional departments with unit-wide performance-based rewards. Thus, again, introducing a process-based organization without mechanisms for collective responsibility (in this case, unit-based rewards) was worse than leaving the functional organization alone. Moreover, offering unit-based rewards in a process-based organization provided more value (in terms of lower throughput times) than offering unit-based rewards in a functionally based organization.

Figure 6.4 **Cycle Times for Departments Varying in Number of People per Job Title**

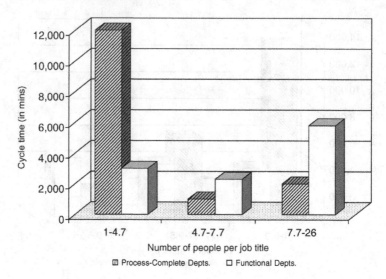

*Source:* Adapted from Majchrzak and Wang (1996). Used with permission of *Harvard Business Review.*

Figure 6.5 **Cycle Times for Departments Varying in Reward Based on Unit Performance**

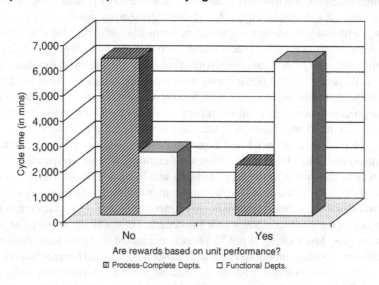

*Source:* Adapted from Majchrzak and Wang (1996). Used with permission of *Harvard Business Review.*

The fourth way to achieve collective responsibility was by establishing a collaborative physical layout. Observers were asked to determine the extent to which a majority of the employees in the department could see how other employees worked. For example, circle or U-shaped layouts

Figure 6.6 **Cycle Times for Departments Varying in Physical Layouts Promoting Collaboration**

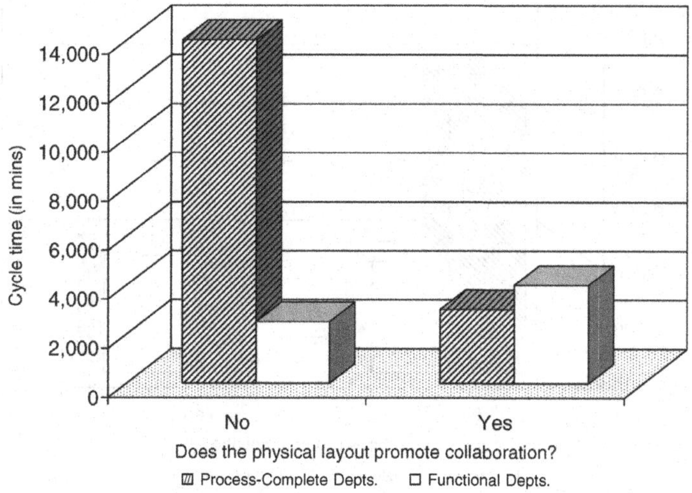

Cycle time (in mins)

14,000
12,000
10,000
8,000
6,000
4,000
2,000
0

No          Yes

Does the physical layout promote collaboration?
▨ Process-Complete Depts.    ▢ Functional Depts.

*Source:* Adapted from Majchrzak and Wang (1996). Used with permission of *Harvard Business Review.*

were more conducive to seeing others' work than assembly-line-style layouts or machines installed back-to-back with control panels facing outward. We found that, of the 31 process-organized manufacturing departments, those with collaborative layouts had substantially faster throughput times than those without (see Figure 6.6). Moreover, process-based departments with collaborative layouts had substantially faster throughput times than functional departments with collaborative layouts. Thus, again, introducing a process-based organization without mechanisms for collective responsibility (in this case, collaborative physical layout) was worse than leaving the functional organization alone. Moreover, a collaborative physical layout in a process-based organization provided more value (in terms of lower throughput times) than a collaborative layout within a functionally organized department.

The fifth way to achieve collective responsibility was through work procedures that encouraged collaboration. Three collaborative behaviors were examined: (1) sharing ideas for improving the process with people in other disciplines, (2) involving everyone affected by a decision in making that decision, and (3) helping others in the department even if it causes one's productivity to suffer. Observers asked employees in each department to complete a survey indicating whether each of these three behaviors was (1) encouraged by management, (2) systematically monitored, and (3) of frequent occurrence. Observers also used their observations of interactions between managers and employees and among employees to determine the extent to which these collaborative work procedures were used. As shown in Figure 6.7, we found that, of the 31 process-organized manufacturing departments, those with collaborative work procedures had faster throughput times than those without. Moreover, process-based departments with collaborative work procedures had substantially faster throughput times than functional departments with collaborative work procedures. Finally, process-based departments without collaborative work procedures had slower throughput times than functional departments without those procedures. Thus, again, introducing a process-based organization without mechanisms for collective responsibility (in this case, col-

Figure 6.7 **Cycle Times for Departments Varying in Collaborative Work Procedures**

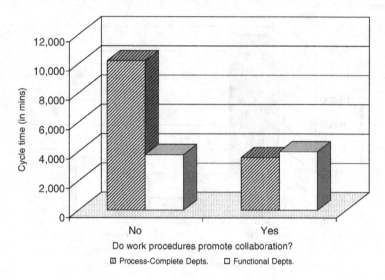

*Source:* Adapted from Majchrzak and Wang (1996). Used with permission of *Harvard Business Review.*

laborative work procedure) was worse than leaving the functional organization alone. Moreover, the use of collaborative work procedures in a process-based organization provided more value (in terms of lower throughput times) than collaborative work procedures within a functionally organized department.

In sum, the study found that process-based organizational structures lead to greater efficiencies than do functional departmental structures, but only if coupled with practices that create collective responsibility. Without such practices, functional departments outperform process-based departments.

## CURRENCY AND GENERALIZABILITY OF THE RESULTS

The existence of functional mind-sets that lead to coordination problems are not the sole province of manufacturing departments. Problems of crossing disciplinary and functional boundaries have been observed in software development (Majchrzak et al., 2005c); technology implementation (Markus and Tanis, 2000); engineering design (Faniel and Majchrzak, 2007; Majchrzak et al., 2005a); new product development (Dougherty, 1992); and customer support for diverse sectors such as banking, insurance, and management consulting (El Sawy and Bowles, 1997).

Reorganizing these functional departments into departments responsible for a complete process is also not the sole province of manufacturing departments. For example, much has been written in the popular press of IBM's need to reorganize its consulting practice away from functional departments (e.g., hardware, software) to customer teams responsible for the complete order fulfillment process. Structurally diverse virtual teams are often created specifically to bring experts familiar with a complete process together (Cummings, 2004; Majchrzak et al., 2004). For example, a team of Unilever Latin American employees responsible for the redesign of a facial cream for Colombia included experts knowledgeable about marketing, suppliers, manufacturing, and packaging for that population of consumers.

Our 1996 findings suggested that process-based organizational redesigns will not succeed without mechanisms in place for collective responsibility. Evidence of the value of these mechanisms in studies since 1996 abounds. For example, in an in-depth study of a process-based new product development virtual team, team success was tied to such mechanisms as frequent virtual team meetings, cocreation of boundary objects, all-member discussions about interpreting events and analytic findings, and having a norm that all information is shared with everyone on the team (Malhotra et al., 2001). In a study of 54 process-based virtual teams, success of the teams was tied to the ability to create a collaborative culture in which members felt included in the decision making and felt connected to other members both during virtual meetings as well as between meetings (Majchrzak et al., 2004). Mechanisms such as overlapping job tasks among members, providing rewards for team (not individual) performance, and work procedures that encouraged collaboration over individual performance were found to be related to higher performance.

In sum, the need to create collective responsibility for process-based organizations to succeed is still a current challenge in transforming businesses.

## ROLE OF INFORMATION TECHNOLOGY IN SUPPORTING COLLECTIVE RESPONSIBILITY

Observers in the 1996 study examined the information systems used by manufacturing employees, among other factors. Information systems were used to support each of the five ways of promoting collective responsibility.

Having employees perform a larger number of tasks required employees to be skilled in a variety of new tasks—skills that often required just-in-time training as employees performed tasks with these new skills. Even in 1996, rudimentary distance learning systems were being put in place at some locations to provide just-in-time training to employees. For example, in one organization, video clips were provided to employees at their manufacturing workstation to be used as job aids whenever they needed to set up a machine for a new manufacturing process.

When employees share the same job titles, not all employees assigned to a particular job title will have the necessary training to perform all of the tasks associated with that job title. Information systems were used to keep track of which tasks in each job title each employee could perform. In some departments, this information was publicly displayed on a spreadsheet posted in a public location. The public display, frequency of updating, and occasional financial incentives for the ability to perform more tasks served to encourage employees to quickly develop their skills. Information systems for keeping this information about employees' task knowledge was critical.

Information systems were also critical to unit-based performance reward systems, because, for such rewards to be effective, employees needed to have the unit's performance monitored and publicly displayed. With such information, employees could react when performance dipped below a target and help the unit to boost performance. Observers commented on the range of information systems used. At the simple end of the spectrum, these systems included mostly manual kanban systems and hourly performance output posted manually by the supervisor in a central viewing place on the manufacturing floor. At the more sophisticated end of the spectrum were highly automated systems (often associated with a flexible manufacturing cell or automated quality inspection system) in which process metrics such as scrapped parts, downed machines, and low-parts inventories were displayed to the departmental employees as audio and visual alarms. In some departments, employees had computer terminals at their manufacturing workstations providing a display—updated several times an hour—on the output of various parts of the manufacturing process relative to target.

Information systems also made it easier to coordinate collaborative work procedures by identifying people in need, contacting them quickly, and providing help virtually if not in person. For example, in one department, manufacturing equipment operators had computer terminals that connected them to the e-mail network and an electronic problem reporting and tracking system. As workers encountered problems with the manufacturing operations, they recorded the problems in the tracking system, which automatically notified departmental support staff such as engineering support and maintenance. The staff had only five minutes to arrive at the operator's terminal to log in and report that the problem was under investigation. Problems left open more than five minutes were automatically routed to the support staff supervisor for review. Workers were also encouraged to comment on the problems of others through e-mail. Finally, the manager actively used the e-mail network to keep workers informed of customer, cost, and market data.

Information systems have evolved substantially since 1996. In the remainder of this chapter, I discuss how information systems can support collective responsibility in process-based organizations. I propose that, following the five mechanisms for promoting collective responsibility, information systems can be designed to similarly support each of these mechanisms. These five mechanisms become design principles for information systems in process-based organizations. In brief, information systems to support collective responsibility should be designed to:

1. Provide real-time training and knowledge about both immediate tasks and the complete process.
2. Provide and maintain a transactive memory of who knows what in the group.
3. Provide real-time monitoring of performance and decision making support.
4. Provide a virtual work space to allow people to see each other's work.
5. Simplify coordination of work.

Each of these design principles is discussed below.

### Design Principle 1: Provide Real-Time Training and Knowledge About Both Immediate Tasks and the Complete Process

In process-based organizations, the broader job responsibilities of each individual can only be effectively performed when individuals understand the broader implications of their work. A customer service team in a bank that understands the full set of financial products to sell to customers and is able to tailor product selection for the customer will provide better customer service than a team in which employees' knowledge is limited to a small subset of the financial products or a small subset of information about the customer. Having the knowledge, though, is insufficient if the team members do not know how to interpret or use the knowledge. Information systems can be designed to facilitate both the provision of the knowledge and training to use it. For example, a customer relationship management (CRM) system can be designed so that the team is given access not only to highly selected knowledge about a customer, but to a complete profile of the customer (including who else has worked with the customer, the various products the customer has been exposed to in the past, and the current results the customer has experienced from past products provided by the organization). Although CRM systems collect that information, it is often not conveyed in its entirety to the customer support team for easy processing, harming the team's ability to service the entire process of providing customer support. Information systems can be designed to help interpret the knowledge. Just-in-time training delivery systems (Davenport and Glaser, 2002) integrated with performing the work are used at Partners Health, for example. In that organization, doctors are given information about possible drug interaction effects when they prescribe a drug. Such a system helps doctors to learn about possible side effects and either alter their prescription decision or note the possible effect for close patient monitoring. At Cisco Systems, just-in-time learning is accomplished through video clips that employees can press anytime they have a question about why a procedure is needed or how to perform the procedure (Kelly and Bower, 2003). Enterprise resource planning (ERP) systems were often criticized in the past because they failed to provide employees with a process-based view of their work. Each screen would surface informing the employee of what information to enter into the system without indicating how that information would affect other information in the system. As a result, employees would inadvertently reenter product numbers without realizing the impact of their decisions (Markus and Tanis, 2000). Thus, an organization transforming to a process-based structure should ensure that the information systems support the complete process by providing just-in-time training and process-based knowledge as the work is performed.

### Design Principle 2: Provide and Maintain a Transactive Memory of Who Knows What in the Group

Information systems can facilitate collective responsibility by offering members of a process-based organization information about the transactive memory of the department. Wegner (1987) first defined a team's transactive memory system as the system by which individuals in a team differentiate which knowledge each should have and develop implicit procedures for encoding new knowledge as it comes into the group, and then allocating that knowledge to the appropriate person. Transactive memories have been found repeatedly in experiments and field studies to facilitate efficient coordination among team members; with well-developed transactive memories, there is less misunderstanding and miscommunication among members as teams perform their tasks (Faraj and Sproull, 2000; Lewis, 2003; Moreland et al., 1996). Information systems can support the development of transactive memories (Anand et al., 1998; Griffith and Neale, 2001). They can document and help to identify who knows what, using corporate directories for static knowledge and dynamic expertise mining of e-mail for dynamic knowledge. If organized appropriately, virtual work spaces can facilitate maintenance of transactive memories as team members update them with their growing knowledge (Griffith and Neale, 2001). Thus, an organization transforming to a process-based structure should ensure that the information systems help employees understand who knows what in the department so that, as problems and opportunities arise, expertise within the department can be collectively utilized.

### Design Principle 3: Provide Real-Time Monitoring of Performance and Decision Making Support

The 1996 study demonstrated that information systems with real-time performance information could enable employees in process-based organizations to intervene and help others when performance fell below targets. In an article on real-time information systems, El Sawy and Majchrzak (2004) argued that, as organizations increasingly struggle to be competitively dynamic, information systems are needed to support real-time decision making. Such systems, called *vigilant information systems* (Walls et al., 1992), provide information to help individuals *observe* (see change signals), *orient* (interpret these signals), *decide* (formulate an appropriate response), and *act* (execute the response selected) in real time. Vigilance means being alertly watchful for any signals of change, detecting weak signals about emerging issues, and initiating further probing based on such detection. Vigilant information systems allow information and business intelligence to be integrated and distilled from various sources and systems; they detect changes, have active alert capabilities, aid issue diagnosis and analysis, and support communication for quick action. Vigilant information systems should support both *sensing* (observe, orient) as well as *responding* (act, decide). A vigilant information system includes functionalities such as the ability to tap into key indicators from core business processes and to integrate information from various systems, graphical dashboard displays, automatic alerts to affected parties, drill-down and slice-and-dice capabilities for databases, analytics for asking "what-if" questions and scenario generation, and enabling communication to others for action and follow-up tracking. One way in which information systems can provide this real-time monitoring and decision-making support is to make the systems adaptive learners by having flexible modular structures that can either learn through machine case-based learning or capture human learning by easily making updates (El Sawy and Bowles, 1997; Markus et al., 2002). Another way is to provide frontline workers with the ability to enter questions and offer comments on their own and others' work, thereby increasing the number of people providing real-time information. A third way is to design systems that facilitate hermeneutic inquiry such that people can quickly represent their current knowledge in multiple ways, compare these perspectives, and challenge each other's assumptions before proceeding to a joint action (Boland et al., 1994). Thus, an organization transforming to a process-based structure should ensure that the information systems provide real-time information gathering and dissemination as the work process unfolds.

### Design Principle 4: Provide a Virtual Work Space to Allow People to See Each Other's Work

Virtual work spaces are increasingly popular technologies for supporting virtual teams (Greenberg and Roseman, 2003). Virtual work spaces provide a virtual "team room" in which members can cocreate their draft work asynchronously, providing automatic sharing, revision history, and indexing capabilities. Team members can coedit synchronously with electronic whiteboards; they can link their room to other applications (such as Excel or CAD systems) to explore alternative scenarios in real time; they can use meeting scheduling, agenda, and minutes templates to simplify meeting coordination; they can link entries in the team room to action items, meeting minutes, and documents to facilitate easy travel between the various elements of a task; they can open and close discussion threads for a topic, linking documents in the team room to the discussion; and they can include voting, voice, desktop videoconferencing, and passing control over the mouse to different members on demand during synchronous virtual meetings to facilitate member inclusion in the discussion. Research on these technologies has demonstrated their value for knowledge sharing, especially when tasks are nonroutine (Majchrzak et al., 2005b). Just as collaborative physical layouts were found to be related to lower throughput times in process-based manufacturing departments, because such layouts allow employees to see each other's work, virtual work spaces allow employees to see each other's work. At a minimum, when all members of a process-based department are not collocated (as is the case for most organizations today), a virtual work space becomes the electronic equivalent of the collaborative physical layout. Virtual work spaces provide additional value than that provided by physical layouts, though. Virtual work spaces have the additional benefit of providing historical information so that past decisions can be more quickly revisited and reevaluated. Virtual work spaces provide the benefit of asynchronicity, allowing time for reflection before commenting. Finally, virtual workspaces link to personal desktop software applications, allowing real-time what-if analysis during decision making (Majchrzak et al., 2000).

**Design Principle 5: Simplify Coordination of Work**

The 1996 study found that collaborative work procedures were facilitated by information systems that made it easy to know when people needed help and readily provided that help. At the simplest level is e-mail, which provides coordination capability, although with little additional support. The use of list servers increases the level of support by providing a ready means to reach all members of the entire process-based department. Departmental Web pages further increase coordination support by enabling members to obtain and share information, maintaining a revision history over time. Most recently, wiki technology and wiki use procedures provide enhanced coordination support (Fenn et al., 2004; Leuf and Cunningham, 2001). Wikis are essentially hyperlinked blackboards that can be accessed and changed using a simple browser-based user interface. The idea behind wikis is to make them as easy to write as they are to read. Any user who looks at any page on a wiki Web site can easily change it, remove it, link from it, or link to it. This ease of use and conceptual simplicity can encourage user contributions (Drakos et al., 2004). Wikipedia is one of the largest voluntary efforts in distributed authorship with more than 85,000 users creating a multilingual online encyclopedia with over 300,000 articles in English and more than 500,000 articles in 82 other languages. Organizations have recently begun to adopt wikis as a way to coordinate their work (Wagner, 2004). Each member of a project team (or process-based organization) makes daily entries into the team's wiki Web site, correcting each other's contributions and moving toward a team-based memory of the evolution of the work. For example, if one member comments that the development of a software component is slowed because of the lack of availability of another component, other members of the team or organization may make comments about this assertion on the Web site. Therefore, differences of opinions are more quickly surfaced and documented.

**CONCLUSION**

Organizations are continuing their transformation from functionally based to process-based structures. A significant challenge in this transformation is breaking down functional mind-sets. My earlier research indicated that functional mind-sets are not broken by restructuring the organization alone. Instead, what is needed is for members to adopt collective responsibility. Managers can facilitate adoption of collective responsibility by broadening job responsibilities, having fewer job titles in the department, using performance-based unit reward systems, having a physical layout that allows employees to see each other's work, and instituting work procedures that encourage collaboration.

Information systems play a key role in achieving collective responsibility. By implementing information systems that are specifically designed to encourage collective responsibility, process organizations are more likely to be successful. Information systems that provide information to workers about tasks and skills, a complete process view, a transactive memory of who knows what, latest updates on unit performance, the progress of others as seen through a virtual work space, and ways to simplify coordination work will help managers foster collective responsibility. Information technology alone cannot solve the problem of functional silos; strong management action is needed. But it can help.

## REFERENCES

Anand, V.; Manz, C.C.; and Glick, W.H. 1998. An organizational memory approach to information management. *Academy of Management Review,* 23, 4, 796–809.

Boland, R.; Tenkasi, R.; and Te'eni, D. 1994. Designing information technology to support distributed cognition. *Organization Science,* 5, 3, 546–475.

Cramton, C. 2001. The mutual knowledge problem and its consequences for dispersed collaboration. *Organization Science,* 12, 3, 346–371.

Cummings, J.N. 2004. Work groups, structural diversity, and knowledge sharing in a global organization. *Management Science,* 50, 3, 352–364.

Davenport, T., and Glaser, J. 2002. Just-in-time delivery comes to knowledge management. *Harvard Business Review,* 80, 7, 107–111.

Dougherty, D. 1992. Interpretive barriers to successful product innovation in large firms. *Organization Science,* 3, 2, 179–202.

Drakos, N.; Linden, A.; Reynolds, M.; and Raskino, M. 2004. Wikis can improve collaborative work and knowledge sharing. Gartner Research Note G00123434, New York.

El Sawy, O.A., and Bowles, G. 1997. Redesigning the customer support process for the electronic economy: Insights from Storage Dimensions. *MIS Quarterly,* 21, 4, 457–483.

El Sawy, O.A., and Majchrzak, A. 2004. Critical issues in research on real-time knowledge management in enterprises. *Journal of Knowledge Management,* 8, 4, 21–37.

Faniel, I., and Majchrzak, A. 2007. Innovating by accessing knowledge across departments. *Decision Support Systems,* 43, 4, 1684–1691.

Faraj, S., and Sproull, L. 2000. Coordinating expertise in software development teams. *Management Science,* 56, 12, 1554–1568.

Fenn, J., et al. 2004. Hype cycle for emerging technologies. Gartner Strategic Analysis Report G00121844, New York.

Greenberg, S., and Roseman, M. 2003. Using a room metaphor to ease transition in groupware. In M. Ackerman, V. Pipek, and V. Wulf (eds.), *Sharing Expertise: Beyond Knowledge Management.* Cambridge, MA: MIT Press.

Griffith, T.L., and Neale, M.A. 2001. Information processing in traditional, hybrid and virtual teams: From nascent knowledge to transactive memory. In B.M. Staw and R.I. Sutton (eds.), *Research in Organizational Behavior.* Stamford, CT: JAI Press, 379–421.

Hammer, M., and Champy, J. 1993. *Reengineering the corporation: A manifesto for business revolution.* New York: HarperCollins.

Kelly, T.M., and Bauer, D.K. 2003. Managing intellectual capital—Via e-learning—At Cisco. In C.W. Holsapple (ed.), *Handbook of Knowledge Management,* vol. 1. Berlin: Springer, pp. 511–532.

Lewis, K. 2003. Measuring transactive memory systems in the field: Scale development validation. *Journal of Applied Psychology,* 88, 4, 587–604.

Leuf, B., and Cunningham, W. 2001. *The Wiki Way: Quick Collaboration on the Web.* Boston: Addison Wesley.

Majchrzak, A. 1997. What to do when you can't have it all: Toward a theory of sociotechnical dependencies. *Human Relations,* 50, 5, 535–565.

Majchrzak, A., and Wang, Q. 1996. Breaking the functional mind-set in process organizations. *Harvard Business Review,* 74, 5, 93–99.

Majchrzak, A.; Chellappa, R.K.; and Cooper, L.P. 2005a. Personalizing knowledge delivery services: A conceptual framework. In K.C. Desouza (ed.), *New Frontiers in Knowledge Management.* London: Palgrave Macmillan, pp. 51–75.

Majchrzak, A.; Malhotra, A.; and John, R. 2005b. Perceived individual collaboration know-how development through IT-enabled contextualization: Evidence from distributed teams. *Information Systems Research,* 16, 1, 9–27.

Majchrzak, A.; Beath, C.; Lim, R.; and Chin, W. 2005c. Managing client dialogues during information systems design to facilitate client learning. *MIS Quarterly,* 29, 4, 653–672.

Majchrzak, A.; Malhotra, A.; Stamps, J.; and Lipnack, J. 2004. Can absence make a team grow stronger? *Harvard Business Review,* 82, 5, 131–137.

Majchrzak, A.; Rice, R.E.; Malhotra, A.; King, N.; and Ba, S. 2000. Technology adaptation: The case of a computer-supported inter-organizational virtual team. *MIS Quarterly,* 24, 4, 569–600.

Malhotra, A.; Majchrzak, A.; Carman, R.; and Lott, V. 2001. Radical innovation without collocation: A case study at Boeing-Rocketdyne. *MIS Quarterly,* 25, 2, 229–249.

Markus, M.L., and Tanis, C. 2000. The enterprise system experience—From adoption to success. In R.W. Zmud (ed.), *Framing the Domains of IT Management.* Cincinnati, OH: Pinnaflex, 173–208.

Markus, M.L.; Majchrzak, A.; and Gasser, L. 2002. A design theory for systems that support emergent knowledge processes. *MIS Quarterly,* 26, 3, 199–232.

Moreland, R.L.; Argote, L.; and Krishnan, R. 1996. Socially shared cognition at work: Transactive memory and group performance. In J. Nye and A. Bower (eds.), *What's Social About Social Cognition?* Thousand Oaks, CA: Sage, 57–84.

Rummler, G.A., and Brache, A.P. 1995. *Improving Performance: How to Manage the White Space in the Organization Chart.* San Francisco: Jossey-Bass.

Wagner, C. 2004. Wiki: A technology for conversational knowledge management and group collaboration. *Communications of the AIS,* 13, article 19, 265–289.

Walls, J.; Widmeyer, G.; and El Sawy, O.A. 1992. Building an information system design theory for vigilant EIS. *Information Systems Research,* 3, 1, 36–59.

Wegner, D.M. 1987. Transactive memory: A contemporary analysis of the group mind. In B. Mullen and G.R. Goethals (eds.), *Theories of Group Behavior.* New York: Springer-Verlag, 185–205.

CHAPTER 7

# ERP-ENABLED BUSINESS PROCESS REENGINEERING

## Implications from Texas Instruments

JOSEPH SARKIS AND R.P. SUNDARRAJ

*Abstract: Despite the widespread espousal of business process reengineering (BPR) in organizations, there have been divergent viewpoints on the process of reengineering and, in particular, on the role of information technology (IT) in BPR. The purpose of this chapter is to shed some light on the latter issue by examining the relationship between BPR and an emergent type of IT—namely, enterprise resource planning systems. We use a case study at Texas Instruments to evaluate commonly held notions about BPR and use the lessons learned to discuss the future prospects of BPR.*

*Keywords: Business Process Reengineering, Enterprise Resource Planning Systems, Information Technology Implementation, Case Study*

## INTRODUCTION

Economic downturns of the 1980s and 1990s led many organizations to think creatively about their business processes. Throughout the 1990s, business process reengineering (BPR) was seen as a means of reducing waste (Hammer and Champy, 1993), and, thus, as a panacea for many organizational ills. This was evident from the cross-section of organizations conducting BPR (Mohsen, 2003), as well as from well-publicized cases of Ford, Xerox, and Detroit Edison reaping disproportionate benefits through breakthrough changes to their processes (Grover and Malhotra, 1997). However, pessimistic statistics paint most BPR undertakings (as many as 70 percent) as failures (Cao et al., 2001).

To those familiar with the BPR literature, such divergent outlooks are hardly uncommon. Even after discounting cynical mischaracterizations that equate BPR with downsizing (Mohsen, 2004), genuine differences exist among researchers on several points. For example, Hammer and Champy defined BPR as a "collection of activities that takes one or more kinds of input and creates an output that is of value to the customer" (1993), whereas Davenport defined it as "a structured set of activities designed to produce a specified output for a particular customer or market" (1993). Among other things, what is different in the second definition is the lack of the word *value,* which has different meanings in the literature (see, for example, Byrnjolffson and Hitt, 2000). In addition, there are different perspectives on information technology's (IT) role in BPR and often diametrically opposed prescriptions for how BPR should be executed.

The purpose of this chapter is to use examples of enterprise resource planning (ERP) implementations to draw implications for BPR in organizations seeking to adopt IT. We review the different perspectives involved in BPR implementations. This review is followed by examples of ERP implementations in the literature, as well as a detailed description of an ERP implementation at Texas Instruments (TI). We then overview some practical lessons learned with these implementations in the context of various BPR myths (Grover and Malhotra, 1997).

## VIEWS OF REENGINEERING

Perspectives on BPR vary widely. The purpose of this section is to bring out the various proposals for BPR execution and the role of IT in BPR.

### The Process of Process Engineering

Some of the most debated elements of BPR are whether reengineering should be revolutionary or evolutionary, whether it should be driven by top management or from the grassroots level, and whether it should be a clean-slate approach without consideration of the as-is status.

The original pioneers have generally tended to be proponents of the revolutionary approach to BPR. Hammer and Champy wrote, "reengineering isn't about making marginal or incremental improvements but about achieving quantum leaps in performance" (1993). A similar point was echoed by Davenport: "Process innovation (i.e., reengineering) is intended to achieve radical business improvements" (1993). This radical change, wrote some authors (Romanelli and Tushman, 1994; Tushman et al., 1986), is often motivated by a proactive response to a potential crisis, or is completed as a result of steady performance degradation that makes the business untenable and uncompetitive. Radical change advocates prefer that the process undertaken be a clean-slate approach wherein the current manner of conducting the business (as-is process) is not considered at all. The detailed analysis and documentation of the as-is process is very time-consuming and, hence, can be a "profound waste of time, [if] you know you are going to start over" (Hammer and Champy, 1993). Further, the as-is study can "anchor" managers onto the current processes and, hence, would limit their ability to think innovatively. Finally, on the issue of BPR leadership, following their prescriptive leanings, Nadler and Shaw (1995) suggest that senior management, with the aid of outsiders, must lead the charge for BPR, providing the vision and the political support to effect the far-reaching changes. They contend that middle managers should even be avoided or excluded from BPR teams.

In contrast to these high-risk, high-reward propositions, evolutionists suggested that radical change can lead to chaos and to a lack of purpose for those serving the organization (Clemons, 1995; Gersick, 1991). Conceivably, any change must be carried out by humans and must unfold from people involved in the process (Beer et al., 1990). Change must be concomitant with the capabilities of the people involved (Cooper and Markus, 1995). As a result, both the as-is process and middle managers are very much part of the decisions; senior management is seen as a facilitator rather than the driver of change.

In terms of practice, research has generally shown that organizations employ a mix of both radical and incremental techniques (Beer et al., 1990). Cooper and Markus's (1995) study of Japanese firms is a case in point. Later, Dennis et al. (2003) and Jarvenpaa and Stoddard (1998) reported similar findings in studies involving North American organizations as well. Not surprisingly, even "Hammer now admits that radicalness is not as important as a solid process-based analysis" (Dennis et al., 2003; Grover and Malhotra, 1997). These joint approaches can usually be observed in organizations where total quality management (TQM) concepts such as continuous improvement work side by side with BPR efforts.

## Role of Information Technology

One view of IT's role is that organizational innovations do not have to involve IT. Some examples of such innovations include: (1) the case of Hughes Aircraft Company, in which non-value-added processes were eliminated without any use of IT; and (2) the case of Promus Company, in which customer turnover was drastically reduced through the empowerment of employees (Grover and Malhotra, 1997).

On the other hand, with the advent of computer and communication technologies, the opposing view is that reengineering is primarily enabled through IT. At the most basic level, IT can be used to support the operational aspects of conducting BPR (Mohsen, 2004); IT can, for example, support in recording the various business processes, in analyzing current and proposed processes, in keeping track of deadlines, in balancing capacities with demands, and in enabling the flow of information and documentation among the various participants. IT can also be employed in a more direct manner, that is, automating a number of processes to obtain productivity gains, although questions have been raised about the value of IT (e.g., the productivity paradox described by Brynjolfsson, 1993).

Despite differences of opinion, the most powerful applications of IT stem not from such incremental, albeit significant, improvements in productivity but, rather, from thinking innovatively about IT (Guimaraes and Armstrong, 1997; Harvey, 1990). Hammer and Champy's (2001) maxim "obliterate, don't automate" is an apt and succinct description of IT's potential role. In other words, one should think of how IT can be used to transform the process strategically, in the sense of Henderson and Venkataraman (1993). While innovation can be thought of at different levels (Swanson, 1994), many examples today include external constituents and could involve, for instance, removing intermediaries (Kettinger and Teng, 1998). Piccoli et al. (2001) gave a pertinent example of British Airways' mobile self-check-in service. In this service, travelers with a wireless device are able to view an actual seating chart for the plane and select their own seats. This way, British Airways not only provided 24-hour service to its customers but also came up with an innovative idea to more or less "obliterate" this time-consuming business process of seat selection management from its organization.

We next discuss how a specific type of IT—namely, ERP systems—can play a role in BPR.

## ERP AND BPR

We first provide some general observations from the literature related to the relationship between ERP and BPR. We then provide some examples of various case studies, followed by a more detailed case study of TI.

### General Observations

The road to the current type of ERP systems was complex. Because of the evolution of IT, a number of legacy systems, created over the years, now pose numerous difficulties for organizations. The term *legacy* is somewhat broad and includes systems that (1) lack the efficiency to scale for the volume of today's data sets, (2) were written for hardware or software that is no longer seen as part of an organization's IT strategy, (3) fail to interoperate with current hardware/software systems, or (4) were tailored for the business rules of increasingly obsolete organizational forms (Alderson and Shah, 1999). Thus, legacy systems are seen as old, inflexible, nonportable, and undocumented and, hence, inhibiting cross-functional integration.

To facilitate integration and corporate reengineering, organizations may now use ERP systems (Soliman and Youssef, 1998). Today, the market for ERP systems is large. ERP systems started off as solutions for large Fortune 100 companies, but have expanded into small and medium-sized companies as well. These systems have business models of industry's "best practices" embedded in them (Soh et al., 2000) and, therefore, represent a hybrid approach between costly customized software and packaged software that cannot be altered to suit business needs (Sawyer, 2000). Through an integrated support of numerous functions and geographically dispersed departments, ERP systems help make operations within and between functions seamless.

Yet the integration of BPR and ERP systems in implementation plans for organizations is a point of research and controversy. One such issue is the relationship between successful ERP implementation and influences by change management programs such as TQM (continuous improvement) and BPR. Schniederjans and Kim (2003) studied the types of changes required of an organization's infrastructure to make ERP and integration projects successful. They focused on the timing and sequencing of these three initiatives such that business performance success occurs. They found that most successful organizational integration started with BPR, with the purpose of making radical change, followed by the implementation of an ERP system, and then followed by a TQM program. Other successes occurred when the sequence is TQM, BPR, and ERP. Both approaches involved the sequence of unfreezing, changing, and refreezing.

Another issue worthy of consideration is whether to change business processes to fit the ERP package or whether to customize the software package to fit the organization's processes (Al-Mashari, 2001). Davenport et al. (2003), in discussing some of the difficulties associated with the downfall of BPR, mention how managers of reengineering projects flocked to the enterprise software vendors such as SAP, Oracle, and PeopleSoft and wrapped up their reengineering and ERP projects into one integrated change program. These companies began to rely heavily on ERP as the way to implement reengineering. These ERP processes were based on best practices and thus were generic rather than customized for an organization. Due to time and cost difficulties in modifying these systems, there may be standardized, albeit ill-fitting, processes, leaving no one with a competitive advantage. This argument was made by Carr (2003) in what he termed the *commoditization* of IT. He argued that organizations should purchase business processes off the shelf, which provides significant cost savings. He stated: "Because most business activities and processes have come to be embedded in software, they become replicable, too. When companies buy a generic application, they buy a generic process as well. Both the cost savings and the interoperability benefits make the sacrifice of distinctiveness unavoidable" (Carr, 2003, p. 45).

Other experts argued that those ERP systems that came in under budget and within schedule (which project managers would view as successes) had characteristics of completing minor BPR efforts up front and had few modifications to ERP software (Mabert and Venkataraman, 2003). However, whether these characteristics help organizations gain long-term success and build competitive advantage is still in question.

## General Examples of ERP Enabling Business Processes

While the literature reports cases of failed ERP systems (see, for example, Appleton, 1997, or Markus and Tanis, 2000, for the well-known case of Fox Meyer Drug), a number of implementations are undertaken to facilitate organizational improvements. We present some general examples drawn from the literature.

Cara Airport Services, a Canadian catering company with sales of over $700 million, supplies more than 100,000 meals each day to more than 50 airlines. Cara's ERP implementation was different from the typical manufacturing implementations; in manufacturing companies, order changes occur infrequently, whereas Cara receives meal-order changes up until the time planes take off. Rather than hedge these uncertainties by making extra meals, Cara's business process for meal plans involves a combination of an ERP system along with supply-chain management tools that allow changes in meal orders to be transmitted to personal computers in the kitchen every 15 minutes. Due to this shortening of the supply-chain and rapid response business processes, savings from the new system were estimated at 7 percent of the $130 million meal-production cost (Stedman, 1999).

The case of Marshall Electronics illustrates how poor business practices are unearthed during an ERP implementation (Willis, 1998). Marshall, a $1.5 billion electronics distributor that sells 200,000 parts and has a customer base of 50,000, discovered, during its ERP implementation, that its goal of achieving a global supply-chain operation was at odds with its commission-based sales system. Salespeople often timed shipments to gain their commissions rather than to meet customers' needs. When made aware of this problem, Marshall's management affected a simple yet dramatic solution: it eliminated commissions and replaced them with profit sharing. This change in the business process boosted the company's sales by 200 percent, making Marshall the fourth-largest electronics distributor in the world.

Eastman Kodak's ERP implementation started with an enterprise-wide BPR effort designed to create a single global business model, regardless of location. The senior managers responsible for the project obtained top management's commitment not only for financial sponsorship of the project but also for leadership in reconciling conflicting procedures. The result, in terms of IT infrastructure, was to replace 2,600 software applications, 4,000 systems interfaces, and 100 programming languages with one integrated system, operating off common global corporate data and thereby presenting a single face to the customer (Stevens, 1997).

The above examples illustrate how ERP systems act as an agent for process change. We next focus on this point in detail by using a case study at TI.

**The Texas Instruments Case Study**

Changes in the manufacturing sector (and in particular the electronics industry) caused TI to critically reexamine its business strategies and to suggest new high-level business process initiatives. To implement the changes suggested by this BPR effort, TI justified, designed, and integrated a new ERP system. A number of difficult decisions had to be made during the course of these activities. We trace the chronology of the various milestones as follows: (1) *strategy formulation,* in which we identify the important business process changes; (2) *system justification,* in which the conclusions at the strategy formulation stage were used to justify an ERP system; (3) *detailed design,* in which we give examples of certain difficult decisions that had to be taken; (4) *system implementation,* in which we outline how the system was actually phased in; and (5) *postimplementation* results.

Information for the materials presented in this section was collected in two stages. In the first, we conducted (1) a number of structured interviews (including a face-to-face informal interview, a written interview, and an open-ended interview); (2) several telephone and e-mail communications; (3) "snowballing" sessions with additional interviews with Andersen Consulting (now Accenture) personnel based on the recommendation of the senior executive; and (4) archival information supplied by TI and other secondary sources. The second stage, which was intended to verify a justification methodology for ERP systems, entailed e-mail exchanges and an online survey; this stage gave us an overview of TI's justification process.

**Strategy Formulation**

Throughout the 1980s and 1990s, markets evolved from accepting one-size-fits-all products to demanding customized products. This mass customization phenomenon challenged TI's leadership in the erstwhile commodity business of Transistor Transistor Logic (TTL) products, and, in turn, led the organization to reexamine its goals and strategies. Unlike the commodity business, the newer types of products, known as Digital Signal Processing (DSP) or Application-Specific Integrated Circuit (ASIC) products, had to be customized to user specifications, which generally undergo subtle variations at different points in time (even for the same customer).

TI had a number of customer needs that could not be easily met. For example, a customer in Taiwan wanted to place all orders in California and would allocate a worldwide destination for the ordered products only at the time of shipping. This operation was difficult for TI to coordinate, because each of the regions was on a separate system, and manual work-arounds and interventions were needed to handle this kind of demand.

According to Phil Coup[1]:

> We had customers tell us that if we couldn't improve, then they were going to do business with other suppliers. In some cases we were taking as long as six months to deliver products that our best competitor can do in less than 30 days.

Thus, the goal was to determine the appropriate processes and systems needed to support agile design and manufacturing strategies. The following quotations from Phil Coup summarize TI's BPR process:

> We went through a major reengineering of our company to become a DSP company, where we are doing a lot of custom products, where we needed much faster cycle time and responsiveness. . . . [We] did a lot of [the BPR] activity [ourselves]. . . .
>
> [The reengineering] was really done for the whole enterprise, because a lot of it is standard process we wanted to do globally. And so, we had to look at how some parts of the business would have to change more than the others, but we really had to do it at the enterprise level. . . .
>
> We made a lot of progress initially, just in changing the processes themselves, then began to bump into a lot of issues with our systems. And then we realized we had to change to a more open software. . . .
>
> Very few [consultants were involved]. We had some work from Michael Hammer and we had some work from some other consultants. Not very much. It was mostly done by TI. . . .
>
> We pretty much knew ourselves.

Two major process changes resulting from this BPR effort were as follows:

• TI wanted to globally manage its inventory and manufacturing processes, so as to support the market trend of short product cycle times.

• TI wanted to leverage the capabilities of the Internet and give visibility to its customers and suppliers, so as to move toward supplier-managed inventory and customer-managed orders.

These changes laid the foundation for the next phases of the case study. Also, as alluded to by the above quotations, the process of TI's BPR involved a mix of revolutionary and evolutionary change, clean-slate and as-is processes, and top-driven and bottom-up initiatives. Later, we will use examples from the case study to illustrate this point.

## System Justification

Next, TI had to justify the systems that were appropriate for supporting their new processes. At that time, TI was operating a number of proprietary mainframe-based legacy systems. First, these systems were incurring huge maintenance costs. Second, and more important, they were incompatible with TI's goal of moving toward a Web-based customer/supplier interaction that was identified above. Third, TI had decided to provide competitive cycle times for its products by globally managing its inventory and manufacturing processes. The implication of a unified global process is that one should have real-time visibility to inventory status and manufacturing capacity at various sites of the organization. As mentioned earlier, legacy systems are inherently not suited for such interoperability, whereas ERP systems' integrative nature facilitates global processes.[2] In summary, according to Phil Coup:

> At the enterprise level it is more like "you have obsolete plumbing and wiring in your house, and you are going to have to replace it. And, therefore, you need to do something new." From a business perspective, it boils down to having key business managers say: "it is obvious we need to do this, we are going to get benefits and we are going to have huge risks if we don't fix the plumbing and wiring in our house." So, whether you think that these benefit numbers are right or not, whether you think it is a bit more or a bit less, it is still a good decision. A lot of the intangibles came into play.

In addition to the above strategic justifications for an ERP system, part of TI's management and development process was to make sure that metrics were used to manage the project. TI is a metrics-driven organization, where strategic goals and objectives are translated into tactical and operational metrics. Due to this fact-based management approach, standard hard justification measures such as return on investment (ROI) and internal rate of return (IRR) were used to ensure the financial viability of the project. Global capacity utilization as a result of the ERP system was also projected, keeping in mind that such projections were only guidelines and could be offset or boosted as a result of other continuous improvement activities in the company. These estimates[3] ranged from 3 percent to 5 percent output improvements based on current assets, which, although seemingly small, amounted to increased profit of several hundred million dollars. A budget of approximately $250 million was set for the ERP implementation.

## Designing Detailed Processes

The goals and processes outlined in the strategy formation stage above are fairly easy to state, but they entailed difficult changes. As mentioned earlier, ERP systems have embedded in them industry best practices for users to perform various operations. Being generic in nature, these practices could sometimes be at odds with the detailed requirements of users at a particular organization. In other words, at the level of the actual users, there are two approaches to employing an ERP system to implement new business processes: (1) customize the system to suit the needs of users and (2) have users follow a combination of the standardized operations embedded within the system. Clearly, there is a trade-off between the systems customization approach and the one involving the standardization of user processes. Because customization is expensive, TI's management wanted to employ it sparingly. As said by Mitch Cline, the Accenture management partner:

> If at any point the planned change in the business [operations] (due to software requirements) was to have a negative impact on a process, it had to be significant for the software to be customized. It could not be "we don't like it." . . . [T]he justification had to be significant, it would have to degrade service to the customer or increase cost to the business, not a slight productivity dip. . . . [A] good example of one such justification, if we can't do supplier managed inventory like the automotive guys like to do it and it's going to cause a burden on these customers. . . . [I]t had to impact the customer or it had to take away capability that would drive up cost.

To illustrate the above guideline, one major customization that TI undertook was the incorporation of Web capabilities into its ERP system. At that time, ERP systems did not have this capability, and this was fundamental in implementing TI's business process of online interactions with customers and suppliers. Another example was in allowing the design department to run its own custom software. Design processes at TI were specialized and different from the best practices found in an ERP system. As such, management felt that the inclusion of design within the scope of ERP would deteriorate the process efficiency of that department.

On the other hand, a number of operations were set according to the prescriptions of the software. First, the number of levels of approval on a purchase order was standardized at four. Some countries had as many as 15 levels. Second, authorization amounts were standardized according to the level of the concerned person in the organization. Third, owing to the adoption of global inventory processes, part numbers had to be standardized. This standardization involved a huge information systems and business effort, because changes had to be made to the databases, the programs supported by them, and some manufacturing procedures. Finally, all systems were mandated to be in English, except for customer-specific information such as addresses used for external communication. That is, if some element of the system is meant for global usage, then it was communicated in English.

## System Implementation

In this phase, concepts and goals must be translated into the tangible implementation of the software. The details below will help sensitize readers about the difficulty of this phase, especially when the software is an ERP system. We describe three subphases of the implementation: start-up, project management, and go-live.

*Start-Up*

Unlike many organizations in which IT departments have to "sell" the implementation of new technologies to business managers, IT projects at TI are initiated and driven by the business units. Given this corporate culture, it is imperative to have the concurrence of the business managers of all units on the design and implementation of the ERP system. Thus, a number of key personnel, along with their families, were expatriated to the United States and stationed in Dallas for a few years.

Second, about 250 people were transitioned from TI to Accenture (i.e., put on Accenture's payroll), which became the main provisioner of ERP system services. This transition was completed after numerous discussions with business leaders and business teams.

*Project Management*

TI adopted a number of different approaches to handle change management. First, CEOs of the solution providers (Sun Microsystems, SAP, etc.) met with TI's information systems and business leaders and sometimes with the president on a quarterly basis. Second, people from other companies that had been through ERP implementation were brought in to relate their experiences. Third, leadership teams were defined for people who were leading key implementation areas for their business units, and executive teams oversaw the performance of the leadership teams with respect to change management. Finally, a process was established to handle problems that arose. The goal of this process was to handle a problem at the lowest possible level, without magnifying it and "sending it up the management chain."

*Handling Go-Live*

To get prepared for "go-live," the key managers who were stationed in Dallas were sent back to their territories for educating the next level of users. Using selected experts, user acceptance scripts were defined and tested. Problems, if any, were resolved according to the process described above. Daily conference calls were set up for 30 days prior to go-live to obtain progress reports.

Based on the results of these checks, a risk analysis was conducted weekly to determine the effects of various potential failures. The implementation plan had a few go-live dates, one after another, but in relatively quick succession. For each of these events, a "war room" was staffed with up to 500 people, including TI's people in addition to consultants from Accenture, Sun, SAP, i2, Oracle, and other suppliers. In the first stage, a prototype of the planning part of the system was released. This was followed by turning on the various modules (e.g., finance, accounting, etc.) of the ERP system. For this stage, TI used a direct conversion method, in which the new system was introduced within about two to three hours of turning off the old system. Finally, the actual planning system was released.

**Postimplementation**

As mentioned in Strategy Formulation, TI had set two goals for its BPR efforts: (1) online interactions with customers/suppliers and (2) global process management in order to reduce inventory and cycle time. We now outline how the results from the ERP system measure up against these goals.

Because performance metrics played a role in TI's decision to justify and implement the ERP system, tangible postimplementation results were important to assess project success. There are around 13,000 users (10,000 TI employees plus 3,000 outsiders) on the system, with concurrent users ranging from 300 to 1,700. The integrated system allowed TI to better manufacture and deliver its 120,000 orders per month involving 45,000 devices.

TI's worldwide external constituents include distributors, customers, suppliers, and field sales-people. Because of its Web capability of the system, over 70 percent of TI's external transactions were conducted electronically. This faster, easier-to-use process reduced order management costs for customers by allowing access to all orders and providing access to real-time global information using open and non-TI-specific systems. Finally, a few months after start-up, some TI factories reported output increases of 5 percent to 10 percent, and up to 15 percent reduction in work-in-process inventory. See Sarkis and Sundarraj (2003) for more details.

## MYTHS OF REENGINEERING: EVIDENCE FROM TI

As mentioned earlier, in practice, reengineering is implemented by a judicious mix of revolutionary and evolutionary approaches. Grover and Malhotra (1997) elaborated on this point and proposed a series of myths pertaining to reengineering. We evaluate these myths in light of the TI case.

### Reengineering Is a One-Time Radical Approach

TI certainly had some elements that can be considered radical. Providing visibility to its customers and suppliers was an innovative idea at the time of early ERP implementations. Global inventory was certainly a radical change, compared to the manner in which TI operated. But the TI case showed a number of evolutionary elements as well. The move toward the ASIC business did not happen in a revolutionary fashion (i.e., overnight). Marketing, customer, and vendor involvement were necessary.

### Reengineering Involves Breakthrough Performance Gains

The evidence from TI suggests that breakthrough gains are not attainable in all cases. Only moderate performance gains were predicted and also recorded at TI. In fact, TI planned for and witnessed "productivity dips" initially (see Ross and Vitale, 2000, for more discussion).

### Reengineering Enables Changes Primarily Through IT

TI's ERP system was key to the reengineering of a number of its areas (e.g., manufacturing, service, finance, and accounting), but it had no role to play in design. This was the case even though design was central to TI's BPR efforts, inasmuch as the designing of ASIC products was central to the organization's customer strategy. Thus, the TI case shows the need for a balanced view in assessing the role of IT.

### Reengineering Should Focus on Cross-Functional Core Processes

TI's global inventory management clearly involved cross-functional processes, but purely departmental processes (e.g., purchase order approvals) were also examined as part of the BPR.

### Reengineering Enhances Individual Capacities Through Empowerment and Teams

Reengineering efforts were completed by teams in TI's ERP implementation, but the issue of whether ERP enhanced individual capacity with team effort was not clear.

**Reengineering Is a Standardized Method Deployed by Armies of Consultants**

TI did not fall into the trap (identified by Davenport et al., 2003) in which BPR was completed to fit with the ERP business process standards. In fact, when key business process changes (e.g., Web capability) were involved, TI went to the extent of customizing the software, although for other lower-level processes, TI tended to adopt the software's recommendations. As for personnel, both consultants and TI employees were involved in the implementation process, but the BPR efforts were primarily driven by TI. In an unusual approach to employee involvement, because of the transfer of employees to Accenture, some of the consultants were employees.

**Reengineering Must Be Conducted from the Top Down**

Again, the practice at TI was mixed. Core decisions such as the strategy to follow the ASIC market and the standardization of business processes were definitely top-down dictates. Also, top management support from the CEO was critical to ensure progress was completed across functions. However, given the involvement of middle managers, the actual design of the process involved a significant bottom-up approach.

In summary, it is clear from the TI case that there were a number of instances in which traditional notions of BPR were not true. However, in the case of nearly all of the above myths, the TI case provided the existence of a countermyth as well. Both have implications for future BPR efforts, even though the evidence cited herein is from a single case.

## CONCLUSIONS

In this chapter, we outlined the relationships between organizational BPR and strategic IT systems such as ERP. After a review of enterprise systems, we outlined examples of ERP implementations described in the literature. This set the stage for our detailed case study at TI. Our example illustrates the central role of ERP technologies in implementing far-reaching BPR goals.

To conclude, a plausible viewpoint about BPR evolution over the years is as follows. In the first generation of BPR implementations, management-supported consultants implemented radical one-time changes through the large-scale use of technologies. Gradually, as the second generation of implementations began to take root, researchers and practitioners challenged these characteristics and identified a set of traditional beliefs that may be false. In this context, what the TI experience suggests for future BPR implementations, albeit through a single case, is that multiple viewpoints (myths and countermyths) can coexist even within the same case. The unifying theme underlying the divergence is that technologies and processes, wherever used, must align with business process changes to meet organizational goals and strategies.

## ACKNOWLEDGMENTS

The authors are grateful to Phil Coup, Texas Instruments Vice President and Open Systems Transition Manager, for enabling access to the details provided in this case study.

## NOTES

1. Texas Instruments Vice President and Open Systems Transition Manager during the planning and implementation of the ERP system.

2. Although design was crucial to TI's BPR, this department was excluded from the ERP system because of the highly specialized nature of operations.

3. It is important to note that estimates are often affected by a number of judgmental biases on the part of the decision maker (Bazerman, 1986), and, hence, debiasing techniques must be applied to improve estimation accuracy.

## REFERENCES

Alderson, A., and Shah, H. 1999. Viewpoints of legacy systems. *Communications of the ACM*, 42, 3, 115–116.

Al-Mashari, M. 2001. Process orientation through enterprise resource planning (ERP): A review of critical issues. *Knowledge and Process Management*, 8, 3, 175–185.

Appleton, E.L. 1997. How to survive ERP. *Datamation*, 43, 3, 50–53.

Bazerman, M. 1986. *Judgment in Managerial Decision Making*. New York: John Wiley.

Beer, M.; Eisenstat, R.; and Spector, B. 1990. Why change programs do not produce change. *Harvard Business Review*, 68, 6, 195–198.

Brynjolfsson, E. 1993. The productivity paradox of information technology. *Communications of the ACM*, 36, 12, 67–77.

Brynjolfsson, E., and Hitt, L. 2000. Beyond computation: Information technology, organizational transformation and business performance. *Journal of Economic Perspectives*, 14, 4, 23–48.

Cao, G.; Clarke, S.; and Lehaney, B. 2001. A critique of BPR from a holistic perspective. *Business Process Management Journal*, 7, 4, 332–339.

Carr, N.G. 2003. IT doesn't matter. *Harvard Business Review*, 81, 5, 41–49.

Clemons, E. 1995. Using scenario analysis to manage the strategic risks in reengineering. *Sloan Management Review*, 36, 2, 61–71.

Cooper, R., and Markus, L. 1995. Human reengineering. *Sloan Management Review*, 36, 2, 39–51.

Davenport, T.H. 1993. *Process Innovation*. Boston: Harvard Business School Press.

Davenport, T.H.; Prusak, L.; and Wilson, H.J. 2003. Reengineering revisited: What went wrong with the business process reengineering fad. And will it come back? *Computerworld*, 37, 25, 48–49.

Dennis, A.; Carte, T.; and Kelly, G. 2003. Breaking the rules: Success and failure in groupware-supported business process reengineering. *Decision Support Systems*, 36, 1, 31–47.

Gersick, C. 1991. Revolutionary change theories: A multilevel exploration of the punctuated equilibrium paradigm. *Academy of Management Review*, 16, 1, 10–36.

Grover, V., and Malhotra, M. 1997. Business process reengineering: A tutorial of the concept, evolution, method, technology and application. *Journal of Operations Management*, 15, 3, 193–215.

Guimaraes, T., and Armstrong, C. 1997. Exploring the relation between competitive intelligence, IS support and business change. *Competitive Intelligence Review*, 9, 45–54.

Hammer, M., and Champy, J. 1993. *Reengineering the Corporation*. New York: Harper Collins, 1993.

———. 2001. *Reengineering the Corporation: A Manifesto for Business Revolution*. New York: Harper Collins.

Harvey, J. 1990. Operations management in professional service organizations: A typology. *International Journal of Operations and Production Management*, 10, 4, 5–15.

Henderson, J., and Venkataraman, N. 1993. Strategic alignment: Leveraging information technology for transforming organizations. *IBM Systems Journal*, 32, 1, 472–484.

Jarvenpaa, S., and Stoddard, D. 1998. Business process redesign: Radical and evolutionary change. *Journal of Business Ethics*, 41, 1, 15–27.

Kettinger, W., and Teng, J. 1998. Aligning BPR to strategy: A framework for analysis. *Long Range Planning*, 31, 1, 93–107.

Mabert, V., and Venkataraman, M. 2003. Enterprise resource planning: Managing the implementation process. *European Journal of Operational Research*, 146, 2, 302–314.

Markus, L., and Tanis, C. 2000. The enterprise system experience—From adoption to success. In R. Zmud (ed.), *Framing the Domains of IT Management: Glimpsing the Future Through the Past*. Cincinnati, OH: Pinnaflex Educational Resources, pp. 173–207.

Mohsen, A. 2003. Information technology and business process redesign. *Business Process Management Journal*, 9, 4, 440–458.

———. 2004. Exploring relationships between information technology and business process reengineering. *Information and Management*, 41, 5, 585–596.

Nadler, D., and Shaw, R. 1995. *Discontinuous Change*. San Francisco: Jossey-Bass.

Piccoli, G.; Spalding, B.; and Ives, B. 2001. The customer-service life cycle: A framework for improving customer service through information technology. *Cornell Hotel and Restaurant Administration Quarterly*, 42, 3, 38.

Romanelli, E., and Tushman, M. 1994. Organizational transformation as a punctuated equilibrium: An empirical test. *Academy of Management Journal*, 37, 5, 1141–1166.

Ross, J., and Vitale, M. 2000. The ERP revolution: Surviving versus thriving. *Information Systems Frontiers*, 2, 2, 233–241.

Sarkis, J., and Sundarraj, R. 2003. Managing large-scale global enterprise resource planning systems: A case study at Texas Instruments. *International Journal of Information Management*, 23, 5, 431–442.

Sawyer, S. 2000. Packaged software: Implications of the differences from custom approaches to software development. *European Journal of Information Systems*, 9, 1, 47–58.

Schniederjans, M., and Kim, G. 2003. Implementing enterprise resource planning systems, with total quality control and business process reengineering: Survey results. *International Journal of Operations and Production Management*, 23, 4, 418–429.

Soh, C.; Kien, S.; and Tay-Yap, J. 2000. Cultural fits and misfits: Is ERP a universal solution? *Communications of the ACM*, 43, 4, 47–53.

Soliman, F., and Youssef, M. 1998. The role of SAP software in business process rerengineering. *International Journal of Operations & Production Management*, 18, 9–10, 886–895.

Stedman, C. 1999. Airline food vendor seeks 7% savings. *Computerworld* (June 14), 73.

Stevens, T. 1997. Kodak focuses on ERP. *Industry Week*, 246, 15, 130.

Swanson, E. 1994. Information systems innovation among organization. *Management Science*, 40, 9, 1069–1092.

Tushman, M.; Newman, W.; and Romanelli, E. 1986. Convergence and upheaval: Managing evolutionary unsteady pace of organizational evolution. *California Management Review*, 29, 1, 29–44.

Willis, C. 1998. How winners do it. *Forbes*, 162, 4, S88–91.

# PART IV

## TRANSFORMATION ACROSS A
## SPECTRUM OF BUSINESS PROCESSES

# CHAPTER 8

# REDESIGNING IT-ENABLED CUSTOMER SUPPORT PROCESSES FOR DYNAMIC ENVIRONMENTS

## OMAR A. EL SAWY

**Abstract:** *This chapter provides insights for redesigning IT-enabled customer support processes to meet the demanding requirements of highly dynamic environments in which fast response, shared knowledge creation, and internetworked technologies are the dynamic enablers of success. The chapter describes the implementation of the TechConnect support system at Storage Dimensions, a manufacturer of high-availability computer storage system products. TechConnect is a unique IT infrastructure for problem resolution that includes a customer support knowledge base in which the structure is dynamically updated based on adaptive learning through customer interactions. The chapter assesses the effects of TechConnect and its value in creating a learning organization. It then draws insights for redesigning knowledge-creating customer support processes for the dynamic business conditions of the electronic economy.*

**Keywords:** *Customer Support Process, Customer Service, Business Process Redesign, Business Process Transformation, Information Technologies for Customer Integration, Fast Response Management, Learning Organization, Fast Learning, Learningful Processes, Knowledge Management, Knowledge Creation, Knowledge Synthesis, Knowledge Sharing, Knowledge-Based Organization, Electronic Business, Interorganizational Information Systems, IT Effects, Expert Systems, Help Desk, Help Desk Software, Problem Resolution Technologies*

## INTRODUCTION

Effective customer support and service is a strategic imperative. Whether a company is in manufacturing or in services, it is not only the quality of the product or service that makes a competitive difference but also the customer support and service built into and around the product (e.g., Henkoff, 1994). Customer intimacy is an acknowledged strategic posture (Treacy and Wiersema, 1995), and the traditional distinction between products and services is increasingly irrelevant (Haeckel, 1994). Companies are moving closer to their customers, expending more effort to find new ways to create value for their customers, and transforming the customer relationship from one of selling and order taking into one of solution finding and partnering. Customer support and service is one of today's most critical core business processes.

Improving the customer support and service process involves both innovative process design and innovative use of information technology (IT). How to do this effectively is well illustrated by the case of Storage Dimensions. My interest in this case was initially triggered by a news item in the September 1995 issue of *Stanford Business School Alumni Magazine* about alumnus Gene Bowles, then Executive Vice President of Storage Dimensions, which, at the time, was a vendor of 24-7 high-availability computer storage products. There was a short description about how the Storage Dimensions troubleshooting knowledge base was able to solve customers' problems in a quick and cost-effective way at the lowest support tier possible, and that it had transformed the customer support process. I was studying how to improve knowledge sharing around business processes in fast response environments, and how to design information systems (IS) to enhance that. I was intrigued by the brief description and contacted Gene Bowles and visited Storage Dimensions in Northern California to understand this innovative practice, and we eventually produced a paper that became a finalist in the 1996 SIM Paper Awards Competition. It did not win a prize in the paper competition, but, after a few revision iterations with the relentless encouragement of then Senior Editor Bob Zmud, the paper was published in *MIS Quarterly*. The story of Storage Dimensions is one that, for me, continues to provide ideas and insights about how to design knowledge-creating business processes for rapidly changing environments that require fast response. A decade later, Storage Dimensions is no more, having been acquired by Artecon, which is now part of Dot Hill; however, the customer support process continues to be enhanced through the technologies and methods that were developed at Storage Dimensions.

## THE EVOLUTION OF CUSTOMER SUPPORT FOR COMPLEX PRODUCTS

Customer support traces its origins to the 1850s when the Singer Sewing Company set up a program that used trained women to teach buyers how to use the sewing machine (Lele and Sheth, 1987). Traditionally, customer support has referred to after-sales support, which is all of the activities that help increase customers' satisfaction after they have purchased a product and started to use it. The marketing literature (e.g., Lele and Sheth, 1987) has differentiated between specific *support services* and *feedback and restitution*. Support services refer to activities such as parts and service, warranty claims, customer assistance and training, technician training, and occasionally trading in older equipment. Feedback and restitution refers to activities such as complaint handing, returns and refunds, and dispute resolution. As manufacturers started to compete by bundling services with products (e.g., Chase and Garvin, 1989; Shostack, 1977), the scope of customer service and support for products expanded cross-functionally to include expert help from the manufacturing, engineering, and R&D functions. More recently, as long-term customer relationships and partnering with customers became more important (e.g., Henkoff, 1994), the notion of customer support expanded beyond "after sales" and has colored the way that customer service is provided. Although the terms *service* and *support* are used interchangeably in some contexts, they are not the same. Customer support has a long-term partnering flavor that signifies that the supplier wants to help customers do their job effectively, and in this age of interdependence and alliances, *customer support* seems to be a more apt term for the bundle of activities that comprise it.

Customer support is more critical and difficult for high-technology complex products—especially with the breakneck speed in new product development for those products. Many customer support innovations and strategies in the past decade originated in the computer and telecommunications industry. They include automated help desks, toll-free hotlines, computer bulletin board systems, 24-7 services, remote online troubleshooting, and use of the Internet. As organizations became critically dependent on IT and telecommunication networks for the operations of their business, the criticality of response time in supporting those products and services rose to unprecedented levels. The cost of providing effective customer support also rose more than proportionately, and the high-technology industry sought solutions, which may have provided ideas for companies in other industries.

To improve overall service levels and reduce overall costs, the IT industry adopted a hybrid model for customer support (Entex, 1994). This model includes having personnel on-site at major customer accounts (for which IBM has traditionally been known), using third-party resellers or other vendors that can provide localized customer support for smaller accounts and consumers, and providing high-tech long-distance remote support through a centralized pool of talent whether in-house or through an external service (very common in commodity and low-margin items such as PC hardware and software). Each of these options has a different cost structure and service advantage. Direct on-site support is expensive but provides superior service; going through resellers requires heavy investments in training and qualification to assure good service, whereas remote high-tech support is a challenge for complex products and can be very impersonal if not carefully managed. Different vendors in various market segments have different hybrid blends depending on their support strategy.

These options are further challenged when products interact with other vendors' products, response time is critical, and the stakes in downtime are very high. Figure 8.1 illustrates how the required customer support level rises quickly when there is an increase in the combination of complexity and connectivity of the product and its criticality to customer operations. For high-end products in heterogeneous networked environments where downtime is prohibitively expensive for the customer, the requisite level of customer support rises exponentially. It requires fast response time, highly skilled personnel, and the ability of customer support personnel to learn quickly about product innovations and quirks in their own products and those of related vendors. Quick learning requires a radical rethinking about how learning occurs during the customer support process. The challenge is to find a way to capture and disseminate new learning around the customer support process quickly to all participants in a simple and cost-effective way.

## THE CUSTOMER SUPPORT CHALLENGE AT STORAGE DIMENSIONS

Storage Dimensions was a vendor of high-availability disk and tape storage for client/server environments. It was founded in 1985 in the heart of Silicon Valley in Milpitas, California, and went public in March 1997. Its 1996 sales were $72 million. The company designed, manufactured, marketed, and supported hardware/software products that provide open systems storage solutions for mission-critical enterprise applications. Its high-end storage solutions were targeted to organizations with enterprise-wide client/server networks that needed mission-critical data protected and available 24 hours a day. The company's customer base was mainly Fortune 1000 companies in information-intensive industries that lived and died by their data, such as airlines, banking, finance, insurance, retail, utilities, and government agencies. Storage Dimensions products were sold through distributors and resellers in the United States, Europe, and the Pacific Rim. The company also had a direct sales force to more effectively serve its key vertical market customers.

Storage Dimensions' products fell into three main categories: high-availability Redundant Array of Independent Disks (RAID) storage systems, high capacity tape backup systems, and network storage management software for multiserver networks. RAID is a fault-tolerant disk subsystem architecture that provides protection against data loss and system interruption and improved data transfer/access rates for large databases. This protection ranges from simply mirroring data on

Figure 8.1 **Customer Support Level Versus Product Complexity, Connectivity, and Complexity**

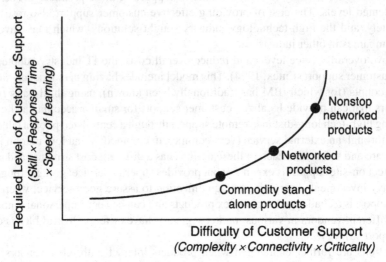

Required Level of Customer Support
*(Skill × Response Time × Speed of Learning)*

Nonstop networked products

Networked products

Commodity stand-alone products

Difficulty of Customer Support
*(Complexity × Connectivity × Criticality)*

*Notes:* A search through the publicly available information systems, operations management, and marketing literature did not uncover any models that captured this dynamic. The graph is meant to illustrate the magnitude of the challenge and what apparent factors appear to affect it rather than to be exhaustive.

duplicate drives to breaking data into pieces and "striping" it across an array of three or more disks; if one drive goes down, the controller instantly reconstructs the lost data and rebuilds it on a spare drive. Other features include a combination of redundant hot-swap hot-spare power supplies, fans, and disk drive components to ensure nonstop operation and continuous access to data.

Following a 1992 buyout from Maxtor, Storage Dimensions refocused to become a higher-end and faster-response industry player. It was clear that exceptional customer support would be essential to success, and a customer support–focused corporate strategy was put in place. The customer support process was reexamined, and it was apparent that it was inadequate for the growing customer base and expanding product line. Furthermore, with increased globalization, the customers were dispersed geographically and in different time zones. The customer support process was too slow (as much as two to three hours to return a phone call in some circumstances), too haphazard (no organized online knowledge base for repeat problem solutions), too expensive (repeat problems frequently escalated to development engineers, long training periods), and stressful to both support personnel (overloaded) and managers (little visibility for the what, who, why, when). Top management saw the need for a radical solution.

Given the mission-critical nature of its customers' network environments, the company expended much effort in providing exceptional customer support. The company differentiated itself in the market by helping customers minimize their total life cycle cost of ownership for network storage in the context of mission-critical applications. A storage systems' total life cycle cost of ownership is much more than the purchase price. Service, support, and downtime for RAID storage systems accounted for 80 percent of the total cost over the life of the system according to a Gartner Group study—and downtime is especially critical to customers. A Computer Reseller News/Gallup Organization 1994 study found that hourly losses due to network downtime in Fortune 1000 companies were $3,000 to $5,000 per hour (median), could often be $10,000, and were sometimes $100,000 or more (6 percent of companies). Storage Dimensions products and solutions were designed to drive down the overall cost of ownership by minimizing downtime, lowering service and support costs, reducing up-front investment costs, and providing a technology migration path. Storage Dimensions instituted several customer support programs and innovations that further enhanced its lower total life cycle cost of ownership customer support strategy:

- *FlexCredit*™: this enabled a customer to trade in their old storage (including those from other vendors) for 50 percent megabyte-for-megabyte credit toward the latest Storage Dimensions RAID storage system with updated warranty coverage. This helped customers upgrade and standardize on new technology storage solutions while recovering substantial value from their existing storage investments.
- *SpeedExchange*: an exchange warranty program that provided a replacement system or components to customers within 24 hours. Warranties went up to five years on disk drive modules. This fast response warranty program minimized the time a company's mission-critical applications went without fault tolerance.
- *TechConnect*: an online technical support system based on an extensive knowledge base with 24-7 access through the Internet and e-mail (described more fully below).

## THE DEVELOPMENT OF THE TECHCONNECT SUPPORT SYSTEM

As the customer support process was reexamined in mid-1992, it became apparent to the management team that an IT-enabled solution with an artificial intelligence component had to be part of the remedy. They put their commitment behind it and a project was initiated. The core management team for the project consisted of the executive vice president for marketing and customer service (who was also the project sponsor), the director of customer service and support, and the director of IS (Figure 8.2 shows organization chart). In addition, a cross-functional task force was formed consisting of three people: one from the customer support group, one from the IS group, and one from engineering. Together, and with input from both customers and others in the company, the management team and the task force came up with a list of the top operational objectives (see Table 8.1) and key technical/usability requirements (see Table 8.2) for what they generically referred to as the customer support management system. They then searched the market for software packages that could help meet those requirements.

The search included various types of artificial intelligence shells, database managers, call management packages, and help desk software—most of which were not the least bit suitable and were quickly eliminated. Only four packages in the help desk software category came close, and these were then evaluated in detail. The help desk software packages were not an off-the-shelf fit to the application context. First, the packages and vendors were mostly geared in their approaches to internal help desks rather than external customer support with different customer types. Second, the knowledge capture/update and key word search capabilities (if any) were too primitive for complex products that changed quickly and had interactions with other vendors' products. Third, Storage Dimensions had a fairly sophisticated client/server network, and it wanted to link the customer support system to its e-mail and to its internal IS and databases in other functional areas. As the help desk software vendors acknowledged at the time, making this linkage would be a stretch.

The four help desk software packages were compared as to how their software features fit the company's operational requirements. The Apriori GT help desk software from Answer Systems (since 1995 a part of Platinum Technology Inc.) was mainly selected based on its unique "Bubble-Up" technique (described below), which could prioritize likely problem solutions, its good incident

## Figure 8.2 **Organizational Chart for Storage Dimensions**

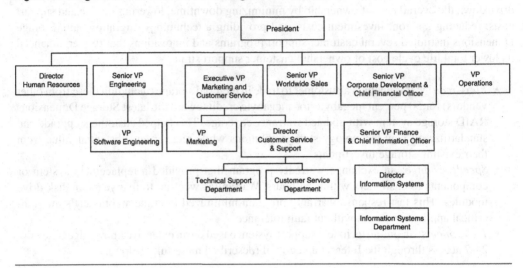

---

Table 8.1

**Top 10 Operational Objectives of Customer Support Management System in Mid-1992**

1. Provide consistent, accurate responses to customer inquiries
2. Document and track all known problems and proven solutions
3. Create centralized sources of information about customers, known problems, solutions
4. Assist in developing solutions to new problems
5. Create a closed-loop escalation process
6. Promote cross-training of support staff
7. Provide remote access for customers of problem solutions
8. Improve call tracking and problem reporting
9. Improve accountability and responsibility with clear audit trails
10. Improve productivity of customer support staff

---

management capabilities, its good reporting capabilities, and its technical compatibility with Storage Dimensions' client/server network infrastructure and the Windows graphical user interface. Other Apriori GT capabilities at the time included call tracking, incident escalation, various search and retrieval features, custom notification and routing, e-mail and fax integration, accountability features, and tailorability for application integration.

While no programming changes were made to the source code, there was much work to be done in structuring Apriori GT to fit the complexity of the Storage Dimensions technical environment and linking it (through Perl scripts and macros) to the internal IS infrastructure and e-mail. For the next 90 days, the task force worked together with the software vendor to install, customize, script, and test the customer support application. Simultaneously, the customer support process and the way it was managed were reengineered to take advantage of this new technology. Much input was sought and enthusiastically received at that stage from various parts of the company, and a pilot test was run with selected customers. Fortunately, implementation was successful both technically and organizationally. TechConnect was online in late 1992.

The TechConnect system was set up on a Sun Sparc 670 MP server and cost $160,000 for hardware and software. It cost $15,000 per year to maintain. The cost justification for TechConnect

Table 8.2

**Technical/Usability Requirements of Customer Support Management System in Mid-1992**

IT Infrastructural/Compatibility Requirements
1. Multi-user, runs off current Ethernet network lines
2. Works under Microsoft Windows with a GUI interface
3. Dial-in capability for remote user access
4. Provides initial access for 25 users, expandable to 50 within one year
5. Must interface with cc:Mail for notification purposes
6. Must have data import/export capability

Usability Requirements
1. Call tracking capability
2. Problem/solution tracking capability
3. Key word search for problems/solutions
4. Must have a method for assisting technical support staff with answering calls (artificial intelligence or other)
5. Must have a report generator with user-definable reports without generating programming code or a script
6. Ability to create and define call queues
7. Have at least five user-definable fields
8. Have automated call escalation process
9. Must have a closed-loop problem-solving process
10. Provides call audit trail
11. Tracks and reports customer configuration data

was not difficult. In the first year alone, the reduced callbacks (due to higher problem resolution rate on first customer call) saved about $70,000 in long-distance phone bills. In addition, the productivity gains obviated the need to hire more technical support engineers to handle the growing customer support load, saving another estimated $150,000.

## THE NEW IT-ENABLED CUSTOMER SUPPORT PROCESS

TechConnect enabled the redesign of the customer support process such that it could be more effective and better managed. Some key aspects of how this new online customer support process was managed were:

- *Improved escalation paths for problem management.* A simplified diagram of the three-level escalation sequence is shown in Figure 8.3. After dispatch, the customer call went to a Level 1 technical support engineer. He or she tried to resolve the problem through an online TechConnect solution document. If it included a request for material authorization, then an appropriate customer service representative was notified through TechConnect. If the problem was not resolved at Level 1, it was automatically escalated and queued (path depends on the operating system used by customer's client/server network hardware) to a Level 2 applications engineer who was more skilled and who investigated it thoroughly. If the applications engineer was unable to resolve the problem, then it was automatically escalated to the problem tracking request (PTR) manager who verified the problem and decided whether to escalate it to a development engineer.
- *Closed loop problem resolution.* As the incident moved along the escalation path, both the caller and the customer support staff along the escalation path (and manager) knew who had

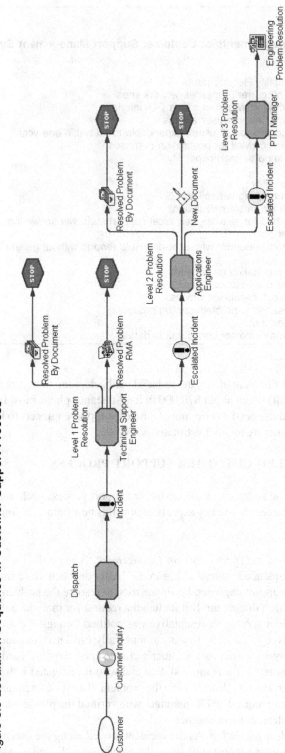

**Figure 8.3 Escalation Sequence in Customer Support Process**

*Source:* Adapted from Answer Systems.

the incident and what its status was. This process also ensured that the customer was informed in a timely manner. TechConnect kept track of all of the information related to the incident and stored it in the TechConnect database.

- *Analysis and reporting capabilities.* TechConnect provided a multitude of management and activity reports that helped manage the customer support process and identify bottlenecks. It also became possible to automatically flag unusual events and for customer support staff to spend more time on proactive rather than reactive customer support.
- *Automatic cross-triggering capabilities.* TechConnect was integrated into the Storage Dimensions network of IS to automatically flag other business areas or IS via e-mail based on problem incidents. This facilitated cross-functional coordination between customer support and other departments.
- *Amplified shared knowledge creation.* The intensity of shared knowledge creation through customer interactions around the customer support process was greatly amplified through TechConnect. The continuous production of online solution documents steadily created a valuable knowledge base that was accessible to all: *everyone could be an expert and everyone could contribute to the learning.* That transformed the way that the customer support process was carried out and managed, as it did its knowledge-creating capacity. That critical aspect is discussed in more detail in the next section.

With the use of the TechConnect system and a transformed customer support process, the customer support department remained at the same size despite increasing sales volume. The group consisted of eight technical support engineers, three applications engineers, and one manager. They worked a basic 11-hour shift among them and also had a 24-hour on-call system.

## TECHCONNECT AS AN ADAPTIVE LEARNING IT INFRASTRUCTURE

The TechConnect system was based on a knowledge base architecture that adaptively learned through its interactions with users. It was based on a unique software-based problem resolution architecture (PRA; see box below) that linked problems, symptoms, and solutions in a document database. All problems or issues were analyzed through incident reports, and resolutions were fed back into the online knowledge base in the form of solution documents. The way that the TechConnect knowledge base learned was through the well-structured dynamic feedback loops managed by the PRA. As problems were analyzed and resolved by technical support specialists, development engineers, and customers, the results were integrated into the knowledge base as solution documents and new knowledge was created and synthesized (see Figure 8.4). As a result, solutions were consistent and readily available to support specialists and customers alike. Solutions were "fresh" (up-to-date), accurate, and based on the latest experience of customers (200 new data points per week). In 1997, support specialists and customers had access to information from over 35,000 relevant incidents. In total, 1,700 solution documents were currently available electronically. Because 80 percent of incoming calls were repeat problems, existing solution documents often provided resolutions within minutes.

---

**Problem Resolution Architecture**

PRA was a software architecture that automated the problem resolution process in help desk environments. It linked problems, symptoms, and solutions in a knowledge base. PRA

Figure 8.4 **TechConnect's Dynamic Feedback Loop for Knowledge Creation**

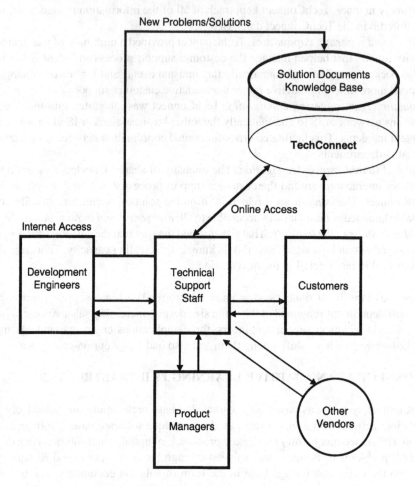

enabled both the automated creation of knowledge bases and the automated maintenance of those knowledge bases. It was able to link one master solution or solution-in-progress with variants of multiple symptoms. This unique many-to-one relationship allowed the help desk to update the solution in a single place in the knowledge base and communicated meaningful updates to users automatically. This streamlined the distribution of information and assured that questions were answered with the most up-to-date information in the knowledge base. Answer Systems received a patent for PRA in October 1995. At that time, PRA and Bubble-Up were the help desk industry's only two patented problem resolution technologies.

Another key feature of the TechConnect system was the "Bubble-Up" solution management technology (see below) that enabled the TechConnect knowledge base to adaptively learn through its interaction with users. It automatically prioritized solution documents based on "usefulness/ frequency of use" in resolving specific problems; the higher-priority solutions rose to the top of the list. This helped less-experienced inquirers to see the most useful solutions and sped up problem resolution. The Bubble-Up process also adaptively changed the structure of the knowledge base continuously with new knowledge.

---

**Bubble-Up™**

Bubble-Up was a patented problem resolution technology embedded in the Apriori product. It enabled an indexing scheme and intelligent filter that caused the most-used solution documents to rise to the surface of the volume of solution documents stored in a problem resolution knowledge base. The index structure of the knowledge base had multiple roots and was not strictly hierarchical. Moreover, it used a proprietary algorithm to automatically modify the structure of the knowledge tree based on "most-used" knowledge elements in the tree. "Most used" was based on a statistical weighting of both the actual usefulness and popularity of a solution document in solving a problem rather than just access (i.e., incorporates a voting heuristic). It did this at any level of the index structure, thus enabling selective filtering. A flowchart illustrating how the Bubble-Up procedure works internally is shown in Figure 8.5.

As new solution documents were created and/or their usefulness in solving problems changed (through user voting when accessed), the knowledge base was able to adaptively learn and automatically changed its structure without any programming, and in a way that was transparent to the user. It was thus able to self-modify through use and learn as new problems, solutions-in-process, or solutions were added.

Bubble-Up was patented by Answer Systems in 1994. It won the 1995 Harold Short Jr. Innovations in Service Award that recognizes tools and services that have a far-reaching effect on service delivery.

---

In combination, the PRA and the Bubble-Up software made it possible for the knowledge base to change its structure dynamically "on the fly" as it gained new knowledge from those who interacted with it. TechConnect learned quickly from customer support specialists, development engineers, and customers. Furthermore, the knowledge was always fresh and usefully organized for rapid problem resolution for less-experienced users.

The TechConnect support system allowed self-help by customers. It could be directly accessed by customers 24 hours a day through e-mail or through the Internet via the Storage Dimensions Web site. To access the knowledge base via the Internet self-help route or e-mail, customers completed a TechConnect search request form that included symptom identifiers. Within two minutes, TechConnect automatically returned a related list of solution documents from which to choose. Thus, through an e-mail or Web page request, TechConnect was able to search for solutions in the knowledge base, select and rank order them based on usefulness, and post them back to the Web page. Although technically possible, the structure of the knowledge base was not updated on the fly through the self-help route in order to protect the integrity of the database from spurious information. New knowledge from self-help incidents was first checked by technical support specialists before being submitted as updates.

The TechConnect knowledge base provided detailed information on installation, compatibility, troubleshooting, and support for Storage Dimensions' systems, as well as related products from other vendors (servers or operating systems or backup software). The customer support Web page

Figure 8.5 **Flowchart of Bubble-Up Procedure**

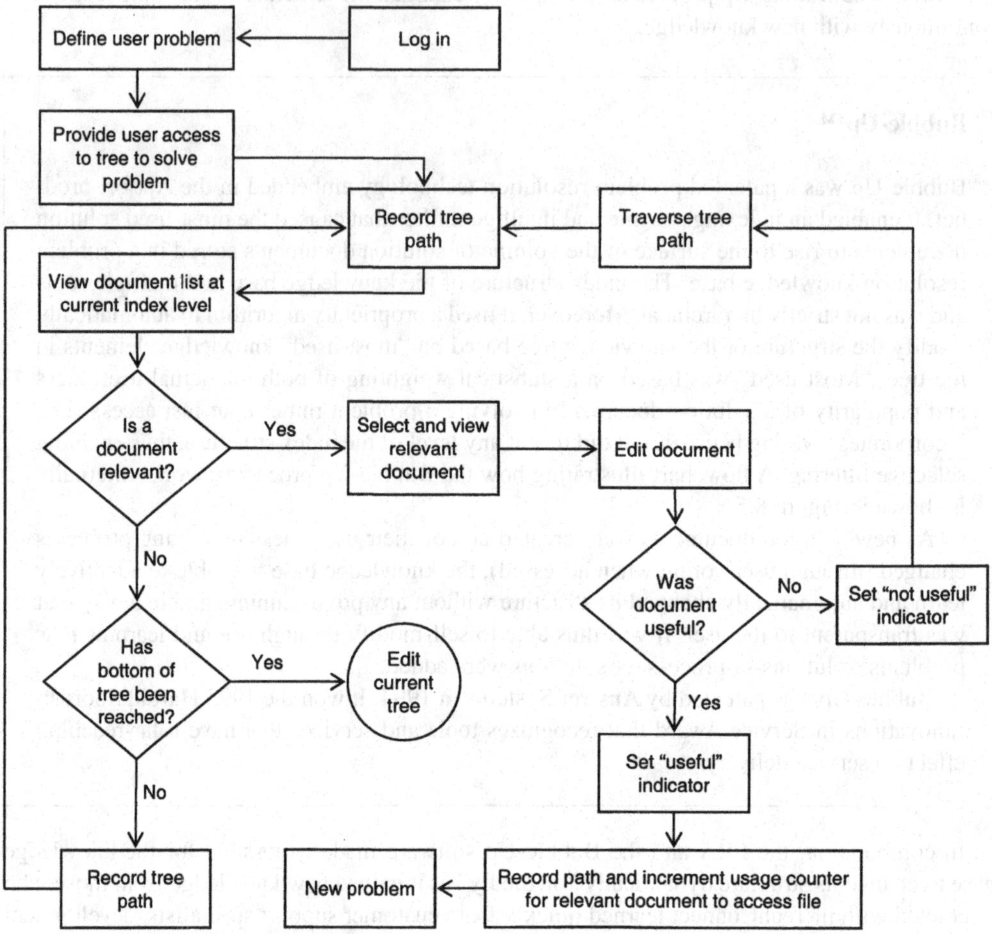

also had hot links to those vendors. Of course, for such a system to work effectively, it had be integrated into a well-structured and managed organizational customer support process. That was a crucial consideration in the redesign of the customer support process at Storage Dimensions. The tightness of integration between the use of TechConnect and management of the customer support process is perhaps best shown through the example below.

**How TechConnect Drove the Knowledge-Creating Customer Support Process**

When a customer called on the phone for support, a Storage Dimensions frontline technical support engineer sitting at a TechConnect screen asked questions about system configuration (enclosure type, operating system, type of drive, etc.) and an incident report was created. Based on the customer's reported problem, the technical support engineer used symptom words to search for an existing problem/solution document. Each solution document had symptom words associated with it that were assigned when the solution document was created or modified, and they were added

Figure 8.6 **TechConnect Screen for Symptom Search**

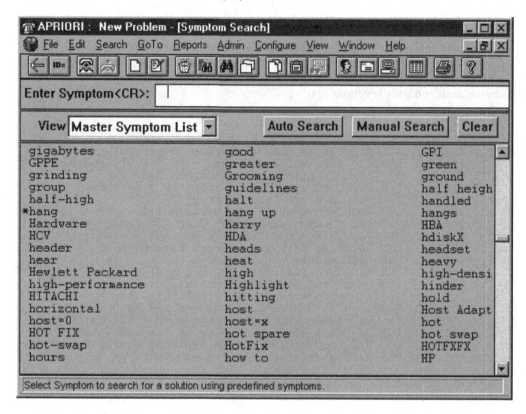

to the master symptom list. On the TechConnect screen captured in Figure 8.6, the word "hang" is selected (note asterisk in the figure) from the master symptom list as one of the symptom words. An "Auto Search" would look for any solution documents linked to the symptom words. A "Manual Search" did the same, but would also prompt the user to iteratively reduce the number of symptom words if no documents were found in the initial search with all of the symptom words.

If the simple indexed search did not locate any solution documents, then a natural language text retrieval search for the symptom words was attempted for all documents in the knowledge base—even documents not contained within the Apriori database (through the icon circled in Figure 8.7). This type of search took more machine time than an indexed symptom word search. Based on the symptom words selected, a listing of problem/solution documents was listed (see Figure 8.7) and then the technical support engineer could view them to see if any apply.

If a solution document could not be found based on symptom words, the technical support engineer would then try to search the index structure of documents using TechConnect's "Bubble-Up" feature. By clicking on the Bubble-Up icon (left circle in Figure 8.8), the technical support engineer saw a hierarchical index structure as shown in the top half of the screen in Figure 8.8. The bottom half of the screen shows the top 12 solution documents for all of the available indexes based (and rank-ordered) on the effectiveness of each solution document. By clicking on any of the index buttons (BBS, Software, Hardware, etc.), the user drilled down deeper into the index. For example, clicking on the "Hardware" button revealed the next index level (Computers, Drives, Tape

**Figure 8.7 TechConnect Screen with List of Possible Problem/Solution Documents**

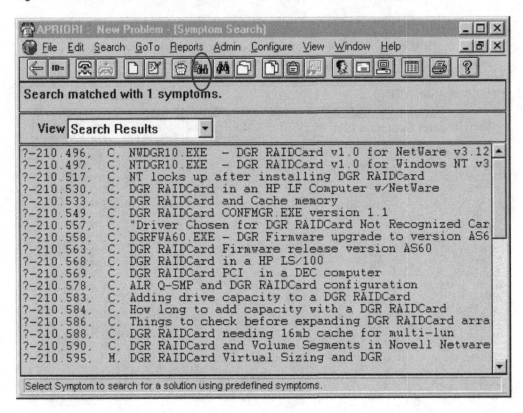

Drives, etc.), and the top 12 documents for those index buttons were listed. He or she could then start examining each solution document from the top of the list and clicking on the most relevant document. (This was a support system that supported, not replaced, the user's thinking.)

As documents were read, the technical support engineer was prompted to vote on the usefulness of the document. He or she was requested to select among "not useful," "useful," and "solved incident." If either "useful" or "solved incident" was selected, the document was moved up higher in the Bubble-Up list. If "solved incident" was selected, then the customer's TechConnect account number became associated with the solution document so that any updates or modifications to the document would generate an automated notification to the customer.

If none of the documents provided a solution to the customer's issue, the technical support engineer would complete a "new problem" report (by clicking on "new problem" icon circled on the right in Figure 8.8). The new problem report was generated whether the problem was resolved or not. If the problem was resolved, then the report also described the solution. If there was no resolution, then recommendations for a solution would be given (update manual, debug software, change hardware, etc.). If a specific index was not specified, then the new problem report would be assigned to the last index visited during the Bubble-Up search. The owner of that index (the applications engineer) would then be notified that a new problem had been submitted.

The applications engineer would then review the new problem and check that no problem/solution document or pending problem existed, that all information was present to replicate the issue

Figure 8.8 **TechConnect "Bubble-Up" Solution Document Listing**

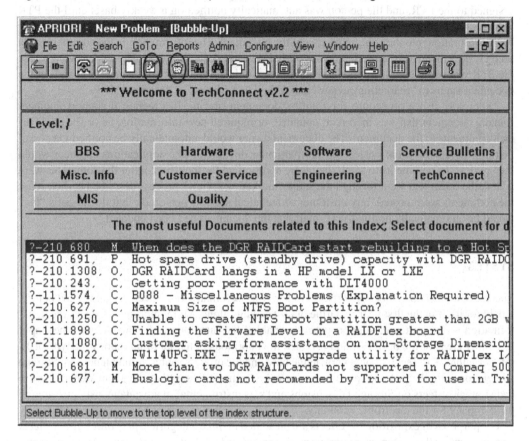

if needed, and that all basic troubleshooting steps had been performed. If a solution was provided, the applications engineer would then verify the validity of the new problem report and edit it for clarity and effectiveness. It was at this time that symptom words were assigned to the document. The document would then be marked with a status of "marketing review" and the appropriate marketing product manager's e-mail address would be assigned to the document, and he or she would be automatically notified that a new document had been created and was awaiting his or her review. Any comments or corrections were then forwarded back to the applications engineer to incorporate into the document. At that time, the document was set to the status of "closed."

If no solution was included with the problem report, the applications engineer would then try to resolve the issue by interfacing with engineering or other departments as needed and/or by replicating the problem by duplicating the installation as close as possible. If the problem was resolved by the applications engineer, then the document would be set to a status of "marketing review" and followed the process explained above. If the applications engineer was unable to resolve the issue or was able to verify a hardware or software issue that required engineering or another department's effort or resources to resolve, then the document was set to a status of "PTR (Open)." PTR (Problem Tracking Report) meant that an issue was not resolved by the technical support department and required resources from another department in the company. After an appropriate person was identified to follow through with resolving the PTR, his or her e-mail address was assigned to the PTR, and the person was automatically notified on a weekly basis until the PTR was resolved. The person could submit comments back to the submitting applications engineer for incorporation into the comments area of the document. The information in the comments area on PTR documents was compiled on a weekly basis and posted for company-wide review. Once the PTR was resolved, the applications engineer would complete the documentation and set the document status to "marketing review" and follow that process as described above.

There was also a procedure for solution document update. If a technical support engineer found a document that was incorrect, outdated, or required new information, he or she could attach comments to the document. The document owner would automatically be notified via e-mail that new comments were posted for that particular document. The applications engineer would then review the comments to see if they were appropriate for inclusion. After the comments were added, the document went through the same "marketing review" process described earlier. After the comments were posted, any customer or technical support person on that document's "list" would be automatically notified via e-mail that the document had been updated.

## ASSESSING THE EFFECTS AND VALUE OF THE TECHCONNECT SYSTEM

The TechConnect customer support system paid for itself many times over. As mentioned before, it paid for itself in the first year by virtue of cost savings alone. More important, it drove the transformation of the customer support process, enabled the integration of valuable customer input into other areas of the business, and revealed the enormous potential of an innovative type of IT infrastructure. The TechConnect knowledge base and the process routes around it became Storage Dimensions' intellectual capital. It is not an overstatement to say that the TechConnect system had strategic effects on Storage Dimensions and was instrumental in advantageously positioning the company for the electronic economy.

For purposes of exposition the effects are presented in three categories: *first-order direct effects* on transforming the customer support process, *second-order effects* related to integrating customer input into other business areas, and *third-order indirect effects* related to building an IT infrastructure for the electronic economy. *First-order effects* are the primary direct effects around transforming the business process and its effectiveness and can be both planned and unplanned. Planned direct effects manifest themselves around whatever performance measures were deliberately set out to be changed (such as response time, less errors, the ability to have the process performed by less-skilled people, lower costs, or increasing "learningfulness" in the process). First-order or direct effects also carry inadvertent or unintended consequences that may be positive or negative (such as extent of IT-enabled group collaboration around the process, different modes of information sharing, or greater transparency through ubiquitous access, etc.). *Second-order connectedness effects* are those that go beyond the confines of improving the targeted primary business process. This is often an impact on another business process that interacts with the primary business process and is perhaps mostly owned by different functional areas within the enterprise (such as customer support processes having an impact on product design process) or that resides within another enterprise in the supply chain (such as self-stocking process transformation in a retail store changing a package design process at a supplier). Finally, *third-order effects* are those that help build a better enterprise-wide IT infrastructure for business process transformation in the long run. These effects are often in the form of organizational learning and the development of distinctive capabilities for IT-enabled business process transformation. As a greater portion of the business processes in an enterprise and the supply chains it participates in are transformed to take advantage of IT capabilities and competencies, the higher the impact multiplier will more likely be in subsequent business process transformations due to connectedness and acquired expertise. Often these will result in the development of dynamic capabilities for business process transformation that may eventually have longer-term strategic effects for the enterprise as the environment changes. Granted that the third-order effects are the most elusive to measure, but they should not detract from their often bigger impacts over the long run.

## First-Order Direct Effects of TechConnect: Transforming the Customer Support Process

A number of first-order direct effects on transforming the customer support process were identified:

- *Faster customer response.* Average time to respond to a customer problem report dropped to 15 minutes—after being as high as two to three hours in some cases prior to TechConnect. Problem resolution time dropped from an estimated four-hour average to a measured 50-minute average: 60 percent of all problems are resolved within 30 minutes, and 70 percent within an hour. Also, about 20 percent of incidents were handled by the self-help route through 24-7 Internet/e-mail with instant response to queries; 80 percent of these self-help incidents were resolved on the first try through online solution documents.
- *Accurate, consistent, and accountable problem resolution.* Due to the real-time currency of the TechConnect knowledge base and rank ordering of solution documents, repetitive problems were solved correctly and at the first level every time—no matter what the skill level of the technical support engineer. If escalation occurred on a difficult new problem, then both the customer and Storage Dimensions knew the progress of the resolution at all times. It became impossible to be unaccountable.
- *Cost-effective problem resolution.* Due to orderly TechConnect escalation processes, valuable development engineer time was conserved. Sixty-seven percent of technical failure incidents were resolved at Level 1—also conserving the time of application engineers. The remaining 33 percent were handled by Level 2 applications engineers who thoroughly researched the problem and solved it about 80 percent of the time. The remaining 20 percent (7 percent of the total) were escalated through the customer support manager to a development engineer. Although a 33 percent escalation ratio may appear high in comparison to traditional internal help desks, it is actually low given the complexity of products and given that related server technology changed every 90 days (paced by Intel's synchronized 90-day release schedule for microprocessors).
- *Leadership in cross-vendor troubleshooting.* Most of the difficult technical problems in client/server environments were related to compatibility issues and integration across storage and server products made by different vendors. Storage Dimensions' capability for cross-vendor troubleshooting was greatly amplified through TechConnect and has eliminated many hours of finger-pointing. There was no quantitative data, but there were many anecdotes about how Storage Dimensions was able to provide a solution document to another vendor's compatibility problem and verify it before the other vendor's technical support person even arrived at the customer site. Such incidents helped establish a reputation for the company as a customer support leader.

- *Vigilant and proactive management of customer support process.* TechConnect collected much data related to problem reports, activity levels, and customers. It easily provided ad hoc management reports for spotting process problems. It flagged problems that required quick management attention and alerted of longer-term capacity and service-level issues. The customer support process had a greater proactive component based on such flagging. A telling (but unscientific) measure of this effect was the director of customer support's likening the discovery of TechConnect's management capabilities to uncovering the Holy Grail—even giving the system the nickname "Galahad."
- *More learningful customer support staff.* The word "learningful" is concocted, but it aptly captures the spirit of TechConnect. TechConnect enabled staff to be more learningful in that they built on each other's knowledge and on that of more experienced senior colleagues and smart customers. Every customer support staff person had access to expert problem solutions through TechConnect—no matter what his or her current expertise level was. Similarly, every customer support person contributed to the knowledge base. The systematic structure through which TechConnect directed the problem resolution process also sharpened problem-solving skills and diagnostic logic. This upped the general skill level of the group and helped new hires ramp up their skills more quickly.
- *More learningful customer support process.* TechConnect had analysis capabilities that enabled staff to uncover patterns and take proactive action for further prevention. This information was also fed back to other areas of the company depending on where action needed to be taken. Actions ranged from changing a confusing paragraph on a page in an installation manual to major redesign of a product component. Over three years, the number of incidents dropped from 7,283 incidents per quarter in early 1993 to 1,715 incidents per quarter in early 1996 (see Figure 8.9). Even as a percentage of installed base, incidents dropped from 1.45 percent to 0.49 percent.

In combination, these direct effects and a qualitatively transformed customer support process translated to more satisfied customers. They also translated to more satisfied customer support staff. The staff (especially the junior staff) appreciated the positive feedback from being able to resolve problems quickly and the clear systematic guidance for the process that TechConnect provided. The turnover rate dropped by about 50 percent in the past four years.

## Second-Order Effects of TechConnect: Integrating Customer Input into Other Business Areas

Changes in the customer support process also had effects beyond its own confines in that customer input was integrated into other business areas of the company. This was facilitated by TechConnect's "trigger" feature, which automatically triggered e-mail to other departments in the company depending on how questions were answered in a problem report. Examples of such second-order effects include:

- *Product improvements.* The number of incidents decreased (see Figure 8.9) partly due to product improvements triggered through TechConnect. This also provided valuable information to better track new products as they were introduced and, on more than one occasion, helped to catch repetitive problems quickly. Proactive tracking of evaluation units at customer sites was now routinely done, and the conversion rate (the conversion of a unit from evaluation

Figure 8.9 **Change in Number of Incidents on a Quarterly Basis**

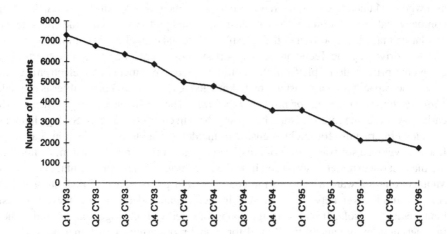

to a sale) increased by 30 percent following the use of TechConnect for that activity. This fostered an appreciation of TechConnect by engineering.
- *Sales lead triggers and marketing support.* As TechConnect kept a record of the nature of customer inquiries, the "trigger" feature automatically passed on any sales leads and provided new knowledge for marketing strategy.
- *Global expansion strategy support.* TechConnect allowed customer support to be easily administered online from one centralized location in Milpitas, California. As Storage Dimensions continued its global expansion, customer support could be provided in any remote location around the world without substantially increasing costs or sacrificing the level of support.
- *Discovering the potential of customer support as revenue-generating business process.* The company did not convert its customer support savvy into a direct source of revenue, although its expertise with solving other vendors' compatibility problems became a source of knowhow that could generate revenue. The challenge was to take advantage of the opportunity without jeopardizing the collaborative cross-vendor problem solving that Storage Dimensions sought to nurture.

These second-order effects were not immediately felt enterprise-wide, but as awareness grew of the cross-functional synergy that the customer process transformation had triggered, the benefits eventually became obvious to all.

### Third-Order Indirect Effects of TechConnect: Building an IT Infrastructure for the Dynamic Electronic Economy

TechConnect also had broader indirect effects on the organizational vision of the company as a whole and its positioning for the dynamic environment of the electronic economy. Although perhaps more difficult to measure, these effects might have been the most profound for Storage Dimensions in the long run:

- *Finding an IT infrastructure that learns quickly.* Somewhat serendipitously, Storage Dimensions discovered an adaptive learning IT infrastructure that could be applied to the company as a whole. Management discovered a concrete practical way to build a knowledge-creating company that learned quickly from its customers and partners. It is a somewhat unexpected revelation that a large portion of the "fresh" intellectual capital of the company grew around and was driven by the TechConnect support system. TechConnect became the foundation of an enterprise-wide IT platform that could be used to compete in the electronic economy where the capacity to learn faster, create knowledge quicker, and be nimbler is critical.
- *Shaping the vision for use of Internet platforms.* The TechConnect experience illustrated early how useful the Internet could be for self-help in customer support. Storage Dimensions expanded Internet use for tracking customer incidents in addition to telephone call tracking. It also developed software that monitored remote network storage at customer sites through the Internet (an extranet of sorts) and linked with Storage Dimensions' VantagePoint product. VantagePoint software monitored the condition and performance of disk storage systems across a multiserver network, collected the performance data, and reported it to a single management console. It had alerting capabilities tied to both pagers and e-mail. The new Internet monitoring capability allowed for global monitoring of customer network storage by Storage Dimensions. The performance characteristics transmitted through the Internet were matched through the software to a database with site configurations (host bus, type of network adapters, type of server, etc.). With the help of VantagePoint, it came up with an error code that provided diagnosis and early warning to the customer support personnel through e-mail—allowing them to take preemptive action. The augmented database, with its automatic and continuous performance data capture, allowed Storage Dimensions to have robust failure predictions based on learning from its own database and to take necessary corrective or preventive action earlier. This capability was fully available for customers in late 1997.
- *Developing customer-facing intranet applications.* The success of the Internet interface as a standard ubiquitous accessible way to communicate with customers prompted Storage Dimensions to develop intranet applications for other functions that interact frequently with customers. The company implemented an intranet system with a standard browser coupled with a customized search engine for salespeople. Through this new application, the approximately 25 Storage Dimensions salespeople gained access while on the road to the latest versions of sales-related documents (such as competitive information, benchmarking data, newsletters).

## INSIGHTS FOR REDESIGN OF KNOWLEDGE-CREATING CUSTOMER SUPPORT PROCESSES

Storage Dimensions was a small company with a total of 240 employees and limited resources. Many Fortune 1000 companies have more people than that solely in their IS departments. The company was also in the frenetically paced IT industry. Furthermore, because of the nature of Storage Dimensions customers' mission-critical applications and product complexity, the customer support requirements were extremely demanding. However, the lessons learned and the insights gained from the Storage Dimensions experience are applicable in any industry to companies of any size that want to have effective customer support and service process in the electronic economy. It is just that the trying conditions in which Storage Dimensions operated drove it to actively search for (and fortunately find) an innovative IT-enabled response to the customer support challenge earlier than other companies.

The insights gained and articulated below are based on four sets of inputs. First, and most influential, is the Storage Dimensions TechConnect experience. Second is the collective experience about customer support and service in technology-based companies. Third is the state-of-the-art knowledge about IT-enabled business process reengineering (e.g., Bennis and Mische, 1996; Davenport, 1993; El Sawy, 2001; Grover and Kettinger, 2000). Fourth is the reports of practitioners and researchers of fast learning and knowledge management through problem resolution systems (e.g., Kirkbride and Deppe, 1995; Nonaka and Takeuchi, 1995). These four sets of inputs are synthesized to produce a generic set of insights for redesigning IT-enabled knowledge-creating customer support processes and the issues around them. Presented below are the top seven insights that "bubbled-up."

> Insight 1: IT's biggest leverage in knowledge-creating customer support processes is in enabling ubiquitous problem resolution—not in providing complex problem routing.

It is better to use IT to make new knowledge accessible to everyone at the front line than to route different problems to different specialists. The biggest payoff from using IT in knowledge-creating customer support processes does not come from call tracking technologies for increasing the speed or automating the complexity by which customer inquiries are routed, queued, or escalated. The biggest payoff comes from IT-based problem resolution systems that enable frontline employees to answer any known question consistently and accurately. The TechConnect system at Storage Dimensions with its solution "Bubble-Up" feature enabled people without advanced expertise (whether a customer support person or a customer) to resolve any problem for which there was already an online solution—and using this philosophy had high payoffs.

The nature of knowledge work is different from operational work and requires different reengineering strategies (e.g., Davenport et al., 1996). A business process can be viewed as a nexus around which knowledge sharing and creation can thrive (El Sawy and Josefek, 2002), and knowledge management can be used as a strategy for business process redesign. Thus reengineering knowledge work requires ways of capturing relevant knowledge from everyone who interacts with the business process. Changing knowledge management around a business process means taking advantage of collective expertise to create, capture, deploy, share, preserve, and reuse knowledge. These strategies include augmenting the interactive analysis and synthesis capabilities around a business process to generate added value. There are three sets of principles and tactics for redesigning and transforming the architecture of business processes. They are principles and tactics based on changing (1) the configuration and structure of business processes, (2) the information flows around processes, and (3) knowledge management around processes by harnessing the collective intellectual assets around it (El Sawy, 2001). These strategies include growing intelligently reusable knowledge around the process through all who touch it; examples of associated tactics include creating communities of practice around the business process, creating expertise maps and "yellow pages" related to the process, and embedding knowledge sharing spaces for interactive dialogues around the process. Knowledge management strategies for business process transformation have also bred personalization approaches in which a business process is made intimate with preferences and habits of participants (whether executors of the process or its customers) such that the process is executed in a personalized way depending on the participant and such that the extent of personalization is iteratively honed over time. It is aided by questioning that helps elicit tacit knowledge and converts it into explicit shareable knowledge that is synthesized so that it is usable by all (Nonaka and Takeuchi, 1995). It also requires different coordination strategies (Rathnam et al., 1995). In high knowledge creation customer support environments, it is not as useful to focus on escalating the problem up to the expert or the right person—the high payoff challenge is to make sure that *everybody* is the right person.

Insight 2: Problem resolution technologies with adaptive learning capabilities are much more suitable than traditional expert systems as IT infrastructures for speeding up learning and creating new knowledge around customer support processes in rapidly changing environments.

The TechConnect experience showed how an IT infrastructure based on adaptive learning problem resolution technology can help create new knowledge "on-the-fly" through customer dialogues and without lag time between the discovery of a solution and its availability to all in an intelligently accessible form. Storage Dimensions considered an alternative IT infrastructure based on expert systems but decided against it. Traditional expert systems, whether rule-based expert systems, case-based reasoning systems, or decision trees, do not work well in situations where conditions change rapidly and a large number of cases or rules must be maintained. They require much up-front development work to develop cases or rules, need skilled knowledge engineers to make changes, and are not suited to contexts that have fluid structures with solutions-in-progress.

As an example, Storage Dimensions has an almost endless number of product permutations because of the way storage systems must work with a variety of other products (something like 10 models × 5–10 storage capacities × 5 operating systems × 3–4 revision levels × ~100 configurations [memory, network interface card, peripherals]). The number of rules would be extraordinarily high. Furthermore, server technology changes every 90 days, paced by Intel's microprocessor release schedule. Designing expert systems for creating knowledge in such a context would mean that by the time we finished redesigning it, its knowledge structure would have to be redesigned again. Kirkbride and Deppe (1995) provide an excellent comparison of the robustness of adaptive learning systems as compared to traditional expert systems. Key features of comparison are captured in Table 8.3.

Insight 3: The World Wide Web's strength as a contact route to a knowledge-creating customer support process is that it can provide powerful remote computational functionality for casual users (customers) through a standardized familiar interface that enables a more active role for customers in solution construction.

The power of the World Wide Web for customer support is not in that it provides worldwide e-mail, fancy multimedia, or brochure-ware capabilities; rather, it provides a standard customer interface through Web browsers that is ideal for capturing input from the *casual user* while enabling a more active role as a customer. A user can submit a request for a complex computational task remotely and receive a response and participate more actively in solution construction. For example, the TechConnect Web access route allowed customers to submit problem symptoms to TechConnect, which then searched its knowledge base, made some computations that went beyond key word search, and returned with a list of probable solution documents. As Java-like capabilities have become more readily available, it has become feasible to have more computational functionality for customer support interactions through the Web. Vendors such as Netscape changed the name of their browser software category from "browser" to "client" (e.g., Muller, 1996, for an analysis of how help desk functionality is being expanded through the World Wide Web).

Insight 4: Use IT to enable as many different types of customer self-help routes as you can to a knowledge-creating customer support process, provided that you understand the prerequisite conditions for success.

Table 8.3

**Traditional Expert Systems Versus Adaptive Learning Systems**

| | Traditional Expert Systems | Adaptive Learning Systems |
|---|---|---|
| Knowledge Capture | Time spent building workable rules and cases is prohibitive. | On-the-fly knowledge capture such that knowledge base learns quickly and easily. |
| Knowledge Retrieval | Unsuited to solutions-in-progress. Requires large number of cases to provide problem-solving accuracy. | Accommodates changing solutions and solutions that have fuzzy and incomplete knowledge. |
| Knowledge Base Maintenance | Very high effort to maintain changing rules with large numbers of cases. | Self-organizing adaptive knowledge structure. |
| Skill of Knowledge Engineer | Requires skilled knowledge engineers to translate knowledge to rules and to develop expert system. | Problem/solution/symptom word structure is intuitive and requires no special skill. |

In 1994, Storage Dimensions tried to give its resellers direct access to TechConnect from their remote computers by making it possible for them to appear like a virtual TechConnect client complete with full GUI features. The technical implementation was superb, but resellers never used it. Apparently, for the casual user trying to play the role of technical support engineer, the functionality and richness of features of TechConnect were beyond what a casual user was willing to remember. On the other hand, the TechConnect e-mail and Internet connection were very successful, as previously discussed, and Storage Dimensions steadily expanded the capabilities of those routes. The difference between those two situations is that Storage Dimensions learned the prerequisites for successful self-help routes. First, the route must fill a need that provides incentive for self-help (such as 24-hour access). Second, the functionality should not be more than a casual user can assimilate (TechConnect self-help did not allow direct knowledge base access). Third, there must be alternate routes with live customer support staff, as self-help is not successful for all types of queries. Thus, self-help should only be attempted after a support staff is in place. Fourth, while the customer should be encouraged to provide new knowledge for the customer support knowledge base, care must be taken to protect its integrity.

> Insight 5: There will be an increasing need in business organizations to have a common interconnected "fresh" knowledge warehouse that captures in near-real-time the knowledge created around all critical interdependent business processes—including the customer support process.

Data warehouses became popular with business organizations because businesses became acutely aware of the criticality of joining data from the various interdependent parts of the organization, and yet being able to serve each constituency in a customized way. There is a knowledge warehouse analogy to that for the dynamic electronic economy that would center around knowledge-in-action captured through various business processes (e.g., Kalakota and Whinston, 1996). The key differences are inferred in Table 8.4.

It is envisaged that such knowledge warehouses would be built around knowledge creation processes rather than data, and there would be a much higher percentage of "fresh" solutions-in-progress (or fuzzy data). A comparison would probably have a higher percentage of interorganizational knowledge creating routes than today's warehouse has interorganizational data feeds. As

Table 8.4

**The Shift to Knowledge Warehouses**

| Data Warehouse | Knowledge Warehouse |
| --- | --- |
| Stable database structure | Emergent database structure |
| Does not learn from user access behavior | Learns from user access behavior |
| Passive; user retrieves information | Active; system may initiate discourse |
| Attribute search | Attribute search and pattern matching search |
| Scrubbed clean data | Fuzzy incomplete knowledge |
| Historical data | Fresh knowledge |
| Constrained interorganizational data feeds | Rich intranet/extranet knowledge creation routes |

Insight 6 suggests, the customer support process may be a promising place to start; however, it would also include knowledge created around other interdependent processes.

Insight 6: Methodologies for redesigning IT-enabled knowledge-creating customer support processes need to cater to both learning changes and process work flow changes.

Business process reengineering methodologies for IT-enabled business processes typically focused on changing the structure of work flow and the information around it. With customer support processes that have a large knowledge creation component given the rapidly changing environment, there is an intimate interdependence between the mode of learning and knowledge creation (e.g., Sampler and Short, 1994). Business process redesign methodologies thus have to move to a higher order of analysis in which the way that the process learns (becoming more learningful) is redesigned.

Insight 7: IT infrastructures and knowledge bases built around adaptive learning PRAs linked to customer support processes can provide the first step toward building the faster-learning knowledge-creating organization.

The Storage Dimensions experience showed that using PRAs based on adaptive learning is one of the most systematic and natural ways that one can structure the way that we learn and create knowledge. It can have well-defined dynamic feedback loops that, when utilized properly, can both speed up the learning process and amplify the shared knowledge creation capability of a network of people. It can have built-in knowledge consistency checks through constant interaction, and it can minimize the time between the creation of new knowledge and its incorporation into the knowledge base in intelligently accessible form. It can accommodate different levels of expertise by assuring that novices are not penalized for their lack of expertise and that experts are not burdened by unnecessary steps. It can be a smart way of creating new knowledge around business processes in action and appears to be one of the most promising paradigms for building IT-based learning organizations. Perhaps, after more than 20 years of trying, artificial intelligence has finally produced an appropriately targeted paradigm that will be of critical and widespread business use.

Furthermore, the customer support process is an excellent context in which to do this knowledge creation, as it is the natural meeting space around which the organization, its customers, its partners—and often its competitors—exchange dialogue about current issues of importance to all of them (e.g., Savage, 1996). It is the swiftest and most obvious context around which to capture shared knowledge creation in action and systematically incorporate it into a corporate knowledge base. Furthermore, the usual lack of physical proximity among different participants and parties makes the use of IT network–mediated exchanges all the more natural.

There is evidence to believe, based on the TechConnect experience, that the combination of using adaptive learning problem resolution IT architectures and the customer support process provides the most promising first step in building a faster-learning knowledge-creating organization. Other areas of the business can be more easily linked through the customer support process than any other critical business process—because of its simultaneous critical intersection with many knowledge sources and its built-in time pressures that can drive participants to augment learning quickly. It also brings into play emergent knowledge processes with high intensity (Markus et al., 2002). And it appears to be the best and fastest space from which to start building the structural intellectual capital of an organization (e.g., Alavi and Leidner, 2001; Grover and Davenport, 2001; Quinn, 1992; Stewart, 1994). It is an excellent arena for building a learning relationship with customers (Pine et al., 1995). Perhaps large management consulting companies have inadvertently shown us that, through being one of the first industries that has tried to build systematic knowledge maps (albeit not with adaptive learning PRAs).

## FURTHER RESEARCH AND CONCLUSION

One critical distinction between a database and a knowledge base that this chapter has taught us is that an IT-enabled knowledge base learns and changes from each user access—even to the point of changing its database structure—whereas a database does not learn. Similarly, a knowledge base may proactively initiate user discourse whereas databases are passive and, typically, it is the user who retrieves the information. This has substantial implications for how knowledge bases and business processes interact, and how business processes can be redesigned and transformed to take advantage of that in IT-intensive environments. The insights in this chapter and the accompanying guidelines for combining learning changes and process work flow changes in business process redesign still remain relatively underexplored. This is a fertile area for both research and practice where many opportunities for advancement exist and are badly needed.

One notable advance around this issue is the work by Nissen (2005) regarding managing dynamic knowledge flows, which combines in a tractable way the elusiveness of tacit knowledge with the nitty-gritty of process flow analysis. Nissen's main thrust is that organizational knowledge moves and flows from how it exists and where it is located to how and where it is needed in order to enable business processes and organizational performance. Nissen has started to address the issue of the "knowledge divide" in the enterprise (the "haves" and the "have-nots") by methods of managing the interactions between knowledge bases and business processes.

Another line of study that requires more attention by both scholars and practitioners is the context of exception processes: How do we design business processes in situations in which a large number of exceptions are likely to occur while the process is being executed? (e.g., El Sawy and Josefek, 2002). Exception processes are messy, knowledge-intensive processes that are constantly being redesigned when environments are turbulent, and they require much interaction with knowledge bases. Practitioners in some industries such as financial services are now designing dual business processes: a simple process that maps the typical way that the process works under normal conditions and a separate exception process that deals with identified and yet-to-be-identified process exceptions and that requires frequent redesigns and much more complex interactions with knowledge bases. There is much research waiting to be done around this issue.

The chapter has also provided a foundation for a better understanding of how to approach real-time knowledge management and quicken action-learning loops (El Sawy and Majchrzak, 2004). Managing enterprises in dynamic near-real-time environments requires the transformation of business processes so they can help an enterprise operate in a sense-and-respond mode and so that the processes include connections to vigilant IS that help provide real-time visibility and early warning across end-to-end business processes (Houghton et al., 2004). The lessons from this chapter have helped shape some of the ways that business processes can be transformed for real-time enterprises.

As we look forward into the future, it is clear that the global business environment will only become more dynamic and turbulent, and increasingly electronically interconnected in rich new ways. It is also clear that agility will need to be substantially enabled through IT infrastructures (Sambamurthy et al., 2003). Having robust internetworked IT-enabled knowledge-creating processes that learn quickly from customers (and employees, partners, and competitors) will not be a strategic choice—it will become a strategic necessity for success. Business process transformation to expand the knowledge-creating capacity of business processes to become more learningful in dynamic environments will be a formidable challenge and opportunity for both practitioners and researchers.

## ACKNOWLEDGMENT

This is an updated and modified version of an article that was published as Redesigning the customer support process for the electronic economy: Insights from Storage Dimensions, *MIS Quarterly,* 21, 4 (December 1997), 457–483. Gene Bowles, former Executive Vice President of Storage Dimensions, was the coauthor of that article. Expanded and revised with permission from the Regents of the University of Minnesota.

## REFERENCES

Alavi, M., and Leidner, D. 2001. Knowledge management and knowledge management systems: Conceptual foundation and an agenda for research. *MIS Quarterly,* 25, 1, 107–136.
Bennis, W., and Mische, M. 1996. Reinventing through reengineering: A methodology for enterprise wide transformation. *Information Systems Management,* 13, 3, 58–65.
Chase, R.B., and Garvin, D. 1989. The service factory. *Harvard Business Review,* 67, 4, 61–69.
Culnan, M.J. 1989. Designing information systems to support customer feedback: An organizational message system perspective. In J.I. DeGross, J.C. Henderson, and B.R. Konsynski (eds.), *Proceedings of the Tenth International Conference on Information Systems.* Atlanta: Association for Information Systems, pp. 305–311.
Davenport, T. 1993. *Process Innovation: Reengineering Work Through Information Technology.* Boston: Harvard Business School Press.
Davenport, T.; Jarvenpaa, S.; and Beers, M. 1996. Improving knowledge work processes. *Sloan Management Review* (Summer), 53–65.
El Sawy, O.A. 2001. *Redesigning Enterprise Processes for e-Business.* New York: McGraw-Hill.
El Sawy, O.A., and Josefek, R. 2002. Business process as nexus of knowledge. In C. Holsapple (ed.), *Handbook of Knowledge Management,* vol. 1. Berlin: Springer, pp. 425–438.
El Sawy, O.A., and Majchrzak, A. 2004. Critical issues in research on real-time knowledge management in enterprises. *Journal of Knowledge Management,* 8, 4, 21–37.
Entex. 1994. Vendor relationships: Trends, options, issues. White Paper, Entex Information Services, New York.
Grover, V., and Davenport, T. 2001. General perspectives on knowledge management: Fostering a research agenda. *Journal of Management Information Systems,* 18, 1 (Summer), 5–23.

Grover, V., and Kettinger, W.R. 2000. *Process Think: Winning Perspectives for Business Change in the Information Age.* Hershey, PA: Idea Group.

Haeckel, S. 1994. Managing the information-intensive firm of 2001. In R.C. Blattberg, R. Glazer, and J.D.C. Little (eds.), *The Marketing Information Revolution.* Boston: Harvard Business School Press.

Henkoff, R. 1994. Service is everybody's business. *Fortune* (June 27), 48–60.

Houghton, R.; El Sawy, O.A.; Gray, P.; Donegan, C.; and Joshi, A. 2004. Vigilant information systems for managing enterprises in dynamic supply chains: Real-time dashboards at Western Digital. *MIS Quarterly Executive* (March), 19–35.

Kalakota, R., and Whinston, A. 1996. *Frontiers of Electronic Commerce.* Boston: MA: Addison-Wesley.

Kirkbride, L., and Deppe, S.M. 1995. Evaluating problem resolution technologies for the help desk. White Paper, Answer Systems, CA.

Lele, M., and Sheth, J. 1987. *The Customer Is Key.* New York: Wiley.

Markus, M.L.; Majchrzak, A.; and Gasser., L. 2002. A design theory for systems that support emergent knowledge processes. *MIS Quarterly,* 26, 3, 179–213.

Muller, N. 1996. Expanding the help desk through the World Wide Web. *Information Systems Management,* 13, 3, 37–44.

Nissen, M. 2005. *Harnessing Knowledge Dynamics.* Hershey, PA: Idea Group.

Nonaka, I., and Takeuchi, H. 1995. *The Knowledge Creating Company.* New York: Oxford University Press.

Pine, J.; Peppers, D.; and Rogers, M. 1995. Do you want to keep your customers forever? *Harvard Business Review,* 73, 2, 103–114.

Quinn, J.B. 1992. *Intelligent Enterprise: A Knowledge- and Service-Based Paradigm for Industry.* New York: Free Press.

Rathnam, S.; Mahajan, V.; and Whinston, A. 1995. Facilitating coordination in customer support teams: A framework and its implications for the design of information technology. *Management Science,* 41, 12, 1900–1921.

Sambamurthy, V.; Bharadwaj. A.; and Grover, V. 2003. Shaping agility through digital options: Reconceptualizing the role of IT in contemporary firms. *MIS Quarterly,* 27, 2, 237–263.

Sampler, J., and Short, J. 1994. An examination of IT's impact on the value of information and expertise: Implications for organizational change. *Journal of Management Information Systems,* 11, 2 (Fall), 59–73.

Savage, C. 1996. *5th Generation Management,* 2d ed. Burlington, MA: Butterworth-Heinemann.

Shostack, L. 1977. Breaking free from product marketing. *Journal of Marketing,* 41, 2, 73–80.

Stewart, T. 1994. Your company's most valuable asset: Intellectual capital. *Fortune* (October 3), 68–75.

Treacy, M., and Wiersema, F. 1995. *The Discipline of Market Leaders.* Boston: Addison-Wesley.

# CHAPTER 9

# TRANSFORMING THE NEW PRODUCT DEVELOPMENT PROCESS

## Leveraging and Managing Knowledge

ANNE P. MASSEY, MITZI M. MONTOYA-WEISS, AND
TONY M. O'DRISCOLL

*Abstract: In response to global competitive environments and technological factors, organizations are examining how they can better leverage knowledge assets for value creation. In this chapter, we describe a business process reengineering effort undertaken by Nortel, a telecommunications equipment manufacturer. Following a knowledge management approach, Nortel transformed the front end of its new product development (NPD) process. NPD is knowledge-intensive work based on the individual and collective expertise of employees. The front-end activities of NPD are commonly referred to as the "fuzzy front end" because they involve ill-defined processes and ad hoc decisions carried out by multiple and diverse performers. This chapter describes Nortel's efforts to transform NPD business process by bringing structure to it, the information technology implementation approach, and lessons learned.*

*Keywords: New Product Development Process, Business Process Transformation, Knowledge Management, Electronic Performance Support*

## INTRODUCTION

Global competitive environments and technological factors are increasingly volatile and evolving rapidly. In response, organizations are examining how they can better leverage knowledge assets for value creation. In highly competitive environments, a firm's long-term viability depends on the successful expansion and exploitation of its knowledge assets. One challenge for business process reengineering (BPR) has been an inability to deal effectively with highly unstructured, knowledge-intensive processes. This challenge has led some experts to suggest that an entirely different approach—a knowledge management (KM) approach—should be taken for improving these processes.

In a business context, knowledge is defined as information that is relevant, actionable, and based, at least partially, on experience (Leonard and Sensiper, 1998). In essence, knowledge is what employees know about customers, products, processes, past successes and failures, and about each other. A KM strategy entails consciously helping people share and put knowledge into action by creating access, context, and infrastructure, and simultaneously shortening learning cycles (Alavi and Leidner, 2001; Davenport et al., 1998; O'Dell and Grayson, 1998; Schultz and Leidner, 2002). A KM strategy takes place within a complex system of organizational structure and culture, and is enabled through information technology (IT). A successful KM strategy identifies a firm's key leverage points for achieving business results. Often, these leverage points reside in core business processes that may be reengineered to capitalize on or expand the organization's knowledge resources and capabilities.

In this chapter, we describe a BPR initiative undertaken by Nortel, a leading telecommunications equipment manufacturer. Following principles of KM, Nortel transformed the front end of its new product development (NPD) process. Continuous innovation through NPD is the foundation of competitive advantage for many companies in today's business environment. NPD is knowledge-intensive work based on the individual and collective expertise of employees (Leonard and Sensiper, 1998). How well a company manages the NPD process is a critical determinant of how successfully organizational knowledge creation can be carried out (Nonaka and Takeuchi, 1995). Nortel applied KM principles to the NPD process in order to transform it and achieve a sustainable advantage.

The rapid penetration of IT into business processes is enabling changes that can significantly enhance productivity and performance and simultaneously manage knowledge (Grover et al., 1997). IT embodied in the form of an electronic performance support system (EPSS) was the key enabler of Nortel's effort to implement their newly designed front-end NPD process. EPSS represents a relatively new paradigm integrating principles found in artificial intelligence, human performance technology, computer-based training, information systems, and user-centered design. An EPSS can be used to capture, store, and distribute individual and corporate knowledge, enabling individuals to achieve desired levels of performance in the fastest possible time and with a minimum of support from others (Raybould, 1995). All software tools are intended to support human performance in some fashion, but an EPSS is distinguished from other approaches (e.g., traditional systems development, expert systems development) by its attention to enabling *performance* in the context of work. That is, the EPSS and work tasks are integrated such that support is provided in the format that best matches the task facing a particular user (Brown, 1996; Karat, 1997).

This chapter describes the elements of Nortel's initiative intended to transform the NPD front-end process, the implementation approach, and lessons learned. We begin with a brief description of the problem background and context of Nortel's initiative. Then, we describe in detail how the EPSS, called *Virtual Mentor,* enabled Nortel to (1) leverage multidisciplinary knowledge assets in the NPD front-end process, (2) improve NPD decision-making processes, and (3) facilitate learning and knowledge exchange. We conclude with a summary of the implications of Nortel's experience.

## PROBLEM BACKGROUND

The divestiture of AT&T in 1984 and the Telecom Reform Act of 1996 spawned intense competition in the telecom industry, yielding an explosion in the development of innovative telecommunications technology. Although Nortel stumbled badly following the dot-com bust in 2000, during the late 1990s, Nortel was a key equipment manufacturer in the industry with employees in over 22 countries. Customers included the interexchange carriers (e.g., AT&T), the Regional Bell Operating Companies (RBOCs), various large corporations, and numerous Internet service providers (ISPs). The new rules of the deregulated telecommunications marketplace forced Nortel to recognize that differentiation through innovation would be a key to its continued success. Continuous innovation through NPD was deemed a mission-critical business strategy. In the 1990s, management attention focused on operationalizing this business strategy, translating it into performance objectives, and implementing it in the work environment.

In the mid-1990s, a senior executive and board member initiated a project to ensure that Nortel could continue to innovate and distinguish itself from competitors. The name given to this effort was "Project Galileo."[1] An internal group was charged with the task of addressing the problem. This task force consisted of representatives from information systems, psychology, business, engineering, marketing, human factors, and new product development. The overarching business objective of the project was to increase the number and market acceptance rate of Nortel's new products. From this objective, the task force determined that the core performance improvement needed was a continuous stream of innovative ideas. The immediate concern of the project sponsors was that Nortel's products and services "idea war chest" was empty and needed to be replenished immediately.

Research into Nortel's NPD process revealed that the organization relied almost exclusively on customer requests for new product/service ideas. Nortel's NPD capability was primarily devoted to developing minor extension products for existing customers rather than researching and developing innovative products and services for existing or new customer segments. After preliminary research, the task force discovered that the generation and existence of innovative ideas within Nortel was not the issue. The problem was that Nortel's existing NPD process had no formal mechanism to systematically deal with internally generated ideas. The lack of use of internal idea sources by Nortel suggested that the company was not fully leveraging its own knowledge base. The competitive environment of the late 1990s mandated that Nortel anticipate new market opportunities, capitalize on emerging technological capabilities, and make more optimal use of its knowledge resources. The task force set out to create and implement a process that leveraged Nortel's knowledge base by cataloging innovative ideas, facilitating idea development, and enabling systematic idea screening for market viability.

## OVERVIEW OF NEW PRODUCT DEVELOPMENT CONTEXT

In general, an NPD project is initiated when a concept is funded and moved forward into development. During development, there are various stages of activities simultaneously involving different functional areas in the organization. Typically, NPD processes feature multiple review points, or decision gates, where projects are evaluated. Figure 9.1 presents a static view of a generic NPD process. In reality, NPD is highly iterative. At each stage of the NPD process, decisions are made to continue, kill, or recycle projects. As projects progress through development, resource commitments increase and decision criteria change. Despite the fact that the front-end concept development and selection activities drive all subsequent decisions, they are the least understood and most poorly managed activities in the entire innovation process (Cooper and Kleinschmidt, 1986; Khurana and Rosenthal, 1997).

The front-end concept development and selection activities are commonly referred to as the "fuzzy front end" because they involve ill-defined processes and ad hoc decisions carried out by multiple and diverse performers (Cooper and Kleinschmidt, 1986). Concept development involves transforming a raw idea into a robust concept through careful definition of the underlying technologies, identification of expected customer benefits, and an assessment of the market opportunity. A product concept should be sufficiently developed so that decision makers can sense whether the newly defined opportunity is worth committing resources for further exploration. Concept selection involves choosing which new product concepts will be funded and initiated

Figure 9.1 **Generic Stage-Gate Model of the New Product Development Process**

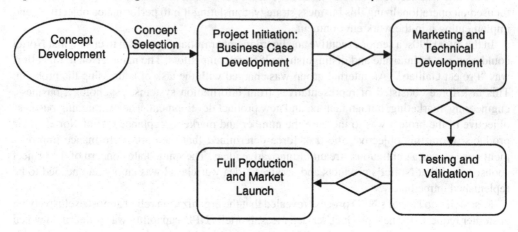

as projects for development. Concept selection decisions dictate all further development activity. And yet studies show that many front-end concept selection decisions are made without the use of objective evaluation criteria (Cooper and Kleinschmidt, 1986). These decisions are often based on informal discussions with no checklists or criteria. Making such important decisions strictly on "gut feel" without any systematic or comparative analysis is not conducive to achieving competitive advantage.

## NORTEL'S FRONT-END NPD PROCESS

At Nortel in the late 1990s, front-end NPD activities were unstructured and ad hoc, and thus the point of optimal leverage to improve Nortel's current NPD process lay there. A great opportunity for improving Nortel's NPD process was better idea-to-concept development and evaluation procedures. Process structuring requires the capture and formalization of task logic—that is, the sequences, relationships, and interrelationships associated with process tasks (Gery, 1991). Therefore, the task force set out to capture external knowledge and surface internal knowledge relevant to the creation of a front-end NPD process. Nortel's knowledge elicitation process determined what screening criteria should be employed by decision makers in concept selection. Standardized criteria would provide structure for the concept selection decision and also provide a consistent framework for concept development.

The task force conducted extensive external benchmarking to gain a better understanding of best-in-class NPD front-end processes. The team conducted case studies with companies renowned for their innovation capabilities (e.g., Hewlett-Packard, 3M, Sun Microsystems, and Kodak). They reviewed academic publications and those of various professional organizations (e.g., Center for Quality Management, Product Development Management Association), and they contracted with outside consultants for objective internal evaluations. After careful study of best practices, the task force developed a four-phase front-end NPD process and a set of standard evaluation criteria. The process consisted of (1) idea qualification, (2) concept development, (3) concept rating, and (4) concept assessment. The task force's research concluded that new product or service concepts should be developed and evaluated according to four categories of criteria: (1) marketing, (2) technology, (3) business analysis, and (4) human factors. The knowledge elicitation process generated detailed information requirements for each category. These requirements would facilitate the development of embryonic ideas into complete and robust concepts that could be subsequently evaluated by decision makers.

## PROCESS IMPLEMENTATION

The task force considered various alternatives for implementing the Galileo front-end NPD process at Nortel. The objective was to identify a solution that best addressed the process goals and organizational constraints, with minimum organizational and human distress, and within time and budget. A particular challenge is that the front-end NPD process is a context in which experts typically do not exist and work practices are not uniform. Traditionally, many diverse people (e.g., engineers, marketers, project managers, executives) are charged with different aspects of the front-end process. Thus, an implementation approach that addressed the divergent needs of the multiple performers was required.

Realistically, using expert cross-functional teams to qualify and develop every submitted idea would be prohibitively costly in terms of time commitment and opportunity cost of pulling individuals away from their jobs for preproject analysis. Therefore, the task force sought an implementation solution that would shift the burden of concept development (Phases 1 through 3) to the original idea generator. The goal was for idea generators to develop robust concepts by conducting a thorough analysis of marketing, technology, business opportunity, and human factors in a standard fashion. Because idea generators (e.g., engineers) typically do not possess sufficient knowledge of all four dimensions, the task force considered three implementation alternatives:

1. Train all employees in the areas of marketing, technology, human factors, and business analysis so that they are able to qualify and develop their own idea.
2. Assign internal subject matter expert (SME) mentors in the areas of marketing, technology, human factors, and business analysis to each idea generator.
3. Capture the expertise of SME mentors and incorporate it into an electronic tool to guide and advise the idea generators, thus providing content knowledge to idea generators.

Each alternative was evaluated according to its cost-effectiveness and feasibility given Nortel's current organizational structure, resource availability, and culture.

Based on this analysis, alternatives that advocated the support of human expertise to implement the process were deemed too costly and difficult to implement effectively. IT could be leveraged to create an electronic version of a human SME and overcome the need to train or buy cross-functional expertise. Such a knowledge-oriented tool would enable the front-end process to be structured, employed, and managed in a consistent fashion across people and over time. IT offered additional benefits in that it could provide efficiencies in process oversight and administration as well as create electronic repositories of the intellectual property (IP) associated with idea generation. It was clear to Nortel that IT would be useful for managing the knowledge inherent in and generated from front-end NPD activities. Yet, for a tool to be successful, human performers would have to employ it in an interactive and iterative manner while performing work. In order to develop their tool, Nortel turned to a relatively new paradigm, EPSS technology.

For Nortel, the attributes of EPSS technology made it an attractive paradigm for building a tool to implement the new front-end NPD process. Whereas KM is a conscious strategy of helping people share and put knowledge into action, EPSS technology provides the means to do so. Each phase of the front-end process could be integrated electronically. Thus, knowledge could be developed, captured, transmitted, and leveraged at each succeeding stage of the front-end process. The goal of an EPSS is to aid *performance* by providing access to integrated information, knowledge, learning experiences, advice, and guidance at "the moment of need" (Gery, 1991). Idea genera-tors and decision makers would have immediate access to consistent expert advice, any time, any place, without the need for intermediaries. Thus, an EPSS-enabled front-end process would facilitate knowledge access, generation, and, ultimately, decision making. Importantly, an EPSS takes a *systemic* view of process tasks, the human performer, and the workplace by recognizing that knowledge is inseparable from the human performers who develop and leverage it in the context of work. Knowledge flows from the processes that help generate and nurture it (Fahey and Prusak, 1998). Thus, the implementation goal was to provide, via one integrated system, performance support for the front-end NPD process for all relevant performer audiences.

Interestingly, although there had been a recent trend in the growth of software tools to support the NPD process (cf. Rangaswamy and Lilien, 1997), no prior research had described a tool or technique specifically designed to support the fuzzy front end of the NPD process. This may be due to the fact that back-end NPD activities such as product development, testing, and launch are better understood and more structured, and are thus more amenable to software support (e.g., project management and decision support tools) (Rangaswamy and Lilien, 1997). However, given Nortel's needs, lending structure and support to fuzzy front-end activities was of paramount importance. The sooner bad ideas could be screened out and good ideas could be detected, the more efficient the R&D resource utilization could be. At the same time, it was important that the resulting structure and technology not constrain the creative processes inherent to the fuzzy front end.

## EPSS DESIGN CONSIDERATIONS

A cross-functional team of process and system development experts was charged with creating Nortel's KM tool, Virtual Mentor. The team identified several general system design requirements:

1. Virtual Mentor should facilitate and oversee the four phases of the Galileo front-end process for each user/performer as appropriate for each phase. Specifically, it should guide and direct an idea generator through the idea qualification, concept development, and concept rating phases. Similarly, it should facilitate and accelerate the concept as-sessment phase for a decision maker.
2. Virtual Mentor should be intuitive and user-friendly for all those who interface with it. It should be "plug and play," requiring no manual.
3. Virtual Mentor should be flexible in use and allow for iterative, rather than forced, se-quential input by an idea generator. In other words, it should allow the idea generator to control and order as much of the flow as possible according to his or her natural thought progression.
4. Virtual Mentor should provide a learning opportunity for performers while doing the task at hand. This attribute offsets the significant costs and productivity loss of sending performers to training courses prior to and during the time that they are working on a new activity.
5. Virtual Mentor should catalog the information associated with all the ideas and keep this information secure. This will provide a record of internal innovation activity and a possible legal safeguard should patent rights become an issue.
6. Virtual Mentor should minimize the administrative overhead associated with overseeing complex systems. Routine tasks such a system monitoring should be automated to allow

Figure 9.2 **General Performance Model**

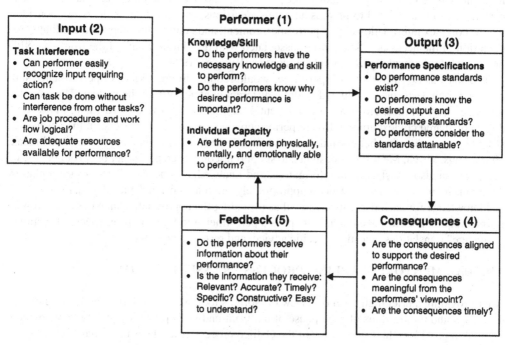

*Source:* Rummler and Brache (1992).

a process owner to focus more on the evolution of the system to ensure congruence with the work activity that it was supporting.

In essence, Virtual Mentor would automate each stage of the Galileo front-end process, support the performance of those individuals working within the process, and manage Nortel's intellectual property. In addition to simultaneously supporting an idea generator and decision maker, Virtual Mentor would support a process owner charged with tracking progress. In order to integrate varied performance requirements into a single, comprehensive tool, the cross-functional team thoroughly analyzed the diverse, yet interdependent, needs of the three performer groups. Nortel's team recognized that individual performance is not simply a function of individual knowledge, skills, or capacity, but rather, there are other factors that can influence individual performance, including the nature of process tasks, performance specifications, consequences, and feedback (Gery, 1997; Rummler and Brache, 1992). The performance support was designed based on an understanding of individual performance within this broader context. Figure 9.2 illustrates the general model (Rummler and Brache, 1992) Nortel used to analyze the needs and environment of each performer.

As shown, in general, process performers are required to process a variety of inputs for which there are desired outputs. For every output (as well as the action required to produce that output) there are consequences that affect the performer. Because consequences are interpreted as either positive or negative, individual behavior is influenced by consequences. Because performers will do things that lead to positive consequences and avoid things that lead to negative consequences, feedback is an essential component. This general model provided Nortel with a useful mechanism for identifying and mapping the knowledge processes, outcomes, and drivers associated with each performer group as related to process activities, decisions, and information flows. By considering the complex interrelationship of performer, content, and context, this approach facilitated the definition of the necessary "know-how" associated with the "know-what" of the front-end NPD process while acknowledging workplace realities (Ruggles, 1998).

The analysis revealed that each performer would require different kinds of performance support, and each performer would add or draw different content to/from the system. Thus, unique interfaces were needed. However, a fundamental intermediate purpose of KM is to build some degree of shared context among diverse performers participating in a process. In the absence of shared context, differing beliefs and meanings may impede decision making (Fahey and Prusak, 1998). Thus, Virtual Mentor was designed to support not only each performer in his or her "local" language but also translate data, information, and knowledge as needed during process phases. All of this required that Virtual Mentor appropriately summarized and depicted data, information, and knowledge for each performer, as well as providing the appropriate context associated with it when required. Virtual Mentor also supported performers through company-specific functional "language" translations, question-specific advice, and resource pointers.

## VIRTUAL MENTOR: ENABLING PROCESS TRANSFORMATION

After providing a brief high-level overview of Nortel's tool, we will describe the specific design objectives and implications of each phase of the front-end NPD process as it was implemented. Figure 9.3 provides a high-level view of the Galileo process as it relates to Virtual Mentor.

An *idea generator* (e.g., an engineer) was the primary performer in the system. It was the idea generator's responsibility to provide the relevant information and knowledge about his or her idea. The primary task required of the idea generator was to create this input by responding to questions presented by the Virtual Mentor. Because idea generators were likely unfamiliar with the marketing, business analysis, and human factors areas, they needed knowledge-based support to understand how to address the questions being asked by the Virtual Mentor. This support is provided on-demand through context-specific advice for each question such that the assistance of a human SME was emulated.

The role of the *decision makers* was to compare and contrast rated concepts and choose concepts for further development. Since decision makers usually had many funding decisions to make with regard to new product/service concepts, they needed decision support that enabled comparing and contrasting the most salient attributes for each concept as they relate to the business imperative of the organization. Virtual Mentor provided this support by codifying and structuring concept information in such a way that it could be evaluated and compared in an objective and consistent manner.

The *process owner* would monitor activity on the system and ensure that Virtual Mentor was congruent with the work environment it was designed to support. Process owners required productivity-based support in order to track the progress of the idea generators and decision makers, provide feedback, and generate relevant reports. Virtual Mentor provided this support via a customized interface to the system that automated many of the search and monitor tasks that would traditionally be carried out manually. As examples, automated reminders could be sent to idea generators who had not been active on the system for over two weeks, usage statistics across geographic areas could be created and graphically depicted to system sponsors, and decision makers could be automatically alerted when a concept that falls within their jurisdiction had been submitted by an idea generator. In the phase-by-phase descriptions that follow, we focus on the idea generator and decision-maker roles.

Figure 9.3 **Overview of Virtual Mentor**

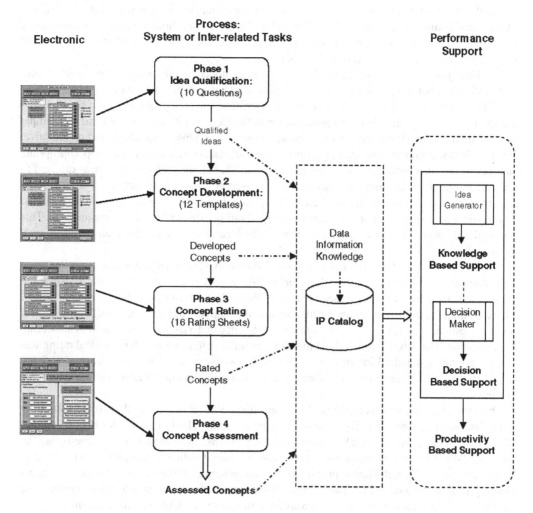

## Phase 1: Idea Qualification

The purpose of the Idea Qualification phase was to effectively prescreen new product or service ideas in a consistent manner at a very high level. The objective was to identify ideas that were the most viable candidates to move to subsequent phases of development. Viability was defined broadly as the degree of perceived market and technological readiness or maturity. The team followed three general process and design objectives for the Idea Qualification phase:

1. Have a standard screening process and evaluation algorithm for all ideas.
2. Validate the idea in the primary areas of market readiness and technical feasibility.
3. Capture the IP associated with every idea submitted.

These objectives ensured that the process and tool provided a quick, structured, and standardized mechanism whereby the many ideas that reside within Nortel could be narrowed down to a few potential candidates for further development. At the same time, all submitted ideas were captured so that those ideas whose "time had not yet come" were collected and managed in the IP Catalog. These ideas would then be readily available to Nortel in the future should market or technological conditions change. Moreover, should legal issues arise over the rights to the IP of any idea, the IP Catalog provided a historical record of the idea.

The Idea Qualification phase began when an idea generator completed a simple ten-question form within Virtual Mentor. The idea generator was presented with an indexed list of the questions that could be answered in any order. Upon selecting a question, the idea generator saw a standardized question screen (see Figure 9.4 for a presentation of the Idea Qualification screen and an example of a question screen). Each question was broken into two sections—qualitative and quantitative. Virtual Mentor prompted the idea generator to use secondary research to develop appropriate answers to various qualitative, open-ended questions. That is, the idea generator was directed to relevant information that may be available via the Web or corporate library (e.g., demographic data, trend forecasts, Forrester Reports, etc.). The quantitative element was a five-point Likert scale that required the idea generator to assign a numerical rating to his or her qualitative answers. This standardized approach to answering questions in the Idea Qualification phase ensured that each question had both a rationale and rating.

For each phase of Galileo, there was a "Guide" button that provided general information about the current phase. There was also an "Advisor" button that provided context-specific assistance to the idea generator for each of the questions in the phase. The Advisor provided (1) the purpose of each question, (2) definitions of any terms that might be unclear in each question, (3) the context of each question, and (4) hyperlinks to sources of reference material that would assist in answering each question. The Advisor also helped the idea generator determine which numerical rating was best by providing standard interpretations for each possible score. This guidance functionality helped to ensure homogeneity across idea generators in providing quantitative ratings within the process.

Once the idea generator completed all ten questions, Virtual Mentor evaluated the idea using a standard scoring algorithm. The total score from the ratings had to be greater than 65 (out of 100) and the idea generator must have answered "don't know" to no more than two questions. The check for "don't knows" is important in this phase because it indicates completeness of the idea. If the idea passed, Virtual Mentor prompted the idea generator to move on to Phase 2, Concept Development. If the idea did not pass, Virtual Mentor prompted the idea generator to investigate specific Idea Qualification questions that warranted further research by providing a summary sheet with the questions in ascending order according to score. Phase 1 was the first step in capturing, accumulating, and documenting internal and external information and knowledge relevant to a new idea.

## Phase 2: Concept Development

The purpose of the Concept Development phase was to assist idea generators in "growing" their embryonic ideas into robust, fully developed concepts. This entailed analyzing the idea in the relevant critical areas (i.e., marketing, technology, business analysis, and human factors). The team followed three general process and tool design objectives for the Concept Development phase:

1. Be well documented, formal, and organized, yet allow for iteration and change.
2. Ensure thorough assessment of each idea in the areas of marketing, technology, human factors, and business analysis.

Figure 9.4 **Phase 1: Idea Qualification**

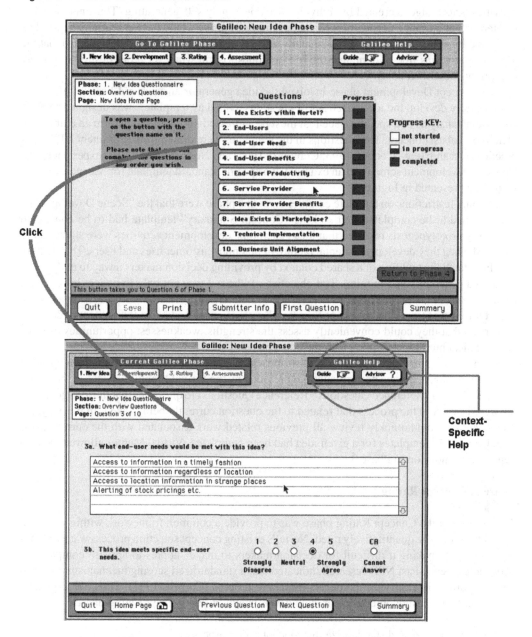

3. Inform the idea generator of the specificity, depth, and detail of the information required to complete the questions in each of the templates.

These objectives ensured that the process and tool were clear and structured, but not to the point that they restricted the innovative creativity of the idea generator. As Leonard and Sensiper pointed out, the process of innovation is a "rhythm of search and selection, exploration and synthesis, cycles of divergent thinking followed by convergence" (1998, p. 116). Through these activities, knowledge is created by individuals and is largely self-generating. Thus, not allowing for iteration and change during this critical development phase would have essentially negated its value and impeded the process. Consequently, this phase of the process was designed so that the idea generator was free to complete the relevant questions in whatever order desired (with two exceptions, described below).

The Concept Development phase involved the idea generator answering 12 sets of questions to more fully develop the idea. Each set of questions, called a "template," was designed to elicit an in-depth analysis of a specific issue that must be addressed in order to transform an embryonic idea into a robust concept. The questions in the templates were drawn from prominent NPD best-practices research (e.g., Cooper, 1993; Crawford, 1994) and Nortel-specific NPD experience. The Concept Development screen and an example of a specific standard template for "Scene Development" are presented in Figure 9.5.

The only restrictions on template completion in this phase were that the "Scene Development" template had to be completed first and the "Concept Summary" template had to be completed last. Early prototype tests revealed that idea generators' development activities were significantly enriched when they developed a mental picture of potential customer uses and users. This activity also facilitated the building of a shared context by providing decision makers a way to understand what idea generators had in mind. The objective of Phase 2 was not only to collect information (which could be disjointed) but, rather, to imbue data and information with decision- and action-relevant meaning. The "Concept Summary" restriction was added at the request of decision makers so that they could conveniently assess the strengths, weaknesses, opportunities, threats, and technical hurdles associated with the concept.

As in Phase 1, the Virtual Mentor Advisor provided context-specific advice for each question in each template. A unique performance aid provided by the Virtual Mentor Advisor in this phase was the access to "Reference Questions." Reference Questions are questions that the idea generator answered earlier in the process that related to the question currently being asked. In this way, the idea generator could quickly review all previous related work associated with the current question. Once all 12 templates for a given idea had been completed, Virtual Mentor allowed the idea generator to move on to Phase 3.

## Phase 3: Concept Rating

The purpose of the Concept Rating phase was to provide a common framework within which all NPD ideas could be quantitatively rated. Nortel's existing concept selection process was predominantly ad hoc, making it difficult for decision makers to make "apples-to-apples" comparisons between concepts. Past NPD research indicated that a standardized scoring mechanism provided the most utility in clarifying the decision-making process (Cooper, 1993). Thus, three general process and tool design objectives directed development of the Concept Rating phase:

1. systematize and standardize the concept rating process,
2. subject the concept to a large set of review criteria,
3. capture rating (quantitative), rationale (qualitative), and confidence data (quantitative) from the idea generator across this large set of criteria.

The Concept Rating phase involved the idea generator rating his or her concept using a standard set of questions in an "Idea Rating Form." The Idea Rating Form was divided into four primary

Figure 9.5 **Phase 2: Concept Development**

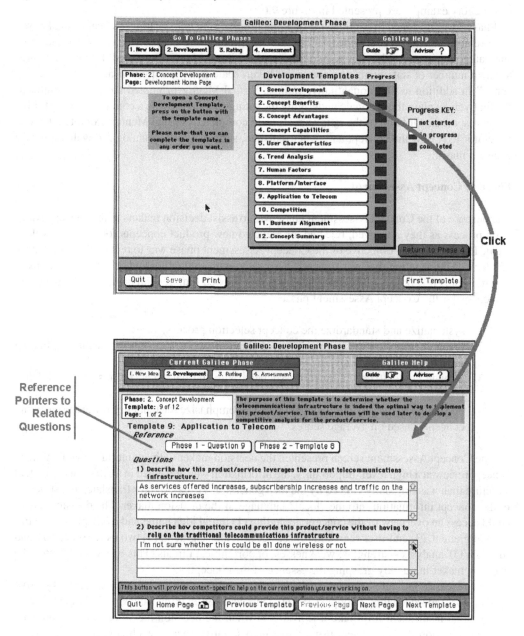

categories: (1) marketing, (2) technology, (3) human factors, and (4) business analysis. Each of these primary categories is, in turn, was divided into subcategories. The Concept Rating screen presented the idea generator with an indexed list of rating sheets. These rating sheet headings were organized into primary categories and subcategories. Again, Virtual Mentor provided context-specific advice and access to reference questions in order to ensure that the idea generator provided the most informed and accurate assessment possible. The Concept Rating screen and a subcategory example are presented in Figure 9.6.

Phase 3 was designed to continue the ongoing process of using, creating, and capturing knowledge relative to an evolving concept. The idea generator could choose to answer the questions and categories in any order. For each rating screen, Virtual Mentor prompted the idea generator to rate a number of statements on a five-point Likert scale from "strongly disagree" to "strongly agree." In addition to these quantitative ratings, Virtual Mentor prompted the idea generator to qualitatively explain the rationale underlying the ratings and to provide a confidence level for his or her responses. Once all of the rating sheets were completed, Virtual Mentor prompted the idea generator to review the concept and, when satisfied, submit it to the catalog for evaluation by a decision maker.

**Phase 4: Concept Assessment**

The purpose of the Concept Assessment phase was to assist decision makers in the concept evaluation process as they approved, rejected, or recycled new product concepts for further development. The overarching objective of the Concept Assessment phase was to reduce the subjectivity and lack of information that was typically associated with evaluation and selection decisions in the front-end NPD process. The development team followed four general process and tool design objectives for the Concept Assessment phase:

1. systematize and standardize the concept selection process,
2. focus attention on the most relevant evaluation issues (i.e., market, technical, human factors, business analysis),
3. provide context (i.e., rationale) associated with the data (i.e., ratings and confidence levels),
4. encourage "why/why not" evaluation and de-emphasize the tendency toward prioritizing concepts based on average scores.

The Concept Assessment screen presented the decision maker with an interface that facilitated concept review at a high level. Importantly, the information was presented in a different contextual structure than was originally created by the idea generator. Virtual Mentor translated the structure of the concept information into the "local" language of the decision maker. The decision maker could access an overview of the concept, including (1) initial idea name and description, (2) strategic alignment, (3) end-user segment, (4) service provider segment, (5) two usage scenarios, and (6) a SWOT analysis—strengths, weaknesses, opportunities, threats. This overview assisted the decision maker in quickly grasping the essence of the concept.

Past research indicates that most decisions regarding new product ideas are subjective "go/no go"-type decisions (Cooper, 1993). This decision-making behavior is largely due to the fact that insufficient information is available when the decision has to be made. Moreover, Nortel's selection decisions were usually executed serially. That is, each concept was assessed independently as opposed to comparatively. Virtual Mentor offered the potential for more effective decision making since the first three phases were designed to generate and codify standard sets of data, information, and knowledge about new product concepts. This presented the opportunity for higher-order "why/why not" decision making that is more comparative in nature. It allowed decision makers to more fully consider specific characteristics of each concept and compare them to other concepts that are codified in a similar manner.

Figure 9.6 **Phase 3: Concept Rating**

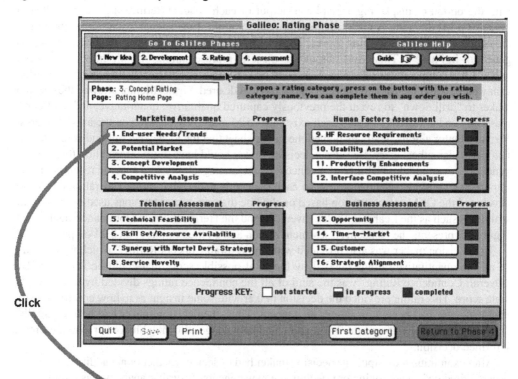

In order to facilitate "why/why not" decision making, Virtual Mentor provided a decision maker with the option of displaying a graphical output of each concept, termed a generic evaluation model (GEM) diagram. A GEM diagram provides a multi-dimensional visual representation of the concept's quantitative rating scores. The axes correspond to the dimensions rated by the idea generator in Phase 3. This GEM output was a useful representation for both individual concept analysis and comparative evaluation. A decision maker could choose to evaluate concepts according to any particular dimension. If deeper exploration was desired, Virtual Mentor allowed the decision maker to "drill down" to reveal the previously captured qualitative, quantitative, and confidence reasoning and knowledge behind each axis on a GEM graph. By clicking on the axis of interest, Virtual Mentor automatically displayed the rating sheet that the idea generator had submitted for that particular subcategory. Because a decision maker could have more information than an idea generator regarding the viability of a concept or the manageability of a specific resource, it was important to provide selective access to each concept's underlying rating and rationale. Nortel developed the GEM representation based on the kite diagram representations used in popular instruments such as the Learning Styles Inventory and the Hermann Brain Dominance Instrument. Figure 9.7 presents the Concept Assessment screen and an illustration of a GEM output.

The decision maker was also provided with an "Overall Concept Rating," which was the sum of all the quantitative ratings divided by the total possible score that could be achieved. The "Overall Confidence Rating" was the sum of all the confidence ratings divided by the total possible score. This rating provided the decision maker with some insight as to how comfortable the idea generator had been with rating the concept. Thus, the decision maker had both qualitative and quantitative context-specific information and knowledge, allowing him or her to make a more informed decision.

After examining the output, the decision maker had to decide whether or not additional analysis was required before approving or rejecting the new concept. If further analysis was required, the concept could be returned to the idea generator for further research. Alternatively, the decision maker could approve the concept in which case it became an input into the company's existing NPD process. If not approved, the concept was stored in the catalog perhaps to be revisited at a later date. Thus, the knowledge generated from the process was either acted upon immediately or stored for future reference. Importantly, the reasoning and knowledge employed by the decision maker in the "why/why not" decision was captured in Virtual Mentor. This provided a mechanism to give idea generators detailed feedback, necessary for learning and continuing incentives to participate. In the performance model analysis of idea generators, Nortel found that feedback about the decision was extremely important to idea generators. Cataloging all concepts regardless of the final decision also avoided "reinventing the wheel" should a cataloged concept be analyzed by a different decision maker in the future. In this way, none of the work conducted within the front-end process would be lost.

**Summary and Outcomes**

For Nortel, the Galileo process and Virtual Mentor tool transformed the front-end NPD process from a relatively ill-structured and ad hoc process to one that was consistent over time and across people. In the end, knowledge assets could be exploited and the performance capability of process performers changed. Table 9.1 summarizes how Virtual Mentor was integrated with and supported the performance model of each performer.

Jointly, the Galileo process and Virtual Mentor provided the work environment necessary to achieve the original performance objective of generating a continuous stream of innovative ideas.

Figure 9.7 **Phase 4: Concept Assessment**

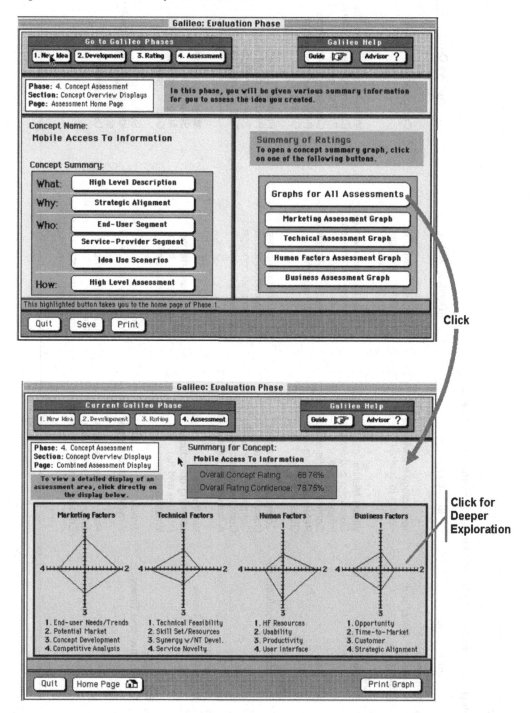

Table 9.1

**Nortel's Mapping of Virtual Mentor to Human Performers**

| Performance Factors | Idea Generator | Decision Maker | Process Owner |
|---|---|---|---|
| 1. Performer<br>Knowledge, Skills, and Capacity | Technology knowledge<br>Dollars to commit | Business knowledge<br>Process knowledge<br>Power to decide | Computer knowledge |
| 2. Input<br>Process Tasks | Virtual Mentor interfaces<br>Questions and templates<br>Process guide<br>Context-specific advice<br>Reference information<br>Glossary | Virtual Mentor interfaces<br>Summary information<br>Process guide<br>Context-specific advice<br>GEM diagrams | Virtual Mentor interfaces<br>Customized report menus<br>Process guide<br>Context-specific advice<br>Reference information<br>Glossary |
| 3. Output<br>Performance Specifications | Completed questions<br>Completed scores<br>Completed templates<br>Completed ratings<br>A "robust" concept | Evaluated concepts<br>Compared concepts<br>Contrasted concepts<br>Chosen concepts | Process reports<br>Process monitoring<br>Tool diagnostics<br>Tool maintenance |
| 4. Consequences<br>Meaningful and Timely | Worthwhile<br>Learning opportunity<br>Intuitive and fun<br>Would do again | Saves time<br>Increases certainty<br>Facilitates decision<br>Would do again | Makes job easier<br>Saves time<br>Automates repetitive tasks<br>Customizable |
| 5. Feedback<br>Constructive and Timely | Timely<br>Why/why not decision<br><br>Rationale for decision<br>Award for participation<br>Encouragement to try again | Timely<br>Why/why not scenario<br><br>Information and knowledge-rich interpretation<br>Immediate access to data, information, and knowledge | System status<br>Idea and concept activity status<br>User questions |

Table 9.2

**Benefits of Nortel's Galileo Process and Virtual Mentor**

| Leverage and growth of Nortel's knowledge base | Standardization of Nortel's front-end NPD process |
|---|---|
| • It captured, stored, and disseminated value-added, insight-laden knowledge.<br>• It improved knowledge transfer across business, technology, marketing, and human factors areas.<br>• It leveraged scarce organizational resources by electronically emulating cross-functional expertise.<br>• It reduced time wasted in finding data, information, or knowledge. | • It facilitated consistent implementation across people and over time.<br>• For idea generators, it "leveled the playing field" and allowed good concepts, not good salespeople, to rise to the top.<br>• For decision makers, it improved the quality and efficiency of concept selection.<br>• For process owners, it improved process control and minimized administrative overhead. |

With its strong emphasis on the link between context and content, Nortel's Galileo process and Virtual Mentor tool encouraged innovation and knowledge sharing. Importantly, senior management perceived that the Galileo process and Virtual Mentor tool gave Nortel the means to achieve a sustainable competitive advantage through innovation. Table 9.2 summarizes the core benefits realized by Nortel. Massey et al. (2002) provide further details regarding the financial and organizational affects of this KM-driven process transformation effort.

**Development Insights**

Not only did the transformation of the front-end NPD process provide many benefits for Nortel but it also created a strong appreciation among top management for the value of consciously managing organizational knowledge and knowledge creation processes. The project also generated insights about how ill-structured knowledge processes can be effectively supported with IT. Several guidelines regarding how to successfully execute a business process transformation using KM approach can be drawn from Nortel's experience with its front-end NPD project.

1. *Focus transformation efforts on critical business issues that have high payoff and are aligned with organizational strategy.* Nortel spent a substantial amount of time defining the business issue, that is, the need to differentiate itself through innovation so that it could generate increasing returns and continuing marketplace advantages. Although they took a KM approach to their transformation efforts, Nortel was more concerned about clearly defining the performance problem than worrying about semantic differences between data, information, and knowledge. By maintaining focus on the business issue, the resulting tool was successfully embedded in the work so that it could help people achieve the performance objective.

2. *Establish enterprise-level support.* A key to the success of Nortel's process transformation initiative was senior management support that provided ongoing funding and investment for necessary human and technical resources. Top-level management support helped send a clear message that managing process knowledge was mission critical. In addition, the development team conducted a careful study of the needs of all process performers—idea generators, decision makers, and process owners. By faithfully incorporating the multiple performer audiences' needs into the

process and tool, Nortel was able to establish bottom-up support for the project. This encouraged participation, knowledge sharing, and use throughout the organization.

3. *Treat knowledge as a process rather than as a "product."* Nortel recognized that knowledge was meaningless when disconnected from the people and processes that generate and use it. Nortel's goal was not only to capture knowledge but also to facilitate the incremental process of knowledge creation. In doing so, the front-end process would be transformed. For example, the Galileo process and Virtual Mentor tool were designed to allow for iterative rather than sequential input so as not to impede knowledge processes. A deep understanding of the front-end process allowed systematic support for and management of its inherent knowledge-intensive processes. Because knowledge develops over time through experience, the Galileo process and Virtual Mentor were designed to provide learning opportunities for process performers while doing their tasks. Nortel successfully created a support tool that embedded and integrated KM capabilities directly into the front-end NPD process.

4. *Take a broader view of process transformation and do not focus solely on knowledge needs and gaps.* Much has been made of the need to assess the "know-what" associated with the "know-how" in knowledge-intensive processes. However, knowledge needs and gaps provide only part of the picture. Other factors affect the use and creation of knowledge by individuals. To truly transform a process, other issues related to process tasks, performance specifications, consequences, and feedback should be considered, as they provide a deeper and broader view of the work and motivational environment in which performers create, share, and use knowledge. The EPSS paradigm for tool development provided Nortel with a useful approach to understanding and integrating the "performance systems" for each target audience. For example, Nortel discovered the importance of depicting information appropriately for each intended user by translating or restructuring content and providing associated context when required.

5. *Avoid "ownership" of the transformation efforts by a specific function.* The success of Nortel's business process transformation came from integrating a range of skills and expertise on the project team. The cross-functional team involved experts from software design and development, technology and marketing research, psychology, training and development, library science, and human factors. Complex interrelationships among people, process, and technology need to be addressed in a balanced manner. As such, transformation efforts must draw from a range of skills, independent from functional influence that may serve to upset the balance.

6. *Recognize that information technology is the medium, not the message, of process transformation.* Nortel deployed technology as an enabler of its new front-end NPD process such that the right information was available to the right performer at the right time, and each could add their insights and experience. Importantly, technology capabilities allow firms to access, embed, and transfer knowledge. As Nortel found, however, the real challenge lies with the complex interplay between content, context, and the performers who pull the business process pieces together. Technology in and of itself is not likely sufficient for effective process transformation. Rather, the key is to create links between technology and the performance system surrounding people. If technology supports the system, then people are more likely to use it.

7. *Strive for parsimony, not excess.* The support process and tool should not create information overload for the performers. It should reduce the time spent searching for information or sifting through irrelevant information to do one's job. The Galileo process and Virtual Mentor tool provided an unobtrusive, common framework for communication and analysis in the front end. Bells and whistles are impressive, but Nortel found that keeping the end-product simple and focused on core functionality was better received throughout the organization.

8. *Prototype fast and frequently.* During development, evolving prototypes of Virtual Mentor were presented for review and discussion to sponsoring executives, SMEs, and the targeted per-

formers. This ensured that the organizational strategy, performance objectives, business process, and supporting technology were in constant alignment. Rapid prototyping allowed for iterative design and development. It also allowed Nortel's personnel to be actively involved throughout the project, which, in turn, resulted in increased confidence in the process and resulting tool.

9. *Do not forget disciplined project management.* Nortel carefully defined the scope of the project, including preliminary and updated cost estimates and launch dates. This is important because sufficient resources are vital to a project's success. The development team was constantly vigilant about the scope of the project. There were many instances when the team was nudged in different directions and encouraged to broaden the scope. It is essential to avoid creep in project scope or it may become prohibitively costly and unwieldy. This can lead to a downward spiral of waning support for a behemoth, never-ending project. To maintain support for the project during development, the team regularly promoted its efforts using early prototypes while being mindful not to "oversell" the potential benefits. It is important to prepare employees for impending organizational or technical change early.

## CONCLUSION

Many organizations continue to search for ways to improve the performance of knowledge-intensive business processes. Oftentimes, these processes are highly unstructured, posing a particular challenge to BPR efforts. This chapter illustrates how a KM approach may facilitate transformation efforts. Guided by principles of KM, Nortel was able to transform the front-end of its NPD from a relatively ill-structured, ad hoc process to one that was consistent over time and across people. In doing so, Nortel could create, capture, transfer, and use its knowledge and NPD capabilities more effectively. Because new products and services are key drivers of growth for sales and profitability, particularly for firms facing intense competition and rapid technological change, creating process structure and providing support were of paramount importance. As illustrated in this chapter, the effective and integrated use of process and IT design was critical to transformation efforts. An awareness of potential opportunities created by IT capabilities can drive organizations to new technologies and shape strategic direction. Importantly, though, technology capabilities are only effective when there is alignment with the business and work processes that will make use of them. We hope that the insights offered in this chapter will help guide and encourage other firms in their own endeavors.

## ACKNOWLEDGMENTS

The research sponsorship of the Advanced Practices Council of SIM is gratefully acknowledged.

## NOTE

1. This name was chosen because Nortel needed a mechanism (like Galileo's telescope) that would enable it to see the "stars" (i.e., high-potential ideas) more clearly.

## REFERENCES

Alavi, M., and Leidner, D. 2001. Review: Knowledge management and knowledge management systems: Conceptual foundations and research issues. *MIS Quarterly,* 25, 1, 107–136.
Brown, L.A. 1996. *Designing and Developing Electronic Performance Support Systems.* Boston: Digital Press.

Cooper, R. 1993. *Winning at New Products.* Reading, MA: Addison-Wesley.

Cooper, R., and Kleinschmidt, E. 1986. Benchmarking the firm's critical success factors in new product development. *Journal of Product Innovation Management,* 3, 3, 71–85.

Crawford, M. 1994. *New Products Management.* Boston: Irwin.

Davenport, T.H.; DeLong, D.W.; and Beers, M.C. 1998. Successful knowledge management projects. *Sloan Management Review,* 39, 2, 43–57.

Fahey, L., and Prusak, L. 1998. The eleven deadliest sins of knowledge management. *California Management Review,* 40, 3, 265–276.

Gery, G. 1991. *Electronic Performance Support Systems: How and Why to Remake the Workplace Through the Strategic Application of Technology.* Tolland, MA: Ziff Institute.

———. 1997. Granting three wishes through performance-centered design. *Communications of the ACM,* 40, 7, 54–59.

Grover, V.; Kiedler, K.; and Teng, J. 1997. Empirical evidence on Swanson's tri-core model of information systems innovation. *Information Systems Research,* 8, 3, 273–287.

Karat, J. 1997. Evolving the scope of user-centered design. *Communications of the ACM,* 40, 7, 33–38.

Khurana, A., and Rosenthal, S. 1997. Integrating the fuzzy front-end of new product development. *Sloan Management Review,* 38, 2, 103–120.

Leonard, D., and Sensiper, S. 1998. The role of tacit knowledge in group innovation. *California Management Review,* 40, 3, 112–132.

Massey, A.P.; Montoya-Weiss, M.; and O'Driscoll, T. 2002. Knowledge management in pursuit of performance: Insights from Nortel Networks. *MIS Quarterly,* 26, 3, 269–289.

Nonaka, I., and Takeuchi, H. 1995. *The Knowledge Creating Company.* New York: Oxford University Press.

O'Dell, C., and Grayson, C.J. 1998. If only we knew what we know: Identification and transfer of internal best practices. *California Management Review,* 40, 3, 154–174.

Rangaswamy, A., and Lilien, G. 1997. Software tools for new product development. *Journal of Marketing Research,* 34, 2, 177–184.

Raybould, B. 1995. Performance support engineering: An emerging development methodology for enabling organizational learning. *Performance Improvement Quarterly,* 8, 1, 7–22.

Ruggles, R. 1998. The state of the notion: Knowledge management in practice. *California Management Review,* 40, 3, 80–89.

Rummler, G., and Brache, A. 1992. Transforming organizations through human performance technology. In H. Stolovitch and E. Keeps (eds.), *Handbook of Human Performance Technology.* San Francisco: Josey-Bass, pp. 32–49.

Schultz, U., and Leidner, D. 2002. Studying knowledge management in information systems research: Discourses and theoretical assumptions. *MIS Quarterly,* 26, 3, 213–242.

CHAPTER 10

# BUSINESS NETWORK REDESIGN METHODOLOGIES IN ACTION

## RAINER ALT

*Abstract:* *Business network redesign (BNR) has been regarded as the logical step following internal business process redesign. Several methodological approaches have emerged to support a variety of interorganizational redesign aspects. These cover either the allocation of responsibilities among the actors in a business network or the allocation of activities within an interorganizational business process. This chapter elaborates on the constitutional elements of BNR methods and uses them to analyze existing approaches. An important result is a methodology that consistently guides the transformation from a business and a technological perspective is still missing. In view of this deficit and the growing adoption of portal systems, this chapter presents a methodology for the implementation of portals in interorganizational business processes. An in-depth case study illustrates the transformation of the spare parts business at Watch Corp. Key enabler is a portal that has been integrated with a business network consisting of internal departments, external service providers, and suppliers. This research shows the application of BNR methodology at Watch Corp. and concludes with a call for more integrated models across the three architectural layers as well as for an integration of architecture and assessment models.*

*Keywords:* *Electronic Commerce, Business Network Redesign, Portal Engineering*

## FROM BUSINESS REENGINEERING TO BUSINESS NETWORK REDESIGN

Interorganizational relationships and interorganizational information systems (IOS) have been discussed extensively since the 1970s (e.g., Marrett, 1971; Stern and Craig, 1971). It is only now that they are converging with internal processes and the integrated information systems (IS) that were designed during the days of business process redesign (BPR) and enterprise resource planning (ERP) systems which emerged in the mid-1990s. The first reason for the late convergence is that many firms are still in the process of completing their internal reengineering and integration projects. Because external linkages have turned out to be technological, organizational, and political challenges, most companies were wary of involving additional external partners (Scheer and Habermann, 2000). Second, ERP systems were not originally designed for exchanging information with external partners (Luttighuis and Biemans, 2000). Due to a lack of standardized data and application interfaces as well as mechanisms for securely managing databases that are distributed among many companies, isolated and incompatible IS prevail, requiring time-consuming manual procedures and entailing problems of redundant information. From a business perspective, the consequences are inventories and long cycle times. For example, Champy (2002) estimated that total inventories in the value chain of the worldwide electronics and automotive industries at any given time top $1.3 trillion. Research has shown that information distortion is a main cause of these inefficiencies and that IOS such as electronic data interchange (EDI) are an effective remedy (Machuca and Barajas, 2004).

The convergence of Internet, ERP, and IOS technologies enables a powerful information infrastructure that has the potential to generate integrative effects in the interorganizational setting. Although BPR authors extended their concepts beyond corporate boundaries (e.g., Champy, 2002; Hammer, 2001a), shaping interorganizational interrelationships by means of information technology (IT) is not new. Ten years ago, Venkatraman (1994) conceived the redesign of (external) business networks as a logical next step in the redesign of cross-functional processes inside an organization (see Figure 10.1). Business network redesign (BNR) not only aims to make processes in existing relationships more efficient but also at changing the "underlying" relationships. Ultimately, new allocations of competencies may redefine roles in business networks and create the basis for new sources of competitive advantage (such as an enhanced service portfolio or reduced costs and cycle times). This evolution from internal to external redesign has been referred to as the *transformation trajectory* by Venkatraman (1994). Vertical disintegration and increased networking with partners may be observed in many industries. For example, the vertically integrated banking industry is increasingly externalizing processes that were considered as core in the past, such as processing payments or securities (Lammers et al., 2004). In the automotive industry, BMW outsourced the entire development and production of its X3 model to its Austrian supplier Magna Steyr (Edmondson, 2003).

IT acts as an important driver in these transformations. The electronic integration effect described by Malone et al. (1987) makes it possible to link the processes of geographically and institutionally distributed organizational units in much the same way as ERP systems have done in the internal arena. Vendors of packaged software such as SAP or Oracle are providing interorganizational connectivity by pursuing two directions: first, service-oriented architectures (Papazoglou and Georgakopoulos, 2003) enable machine-to-machine linkages by using standardized interfaces that follow industry norms. In standardizing processes and semantics, they go beyond the syntactical EDI standards and promise to lower interorganizational coordination costs as well as the degree of vertical integration (Hagel and Brown, 2001). Because service-oriented architectures are still immature and mainly target high-volume transactions with little variance, the second option for achieving interorganizational linkages are man-to-machine linkages. In this field, portal solutions integrate distributed applications via a common desktop. Portals are helpful in bundling functionalities from internal and external application systems according to various user roles. From a BNR perspective, portals are powerful instruments for making information from interorganizational processes available for the participants at little coordination cost (Dias, 2001).

Again, BNR is not primarily technological in nature as the transformation toward networked organizations requires a close alignment of these technologies with business strategies and processes. For this purpose, many classic BPR approaches have proposed methodologies that structure and guide the transformation. They decompose the projects into a suitable logic of activities and offer instruments that are useful in conducting the transformation. However, established BPR methodologies are limited in their treatment of the change in roles between business partners and in discovering services that could be offered within a business network. This is the area of BNR that includes *all methodological instruments for conceiving and improving business relationships and processes between companies*. Although BNR is also possible without IT to support it, such BNR

Figure 10.1 **Levels of IT-Enabled Business Transformation**

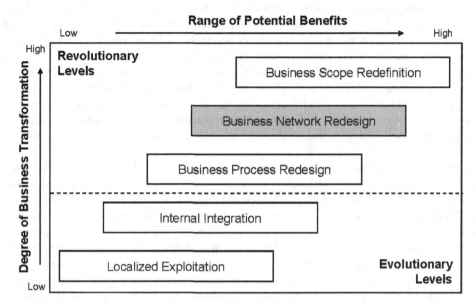

*Source:* Venkatraman (1994, p. 74, figure 1).

is excluded from the present discussion. Below, we establish elements from BPR methodologies that are combined with BNR-specific requirements to obtain criteria for analyzing existing BNR methodologies. We then describe and illustrate a methodology that shows how companies may transform their business network on various levels of design using portal solutions.

## APPROACHES TO BUSINESS NETWORK REDESIGN

As BNR is neither a new field in practice nor in research, a variety of methodologies are available today to address interorganizational redesign issues. The following section first derives redesign and methodological criteria that are used in a second step to compare established approaches.

### Elements of Redesign Methodologies

Methods and methodologies are used synonymously to define rules, tools, and the vocabulary to carry out a certain task. In software engineering, for example, "methodology is a codified set of practices (sometimes accompanied by training materials, formal educational programs, worksheets, and diagramming tools) that may be repeatably carried out to produce software" (Wikipedia, 2005). In BPR, methodologies have proved helpful to systematically address the critical design issues, to leverage experience in prior projects, and to ensure proper documentation for future projects. Comparisons of these methodologies show that, although they propose similar steps for proceeding in a BPR project, they differ in their level of detail and the operational project support. As described by Kettinger et al. (1997) and Motwani et al. (1998), we find conceptual frameworks, success stories ("how we did it"), project manuals, and checklists, as well as measurement methodologies such as benchmarking.

Most of these BPR approaches propose activities and a sequence for the redesign procedure that ranges from understanding a problem, to transformation, implementation, and, finally, evaluation (Motwani et al., 1998). Kettinger et al. (1997) discovered considerable differences regarding the (re)design objects and results that are usually shaped within each activity. For example, organizational forms, metrics, IS, or cultural issues are not explicitly considered in many approaches. In addition, the purpose of the various methodologies has to be taken into account. For example, software engineering distinguishes "thin" and "thick" methodologies. Whereas the former deliberately avoid high formalization and documentation, only the latter aim at developing a solution following engineering principles. Although each approach has its merits, this chapter concentrates on engineering methodologies that produce results that are comprehensive, reproducible, and traceable.

In analogy to the natural sciences, engineering approaches such as "business process reengineering" or "business engineering" (BE) go beyond thin methodologies such as success stories and top-level checklists. They support the staff involved in transformation projects with predefined templates for conducting, elaborating, and documenting the redesign activities. Although creativity and domain specificity call for a methodology's customization, engineering methodologies extensively structure the complexities of organizational transformation projects. Similar to a toolbox, they offer a broad coverage of the major transformation issues. The goal is to produce unambiguous results using a common language that facilitates the communication between people with heterogeneous backgrounds, an inherent feature in interorganizational relationships. Two established engineering approaches subsequently serve to derive the methodological design elements: BE for the redesign levels and method engineering (ME) for the methodological elements.

*Business Engineering*

A key idea of BE is to systematically develop a future business solution. It recognizes business processes as the main lever of change—that is, starting from a future process configuration, the implications are derived for business strategy and the required IS. The way in which this process vision is shaped has to be based on corporate strategy and include the new technological potential. Therefore, most BE methodologies (e.g., Janssen et al., 2003; Österle, 1995; van Meel and Sol, 1996) envisage the translation of top-level (strategic) requirements into specific process and systems architectures, thereby achieving an alignment of business and IT (Henderson and Venkatraman, 1999). Because processes are recognized as a separate dimension that connects business strategy and IT, BE methodologies often distinguish three levels—strategy, process, and (information) systems (e.g., Österle, 1995, p. 25). For formalization purposes, architectures that map the elements involved and show their interrelationships (Cook, 1996) are defined on each level. Achieving consistency across business, process, and systems architectures is an important goal in BE. Due to criticism regarding the neglect of "soft" issues that are critical in transformation processes, a change dimension has also been added to some BE methodologies, which addresses culture, values, and power bases.

*Method Engineering*

In addition to BE, ME is a field that ensures the systematic development of engineering-oriented methodologies (e.g., Brinkkemper, 1996; Heym and Österle, 1993). Following ME, methodologies consist of (1) A *procedure model* that defines the recommended sequence of activities within a transformation project. For example, a BPR methodology may start with a preliminary potential analysis, formulate a scenario of a redesigned process, and, finally, elaborate it in detailed architecture models. (2) Generic templates for these architectures are predefined as *result documents*. For example, the result documents of a BPR methodology are the process architecture showing all processes involved in the redesign effort or activity chains that detail the sequence of activities within a process. (3) To complete the result documents, *techniques* propose the necessary steps and provide useful hints. For example, a technique for designing an activity chain would provide guidance regarding the granularity of the steps and on how to derive them from a more general process architecture. (4) *Roles* describe which members of the organization (e.g., management or IT staff) are necessary in the project at a given stage. They are determined by the decisions that have to be made and the knowledge required to complete the result documents. (5) Finally, a *meta model* contains an ontology of the main design objects used in the result documents and describes the relationships between these objects. For example, a BPR method would specify that processes produce outputs and consist of various activities.

**Existing Approaches to BNR**

Available BNR methodologies come from diverse disciplines such as production operations management and logistics (e.g., inventory management), marketing (e.g., efficient consumer response), and information management (e.g., EDI, IOS) (Christiaanse and Kumar, 2000). Depending on their origins, the methodologies have been termed *interorganizational BPR* (Clark and Stoddard, 1996), *business network redesign* (Kambil and Short, 1994), *business network engineering* (Franken et al., 2000), *modular network design* (Hoogeweegen et al., 1999), *supply-chain restructuring* (Kopczak, 1997), *customer relationship reengineering* (Massey et al., 2001), *EDI-induced redesign* (Sheombar, 1997), or *supply-chain redesign* (Handfield and Nichols, 2002). These approaches are heterogeneous in nature and underscore the fact that an accepted methodology for BNR is yet to emerge. The differences are analyzed below with respect to four areas—unit of analysis, scope of redesign, methodological support, and assessment criteria. Figure 10.2 provides a summary of 17 approaches.

*Unit of Analysis*

Following the emerging theories on IOS, several units of analysis may be distinguished when shaping interorganizational relationships. For example, the model of Gregor and Johnston (2001) consists of an enterprise and an industry group as well as an external environment perspective. Reimers (2002) goes further and describes four units of analysis: (1) the individual transactions on an operational level; (2) the longer-term business relationships, which include a set of transactions; (3) the focal firm and the supply chain, which covers multiple relationships; and (4) entire industries, markets, and economies, which include multiple supply chains. Among the BNR approaches two clusters may be observed: institutional approaches, which focus on determining the actors within a network, and process-oriented approaches, which discuss the distribution of activities within a specific process.

Institutional BNR approaches address the distribution of roles between companies and the shape of organizational forms. The major design elements are the companies involved in business networks, the nature of relationships between these actors, each player's role, and the major services provided within the business network. For example, Short and Venkatraman (1992) describe the implications of Baxter's ordering system for industry structure. Multiple market-like supplier relationships were redesigned to become longer-term cooperative arrangements. From

Figure 10.2 **Assessment of BNR Approaches**

| Redesign Approach | Unit of Analysis | | Scope of Redesign | | | Methodological Support | | | | | | | | Assessment Criteria | |
|---|---|---|---|---|---|---|---|---|---|---|---|---|---|---|---|
| | Network | Process | Strategic | Efficiency | Change | Strategy | Process | System | Meta Model | Result Docs | Role Model | Proc. Model | Techniques | Qualitative | Quantitative |
| Short and Venkatraman (1992) | √ | X | √ | X | X | √ | X | ∀ | X | ∀ | X | X | X | √ | X |
| Kambil and Short (1994) | √ | √ | √ | X | X | √ | X | X | X | ∀ | ∀ | X | X | √ | X |
| Clark and Stoddard (1996) | X | √ | X | √ | X | X | ∀ | X | X | X | X | X | X | X | √ |
| Kopczak (1997) | X | √ | X | √ | X | √ | X | X | X | ∀ | X | ∀ | X | X | √ |
| Sheombar (1997) | X | √ | X | √ | X | ∀ | X | X | X | X | X | X | X | X | √ |
| Hoogeweegen et al. (1999) | ∀ | √ | ∀ | √ | X | ∀ | ∀ | X | X | ∀ | ∀ | ∀ | ∀ | ∀ | ∀ |
| Christiaanse and Kumar (2000) | ∀ | ∀ | ∀ | ∀ | X | ∀ | ∀ | ∀ | X | ∀ | ∀ | √ | X | ∀ | X |
| Klein and Schad (1997) | √ | √ | √ | ∀ | ∀ | ∀ | √ | √ | X | ∀ | X | X | X | √ | ∀ |
| van der Vorst and Beulens (1999) | X | √ | X | √ | X | ∀ | ∀ | ∀ | X | ∀ | X | X | X | ∀ | X |
| Franken et al. (2000) | √ | √ | √ | √ | X | ∀ | √ | √ | X | X | X | X | X | X | X |
| Hammer (2001b) | ∀ | √ | X | √ | X | √ | ∀ | X | X | X | X | ∀ | X | ∀ | X |
| Piccoli et al. (2001) | X | √ | ∀ | X | X | X | ∀ | X | X | X | X | X | X | ∀ | X |
| Kenyon and Vakola (2001) | X | √ | √ | X | X | X | ∀ | ∀ | X | X | X | X | X | ∀ | X |
| Massey et al. (2001) | X | √ | X | √ | X | X | ∀ | ∀ | X | X | X | X | X | X | ∀ |
| Frank (2002) | X | √ | X | √ | X | X | ∀ | ∀ | ∀ | √ | X | ∀ | X | X | X |
| Handfield and Nichols (2002) | ∀ | √ | X | √ | ∀ | X | √ | X | X | X | X | ∀ | X | X | ∀ |
| Toncia (2004) | X | √ | X | √ | X | ∀ | √ | X | X | √ | X | √ | √ | X | X |

*Notes:* √ existing; ∀ partially existing; X not or only rudimentary existing.

the methodological perspective, the work of Kambil and Short (1994) goes beyond mapping the actors and the flows of goods. Their "roles linkage model" (upper half of Figure 10.3) provides a framework for structuring the coordination mechanisms ("linkages") among the various roles in a given industry. To determine the type of linkage, a decision tree based on transaction cost economics is used. Although the "roles linkage model" is useful in mapping relationships and their institutionalization, it does not lead to more detailed specifications at the process and systems levels.

By contrast, process-oriented approaches focus on (re)designing the activities and flows between organizations. Most process-oriented approaches visualize how activities are linked by flows of information and physical goods. As Clark and Stoddard (1996) illustrated, the largest impact on business performance is created when innovations in IT and processes occur in tandem (see also Clark and Hammond, 1997); for example, a new process scheme such as continuous replenishment combined with the introduction of EDI. Most process-oriented BNR approaches focus separately on designing information processing (coordination) and physical activities. They cover the well-known redesign activities (parallelize, sequence, eliminate, combine) and identify suitable forms of organization (e.g., internal, market, cooperation) (e.g., Christiaanse and Kumar, 2000; Klein and Schad, 1997; Sheombar, 1997). The lower part of Figure 10.3 shows the allocation of activities within a transportation process where an air cargo carrier has integrated the forwarder activities (Hoogeweegen et al., 1999). Contributions from the logistics area mainly focus on redesigning transaction processes, whereas authors from the marketing field choose similar procedures from a customer perspective (Kenyon and Vakola, 2001; Massey et al., 2001; Piccoli et al., 2001). Here, the contact points to the company—that is, the individual steps in the customer process—are investigated with respect to possible improvements.

*Scope of Redesign*

A second way to analyze BNR methodologies concerns the *scope of redesign*. Typically, radical approaches to process redesign lead to the formulation of new strategies, and gradual approaches lead to enhanced efficiencies. Christiaanse and Kumar observed that the literature on process-oriented BNR "takes the existing supply chain as given and attempts to optimize either the material and information flows, or inter-partner relationships in the extant supply chain structures" (2000, p. 269). Some authors note similar risks in classic BPR, where radical redesign claims are sacrificed for gradual changes (Jarvenpaa and Stoddard, 1998). Because institutional BNR approaches use relationships and networks as their main unit of analysis, changes in this "big picture" (e.g., adding new types of partners) are more likely to have a radical effect than isolated improvements of transactions, which are the domain of the more operational process-oriented approaches. The latter are vital for identifying the potential for efficiency gains (e.g., eliminating manual reentry of data) and competitive advantage within a given strategic option shaped by institutional approaches (e.g., creating new services for an activity in the customer process). In this sense, Klein and Schad (1997) conceive interorganizational BPR as changes in stable long-term networks with existing partners and BNR as changes in networks that involve new partners.

Both views are not mutually exclusive. Redesign projects often start by developing the "big picture" followed by elaborating a specific or multiple "to-be" scenarios. For example, Hammer (2001b) recommended first selecting "high-level" process candidates (processes with high internal efficiency potential and a suitable partner), then determining the form of institutionalization (e.g., a joint steering committee), and finishing with traditional redesign and stepwise implementation.

214

Figure 10.3 **Examples for BNR Documentation**

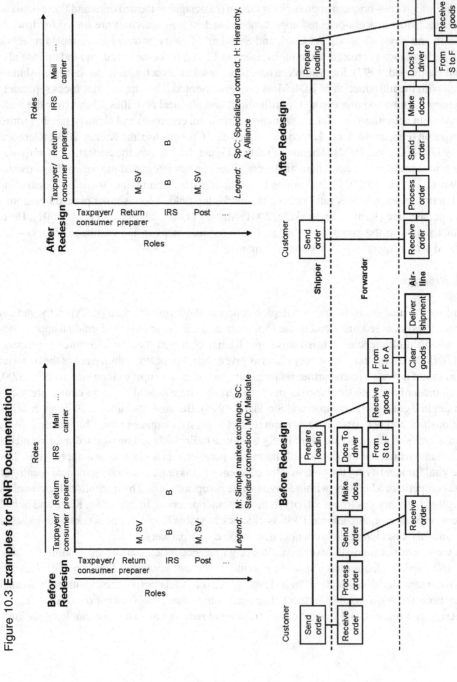

*Sources:* Kambil and Short (1994, p. 71) (top); Hoogeweegen et al. (1999, p. 1086) (bottom).

*Methodological Support*

A third way to analyze BNR methodologies picks up on the elements of an engineering-oriented methodology. As described above, four redesign levels (strategy, process, systems, and change) and five methodology elements (procedure model, techniques, result documents, role, and meta model) may be distinguished here. Using these criteria, most of the 17 BNR approaches investigated (see Figure 10.2) focus on one level and neglect the methodological elements. Initial explanations are the narrative nature of some contributions and the focus on quantitative models of others.

The analysis on the redesign level shows an interrelationship with the unit of analysis and highlights the fact that most approaches are limited to either the strategic or the process level. Although many approaches recognize the relevance of IT, they often neglect the formulation of system architectures. Only the approaches of Frank (2002) and Franken et al. (2000) feature an integrated and coherent picture across several levels. These models not only enable the design of strategies, processes, and systems issues, but they also make it possible to handle interrelationships, such as indicating the implications of a direct sales strategy for the application architecture. Although they are helpful in the documentation of redesign projects, they provide neither an explicit redesign procedure nor metrics for comparing the solutions developed. In addition, predefined scenarios that reduce the effort involved in negotiating a new interorganizational solution with regard to pragmatics, semantics, and syntax are not available. Here, a combination with standardization initiatives such as RosettaNet or BPEL (business process execution language) is required.

Even more heterogeneity may be observed when looking at the methodology elements of the BNR approaches. Only one contribution from the modeling area explicitly mentioned a meta model (Frank, 2002), and only one provided techniques for more detailed guidance during the redesign project (Toncia, 2004). Most authors present a top-level procedure model consisting of four to ten activities (e.g., Handfield and Nichols, 2002; Hoogeweegen et al., 1999; Kenyon and Vakola, 2001; Piccoli et al., 2001; Toncia, 2004; Van der Vorst and Beulens, 1999). Result documentation is also a part of many methodologies. However, architecture models that are integrated and consistent across multiple design levels are rare (e.g., Frank, 2002; Franken et al., 2000; Toncia, 2004). Most methodologies use documentation to illustrate exemplary results on the redesign level they emphasize, but they are not claiming to provide a generalized modeling language. This may also explain why explicit meta models are rare. Other missing elements are role models and techniques. Both deliver operational support in projects and are usually contained in more comprehensive handbooks that are not available in the BNR area.

*Assessment Criteria*

A fourth way to analyze BNR methodologies relates to how the advantages of a new solution are determined. These criteria may be qualitative or quantitative in nature. Qualitative approaches mainly apply transaction cost theory (e.g., Christiaanse and Kumar, 2000; Klein and Schad, 1997), whereas more quantitative approaches use process measures such as throughput time, process costs, or inventory levels (e.g., Hoogeweegen et al., 1999; Kopczak, 1997; Van der Vorst and Beulens, 1999). There is a correlation between institutional BNR approaches and the use of qualitative metrics as well as between process-oriented BNR approaches and quantitative measurements. In view of the unconnected architecture models on the strategy and process level, aligned redesign criteria are still lacking.

In summary, existing BNR approaches paint a heterogeneous picture. The documentation of changes with regard to the business partners involved, their roles and responsibilities, or the activities these actors perform seems to be the least common denominator. While the IOS literature focuses on institutional BNR, the enhanced BPR approaches concentrate on procedure models for developing lean integrated processes, and the logistics literature focuses on measuring and simulating future process designs. Due to the partial representation of IT issues, new technological developments, such as portals or service-oriented architectures, are not systematically included.

**Structure of a BNR Method**

The following discussion describes a first step toward a BNR methodology that addresses many of the shortcomings that were identified above. In view of the broad BNR field, several requirements were necessary. The methodology should (1) be relevant to practice, (2) cover strategy-oriented redesign of networks as well as efficiency-oriented redesign of processes, and (3) provide broad coverage of redesign levels and methodological elements (combined as methodological support). Although a list of qualitative and quantitative redesign criteria has been used to assess the "to-be" scenarios, the focus was not on developing mathematical optimization models.

*Research Methods*

To ensure a close link to requirements in practice, a research methodology was chosen that uses elements from action research (Checkland and Holwell, 1998) and design science (Hevner et al., 2004). The former postulates that the researcher becomes part of the project team and refines his or her findings in multiple iterations with the team members. The latter explicitly recognizes artifacts such as architectures, methodologies, or prototypes as legitimate outcomes of scientific research besides the more theory-oriented behavioral styles used in the natural sciences. For the present research, this implied a close collaboration with nine companies[1] during a two-year multilateral project (Alt et al., 2001). The researchers were involved in bilateral projects with each company, which also comprised designing parts of the solution. The case of Watch Corp. included in the remainder of this chapter describes the activities undertaken in one of these bilateral projects. Experiences from all bilateral projects were generalized and verified in quarterly workshops with representatives from all nine partner companies. This led to the formulation of the BNR methodology for portals described in this chapter.

*Unit of Analysis and Scope of Redesign*

The comparison of BNR methodologies above showed an interrelationship between the unit of analysis and the scope of redesign. Approaches that focused on the network as unit of analysis also had a strategic scope of redesign. Likewise, process-oriented approaches concentrated on (gradual) redesign within a specific process. In a first step, the criteria unit of analysis and scope of redesign were combined. A second step established a link to customer-oriented process portals: customer orientation was regarded as a main strategic BNR driver and process portals as an efficient means to implement this vision.

Customer orientation is a classic strategic goal for redesign efforts. According to Davenport, "processes at the customer interface are perhaps the most critical to an organization's success" (1993, p. 270). As described by Treacy and Wiersema (1993), customer intimacy is one strategic option for attaining market leadership alongside product leadership and operational efficiency. Building on these strategies, Hagel and Singer (1999) explained that traditional companies consist of three businesses that, due to their incompatible goals, will lead to an unbundling in the future. The customer relationship business will evolve separately from the product innovation and infrastructure businesses. This chapter only focuses on customer relationship businesses that "seek to offer a customer as many products and services as possible" (Hagel and Singer, 1999, p. 136). Because these offerings are often highly customized, these companies are also referred to as service integrators (Österle, 2001) or orchestrators (Hinterhuber, 2002). Following the literature on customer relationship management (CRM) (Romano and Fjermestad, 2002), customer business networks generate customer value by closely supporting customer processes.

Portals are important in bundling content from heterogeneous sources to support users who fulfill a certain role. Following Kalakota and Robinson, they offer an "aggregated set of services for a specific well-defined group of users" (2001, p. 87). For this purpose, standard portal software packages feature navigation, interaction, personalization, security, as well as user administration functionalities (e.g., Davydov, 2001; Dias, 2001). Besides popular theme and search portals such as Yahoo! and Google, process portals have emerged as a type of portal that provides support along the business processes of specific user groups (Puschmann and Alt, 2005). Customer process portals bundle services along the entire customer life cycle (CRLC) (e.g., Lightner, 2004; Piccoli et al., 2001) from applications that are internal as well as external to the company running the portal and provide a single point of contact. Redesigning these processes means obtaining an in-depth understanding of customer problems and creating enhanced customer value via (electronic) services within the process portal (Österle, 2001).

*Methodological Support*

Following BE and ME, engineering-oriented methodologies consist of redesign levels and methodological elements. The former structure the relevant redesign issues. On the strategy level, the business network is analyzed with regard to actors and customer segments, as well as the flow of goods and information. On the process level, the front-end and back-end processes are modeled together with the required services. On the systems level, the (technological) portal architecture specifies the internal and external application and integration components. The latter define the building blocks of the methodology. As shown in Figure 10.4, the procedure model comprises the three phases business network strategy, business network processes, and business network architecture. Each contains two techniques that describe the activities for completing result documents. The case study in the following section goes through each technique and presents exemplary result documents.

Each technique also comprises a role model that shows the necessary participants within each organization. As the role models are similarly structured, only an exemplary specification will be included in this chapter (see Table 10.1). On one hand, the general roles within a project are listed (e.g., moderator, decision maker, supporter) and, on the other hand, the roles relating to the portal's design (portal initiator, portal partner). The methodology recognizes that portal partners are important for preparing the successful roll out of a final solution (Czuchry and Yasin, 2003).

Finally, the meta model depicts the constituent parts of the methodology. Figure 10.5 shows the meta model at all redesign levels with its entities and relationships. Because the formal requirements of architectural design are not applicable to the change level, the meta model is limited to the levels strategy, process, and systems that are also discussed in the case study of Watch Corp.

## Business Network Redesign at Watch Corp.

As mentioned earlier, the BNR methodology for process portals is based on close collaboration with nine companies. It reflects the experiences obtained in bilateral projects that all started from the same methodological foundation—that is, BE and ME. The following provides an overview

Figure 10.4 **Procedure Model of the BNR Method**

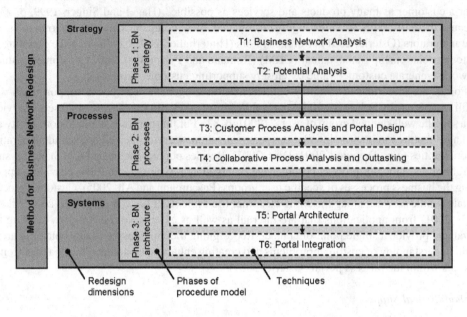

Table 10.1

**Roles of "T3: Customer Process Analysis and Portal Design"**

| Roles in General | Portal Initiator | Portal Partners |
|---|---|---|
| Moderator | Internal or external consultant | |
| Decision Maker | Management representative (marketing and sales) | Management representative |
| Responsible Person | Managers of marketing, sales, customer service departments | Managers of procurement and other departments involved in portal usage |
| Supporter | CIO, representative of IT department | CIO, representative of IT department |

of the major activities and result documents that are contained within each phase of the procedure model (see Figure 10.4). To understand the case, the next subsection introduces the company as well as the main problems prior to BNR.

*Company Profile and Initial Situation*

Watch Corp. is one of the world's largest manufacturers of watch movements. The company has more than 15 production sites in Switzerland, Germany, France, Thailand, Malaysia, and China. About 8,000 people are employed worldwide with movements and spare parts being supplied to several internal and external watchmakers (brands). Watch Corp. is a subsidiary of a watchmaking group that comprises a variety of watch brands as well as products in the area of microelectronics, micromechanics, and telecommunications. The focus of this case study is the distribution of spare

Figure 10.5 **Meta Model on Upper Level**

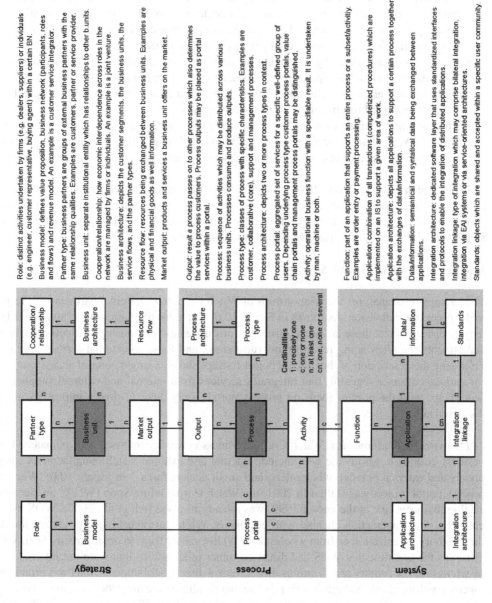

**Strategy**

Role: distinct activities undertaken by firms (e.g. dealers, suppliers) or individuals (e.g. engineer, customer representative, buying agent) within a certain BN.

Business model: defines value proposition, business network (participants, roles and flows) and revenue model. An example is a customer service integrator.

Partner type: business partners are groups of external business partners with the same relationship qualities. Examples are customers, partner or service provider.

Business unit: separate institutional entity which has relationships to other b.units.

Cooperation/relationship: how economic interdependence across roles in the network are managed by firms or individuals. An example is a joint venture.

Business architecture: depicts the customer segments, the business units, the service flows, and the partner types.

Resource flow: resources being exchanged between business units. Examples are physical and financial goods as well information.

Market output: products and services a business unit offers on the market.

**Process**

Output: result a process passes on to other processes which also determines the value to process customers. Process outputs may be placed as portal services within a portal.

Process: sequence of activities which may be distributed across various business units. Processes consume and produce outputs.

Process type: classes of process with specific characteristics. Examples are customer, collaborative (core), support and management processes.

Process architecture: depicts two or more process types in context.

Process portal: aggregated set of services for a specific well-defined group of users. Depending underlying process type customer process portals, value chain portals and management process portals may be distinguished.

Activity: operational business function with a specifiable result. It is undertaken by man, machine or both.

**Cardinalities**
1: precisely one
c: one or none
n: at least one
cn: one, none or several

**System**

Function: part of an application that supports an entire process or a subset/activity. Examples are order entry or payment processing.

Application: combination of all transactions (computerized procedures) which are implemented on an IS to support a given area of work.

Application architecture: depicts all applications to support a certain process together with the exchanges of data/information.

Data/information: semantical and syntatical data being exchanged between applications.

Integration architecture: dedicated software layer that uses standardized interfaces and protocols to enable the integration of distributed applications.

Integration linkage: type of integration which may comprise bilateral integration, integration via EAI systems or via service-oriented architectures.

Standards: objects which are shared and accepted within a specific user community.

parts from Watch Corp.'s customer service department (WCS) to business customers worldwide. WCS is responsible for the worldwide sales of watch spare parts, movement repairs, and technical customer service. In 1996, WCS conducted customer interviews and internal process analyses that yielded the following problems:

- As many watch movement components were not only used in one movement ("caliber") but in an entire caliber family, customers had no information about the interchangeability of (spare) parts. Frequently, they lacked up-to-date technical documentation, including exploded diagrams and drawings of individual parts plus service instructions.
- Customers often ordered by describing the required products over the telephone or by fax. WCS then had to find the appropriate part numbers. The consequences were high lead times for orders as well as frequent misunderstandings and incorrect deliveries. Long cycle times were also reported for the repair of watch movements.
- There was no transparency regarding the status of spare parts and repair orders for either customers or WCS staff. In the absence of IT support, article master data were merely recorded in an index card system, and even pricing and discounts were neither uniform nor transparent.

When Watch Corp. started its BNR project in 1996, the highest-ranked strategic goals were to create a new distribution strategy for spare parts and to install a new distribution channel for spare parts. Ultimately, WCS was to be positioned as a service center for spare parts that efficiently handles all of the needs of a customer within his or her spare parts business.

*Redesign of Business Network Strategy*

The strategy level analyzes the relationships of Watch Corp. to its external partners with respect to the process portal vision. As shown in Figure 10.6, four areas of relationships (numbered 1–4) may be distinguished: those facing the customer (downstream), relationships with other (internal) departments, supplier-facing relationships (upstream), and those to external service providers. Following the description of the process portal concept above, a single point of access is created for various customer segments that integrates services from internal and external suppliers. In accordance with the present focus on process portals, only these IT-driven improvements are discussed next.

*Downstream Relationships.* Watch Corp.'s business network comprises approximately 1,500 business customers worldwide who include internal and external watch manufacturers (group brands and external brands), wholesalers, and small dealers (area 1 in Figure 10.6). When the process portal project was started in 2001, the Watch Corp. Online Shop (WOS), an electronic catalog that went live at the end of 1999, was already in place (Alt et al., 2002). WOS mainly created a direct interaction channel with customers. While customers usually ordered through their country organization or from wholesalers, WOS enabled them to order directly from WCS. This was the first time that WCS had direct customer relationships that were not intermediated by wholesalers or country organizations. In addition, a direct distribution channel was established together with a centralized high-bay warehouse that eliminated the inventory of country organizations and reduced wholesalers' stocks to some extent as well. By 2002, approximately 60 percent of all spare parts transactions were handled via WOS. However, WOS mainly covered transaction handling, and activities before as well as after the purchase were not being addressed. In order to shift more transactions to the electronic channel, Watch Corp. management decided to design

Figure 10.6 **Business Network of Watch Corp. and BNR Areas**

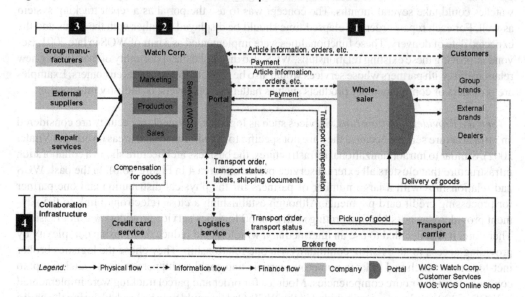

*Legend:* ——► Physical flow   ---► Information flow   ·····► Finance flow   ▮ Company   ◗ Portal   WCS: Watch Corp.
Customer Services
WOS: WCS Online Shop

a process portal that would enhance the WOS and establish closer ties to customers. A first rough segmentation distinguished four customer segments: (1) potential customers, that is, unregistered users; (2) registered component customers, that is, the dealers worldwide and external watchmakers; (3) other business units within Watch Corp., that is, production or sales; and (4) the internal WCS staff. By offering customized services for these customer segments, an intensified interaction was to be obtained via the process portal. Thus, the strategy was not primarily to attract new customers but rather to strengthen existing relationships and to make them more efficient. The first version of the Watch Corp. Customer Portal (WCP) went live on February 6, 2004, and approximately 70 percent of the entire parts transaction volume was handled via the electronic channel until late 2004.

*Internal Relationships.* Although WCP was conceptualized by WCS, the claim to cover large parts of the user processes called for closer relationships to internal departments—namely, marketing, production, and sales (area 2 in Figure 10.6). In particular, these departments started their individual IT projects in the late 1990s: marketing created a master database of all Watch Corp. products (e.g., article numbers, technical specifications, and drawings), production implemented an ERP system to handle the entire order process for nonspare parts, and sales worked on a solution for CRM. As information on products, orders, and customers, to a large extent, was stored redundantly in the WOS, regular meetings were initiated with these departments. On one hand, the portal should enable users from other departments within Watch Corp. to easily access spare parts information and, on the other hand, it should integrate information from other departments' IS on an automated basis. While a dedicated integration project was started for the ERP system, the areas of a joint master database for product data and the implementation of a CRM strategy were left to a later integration step.

*Upstream Relationships.* It is in the nature of the spare parts business that demand is in small quantities and unstable across products. Because most parts of watch movements are made in-house, external supplier relationships of the WCS (area 3 in Figure 10.6) are limited to subcontractors for

the repair of watches. These relationships were highly intransparent and the repair of expensive watches could take several months. The concept was to use the portal as a repair tracking system as well. For each repair order the elapsed time should be displayed together with the status and the expected date of delivery. These functionalities were implemented as a part of WOS in late 2001. Beyond improving these existing relationships, WCS also discussed the opportunity of establishing new relationships with partners whose services would also be relevant to spare parts customers. Examples are providers of complementary products such as batteries, top covers, or industry information.

*Service Provider Relationships.* Services such as logistics, payment, or security are considered an infrastructure service because they are not specific to certain functional areas (Weill and Vitale, 2002). Similar to intraorganizational infrastructures, the business architecture shows a collaboration infrastructure that clusters all external service providers (area 4 in Figure 10.6). In the past, WCS had relationships with a large number of partners for the physical distribution and one partner for processing credit card payments. Although establishing a close (electronic) link to the payment provider was possible, integrating with over 50 logistics service providers was not feasible. Therefore, it was decided to use an intermediary, which would reduce relationship complexity by providing access to an existing community via one relationship. They chose the logistics broker inet-logistics, which had links to numerous carriers and enables shippers such as Watch Corp. to concentrate on their core competencies. Modules for order and parcel tracking were implemented in WOS in 2001 and were also included in the WCP. Orders could now be tracked during the entire order cycle, including the activities of the various logistics providers.

**Redesign of Business Network Processes**

From a strategic viewpoint, the existing relationships within Watch Corp.'s business network shifted toward more cooperative arrangements with new relationships being added on the supplier and service provider side. Pursuing the WCP vision was an important driver that was continued in greater depth on the process level. Two main categories of processes were distinguished: (1) customer processes, which relate to the user's activities at the front end or the customer interface, and (2) collaborative processes, which integrate internal processes and those of suppliers and external service providers (Holstrom et al., 2002). Following the procedure model in Figure 10.4, a separate technique was defined for both categories.

*Customer Processes*

Watch Corp. started the customer process analysis in 2001 with a workshop that brought together several representatives from all four customer segments defined at the strategy level. The purpose was to obtain detailed opinions from potential portal users regarding the goals and the services they associated with the portal as well as to understand the work situations that should be supported by the portal. This analysis included:

- *The collection of the portal goals and drivers.* Each representative was asked to formulate his expectations regarding the portal and to assess potentials and inhibitors. The goals included projecting a more professional image toward customers, achieving higher process transparency, and the fact that IT operations had to remain inside WCS. So-called portal drivers were used to structure the factors that positively or negatively affected the process portal's implementation and adoption. The answers were clustered in six categories such as technological, political, or project drivers for that purpose.

Table 10.2

**Customer Process Categories and Customer Requirements**

| Customer Process Category | Services Required by Customers |
|---|---|
| Technological Support | Technological information, inventory and stock policy, support of watch development, technological FAQs, insert manuals, information on reported problems, complaints management |
| Product Information | Availability of discontinued movements, new movements in the program, production plans and capacities |
| Sales (order processing/transport) | Interchangeability of parts, parcel tracking, available to promise, order tracking, personalized shopping basket, credit card payment, tool catalog, delivery and payment conditions |
| Marketing | Events, industry news, magazines/links, reference list |
| Repair | Repair tracking, classification of defects, chat forum |
| Financial information | Customer turnover, customer profile |
| Company information | Company presentation, contact partner, location, telephone list, addresses, process maps |

- *The definition of the customer process vision.* In a next step, a catalog of potential services that could be offered in a process portal was identified. This led to several customer process categories that are summarized together with the individual services in Table 10.2.
- *The documentation of typical customer processes per customer segment.* Classical context diagrams that show one process with its process environment (Österle, 1995, p. 79) were enhanced to include the eight to ten most important activities of one customer process. These served to document the operational processes of each customer segment. The typical daily work processes were used to derive the customer process. An example of the customer segment "component customer" is shown in Figure 10.7. The picture can be supplemented with a separate table that helps to document and prioritize each service in more detail.
- *The identification of portal services and categories.* Using future customer process categories and the customer process steps, the portal services were identified and grouped in portal categories (see Figure 10.7). For the portal categories, two design decisions were necessary. The first concerned which customer segment should be authorized to access a certain category and to what extent. For example, potential customers should only access public categories ("About WCS," "Help&Contact," "News&Links"), component customers could also access the categories "Products&Services," and internal WCS users could access all functionalities except "Products&Ordering." The second decision referred to how the categories are linked. One option is a loose collection of links such as the Yahoo! Catalog; another is a tight coupling as a work flow. WCS used work flows for ordering procedures that were already defined in the WOS, and all other services were implemented as link collections.

*Collaborative Processes*

Compared to the redesign of (vertical) customer processes, the *collaboration process analysis* discusses the (horizontal) design of processes across the internal and upstream network. Figure 10.8 visualizes the main transaction processes order planning and order execution with an emphasis on the electronic support and the organizational boundary. A large number of IT-supported activities

Figure 10.7 **Customer Process Architecture at WCS**

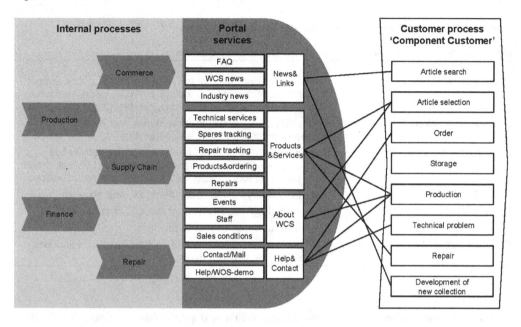

Figure 10.8 **Collaboration Processes at WCS**

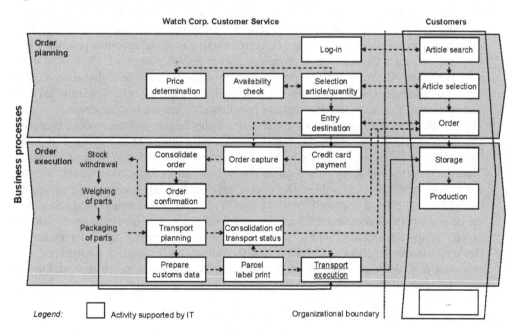

indicate efficient "real-time processes," and the number of interactions at the interface between WCS and the customers indicates a strong involvement of the customer.

To identify activities in customer and collaboration processes that may be outsourced to external service providers, Keen and McDonald (2000) suggested the concept of *outtasking*—that is, small standardized activities performed by external providers that are tightly integrated in the overall process. Watch Corp.'s goal was to keep core activities in-house and to externalize standard services. Services with a high potential for outtasking were those that (1) were not electronically available in-house, but were required by customers; (2) were already available externally on a time or transaction basis; (3) had low resource specificity; and (4) were not strategically relevant. Among the candidates for outtasking within the customer process category were services for article availability, credit card payment, order tracking, industry information, and magazines/links. Examples in the collaboration processes included transport planning, parcel label print, transport documentation, preparation of customs data, and consolidation of order status via multiple transport carriers.

When selecting the providers for services with a high outtasking potential, the external service fees were compared against today's costs, which were calculated from cost center accounting, personnel costs, material costs, and transaction volume. For example, a parcel delivery was not to exceed CHF 30 (USD 23). In addition to cost, criteria such as economic stability of the provider, reference customers, and security levels were evaluated. Today, two external services are used: inet-logistics in the logistics area and Telekurs Card Solutions for credit card and electronic payments. Implementing these partners was not a "plug-and-play" procedure but required a joint project effort. Figures 10.9 and 10.10 indicate significant changes in the collaborative processes with the future activity chain featuring more IT-supported and parallelized activities. At first sight, this implied more complexity because increased interaction occurred between the actors involved and because additional activities were integrated. This is also in line with the shift toward structures with higher coordination intensity as suggested by Malone et al. (1987), which, in the end, has the potential to yield more customer value. In fact, the following benefits were observed at Watch Corp.

- The electronic catalog reduced article search times per order position by 90 percent due to unique article identifiers in the order process and the elimination of mapping efforts into Watch Corp.'s internal numbering system.
- The integration of the logistics provider reduced the time to complete transport documents by 10 minutes per document.
- Customer inquiries at the call center, which amounted to an average of 15 minutes per call, were reduced due to the available tracking functionalities that substituted most telephone contacts.
- Finally, total order cycle time (time span between order entry and invoice date) was reduced by at least 60 percent. In view of delivery times of two weeks or more in the past, this turned out to be an important selling proposition for the electronic channel.

**Redesign of Business Network Systems**

As outlined above, the first step toward BNR was the implementation of the WOS in 1998. At that time, the decision was made in favor of a proprietary shop solution because the "time to market" of a packaged and integrated solution was estimated as longer and the initial transaction volumes were estimated as low. Although this solution was enhanced twice (versions 2 and 3), additional functionalities and external content (e.g., industry information, events, and experiences) were dif-

## Figure 10.9 **Activity Chain for Order Execution at WCS Without Outtasking**

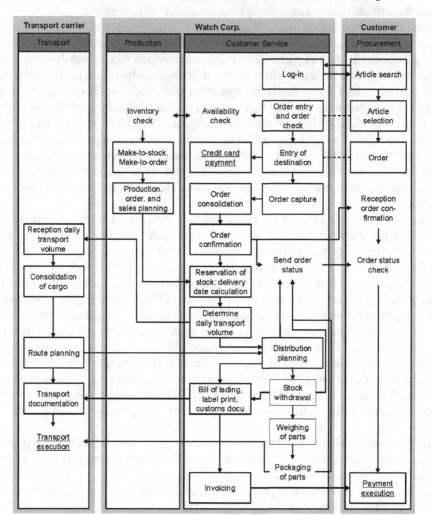

*Legend:* ☐ Activity supported by IT   ⟶ Sequential execution of activities   - - - - Parallel execution of activities

ficult to include. For the design and implementation of a portal-based systems architecture (see Figure 10.11), three major steps were taken.[2]

First, the functional requirements for the process portal were derived from the process architecture and used in the evaluation of the portal software and the possible WOS migration paths. The evaluation list initially contained seven software providers. Three of them were short-listed in a preliminary analysis. In the second round, the detailed provider was evaluated jointly by WCS and brand representatives. In addition to the three providers from the first WCS evaluation, the brands put forward another two providers. The best to emerge from the five alternatives was Microsoft's Commerce Server 2002 as a shop application in combination with the open source portal application IBuySpy from Microsoft. A Microsoft SQL database contained the portal content, and Microsoft Active Directory Services were used for user management.

Figure 10.10 **Activity Chain for Order Execution at WCS with Outtasking**

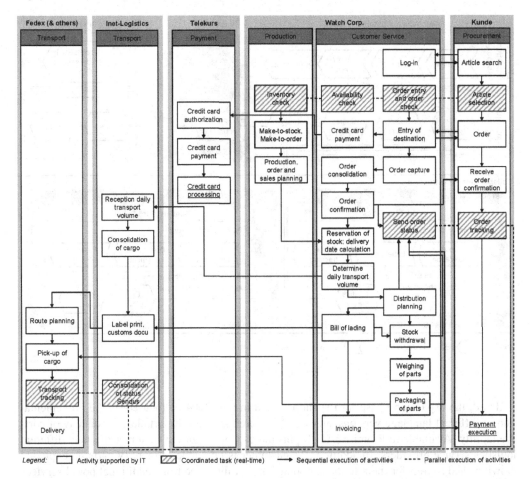

Second, after the software platform decision, interfaces with both internal systems and with applications from external service providers were designed. The existing WOS and the different tracking modules were integrated into the Watch Spares Portal (WSP) and the proprietary WOS (Active Server Pages on Site Server Commerce Edition) being migrated to the MS Commerce Server. When implementing the portal application, the front-end design was aligned with corporate identity, and portal services were matched with preconfigured portal modules. During this period, members of WCS worked closely with the IT department. After integrating the back end (WOS, tracking systems), the portal implementation was finished within 18 months, and the WSP went live on February 6, 2004. As version 1.0 comprised only the most important services, such as technical documents, mailings (referred to as "CS News"), or price lists, the next steps were to include the services with the next highest priority. The first expansion of WOS V3.0 was completed at the end of July 2004 and covered the migration to MS Commerce Server 2002, a graphic redesign and integration into WSP by means of Single Sign On (SSO). The tracking modules, which were still part of the shop, were also migrated to the .NET technology and integrated into WSP as independent portal services.

Figure 10.11 **Systems Architecture at WCS**

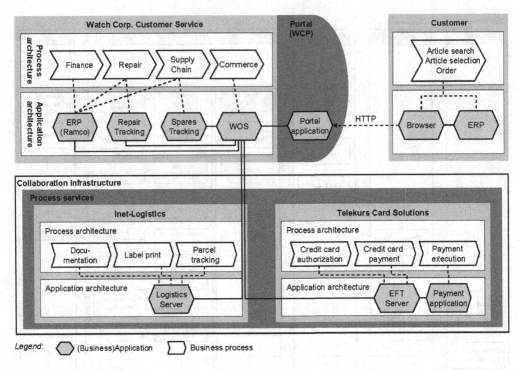

Third, the expansion phase for the shop started in mid-2004. It focused on the implementation of different language versions, an extended search function for articles, the display of parts availability (Available to Promise [ATP]) plus the capability for the customer to select different logistics service providers. In addition, the customer is now able to identify parts on exploded drawings and to transfer them to the shopping cart. At the same time, additional portal services included personalized push information in the form of portlets or e-mail newsletter, Frequently Asked Questions (FAQs), and a complaints tracking module.

## SUMMARY AND CONCLUSIONS

After redesigning their internal processes, many companies are now targeting the potential in their processes with customers, suppliers, and service providers. Existing BPR methodologies only support this purpose to a limited degree because neither the institutional redesign, nor the allocation of activities among multiple actors, nor the implications of portal technologies is taken into account. Several authors have recognized these shortcomings and have suggested methodologies for BNR that, depending on the author's background, are institutional or process oriented in nature. Although researchers from the field of enterprise modeling or enterprise architectures aim to systematically link strategic and technological design, they often neglect a procedure model and decision-making support, such as model assessment with respect to efficiency or strategic recommendations. In order to address these problems, this chapter proposed a methodology that (1) meets the requirements for systematic redesign methodologies, (2) specifically considers the configuration of customer-oriented networks, and (3) introduces the concept of process portals and portal technologies.

This methodology has been developed together with Watch Corp. and a group of other companies. Watch Corp. is a traditional manufacturing company that has been gradually transformed. The process was started with a typical electronic catalog covering only a small part of the customer process. By extending the functionality of the WOS, more activities of the customer process ("breadth of customer process coverage") with more functionalities ("depth of customer process coverage") were covered. This involved redesign decisions at the strategy, process, and systems levels.

**Strategy Level**

On the strategy level the flows in the business network were improved step by step. The downstream flows of goods and information were redesigned with a direct sales and direct distribution solution. This encompassed a change of roles because (1) the customer performs activities that were previously carried out by WCS (e.g., article search and selection), (2) WCS eliminated warehousing activities in regional and country organizations, and (3) new actors were involved for physical and financial logistics. According to Kumar and Van Dissel (1996), integrators are important in reducing dependencies in a business network. From this perspective, the logistics service led to an intermediation, which decoupled WCS from the carrier community. In the long run, WCS may follow the arguments of Hagel and Singer (1999), who expected separate customer-oriented companies to emerge. For example, WCS might offer spare parts services to other watch brands or even other industries on the market. Clearly, this vision goes beyond BNR, thus pointing toward business scope redefinition (see Figure 10.1).

**Process Level**

On a process level, the development of the process portal strategy encompassed, on one hand, the design of customer-oriented processes and the associated portal services ("front-end perspective") and, on the other hand, the processes required for organizing these processes in the partner network ("back-end perspective"). Based on documentation models from established BPR methods, an enhanced form for depicting the customer process and for documenting collaborative processes was proposed. This collaborative process architecture was also used to assess outtasking potentials. Here, established BNR criteria from transaction cost theory have been used, such as strategic relevance and resource specificity. However, assessing small activities within processes (e.g., printing bar code labels or consolidating status information from various carriers) also revealed a dilemma of existing BNR approaches: although institutional approaches analyze the roles among companies, they lack a comprehensive process analysis, thus making it impossible to know all relevant activities. Process-oriented approaches, for their part, map the relevant processes but neglect the institutional decisions. Because many institutional decisions arise only after the process level has been reached, considering institutional criteria here as well seems one possible solution.

**Systems Level**

Many of the above-mentioned concepts have their "reality check" at the systems level. For example, automated processes are invariably associated with homogeneous master data, the availability of services in a digital form, and agreed-upon collaborative processes as well as the interfaces within these processes. Redesign of the systems architecture mainly meant selecting software packages according to functional requirements and embedding the portal in an existing application landscape. WCS decided on proprietary solutions largely because of the lack of economically viable standardized solutions. However, it is clear that standard business applications (e.g., electronic catalogs, portals) as well as standards in the area of collaborative processes can have a positive effect on development and implementation costs.

In summary, the case study shows the role of IT as strategic enabler, on one hand, and the nontechnical nature of most success factors, on the other hand. This observation refers to internal support for establishing homogeneous master data, responsibilities between marketing and IT for the design and operation of the electronic channel, and the acceptance of supply-chain partners and customers. For this purpose WCS involved pilot partners in the development and formulation of "win-win situations." These situations were elaborated in terms of improved effectiveness (guaranteed delivery times, higher information level, transparent order tracking information, interchangeability information for customers of the electronic solution) and higher efficiency (lower order fulfillment costs for Watch Corp. and cost-saving potentials for the brands' local warehouses).

As described in the initial overview of existing BNR methodologies, research in this area is still at an early stage. This chapter suggests two directions for future research. First, integration on a vertical scale is needed for developing architecture models across multiple layers. It should be possible to easily identify and assess the implications of redesign actions on these levels (e.g., the externalization of an activity to an external service provider or the offering of new services). Promising work is taking place in the field of enterprise modeling and architecting as well as in the standardization field with initiatives from RosettaNet and other industry organizations (e.g., http://bpmi.org, http://oasis.org). Beyond conceptual work regarding meta, documentation, role, and procedure models, the development of appropriate modeling tools will also be an important requirement as well. Second, integration on a horizontal scale is needed for linking the architecture models with assessment criteria and simulation facilities. Here, a combination of quantitative and qualitative analyses will be important, because many BNR initiatives are doomed to failure as a result of politics, strategic uncertainties, or project complexities.

## NOTES

1. Partner companies were DaimlerChrysler AG, Deutsche Telekom AG, emagine GmbH, Watch Corp., Hewlett-Packard (Switzerland) AG, Hoffmann-La Roche Ltd., Robert Bosch GmbH, SAP AG, and Triaton GmbH.

2. Portal architectures provide an integrated view on presentation, applications/functionality, and data (Puschmann and Alt, 2005).

## REFERENCES

Alt, R.; Fleisch, E.; and Österle, H. 2001. Introduction—Chances and challenges in business networking. In H. Österle, E. Fleisch, and R. Alt (eds.), *Business Networking: Shaping Collaboration Between Companies*. Berlin: Springer, pp. 1–13.

Alt, R.; Reichmayr, C.; Cäsar, M.A.; and Zurmühlen, R. 2002. Evolution of electronic catalogs to customer process portals—A structured approach at ETA S.A. In C. Loebbecke, R.T. Wigand, J. Gricar, A. Pucihar, and G. Lenart (eds.), *eReality: Constructing the eEconomy—Proceedings of the 15th Bled Electronic Commerce Conference.* Kranj: Moderna Organizacija, pp. 192–213.

Brinkkemper, S. 1996. Method engineering: Engineering of information systems development methods and tools. *Information and Software Technology,* 38, 4, 275–280.

Champy, J. 2002. *X-Engineering the Corporation: Reinventing Your Business in the Digital Age.* New York: Warner Books.

Checkland, P., and Holwell, S. 1998. Action research: Its nature and validity. *Systemic Practice and Action Research*, 11, 1, 9–21.

Christiaanse, E., and Kumar, K. 2000. ICT-enabled coordination of dynamic supply webs. *International Journal of Physical Distribution & Logistics Management*, 30, 3–4, 268–285.

Clark, T.H., and Hammond, J.H. 1997. Reengineering channel reordering processes to improve total supply-chain performance. *Production and Operations Management*, 6, 3, 248–265.

Clark, T.H., and Stoddard, D.B. 1996. Interorganizational business process redesign: Merging technological and process innovation. *Journal of Management Information Systems*, 13, 2 (Fall), 9–28.

Cook, M.A. 1996. *Building Enterprise Information Architectures: Reengineering Information Systems*. Upper Saddle River, NJ: Prentice Hall.

Czuchry, A.J., and Yasin, M.M. 2003. Improving e-business with a Baldrige-based methodology. *Information Systems Management*, 20, 3, 29–38.

Davenport, T.H. 1993. *Process Innovation: Reengineering Work Through Information Technology*. Boston: Harvard Business School Press.

Davydov, M.M. 2001. *Corporate Portals and e-Business Integration*. New York: McGraw-Hill.

Dias, C. 2001. Corporate portals: A literature review of a new concept in information management. *International Journal of Information Management*, 21, 4, 269–287.

Edmondson, G. 2003. Look who's building bimmers. *BusinessWeek* (December 8, 2003), 18–19.

Evans, G.N.; Towill, D.R.; and Naim, N.N. 1995. Business process re-engineering the supply chain. *Production Planning & Control*, 6, 3, 227–237.

Frank, U. 2002. Multi-perspective enterprise modeling (MEMO)—Conceptual framework and modeling languages. In R.H. Sprague Jr. (ed.), *Proceedings of the 35th Annual Hawaii International Conference on System Sciences*. Los Alamitos, CA: IEEE Computer Society. Available at http://csdl2.computer.org/comp/proceedings/hicss/2000/0493/03/04933021.pdf.

Franken, H.M.; Bal, R.; van den Berg, H.; and de Vos, H. 2000. Architectural design support for business process and business network engineering. *International Journal of Services Technology and Management*, 1, 1, 1–14.

Gregor, S., and Johnston, R.B. 2001. Theory of interorganizational systems: Industry structure and theory of change. In R.H. Sprague Jr. (ed.), *Proceedings of the 34th Annual Hawaii International Conference on System Sciences*. Los Alamitos, CA: IEEE Computer Society. Available at http://csdl2.computer.org/comp/proceedings/hicss/2001/0981/07/09817005.pdf.

Hagel, J.I., and Brown, J.S. 2001. Your next IT strategy. *Harvard Business Review*, 79, 9, 105–113.

Hagel, J.I., and Singer, M. 1999. Unbundling the corporation. *Harvard Business Review*, 77, 2, 133–141.

Hammer, M. 2001a. *The Agenda: What Every Business Must Do to Dominate the Decade*. New York: Crown Business, .

———. 2001b. The superefficient company. *Harvard Business Review*, 79, 8, 82–91.

Handfield, R.B., and Nichols, E.L.J. 2002. *Supply Chain Redesign: Transforming Supply Chains into Integrated Value Systems*. Upper Saddle River, NJ: Prentice Hall.

Henderson, J.C., and Venkatraman, N. 1999. Strategic alignment: Leveraging information technology for transforming organizations. *IBM Systems Journal*, 38, 2–3, 472–484. [Originally published 1993 *IBM Systems Journal*, 32, 1, 4–16.]

Hevner, A.R.; March, S.T.; Park, J.; and Ram, S. 2004. Design science in information systems research. *MIS Quarterly*, 28, 1, 75–105.

Heym, M., and Österle, H. 1993. Computer-aided methodology engineering. *Information and Software Technology*, 35, 6, 345–354.

Hinterhuber, A. 2002. Value chain orchestration in action and the case of the global agrochemical industry. *Long Range Planning*, 35, 6, 615–635.

Holstrom, J.; Framling, K.; Tuomi, J.; Karkkainen, M.; and Ala-Risku, T. 2002. Implementing collaboration process networks. *International Journal of Logistics Management*, 13, 2, 39–50.

Hoogeweegen, M.R.; Teunissen, W.J.M.; Vervest, P.H.M.; and Wagenaar, R.W. 1999. Modular network design: Using information and communication technology to allocate production tasks in a virtual organization. *Decision Sciences*, 30, 4, 1073–1103.

Janssen, W.; Steen, M.W.A.; and Franken, H.M. 2003. Business process engineering versus e-business engineering: A summary of case experiences. In R.H. Sprague Jr. (ed.), *Proceedings of the 36th Annual Hawaii International Conference on System Sciences*. Los Alamitos, CA: IEEE Computer Society. Available at http://csdl2.computer.org/comp/proceedings/hicss/2003/1874/07/187470185c.pdf.

Jarvenpaa, S.L., and Stoddard, D.B. 1998. Business process redesign: Radical and evolutionary change. *Journal of Business Research,* 41, 1, 15–27.

Kalakota, R., and Robinson, M. 2001. *e-Business 2.0: Roadmap for Success.* Upper Saddle River, NJ: Addison-Wesley.

Kambil, A., and Short, J.E. 1994. Electronic integration and business network redesign: A roles-linkage perspective. *Journal of Management Information Systems,* 10, 4 (Spring), 59–83.

Keen, P.G.W., and McDonald, M. 2000. *The eProcess Edge: Creating Customer Value and Business Wealth in the Internet Era.* Berkeley, CA: McGraw-Hill.

Kenyon, J., and Vakola, M. 2001. Evolving the customer relationship management paradigm in the retail industry. *Customer Relationship Management,* 3, 4, 313–332.

Kettinger, W.J.; Teng, J.T.C.; and Guha, S. 1997. Business process change: A study of methodologies, techniques, and tools. *MIS Quarterly,* 21, 1, 55–80.

Klein, S., and Schad, H. 1997. The introduction of EDI systems in healthcare supply chains: A framework for business transformation. *International Journal of Electronic Commerce,* 2, 1, 25–44.

Kopczak, L.R. 1997. Logistics partnerships and supply chain restructuring: Survey results from the U.S. computer industry. *Production and Operations Management,* 6, 3, 226–247.

Kumar, K., and Van Dissel, H.G. 1996. Sustainable collaboration: Managing conflict and cooperation in interorganizational systems. *MIS Quarterly,* 30, 6, 484–497.

Lammers, M.; Loehndorf, N.; and Weitzel, T. 2004. Strategic sourcing in banking—A framework. In T. Leino, T. Saarinen, and S. Klein (eds.), *The European Information Systems Profession in the Global Networking Environment* (ECIS 2003). Turku: ECIS, pp. 1–13.

Lightner, N. 2004. Evaluating e-commerce functionality with a focus on customer service. *Communications of the ACM,* 47, 10, 88–92.

Luttighuis, P.O., and Biemans, F. 2000. *ERP in the E-Commerce Era.* Enschede, Netherlands: Telematics Institution.

Machuca, J.A.D., and Barajas, R.P. 2004. The impact of electronic data interchange on reducing bullwhip effect and supply chain inventory costs. *Transportation Research: Part E,* 40, 3, 209–228.

Malone, T.W.; Yates, J.; and Benjamin, R.I. 1987. Electronic markets and electronic hierarchies. *Communications of the ACM,* 30, 6, 484–497.

Marrett, C.B. 1971. On the specification of interorganizational dimensions. *Sociology and Social Research,* 56, 1, 83–99.

Massey, A.P.; Montoya-Weiss, M.M.; and Holcom, K. 2001. Re-engineering the customer relationship: Leveraging knowledge assets at IBM. *Decision Support Systems,* 32, 2, 155–170.

Motwani, J.; Kumar, A.; and Jiang, J. 1998. Business process reengineering: A theoretical framework and an integrated model. *International Journal of Operations & Production Management,* 18, 9, 964–977.

Österle, H. 1995. *Business in the Information Age: Heading for New Processes.* Berlin: Springer.

———. 2001. Enterprise in the information age. In H. Österle, E. Fleisch, and R. Alt (eds.), *Business Networking: Shaping Collaboration Between Companies.* Berlin: Springer, pp. 17–53.

Papazoglou, M.P., and Georgakopoulos, D. 2003. Service-oriented computing. *Communications of the ACM,* 46, 10, 24–28.

Piccoli, G., Spalding, B.R., and Ives, B. 2001. The customer-service life cycle: A framework for improving customer service through information technology. *Cornell Hotel and Restaurant Administration Quarterly,* 42, 3, 38–45.

Puschmann, T., and Alt, R. 2005. Developing an integration architecture for process portals. *European Journal of Information Systems,* 14, 2, 121–134.

Reimers, K. 2002. The unit of analysis in e-commerce studies. Discussion Paper, School of Economics and Management, Tsinghua University, Beijing.

Romano, N.C., and Fjermestad, J. 2002. Electronic commerce customer relationship management: An assessment of research. *International Journal of Electronic Commerce,* 6, 2, 61–113.

Scheer, A.-W., and Habermann, F. 2000. Making ERP a success. *Communications of the ACM,* 43, 4, 57–61.

Sheombar, H.S. 1997. Logistics coordination in dyads: Some theoretical foundations for EDI-induced redesign. *Journal of Organizational Computing and Electronic Commerce,* 7, 2–3, 153–184.

Short, J.E., and Venkatraman, N. 1992. Beyond business process redesign: Redefining Baxter's business network. *Sloan Management Review,* 34, 1, 7–21.

Stern, L.W., and Craig, C.S. 1971. Interorganizational data systems: The computer and distribution. *Journal of Retailing,* 47, 2, 73–91.

Toncia, S. 2004. Methodology for process management design and implementation. In S. Toncia and A. Tramontano (eds.), *Process Management for the Extended Enterprise: Organizational and ICT Networks.* Berlin: Springer, pp. 29–46.

Treacy, M., and Wiersema, F. 1993. Customer intimacy and other value disciplines. *Harvard Business Review,* 71, 1, 84–93.

Van der Vorst, J.G.A.J., and Beulens, A.J.M. 1999. A research design for the redesign of food supply chains. *International Journal of Logistics: Research and Applications,* 2, 2, 161–174.

Van Meel, J.W., and Sol, H.G. 1996. Business engineering: Dynamic modeling instruments for a dynamic world. *Simulation & Gaming,* 27, 4, 440–461.

Venkatraman, N. 1994. IT-enabled business transformation: From automation to business scope redefinition. *Sloan Management Review,* 35, 2, 73–87.

Weill, P., and Vitale, M.R. 2002. What IT infrastructure capabilities are needed to implement e-business models? *MIS Quarterly Executive,* 1, 1, 17–34.

Wikipedia. 2005. *Methodology.* Available at http://en.wikipedia.org/wiki/Methodology (accessed on August 17, 2005).

# PART V

## SUCCESS AND FAILURE IN BUSINESS PROCESS TRANSFORMATION

# CHAPTER 11

# SUCCESSFUL BUSINESS PROCESS TRANSFORMATION AT J.D. EDWARDS

## DURSUN DELEN AND NIKUNJ DALAL

**Abstract:** *In order to succeed (or merely survive) in today's turbulent business environment marked by increasing levels of competition and ever-changing market conditions, enterprises have to change their processes to quickly and efficiently adapt to the changing needs and wants of the marketplace. This is especially true for industries where information technology (in the form of hardware and software) is the main product. Arguably, the most radical response of an enterprise is business process reengineering (BPR). In this chapter, we examine and report on a successful BPR project conducted internally by J.D. Edwards called Project PROOF. Specifically, we present the context in which the BPR project was carried out, describe the project implementation, report on the results of the project execution, and conclude with lessons learned in the context of prior research on BPR success factors and implications for research and practice.*

**Keywords:** *Business Process Reengineering, Business Process Transformation, Critical Success Factors, Enterprise Resource Planning, Case Study*

## INTRODUCTION

Today's business environment is characterized by increasing levels of competition and ever-changing market conditions. This is especially true in industries where information technology (IT), in the form of hardware or software, is the main product. In the face of dramatic turbulence in the environment, an enterprise's ability to adapt, respond, and align itself with its business needs is critical for its survival and success. But how should an enterprise respond?

Among various responses, business process reengineering (BPR) offers radical solutions possibly as dramatic as the challenges. BPR can be defined as the "fundamental revision and radical redesign of processes to reach spectacular improvements in critical and contemporary measurements of efficiency, such as cost, quality, service and quickness" (Hammer and Champy, 1994). However, modern BPR in practice is a combination of radical and incremental changes. While the focus of BPR is on *business processes,* many BPR practitioners have indicated that the application of IT is critical to the success of BPR (Kettinger and Grover, 1995; Tapscott and Caston, 1993). Hammer stated that "a company that cannot change the way it thinks about information technology cannot reengineer" (1990). He described the implementation of state-of-the-art IT as an essential enabler of successful reengineering.

BPR efforts are reported to fail at meeting their goals at a rate of 70 percent (Champy, 1995). The salient observation about this statistic is that an enterprise would have to be facing critical business issues or have considerable problems to attempt a high-risk, highly visible BPR project, given these significant chances of failing. However, a closer examination of this failure statistic is warranted to provide meaning into how to reduce this statistic. According to Mayer and deWitte (2000), there are three primary reasons attributed to failing BPR efforts. The first reason is the lack of an adequate business case resulting in unclear, unreasonable, or unjustifiable expectations for what is wanted or expected to result from a BPR effort. Symptoms of the lack of such an understanding include an overemphasis on radical change without adequate focus on existing processes, underestimation of issues related to people and organizational change, and insufficient support and commitment from top management. A second reason can be the absence of robust and reliable technology and methodologies for performing BPR so that there is a failing in executing BPR efforts. A third reason is incomplete or inadequate implementation.

Reorienting a traditional organization from a function to a process focus requires a major cultural change (Majchrzak, this volume, pp. 125–139; Mayer and deWitte, 2000). It also requires major change to the information systems that support the organization. Organizational members do not know what to expect and are often surprised, angered, or threatened by the change proposed. If the project does not correctly manage their expectations, it will not be allowed to continue. Finally, inadequate carry forward of "lessons learned" and "how-to" knowledge from project to project significantly increases the chance of failure.

In recent years, enterprise resource planning (ERP) software has been the most commonly used IT paradigm in BPR implementation efforts because ERP systems are process oriented and presumably capture best business practices. Given the power of modern ERP software, is the successful implementation of an ERP system synonymous with successful business process transformation or is ERP just an enabler of the BPR implementation? If the latter is true, what are the factors that make an ERP-enabled BPR project successful?

This case study examines a business process transformation project conducted internally by J.D. Edwards in 2001. J.D. Edwards was a well-known provider of ERP and collaborative commerce solutions until 2003, when the company was acquired by PeopleSoft, which, in turn, was taken over by Oracle in 2004. The case study highlights a BPR project, which, despite its relative success, could not prevent the takeover of the company.

This chapter is organized as follows. In the next two sections, a project overview and company background are presented. This is followed by other project details: the motivation for the project, its inception, its execution, and finally, the results. The final section reviews the lessons learned in the context of prior research on BPR success and implications for research and practice.

The material for this case study was collected by the second author while on a year-long sabbatical assignment at the J.D. Edwards headquarters in Denver, Colorado, during the academic year 2001–2. The purpose of this study was to explore managerial, technical, and organizational factors that might have affected the outcome of the process transformation and ERP implementation project carried out by J.D. Edwards. Data were collected by means of structured and open-ended on-site interviews of key people in the project, which included the company CIO, vice presidents, project manager, and training manager, among others; nonparticipant observation of the proceedings of project meetings; and examination of secondary data, which included presentations, minutes of meetings, project plans, and company reports. Besides textual data, multimedia data in the form of video interviews and PowerPoint presentations were also collected.

## PROJECT OVERVIEW

Project PROOF was a business process reengineering effort initiated in June 2001 by J.D. Edwards. One purpose of PROOF was to reengineer major internal business processes within J.D. Edwards by successfully upgrading to the latest enterprise software the company planned to sell to the world. The acronym PROOF reflected the organization's focus on *Process Reengineering and Optimization for Operational Functionality*, although the strategic objectives of the project went beyond process improvement. The offerings of J.D. Edwards included comprehensive applications for ERP, supply-chain management (SCM), knowledge management, customer relationship management (CRM), collaboration and integration, business intelligence, tools, and services.

J.D. Edwards historically used its own AS/400-based enterprise solution called WorldSoftware as the foundation for the company's internal operations and processes. The company started selling customers its client-server-based OneWorld® enterprise solution in 1996. However, the company was not able to keep up to date internally with its latest releases to customers. Moreover, OneWorld Xe, a completely Web-enabled solution, was released in 2000. When they decided to sell these new software releases, the top executives at J.D. Edwards felt that a radical step within the company was necessary to achieve internal information integration and best business practices.

### Company Background

Project PROOF's roots were in the turbulent environment of the late 1990s when the economy hit the whole IT sector hard. Since its inception through 2001, J.D. Edwards had enjoyed compound annual revenue growth of about 43 percent and logged revenues of about $874 million for fiscal year 2001. In 2002, the company had more than 6,000 customers with sites in approximately 100 countries and over 5,000 employees worldwide. From more than 100 ERP providers worldwide, SAP AG, Oracle, J.D. Edwards, PeopleSoft, and Baan—collectively called the "big five" of enterprise software—held roughly 70 percent of the ERP market share in 2000.

The beginnings of the company were modest. J.D. Edwards started in 1977 in Denver as a vendor of packaged financial software running on several small and medium-sized computers, eventually focusing on the IBM System/38 in the early 1980s. Their flagship enterprise software product, called WorldSoftware, brought success to the company. By the mid-1980s, J.D. Edwards was being recognized as a leading supplier of applications software for the highly successful IBM AS/400 computer, a direct descendant of System/38. In June 1996, the company started selling OneWorld, a GUI-based configurable enterprise solution. OneWorld combined a full range of platform-independent applications with an integrated tool set, which permits organizations to configure their systems and applications as their needs changed. In addition, OneWorld integrated with WorldSoftware, allowing existing WorldSoftware customers to preserve their investment with an easy migration path to the advanced, open systems functionality of OneWorld. In the late 1990s, as users turned their attention to integrated front-to-back-office application suites—a key requirement of ERP II—Ed McVaney (a company founder) foresaw the trend, and his team took important steps in this direction.

> Collaborative commerce will be the next high-growth market for developers of business software. And three things have come together to catapult J.D. Edwards into a leadership position in this burgeoning market: an integrated supply chain planning and fulfillment

engine, a fully Web-enabled version of our product OneWorld Xe, and technologies that break the bonds of traditional proprietary software and afford the freedom to choose what's best for business. Armed with these advantages, J.D. Edwards went from an ERP company working to shake off the effects of the Y2K problem to a leading provider of collaborative supply chain solutions almost overnight.[1]

J.D. Edwards distributed, implemented, and supported its software worldwide through 55 offices in the United States, Europe, Middle East, Asia, and Latin America, and more than 350 third-party business partners. To help achieve maximum benefit from its software, the company provided implementation, education, and support services through its own direct services organization called Global Enterprise Solutions (GES) and business partners. Over the years, J.D. Edwards entered into strategic partnerships with consulting partners who provide consulting expertise in J.D. Edwards applications and technologies, product partners such as Ariba to extend and enhance enterprise solutions, and technology partners such as IBM who provide hardware and network solutions. In addition, J.D. Edwards had partnerships with leading applications service providers (ASPs) and hosting/outsourcing companies to offer their enterprise software in a third-party hosted environment.

**Project Motivation**

PROOF was initiated at a time when the company was going through global restructuring made necessary by declining revenues, increasing competition, and a turbulent economic environment. During company-wide restructuring in 2000, the top management of J.D. Edwards refocused its corporate vision to: *We deliver agile, collaborative solutions for the Internet economy.* But the company had to first make sure its own house was in order. Mark Endry, CIO of the company, did not see the project as merely an internal ERP implementation:

> OneWorld is a flexible, highly functional solution that's perfectly suited to the way we run our business. We want to realize the same benefits we preach to our prospects and help mature our Web product so it better meets their needs. This makes Project PROOF a high priority for the whole company.

In a similar vein, an internal management report envisioned the strategic benefits of PROOF:

> We already have one of the largest Web implementations in the world; the next step is to make it one of the most effective Web implementations in the world. The OneWorld product provides everything required in a technical infrastructure to achieve this—and the necessary applications implementations and process changes are underway. Once all of the applications infrastructure is in place, in combination with the process flexibility the OneWorld Xe system affords, J.D. Edwards operations groups will be well positioned to provide the level of organizational agility, flexibility, and responsiveness we need to continue to prosper in the new economy.

The goal of Project PROOF was to implement vanilla OneWorld Web worldwide for internal use by over 5,000 employees of the company. The project had to fit with the business needs of the company.

Facing increasing competition from other enterprise software vendors and from supply SCM and CRM vendors, the management of J.D. Edwards identified four focused strategies for the company during the global restructuring of the company in May 2000: operational excellence, focused revenue growth, knowledgeable and committed workforce, and world-class marketing.

1. *Operational excellence.* Deliver high productivity and profitability by institutionalizing processes and tools, instilling discipline and accountability, and creating highly effective and efficient organizations.
2. *Focused revenue growth.* Maximize revenue from growth products such as Advanced Planning Solutions, CRM, the installed base, and Services. Increase revenue contribution from new products.
3. *Knowledgeable and committed workforce.* Build a world-class leadership team. Implement employee rewards programs tied to performance and business objectives. Deploy a company-wide communications process. Redefine and enforce company culture.
4. *World-class marketing.* Build a world-class marketing organization to drive the product/ segment strategy. Develop visionary, leapfrog solutions. Institute leadership marketing—inside and outside the company.

Each of the strategies was spelled out in terms of key performance indicators, financial targets, and strategic imperatives with clearly defined responsibility centers and due dates for deliverables.

Advised by Endry, J.D. Edwards's top management recognized that supporting these strategies would require standardized, streamlined processes based on a new level of systems and organizational integration and a new technological infrastructure. Although J.D. Edwards had always used its own ERP software to support back-office operations, implementation of various applications over the years had evolved into "silos" mirroring the growth of the organization. The use of enterprise software does not *guarantee* integrated implementation. Some production systems were based on WorldSoftware and others were using OneWorld. Thanks to the coexistence capabilities of these products, it was possible for them to use a single integrated database. But the original implementations focused on the specific applications they were intended to serve and did not take advantage of the degree of integration afforded by OneWorld. Information fragmentation and duplication were pervasive. The use of third-party software was not uncommon. Project PROOF was specifically intended to address issues such as information integration and standardization of processes. There were also the obvious benefits of lowered software deployment and maintenance costs of a Web-client rather than a fat-client environment.

It was clear to Endry and his management team that enterprise systems were not only technologies but also had to be seen as holistic solutions. A company report on the project clarified this systems perspective:

> The key word in "showcasing solutions" is solutions—which means not only the OneWorld product itself, but also the people, processes, and procedures that collectively generate the business value enabled by an enterprise system. An integral component of this solution is the global implementation methodology and the solution kits that the company was advocating to its clients.

This perspective meant that the PROOF implementation process would serve as a reference to customers for the J.D. Edwards implementation methodology. Among other things, this implied that the company would treat this project as it would a customer's and involve its own field consulting organization and business partner consultants.

**Project Inception**

A high-powered cross-functional project steering committee was constituted to ensure that the project direction fully supported the corporate strategy. The PROOF steering committee was in charge of defining priorities, allocating resources, and approving policies and strategies. A program manager (Mary Henneck) with experience in project management, client management, consulting, and managing OneWorld implementations was appointed. Besides Endry and Henneck, the steering committee included senior executives responsible for each division affected by PROOF: CFO, CIO, executive vice president of sales and services, CTO and group vice president of development, vice president of human resources (HR), vice president of customer advocacy, director of international operations, a field consulting services manager, and a field global enterprise manager. The committee met at least once a month.

Early on during the initiative, business process owners knowledgeable in their specific domains were identified and recruited to lead the effort to change business processes. On May 15 and 16, 2001, project planning meetings were conducted for planning and organizing the effort. Participants from key groups at J.D. Edwards were present: IT, GES, business process owners, and development. The internal IT department would provide technical and application support for the deployed software. GES would play the consulting role. The internal development group would make sure the Web product worked as intended. Representatives from all geographies in which J.D. Edwards operated were included on the PROOF team.

The objectives of Project PROOF were clearly developed in various meetings as follows.

- Drive internal business processes toward best business practices already supported by vanilla OneWorld web product.
- Build a reference site for showcasing OneWorld Web and implementation methodology.
- Facilitate maturing of the OneWorld Web product.
- Lay the foundation that enables the company to meet information system needs and take advantage of new OneWorld functionality in later releases of the software.

The management felt that it was important that the objectives of Project PROOF should mesh with its strategic goals. In a memo to company employees, Endry clearly spelled out the relationship between Project PROOF and the overall company strategies of focused revenue growth, operational excellence, a knowledgeable and committed workforce, and world-class marketing. It was shown how PROOF contributes to all of them, but most significantly to the last three.

A key focus of PROOF was on a "plain vanilla" implementation. Lloyd Mitchell, enterprise manager for the project, explained the thinking:

> Permitting modifications to standard system code is the major contributor to prolonging outmoded processes and practices. In implementing an enterprise system, resistance to change is normal and it is usually easier to have a technical person write a modification to support an existing practice than to investigate, define a new process, and deal with the ripple effect. Unfortunately, this mode of action significantly dilutes the realized benefits of the new system and perpetuates the very inefficiencies the company was trying to eliminate. The only way to eliminate those inefficiencies is to adopt the mind-set that anything less than best business practices is unacceptable.

## Processes Affected

The scope of this project was to migrate all users and functionality from WorldSoftware to One-World Web globally across the enterprise. In all, the project affected five main groups of business processes:

1. Order to cash: deployment of sales order processing, maintenance billing, call handling, and pricing, among others.
2. Services: employee self-service time entry, contract service billing, and job cost.
3. Procure to pay/asset management: procurement, accounts payable, fixed assets, and property management.
4. Manage the business: general ledger, accounts receivable, and financial and operational reporting.
5. Workforce management: payroll and HR.

## Project Team

About 200 employees were assigned to Project PROOF, some full time and others part time, about 125 full-time equivalents in total. Considering the key objective of driving internal processes toward best business practices, it was critical to identify senior managers in user departments to serve as process owners for the major process areas. Process owners had responsibility for leading the effort to change business processes and effecting process integration across functional boundaries. Process owners, in turn, identified the people within their own organizations who would participate.

According to the project organization, for every process area there is both a process owner (representing the user organization) and a process team leader (from IT). Under the team leaders are IT specialists and consultants responsible for the software configuration and implementation as well as subject matter experts (SMEs) responsible for process validation and testing. Collectively, all process owners and team leaders worked to ensure that the final product supported the targeted levels of integration across functions, geographies, languages, and cultures.

PROOF was based on a methodology recommended by the company to its customers—J.D. Edwards implementation approach—and specifically included a key aspect for integrated multi-national implementations called the model company approach.

The premise of the model company approach was to define worldwide processes, procedures, practices, and requirements up front, roll the system out to a pilot site, learn from the experience, and eventually roll the system out in a phased manner to the remaining sites. Mitchell focused on the user participation aspect of this approach:

> In a nutshell, the model company approach means that all eventual users are involved in defining as many requirements as possible in the early stages of design. The initial "model company," in this case for U.S. and Canada, is defined primarily focusing on the needs of those countries but taking into consideration all requirements so far identified. With this approach, the initial model company was expanded to accommodate EMEA [Europe, Middle East, and Africa], and then further expanded to accommodate Asia Pacific and Latin America—and, in each case, the job is simplified thanks to early consideration of global localization and integration issues.

Modeling processes was integral to process reengineering and streamlining. Most groups modeled "as-is" and "to-be" processes.[2] The PROOF team decided to use OneWorld Solution

Modeler, a process modeling tool, to determine the processes to change, to define new processes, and to communicate the overall process flow for review or approval. Using Solution Modeler, the team translated the best business practices supported by OneWorld into graphical process models required for these applications. The team started with default models and modified them to fit J.D. Edwards's process flow requirements (see Figure 11.1 for a sample Solution Modeler screen). For new elements, the PROOF teams defined the link between the model and OneWorld. Eventually, the team expected to print OneWorld reports directly from any proposed model.

Viewing as-is process models enabled users to examine flaws in existing processes and to develop better to-be models. A company document notes one such instance:

> The Financial organization spends significant effort wrestling with service billing. This includes, with help from the Engagement Managers, reviewing financials, determining accuracy, checking invoices, verifying invoices, and sending confirmations. The Solution Modeler approach revealed this process left standardization incomplete, inconsistent procedures across geographic regions, and flaws in checks and balances. In the worst cases, it was concluded that audit rules were violated when the same person could potentially make time adjustments, send invoices, and manage received payments.

Some teams (particularly the Services team) observed firsthand the effect of communicating with user representatives using well-designed graphic process models.

> Where employees once thought, "How can I get a quick fix for this problem?" they soon approached the project thinking, "What process flows would provide an efficient overall solution?" . . . The opinions and knowledge of representatives from EMEA, Asia Pacific and the U.S. were easily reviewed and inserted to the new process flows for time entry and services billing. This example of focused accomplishment is exactly the kind of motivation we want to provide customers with needs similar to J.D. Edwards.

## Implementing BPR

As the implementation of Project PROOF started, Endry added to his foundational roles of sponsor and cheerleader by guiding and coaching the project management staff (and cooking hamburgers when the project celebrated a milestone). He recalled some of the challenges at the beginning of the project:

> Several departments were concerned about "what was in it for them," resisting attempts to move through the early stages of the project while that was being defined. Once we got to the point where that was defined, some departments were concerned about their items having a lower priority. Focusing people on cross-department processes helped them see the larger picture.

Resistance to change was a major challenge. As noted in a company document:

> Like many of our customers, we discovered that in spite of the flexibility and capabilities of our underlying technology, because process standardization is much of a people issue, purely technology focused process change management did not progress as smoothly as we planned.

Figure 11.1 **Solution Modeler Screen**

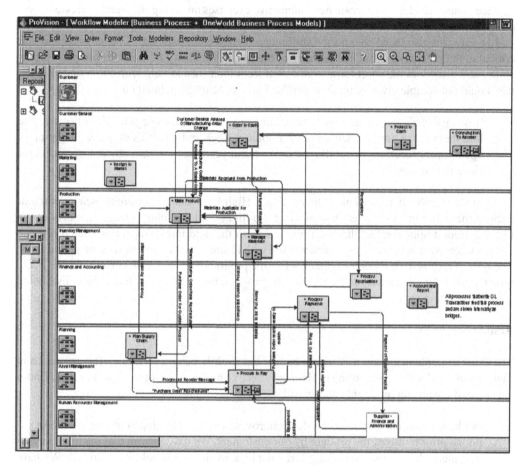

The initial process standardization plans involved far more changes than the process users were willing to accept, and it became apparent to the team that forcing extensive process standardization would seriously affect the delivery of the operational services for which the users were responsible. Hence, the project team had to reprioritize and shift focus from parallel to sequential process integration.

Clear communication was a high priority. An integrated communication plan was drawn out to complement the PROOF project and education/training plans. Communication was achieved with the use of the company intranet (called Knowledge Garden®), executive Webcasts, internal company publications, and meetings. Internal communication among PROOF team members was facilitated by frequent meetings of various groups, presentations by coordinators at cross-functional meetings, and postings of status reports and other documents in a single PROOF folder located on a company server.

The end-user training strategy was dependent upon the applications being deployed. There were some applications such as accounts payable that were specific to very few users. Those users were sent to classroom training. Other applications, such as time entry, which every employee needed to use, required a different training approach. Web-based training (WBT) courses were developed for this purpose using the native J.D. Edwards WBT authoring tool. This tool was versatile: it enabled course developers to create new interactive exercises involving software, to create review questions for trainees, and to easily integrate existing content into a Web-based course.

J.D. Edwards also faced unexpected staffing problems on the user side. User engagement was critical to the success of PROOF, but many of the people necessary to maintain company profitability and growth in the short term were called from their jobs to help with PROOF. However, they could not completely give up their regular jobs. As Mitchell pointed out:

> It is a real challenge in our case to schedule things with the user organizations because you lose them at the end of each month for about a week and a half as they get caught up in operational processing . . . at the end of the fiscal year, they are basically out-of-pocket for close to two months.

Even so, the PROOF management did not flinch. High-level managers were chosen to represent each of the major process areas. A number of top-flight field consultants were members of the PROOF team despite the fact that their absence from the field might impact mandated revenue targets. Users were actively engaged and worked with IT implementation teams as integrated units. The project received a temporary setback when the program manager took personal leave. In the time it took to find a new person for the job, the program manager's work had to be redistributed among other employees.

## Results

The PROOF implementation was within budget but slightly behind schedule. The project team saw a lot of good results. According to Henneck, "We've broken some of the ground rules." Endry categorized the project as "highly successful":

> We have identified numerous product improvements that Development was able to incorporate prior to use of the product by our customers. We have proven that the implementation methodology our consulting force deploys works and should be followed. We have improved the understanding of business processes across the company. This is contributing to the objective to become more of a process driven company. We have experienced what our customers experience and as a result have improved many of our processes. We have been able to stick to a very vanilla implementation. This significantly speeds up the implementation of new releases and reduces the level and cost of ongoing maintenance support. Also, it has helped us focus on process improvements instead of customizing to automate broken processes.

J.D. Edwards saw many benefits due to reengineered, improved, and streamlined business processes. Within the order-to-cash process, the PROOF implementation provided a degree of integration that had not existed before, which translated to a significant reduction in redundant actions and an increase in speed of handling cross-functional transactions. Moreover, the new system provided much better information regarding revenue-by-product and profitability-by-product—both of which would have required additional overhead to produce under the old system. A few processes have seen more radical changes. For example, in Services, the redefined processes altered how profitability is measured on the job, how contracts on the services are obtained, and how invoices are reviewed. While defining to-be processes, the financials team recognized the full repercussions of customers receiving bad invoices. The impact of invoice mistakes was felt downstream where the company could not collect on receivables as quickly due to disagreements and verification delays. After redefining the processes, the cleanup of invoices was moved to the front end and the accountability for this task was assigned to the engagement manager who deals with customers. A company document described the process change:

> After the planning and refining was done, the PROOF team proposed a redefinition of the engagement manager role. The PROOF team used Solution Modeler to cancel out any pre-conceptions of how the job was done before, and redefined the entire process and job-related responsibilities. Now it's possible for engagement managers to have full visibility of, and responsibility for, all aspects of managing a project from conception through completion. The role shifts from accounts management to project management. This frees up time of corporate staff, permitting twice-monthly invoicing. Increasing invoicing frequency increases cash flow.

PROOF was expected to result in a reduction of costs due to improved processes. For example, within HR, current annual operational costs for hiring, terminating (voluntary and involuntary), and status changes total almost $1.5 million. Project savings through implementation of various phases of PROOF were projected to range from 5 percent initially to over 20 percent once work flow (in combination with previous process improvements) is implemented. Similar cost reductions were expected for other processes. The next phase would have focused on additional process improvements and enterprise-wide process integration, had the company not been acquired.

## Implications for Successful Process Transformation

What does the experience of J.D. Edwards imply for other organizations considering similar process transformation projects? As a technology company involved in implementing its own software product that it would sell to its external customers, J.D. Edwards had the advantage of the presence and ready availability of in-house consulting and technical expertise. Nevertheless, there were several other key factors that led to successful process transformation at J.D. Edwards that may be generalized to other organizations. Many of these factors have been identified in other published case studies examining the common features of successful process transformation efforts (Bullington et al., 2002; Jarrar and Aspinwal, 1999; Mayer and deWitte, 2000; McAdams and Leonard, 1999; Mohney, 1995; Smith, 2003).

### Top Management Support

Top management support was absolutely vital to the success of the J.D. Edwards project. The project's executive sponsor, the CIO, had a clear vision and a plan in place prior to analysis work. He put together a cross-functional project steering committee to make sure that the project was fully supported by all of the different areas/departments within the company. The committee was responsible for defining priorities, allocating resources, and approving policies and strategies related to the reengineering project. When the project needed additional financial resources toward the end of the project, the committee was quick to give its approval to see the project through.

### Alignment of Project Goals with Overall Company Strategy

The project steering committee clearly spelled out project objectives in alignment with the strategic corporate goals. Each project objective was explicitly linked to overall company strategy.

*Focus on Business Processes Rather than Business Functions*

The initiative at J.D. Edwards was successful because it was not constrained by the boundaries of the individual business functions; rather, it was designed (and implemented) as a cross-functional transformation of the existing business process to meet (and exceed) the requirements of the ever more volatile ERP marketplace. The company maintained a clear process orientation throughout the project. Process owners were an important part of the project organization. Different stakeholders from functional departments constituting the process were consulted. Business process modeling and study of the existing system uncovered inefficient business practices. The end result of this process orientation was significantly improved business processes.

*Effective Organizational Structure for Project Management*

With cross-functional teams containing internal and external (consultants) members and process owners, the organization of the project was in tune with the overall holistic process orientation.

*Use of a Proven, Structured Methodology That is Aided by a Powerful Set of Methods and Supporting Tools*

Going in, the company worked with a clear implementation methodology, although it was later combined with a newer methodology, utilizing whichever methodology had the most strength for a given problem. Modeling tools were used as needed. Although user buy-in waned a little because of the length of the project, intermittent delays, and staffing and other implementation issues, a phased approach helped make the process transformation less disruptive to the enterprise overall and easier to manage.

*Minimal Software Changes*

Minimizing customization (keeping the implementation as "vanilla" as possible) was crucial to the process standardization envisioned by the company.

*A "Think Globally, Act Locally" Approach*

The "model company" approach helped J.D. Edwards to think globally and holistically of worldwide requirements while implementing its ERP system in a geographically phased manner.

*Customer Focus*

The customer focus is evident in the marketing objectives of the project and the CIO's exhortation of the team to "step inside the customer's shoes."

*Change Management Culture*

Perhaps the most important factor for the success of project PROOF was the way change was managed within the company. The company instituted a change management culture, which, among other things, included effective communication with employees, the involvement of users during the analysis and implementation of the system, an emphasis on training, and continuous monitoring of performance with the help of milestones and metrics.

## CONCLUSIONS

Project PROOF was a BPR effort undertaken by J.D. Edwards in the 2001–2 period. The goals of PROOF were to (1) reengineer major internal business processes within J.D. Edwards by successfully upgrading to the latest vanilla enterprise software the company planned to sell to the world, (2) to serve as a reference site for showcasing its software product and its implementation methodology to external customers, (3) to improve the product as needed, and (4) to lay the process foundation that would enable the company to meet its present and future information needs. These objectives were largely met and the project was a success despite later events that led to the acquisition of J.D. Edwards by bigger competitors. In a nutshell, key factors that led to a successful process transformation were top management support, process orientation, effective project organization and implementation, and a changed management culture.

As evidenced in Project PROOF, because of the size and complexity of BPR projects, the BPR project should be managed as a process, much like the way business processes are managed in BPR. How to implement this "project-as-process" approach is an issue for further research.

A clear implication for practice is that the radical change resulting from BPR should be leveraged for future incremental improvements and as a foundation for strategic change. In the case of PROOF, had the company survived, this would have meant using the successfully implemented ERP platform as a foundation for true enterprise-wide integration, improved and new processes, and future SCM and CRM strategies.

An important implication for practitioners is that ERP-integrated IT solutions can increase the chance of success, but they are not sufficient. Successful implementation of BPR requires the smooth integration and transformation of IT into the system users' daily tasks. Finally, we note that even successful BPR might not guarantee a company's survival.

## ACKNOWLEDGMENTS

This chapter is based on an ERP-oriented case study by N.P. Dalal, Project PROOF: Learning lessons from process reengineering at J.D. Edwards, *Communications of the AIS,* 13 (2004), 486–507. Revised and expanded with permission from the Association for Information Systems (AIS).

## NOTES

1. Internal company report, J.D. Edwards and Company, 2002.
2. There were a few groups who did not see the need to model "as-is" processes due to the time crunch and the significant reengineering occurring in their areas.

## REFERENCES

Bullington, S.F.; Easley, J.Y.; Greenwood, A.G.; and Bullington, K.E. 2002. Success factors in initiating versus maintaining a quality improvement process. *Engineering Management Journal,* 14, 3, 8–15.
Champy, J. 1995. *Reengineering Management.* New York: HarperCollins.
Hammer, M. 1990. Reengineering work: Don't automate, obliterate. *Harvard Business Review,* 68, 4, 104–116.
Hammer, M., and Champy, J.A. 1994. *Reengineering the Corporation: A Manifesto for Business Revolution.* New York: Harper Business.

Jarrar, Y.F., and Aspinwall, E.M. 1999. Business process reengineering: Learning from organizational experience. *Total Quality Management,* 10, 2, 173–185.

Kettinger, W.J., and Grover, V. 1995. Toward a theory of business process change management. *Journal of Management Information Systems,* 12, 1 (Summer), 1–30.

Majchrzak, A. 2008. Breaking the functional mind-set: The role of information technology. In V. Grover and M.L. Markus (eds.), *Business Process Transformation. Advances in Management Information Systems.* Volume 9. Armonk, NY: M.E. Sharpe, pp. 125–139.

Mayer, R.J., and deWitte, P.S. 2000. Delivering results: Evolving BPR from art to engineering. White paper, Knowledge Based Systems, Texas A&M University and Knowledge Based Systems Inc., College Station. Available at www.idef.com/pdf/bpr.pdf (accessed November 8, 2007).

McAdam, R., and Leonard, D. 1999. The contribution of learning organization principles to large-scale business process reengineering. *Knowledge and Process Management,* 6, 3, 176–184.

Mohney, R.W., Jr. 1995. Reengineering the new business process: Lessons learned from refocusing on the customer. *Journal of the American Society of CLU & ChFC,* 49, 5, 90–94.

Smith, M. 2003. Business process design: Correlates of success and failure. *Quality Management Journal,* 10, 2, 38–49.

Tapscott, D., and Caston, A. 1993. *Paradigm Shift.* New York: McGraw-Hill.

# CHAPTER 12

# A CASE STUDY OF BUSINESS PROCESS REENGINEERING FAILURE

SUPRATEEK SARKER AND ALLEN S. LEE

*Abstract:* *This chapter depicts a business process reengineering (BPR) initiative undertaken by a U.S. telecommunications company (TELECO) in response to imminent survival—threatening competitive pressures in its traditionally monopolistic market. The case study first highlights some of the seldom talked about problems faced during the redesign of business processes such as lack of detailed knowledge about functional areas, hidden agendas of top management, lack of knowledge of (and overreliance on) computer-based BPR tools, poor choice of metaphors in organizational language, and lack of communication. Thereafter, the case study identifies critical problems faced in implementing redesigned processes. These problems include difficulty creating an atmosphere of open communication, pressures against selecting information technology (IT) vendors on merit, lack of awareness of the lead times associated with IT, uncoordinated implementation of human resources and IT strategies, and discontinuities in leadership. Although we hope that the reader will individually derive lessons from the case for application in other contexts, we nevertheless provide a discussion on three issues (leadership, communication, and IT knowledge and management) that, in our opinion, significantly contributed to "failure" of the initiative at TELECO.*

*Keywords:* *Business Process Reengineering, Information Technology, Management of Information Systems, Organizational Transformation, Failure, Case Study*

## INTRODUCTION

This chapter describes a business process reengineering (BPR) or radical business process change (BPC) initiative undertaken by a U.S. telecommunications company (TELECO; a pseudonym) in response to imminent survival-threatening competitive pressures in its traditionally monopolistic market. It traces the sequence of events that led to failure and subsequent abandonment of the BPR project. The case narrative is based on a series of interviews conducted by the first author in the role of external researcher. Interviewees included organizational members at different levels and departments that had participated in (or had been affected by) the BPR initiative to different extents (see Table 12.1).

The specific issues discussed in any interview depended on the role of the individual, the stage of the project, information learned from other stakeholders, and the extent of rapport between the interviewer and the interviewee. The formal face-to-face interviews were conducted in some depth by the first author and typically lasted between one and two hours. The interviewer attempted to capture facts and emotional responses of the interviewees regarding different aspects of BPR and

Table 12.1

TELECO Interviews

| Interviewee | Number of formal interviews | Number of informal interviews |
|---|---|---|
| 1. VP or Process Owner (1) | 1 | 0 |
| 2. VP or Process Owner (2) | 1 | 1 |
| 3. BPC Team Member (1) | 2 | 1; telephone |
| 4. BPC Team Member (2) | 2 | 1 |
| 5. Marketing Executive | 1 | 0 |
| 6. Union Executive VP | 1 | 0 |

to coconstruct meanings jointly with the interviewees. The other informal interviews, including those conducted over the telephone, were for clarification purposes. The entire set of data was collected in the latter half of 1996.

## COMPANY BACKGROUND

In 1993, TELECO was an independent telecommunications company with a workforce of approximately 3,500 employees, based in a prominent U.S. city. For several decades, it had provided telephone service for businesses and residences in the city and adjoining areas.

### The Culture: Monopolistic, Technocentric, and Territorial

TELECO's culture was described by many organizational members as "monopolistic," and many of the company's practices reflected its noncompetitive environment, as it served a captive market. TELECO was also clearly an "engineering-driven" organization, and a technocentric approach to operations was evident from the way TELECO's new products and services typically originated. For example, according to a sales manager, TELECO would acquire a switch from AT&T, "find out what it could do, and then try to force-feed an application to the user," rather than find out what the customers needed and then implement a suitable technology. TELECO's priorities were greatly influenced by the regulatory environment (e.g., the Public Utilities Commission), which provided the telecommunications company with a guaranteed client base, but required it to measure service levels using "standard" indicators and to demonstrate high performance on the indicators in areas such as directory assistance and response to customer complaints. The resulting service measurement orientation in the company encouraged a fragmented accountability system and quick fixes to symptoms of larger systemic problems by "throwing people at a problem" to boost service levels.

Another dysfunctional aspect of the organization was the existence of cross-functional barriers that encouraged territorial behaviors among the employees. For instance, a vice president (VP) described difficulties arising in her area because of "finger-pointing" between circuit designers and circuit testers. Similarly, another VP expressed concern over the "total lack of cooperation" between field staff and the central office staff. In his words:

> There was a political wall, you might say, between the "inside" folks and the "outside" folks. The people outside were not allowed to come into the central office and do the . . . work required to provide the service.

## Antiquated Information Systems

A great deal of dissatisfaction also existed in the management ranks regarding TELECO's information systems (IS). There were "islands of automation" in the company, and many computer systems were unable to communicate with each other. TELECO was struggling with its legacy systems, some of which were proving to be significant barriers to responding promptly to customer inquiries and needs. A sales manager, for example, complained about the inability of the billing system to provide a detailed itemized record for any sale:

> Our billing is severely limited. . . . We could not tell you what serial numbers and which circuit pack there was on a PBX [Private Branch eXchange]. . . . We would have a single line on the bill that would say "Equipment," which, downstream, produced a huge problem. . . . Account reps spend 80 percent of their time answering questions about the bill.

He added:

> In the telephone company, there was never . . . a huge perceived need to change any of the existing systems . . . COBOL based mainframe type of systems. . . . We didn't keep up. . . . Why . . . because it always cost too much to keep up; alright, without us looking at the cost of not keeping up.

## Changing Context and Anticipated Organizational Crisis

As long as TELECO had a guaranteed customer base and faced no competition, the problems outlined above merely irritated the managers, employees, and customers. However, several managers at TELECO were beginning to realize that the "irritants" would have more serious consequences in the future, especially if the anticipated regulatory changes opened up the telecommunications market.

In early 1993, in light of the perceived inevitability of changes in the organization's external environment, wherein TELECO would be forced to compete with utilities, cable companies, and long-distance carriers for a large portion of its business, the company's president commissioned a five-member self-study team. This team was to take "a hard look" at the changing environment, evaluate TELECO's cost structures and market penetration, and provide recommendations to the president. Around the end of 1993, after several months of study and deliberation, the team came to the conclusion that

> The whole telecommunications world is changing very rapidly. . . . Competitors will start to be numerous. . . . The technology is changing in such a way that allows competitors to take away business without making gigantic investments. Our cost structures . . . we need to get those down to be competitive . . . we need to really make sure that our business is streamlined and efficient and focused on serving the customers. . . . *What we need to do is reengineer our entire company.*

## THE REENGINEERING DECISION

It was becoming apparent to the TELECO top management that drastic changes had to be initiated and implemented with extreme urgency or else the very survival of the organization would be in question. The leadership determined that an organization-wide radical change initiative was required, during which the existing organization would be dissolved and all work processes would be restructured such that organizational performance in terms of *speed, quality,* and *service* (and, thus, *value* for the customer) was significantly enhanced. Once the appropriate work processes were in place, a new organization would be built around them. Thus, the reengineering team members at TELECO would have to redesign not only the business processes but also the organizational structures supporting the business processes.

An internationally renowned consulting company was hired and entrusted with the responsibility of leading TELECO through the steps of reengineering. This was possibly prompted by the belief among top management that consultants had "broad exposure to leading-edge management ideas," "specific knowledge of IT [information technology]-enabled change," and "experience in guiding other firms" through similar initiatives, and that their expertise could be drawn upon to "translate concepts of IT-enabled change into actionable plans" and to implement the plans thereafter (Tillquist, 2000, p. 116).

Next, the top management selected 25 "privileged" individuals from different functional areas in TELECO as members of the reengineering team. These individuals were believed to have substantial expertise/experience in multiple functions within the organization at different levels. Soon after their selection, the reengineering team members were relieved of their normal job responsibilities and, along with the consultants, were relocated to the top floor of the company building, completely isolated from the other employees. In light of confidentiality and possible insider-trading concerns, the team members were instructed not to discuss sensitive information related to the BPR initiative with other employees of the organization. The team was entrusted with the goal of redesigning the entire company within one calendar year—*all processes, all departments, and all personnel.*

## THE REDESIGN PROCESS

The first step in the redesign phase was to divide TELECO into what appeared to be business processes and assign "process chunks" for detailed study to a subgroup in the reengineering team. As part of this information gathering effort, the reengineering team members interviewed over 1,500 TELECO employees from different parts of the company within a period of one month.

### The Use of Alienating Forms of Symbolism

The next step was to conduct a "problem identification root cause analysis" where the fundamental cause of problems in each process area was identified. This step also led to the isolation of some problems that could be fixed immediately. A team member explained:

> Some of the things that we found can be fixed immediately. . . . I call it the hatchet in the head. . . . If somebody has a hatchet in their head, pull it out. . . . Sometimes they are called quick hits . . . low-hanging fruit.

It was around this time of root cause analysis that some backlash started. TELECO employees resented metaphors such as *low-hanging fruit, hatchet in the head,* and *quick hits* that were diffusing into the language of the reengineering initiative, and these terms had to be hastily withdrawn. A manager who was sensitive to such "soft" issues recalled:

> "Quick hits" was our consultants' lingo. . . . Our employees reacted very negatively because in some situations, what we were "hitting" was . . . people. So the terminology was changed to . . . "immediate opportunities."

Also, the shroud of secrecy around the initiative, due to confidentiality issues as well as insider trading concerns, was making TELECO employees suspicious of the intentions/agenda of the organizational leadership and the reengineering team. In the words of a reengineering team member:

> Basically what they did is to set up a group of people [away] from the rest of the organization . . . and a lot of what we were working on was extremely confidential in terms of the goals we were trying to achieve . . . and other employees would ask us questions about things that we couldn't really answer . . . because of the insider trading, confidentiality, and all the other things that went on . . . so then mistrust started developing.

## Clean-Sheet Approach?

With growing uneasiness, the reengineering team members continued their analysis and consolidation of information gathered through interviewing, gaining a fairly detailed understanding of TELECO's current business processes and the problems with them. Interestingly, at this point, the process redesigners[1] took a "clean sheet of paper" approach and started building the "process visions" from "scratch" rather than working on the identified problems with the existing processes. A redesigner described how he envisioned order processing in TELECO:

> I guess you always start with what you know. . . . Okay . . . you envision someone sitting at the desk knowing everything about a customer . . . you envision them pointing and clicking and ordering a [telecommunications] service . . . and that order being placed does not have to touch anyone along the way. . . . And the next thing you know is the happy customer at the other end because technicians are out there installing the service.

## Designing IT-Enabled Processes Without Sufficiently Understanding IT

As the team started redesigning the company's processes, the potential of IT in enabling more efficient work processes became increasingly evident. Interestingly, all except one reengineering team member had "no particular knowledge or deep understanding of IT," and even that member (an IS director who had the necessary expertise but was on the team as a redesigner and not as an IS consultant/advisor to other redesigners) felt uncomfortable in advising his teammates regarding the (in)feasibility of their visions. Also, because of confidentiality issues, other IT experts could not be made available for advising the reengineering team. As a result, the team members stated in simplistic terms what they wanted IT to accomplish in order to realize their vision.

## Computer-Based BPR Tools: Passive Assistants or Active Manipulators?

Members of TELECO's top management appeared to have much faith in the use of IT tools for supporting BPR activities, and, on their recommendation, the reengineering team had made extensive use of IT tools for creating and representing the redesign. Most of the team members, who saw computer-based BPR tools as assisting them in efficiently representing elements of the redesigns, seemed to have a positive disposition toward the tools. One of them said:

> We used Visio [flowcharting software] to create all the process flowcharts. . . . It was just fantastic . . . and Project [project management software] . . . we used it to integrate plans across all the people involved. . . . I would say that the design would not have been as effective without the use of tools.

However, one of the team members indicated severe frustration regarding his experience with BPR tools in producing the redesign documents:

> we did more damn presentations to try and get a buy into what we were doing that we spent too much time producing those things. The business of producing and documenting was very cumbersome. . . . We refined the hell out of this thing.

It appeared that the BPR tools had been instrumental in creating an expectation among top management: (1) attractive diagrams and documents could be created and modified with ease, and (2) they could influence redesigns/visions by merely dictating changes on abstract representations of visions, plans, and schedules without really engaging in the redesign process with the reengineering team. This, in turn, resulted in significant changes in the nature of the reengineering team members' responsibilities, from the *creative development* of visions and plans guiding the organizational change process to the *production* of documents for presentation to top management. As a BPC team member reported:

> Ideally, you document the existing situation, you sit up and brainstorm about how things might change. . . . I did not sit into any brainstorming session . . . I can tell you . . . at the point we were . . . put[ting] together presentations to present to all the . . . managers.

The top management preoccupation with fancy "process binders" consumed a great deal of time and money, and left some reengineering team members feeling severely manipulated.

## Top Management Focus: Head Count Reduction and Self-Preservation

As the process visions started becoming more concrete, they were presented to members of TELECO's top management, including the president, the VPs, and the directors. The top management, in turn, asked the redesigners to make cosmetic as well as substantive changes to the redesigns. From the point of view of the redesigners, much of the design modifications mandated by the top management seemed to reflect their hidden agenda of self-preservation and downsizing rather than the espoused objectives of process orientation or the organizational values of service, quality, speed, and value addition. One reengineering team member, who had spent considerable time and energy in redesigning TELECO's business processes, expressed his frustration in this regard:

> talk about political . . . you come back with eight processes and they say no . . . you got to have 12. . . . Why? . . . Guess what . . . because there are 12 people [VPs] I see on the sheet who need [process owner] jobs.

The top management members also appeared to completely ignore the potential costs of IT and seemed obsessed with the savings from the head count reduction expected to result from the implementation of the proposed systems. A reengineering team member indicated that his teammates, under pressure from the top management, were "banking too much on the system" and hoping to save as much as 50 percent in costs, even though the consultants said that "typically it's [cost savings arising from IT are] 20 percent or less." One of the middle managers involved in the redesign provided a cynical account of the redesign process, which had degenerated into head count reduction:

the actual practice became . . . reduce head count . . . we know going in we need to get to a certain number [head count]. . . . Okay . . . if you came in with a reengineered process and you were not meeting the number, you were asked to go back and rethink the process to meet the number. . . . So, in other words, we started with a number . . . and backed into that number, and called it reengineering.

### Futile Attempts to Prioritize an Unrealistic Set of IT Projects

The overreliance of the redesign team on IT was also becoming evident to some reengineering team members, especially the IS director, who knew about the large price tags and the long lead times that were required to make major IS operational. As the IS director sat through the presentations of his reengineering teammates on redesigned processes and the IT required to enable them, he started getting a "sinking feeling":

> [As] I sat through this vision presentation for all the processes. . . . I had a paper in my notebook and every time somebody would say, "I want to put in a new system" or "I want to make major enhancements," I just started writing a little line. I thought I'll just capture these five or six items. By the time I got done, I had 130 items that were entire systems projects that these people were expecting to happen to make their process come true. I took that list . . . and wrote a proposal and said, "Somebody [listen] immediately, a team needs to be formed to start interviewing these people, to say: *What do you really need? What are the systems in practice? How's that going to work? What kind of budget do you need to make this happen?* . . . and start digging and doing at least some of the analysis . . . or these things are never going to happen."

The proposal was forwarded to the VP of IS, who immediately realized the gravity of the situation and created a five-member *IT transition support team.* Soon after the formation of this team, its members started interviewing the reengineering team members regarding the IT specified as part of their visions. TELECO management expected the IT transition team to make accurate projections regarding cost and time based on the interviews, virtually ignoring the transition team members' arguments that their analysis would be too "premature" for such projections, even after the interviews.

Reluctantly, the transition team members used historical evidence and came up with their best guess for the cost, which was a "gigantic number." This number clearly indicated that *all of the systems could not be implemented.* The team therefore directed its attention toward devising some way to be able to prioritize the systems and allocate resources to them. A 3-by-3 matrix that had "criticality to vision" (i.e., how important the envisioned process change was to TELECO's strategic goals) and "cost to implement" as its two dimensions was designed by the transition team members and eventually accepted by all parties concerned (see Table 12.2).

All proposed systems projects were to be mapped into one of the nine cells based on the projects' criticality to the vision and the expected implementation costs. The cell marked "A" in Table 12.2 is clearly the "worst" cell, because projects in it have the lowest criticality to the vision and have the highest expected implementation costs associated. In contrast, the cell marked "I" is the "best" cell because projects mapped to this cell are the most critical to the vision, whereas the implementation costs are expected to be the lowest. The transition team members proposed that systems in only the "best" three cells[2] (I, F, and H) should be pursued. This seemed to be a reasonable strategy for prioritizing systems development/implementation resources.

Table 12.2

**A Matrix to Prioritize Systems Projects**

| Estimated Cost of Implementation | Criticality of Vision | | |
| --- | --- | --- | --- |
| | Low | Medium | High |
| High | A | B | C |
| Medium | D | E | F |
| Low | G | H | I |

In practice, dropping IS projects that were mapped in the six remaining cells (A, B, C, D, E, and G) turned out to be completely unacceptable to most of the reengineering team members, because discarding those projects would mean that most of their creatively envisioned processes would not be implemented. After much negotiation, it was finally agreed that projects in the "worst" cell (A) would be discarded. Unfortunately, the problem now was coming to an agreement as to which projects actually deserved to be in that cell. The redesigners would argue regarding the projects that were mapped in the "worst" cell (A): "Well, that [project] is not really there, it should move up . . . it's more important." As a result, hardly any project could be rejected at this stage.

**Creating Voluminous Reengineering Plans to Which Management Had Little Commitment**

Next, the reengineering team started designing the organization around the business processes that had been envisioned, staying within the head count targets approved by the top management for each process. Job descriptions were written up in detail for every position required. Thereafter, the team started working on the implementation plan that included detailed schedules for recruitment into new positions, systems delivery, training, layoffs, and retirements, and highlighted the dependencies among different events or activities. This was an enormous undertaking, given the number of processes being redesigned and the number of IS surviving elimination in an earlier step (using the 3-by-3 matrix discussed in the previous subsection).

All of the work that had been done for each process was now consolidated into "process owner binders." The binders included a description of the processes before reengineering; problems that were found; new processes and their key characteristics, objectives, and assumptions made by the redesign team; personnel required and their job descriptions; organization structure; and, finally, implementation plans, sometimes presented as Gantt charts. While each binder was impressive in terms of its large size and elaborate use of graphics, a reengineering team member lamented that there was a "limited amount of teeth in the plan that we rolled out." That is, the plans in the process owner binders did not have the full support of the process owners and were thus often not adhered to during the implementation phase.

**IMPLEMENTATION OF THE REDESIGNED PROCESSES**

With the redesign phase of the BPR initiative completed, the reengineering team members directed their attention toward the implementation of their visions. The implementation phase, however, turned out to be more problematic than the smooth process the team had envisaged. The problems originated in a series of different factors ranging from lack of trust and coordination to design inconsistencies, poor IT delivery, and management discontinuity.

## Expecting Employees Whose Jobs Were at Risk to Communicate "Openly"

The first step for the reengineering team was to establish lines of communication with other TELECO employees. An important aspect of the communication program was to have a "reality check" on the redesigned processes based on the feedback of people who were specialists in the tasks pertaining to those processes. Such feedback was obtained in "quick-look sessions," which were described by the facilitator (a reengineering team member) as follows:

> I would get all the people in a room . . . we had a technical writer there . . . and I would say, "Let's start off with a concept of the system [for a specific process]" . . . and the people said, "That won't work because of this," or "That's good," . . . and then we'd go through . . . how many people are we going to save? . . . [And they would say] "Oh, I don't agree with those numbers at all . . . this part is OK, that part is not right."

Some valuable feedback could be obtained during these sessions, and as a result, some of the projects changed in scope, though marginally. However, in most quick-look sessions, the participants hardly ever challenged the feasibility of the process or even the estimates of the number of employees necessary to run a process smoothly. This made the facilitator quite uncomfortable, and, as he reflected, he realized that the quick-look sessions had not been able to serve their purpose at all. He explained:

> This is how it would have felt to one of those people in my session. On Monday, in the newspaper you read, "[TELECO] is going to eliminate 800 jobs." On Wednesday, I call you to the meeting, and say, "Can we make these reductions . . . do you believe in my project?" People were reluctant, for fear of losing their jobs, to say "no." Because the backdrop they were working in was . . . "Well, if I say that we can't do this, I am not going to be picked into a new position, and I may be one of these 800 people that gets cut." Plus, what we had been pumping the company full of, is, "Stretch, go aggressive, reach for the stars, let's break our own mind-set." . . . So people were trying to change their culture and say, "We can't be comfortable with everything, we'll give it a try." They were trying to do all the things that we were asking them to do. . . . There were a number of people in these quick sessions that if they would have known . . . that they were secure . . . they might have spoken up more.

The other objective of the communication program was to inform employees that the entire organization (as it existed then) would be dissolved, and current employees would have to apply anew for jobs that had been created and posted by the reengineering team. Employees were also told about the "attractive" voluntary retirement option available for those who qualified.

## IT Sourcing: Biased Vendor Selection and Unclear Systems Specifications

In parallel, the reengineering team was involved in the selection of IT vendors who could provide the systems required to implement the visions within the scheduled dates. Standard company procedures appeared to have been followed for vendor selection, although, according to a member of the reengineering team, a majority of large contracts were preferentially awarded to TELESYS (a pseudonym), a company owned by TELECO's parent company. TELESYS enjoyed a good reputation overall in the software development industry but was known to have treated TELECO as a low-priority customer in the past:

> a problem with our sister company [TELESYS] . . . well you kind of give the business to them . . . to those people. And it is kind of expected, you know . . . they know they got a captive customer and they charge us a lot . . . and are slow in implementing.

In addition to possible irregularities in vendor selection, the contract development process also appeared to be seriously flawed. Because of the large number of systems to be developed and the superficial nature of systems functionality specified by the reengineering team members, the contracts with the vendors ended up being very open-ended, thus making it difficult to make vendors accountable for their deliverables. A VP remarked:

> I think the vendors were only spoken to at a high level. Had more people been involved in fleshing out the systems . . . [the systems] would have been feasible. . . . I think [the vendors] were not given the complexity of the systems environment in which we operate.

### Transitioning to the "New" Organization with a "Parking Lot" Strategy

The physical transition to the envisioned organization began in early 1995. Staffing for the redesigned organization was done using a "parking lot" strategy. This involved relieving all employees from their present positions and then restaffing the new positions by drawing from the pool of available employees (assembled in the "parking lot"). Selection of employees for new positions within each process was done by its process owner (a VP) in consultation with other members of the management who had already been selected for a position in that process. Interestingly, reengineering members were apparently kept in the dark regarding the transition plans. One team member reported that "we had no [prior] knowledge that we were going to do a parking lot restaffing of the whole company."

During this entire period, the anxiety level of all organizational members, including those who had redesigned jobs, was extremely high. Everyone was worried about the possibility of not being picked for any new job, and it was particularly stressful for the redesigners who had to eliminate their friends' or (even) their own positions:

> To give you an idea . . . in about six weeks, I lost 16 pounds. . . . There were many people who had nervous breakdowns during this. . . . I basically eliminated my own position . . . which is a scary thought . . . and by the way, when you are finished, apply for a job.

The staffing process of nonmanagement employees was perceived as being unfair and almost resulted in a major strike:

> People didn't get jobs that they wanted . . . there was a big meeting when all the management supervisors went in and said, "Well, I want this person in my area . . . I want [that] person in my area," and basically the people who didn't get picked were put on the overflow program and either they had to find a place for themselves or they were shown the door. So that was the basis for a lot of union grievances . . . we had a big contract negotiation with the union . . . they almost went on strike.

**Transitioning While Carrying Out Responsibilities of the "Old" Organization**

The transition from the "old" to the "new" organization did not occur on a particular cutoff date but, rather, over a period of few months, as different processes were staffed, and in some cases, as enabling IT was implemented. However, because different parts of the organization attempted to make the transition at different times, new positions within the redesigned business processes could not, in many cases, be immediately filled by employees selected because there was no one available to take over the selected employees' previous jobs. In the words of a reengineering team member:

> people kind of had to continue their old stuff until they could be freed up. . . . It's like, I can't leave to go to my new job until a person comes to replace me. And then that person says I can't come to replace you until this person comes to replace me. It just kept going around like this, and nobody could move.

Consequently, the envisioned processes could not be made operational, whichresulted in a kind of organizational "gridlock." Around May 1995 the "gridlock" had been somewhat resolved through informal means, and people started moving to their new roles while also performing some of their old job-related tasks. The entire organization was described as being in a "churn" with some people leaving the organization, different groups of consultants and part-time workers coming in, and the remaining TELECO employees having to learn about their new jobs almost overnight without training or support. A manager complained about the "lack of full-time transition positions" and described this mode of transition as "building the [Boeing] 747 in flight," wondering if such a transition was at all possible.

**Inconsistencies in the Redesign**

Another significant problem that became evident as the new organization was coming alive was the large number of gaps in the redesigned processes, due to which unanticipated problems arose during the actual transition. A VP felt that the "holes" had arisen because "all disciplines weren't represented" in the reengineering team and argued that it was impossible for individuals unfamiliar with a particular business area to effectively redesign that area based on some interviews: "If I know nothing about your area of expertise, I start asking you questions, you give me answers, I can come up with a totally wrong picture."

Several incidents demonstrated the limitations of envisioning business processes without having a detailed knowledge of the process elements (e.g., tasks) and the interdependencies among them. As an illustration, one VP talked about a process in which long-contested boundaries between the "outside people" (field personnel) and "inside people" (the central office employees) had been redefined for greater "effectiveness." Prior to reengineering implementation, an "inside person" was responsible for "running the jumpers" (i.e., making the connection between the horizontal and vertical side of the communication mainframe) on behalf of all "outside people." In the reengineered organization, "outside people" were expected to "run the jumper" in order to complete an order after they had completed the necessary installations in the field, and this resulted in enormous confusion:

> The day the transition was supposed to happen . . . all the installers [historically "outside people"] who were out doing their service orders are supposed to come into the central

office . . . to run what we call a "jumper" [a wire] on our mainframe. Our mainframe is about . . . 200 feet [long], and about 30 feet high. There is a ladder there, and there is reel of tape. You have to make a cross-connection from the vertical part of the mainframe to the horizontal side. . . . [Before this reengineering initiative] . . . there used to be a person in that office who did all that work for the outside people. . . . Now all these outside people are supposed to come in that morning . . . there's about 10 or 15 ["outside"] people that all have orders due . . . they all try to come into the central office at the same time. There aren't 15 places to park in the parking lot. There's only one ladder and there's only one reel of jumper wire on that mainframe . . . and there's 15 people trying to get to it. Meanwhile the telephone is ringing off the hook, because someone downtown wants the circuit tested, nobody wants to pick up the phone because it is not for them . . . they got to run their jumpers.

## Uncoordinated Implementation of Human Resources and IT Strategies

A basic assumption of the reengineering team in justifying the head count reduction was the availability and successful implementation of certain IS, which was reflected in implementation planning through dependencies in the schedule. Unfortunately, during implementation, these dependencies were not respected, primarily due to pressure from the top management. For example, when implemented, one of the systems proposed, an enhanced billing system, was expected to make about 50 customer service representatives redundant. The original plan documented in the process owner binder clearly recognized the fact that the 50 employees would lose their positions *only after* the new billing system was implemented. However, on the scheduled date of billing system implementation (as per the original plan), the human resources (HR) department, fueled by top management insistence on adherence to the original downsizing plan, laid off 50 customer service representatives, even though the new billing system was still in its early phase of design. This led to a disastrous situation in which very few customer service agents were available to serve the entire customer base using the old billing system, resulting in a rapid deterioration of service. Adding to this problem, the number of employees choosing to retire far exceeded the company's estimate (and desired number) of voluntary retirees and, as a result, left the company severely depleted of experienced HR. This problem arose in part because the TELECO management and the HR specialists, in an effort to pacify the union and to offer a "humane" way to downsize, had created a retirement package that was too attractive for the qualifying employees to "resist."

## Major Systems Not Delivered on Time by Vendors or the In-House IS Department

Most organizational members, including the process owners (VPs), attributed the "debacle" during implementation to the nondelivery of IT by the vendors. Only a handful of systems, most of them involving minor in-house enhancements of existing systems, had been successfully implemented. Many of the large systems that were expected to contribute substantially to the downsizing goals were in the analysis, or, at best, in the design phase around their scheduled delivery dates. Reflecting on the problems during implementation, a process owner explained:

a lot of the restructure or redesign was dependent on the major systems . . . coming to fruition. We have found that almost every single one of those are well behind schedule. Either they were too big, not well thought out enough . . . all required much more homework and analysis to really arrive at . . . or to be able to implement than we anticipated. . . . You need a lot of homework, I think, in the IT area. Either we as a company have a dismal track record . . . of implementing solutions, or everybody promises that, yeah, I have got this, or we can do this, but when it really comes down to delivering, you don't get what you expected and it takes longer and costs more.

A reengineering team member felt that TELECO had completely underestimated the importance of IT in the reengineered organization: "IT plays a huge, huge role in organizations . . . systems can make or break an entire company." The IS director felt that lack of appropriate technological infrastructure explained a lot of delays and problems in implementation:

some areas . . . we did have infrastructure in place and those were the areas where we tended to be more successful in our execution. The areas where we tended to be less successful is where we were trying to forge that infrastructure . . . we were forging new grounds, putting [in] tools we had never worked with . . . [resulting in] delay, frustration.

Many of the projects requiring the extension of older mainframe applications had been completed within the deadline due to TELECO's existing infrastructure and expertise in mainframe programming. Similarly, because of penetration of networked personal computers into the top layers of management, projects concerned with making corporate reference documents available online for all employees or with electronic delivery of documents at different levels of the organization could be implemented without significant difficulties and on schedule. However, projects based on the three-tier client-server architecture, with which TELECO had no prior experience, proved a more formidable challenge and, consequently, were significantly behind schedule.

## Leadership Discontinuity

A major change in TELECO's leadership at this time further worsened the personnel problems. The president, who had sponsored the reengineering initiative and supported the downsizing approach, retired around this time (early 1996), and a new president, who believed more in growth and expansion than in downsizing, assumed control of the organization. Also around this time, top management realized that some of the assumptions on which the reengineering initiative was based had not really materialized. Competition had not arrived, and, in fact, some of the potential competitors had announced that they were not interested in entering TELECO's market. In addition, other high-growth markets such as Internet services had opened up and, led by the new president's enthusiasm for growth, TELECO had entered these markets aggressively and with great success.

## DECLARING BPR "A FAILURE"

With changes in the environment and in leadership, there was much speculation regarding the fate of the reengineering initiative. A VP explained that the new president would support the reengineering plan to the extent that it would allow TELECO to "fuel the growth plans that he wanted for the business." Another VP said that, given that the competition had not arrived and that TELECO had experienced such rapid growth, the reorganization initiative as planned by the reengineering team, including the consultants, had been "outlived" but not "abandoned." He also added that the reengineering team should not be blamed for all the problems encountered during the BPR initiative:

I think the reengineering process was based on perfect conditions or utopia that really doesn't exist or never will exist . . . [but] they [members of the reengineering team] weren't so far off that things were a disaster. They were on target except they didn't hit the bull's eye, because of certain assumptions that did not materialize . . . hindsight would say you do things differently, but hindsight wasn't available. . . . I could sit here and play Monday morning quarterback, they should have done this, they should have done that, but they simply didn't know. There were some areas that they missed, but there were no ship sinkers out there.

Around the middle of 1996, the new president delivered the final blow to the reengineering initiative in a company-wide meeting where he spoke about TELECO's current state of affairs and future directions. After attending the meeting, many reengineering team members were convinced that the BPR initiative was "over." According to one, terms such as "not abandoned" and "outlived" were merely "euphemisms," and in his opinion:

The President basically said . . . "No more anything on this reengineering project. We are no more doing anything that process owner binder says" . . . pointing out that this initiative is a failure . . . it worked to get people off the payroll and that's about it.

## DISCUSSION

Many insights can be derived from the case study, and we encourage readers to formulate lessons most applicable for their own purposes. In this section, we discuss three fundamental issues that, we believe, had a significant influence on the process and outcome of TELECO's BPR initiative—top management leadership, communication, and IT knowledge and management. In this discussion, we briefly review the literature on each issue and use aspects of the TELECO case study to refine the relevant body of knowledge. We then summarize the essential elements of our knowledge on each issue in the form of diagnostic questions.

### Top Management Leadership

The existing BPR literature has recognized the critical role of leadership in BPR initiatives (e.g., Sarker and Lee, 2002). Specifically, Hammer and Champy (1993, p. 107) state that "most reengineering failures stem from the breakdowns in leadership." The importance of leadership is further highlighted in one of the "morals" of reengineering: "If you proceed to reengineer without proper leadership, you are making a fatal mistake" (Hammer and Stanton, 1995, p. 23).

Top management must formulate and communicate the vision for the reengineered organization and, through their transformative leadership, create a sense of mission among organizational members (Carr and Johansson, 1995; Hammer and Champy, 1993). Based on their detailed case study of a BPR initiative at CIGNA, Caron et al. also observed that, for successful radical change, members of the senior management must be committed to the initiative and must demonstrate their commitment "by being visibly involved with the project" (1994, p. 247). Finally, top management must view their organization not only as an economic entity whose health can be judged based on quarterly financial reports (Carr and Johansson, 1995) but also as a social system that consists of individuals trying to cope with the sweeping changes in their lives due to BPR and the resulting low morale in their workplace (Hammer and Champy, 1993; Hammer and Stanton,

1995). An implication of viewing the organization as a social system is that managers need to make careful use of "signals" (clear and explicit messages), "symbols" (actions that indirectly reinforce the signals), and "reward systems" to manage the reengineering process (Hammer and Champy, 1993, pp. 105–106).

The TELECO case study provides considerable support for the kind of guidance given in the literature. Throughout the life of the reengineering project at TELECO, top management commitment and sincerity were not in evidence. Initially, the president, it appears, was inclined toward downsizing while publicly espousing ideas of process-oriented organization and notions of cost, service, speed, and value. Also, the role of top management was very "hands-off" during the redesign as well as the implementation phases, which was evident from the nature of feedback given to the redesigners about their process visions. Almost all of the feedback was related to increasing the number of people who could be eliminated from the new processes. In one instance, the feedback was related to ensuring that the number of process owners in the final redesign should be the same as the number of VPs, thereby revealing the self-centeredness and insincerity of top management to the reengineering team members. It is also worth noting that, although the top management seemed to rely a lot on the consultants, they did not seriously consider their advice when it was not consistent with their single-minded drive toward downsizing and IT implementation. Consultants had indicated that expecting cost reductions of 50 percent through IT substitution of HR may not be feasible, and "no one's pulled [such an aggressive plan] off." In fact, a reengineering team member observed that it was difficult for the consultants to present and enact an "objective view" that they are expected to bring in because "the consultants are being paid by the people [i.e., the top management] that have the culture that you [are] trying to change." Commitment to downsizing and not to the espoused goals of reengineering was particularly evident when the HR department, prompted by top management, eliminated people from the organization as scheduled, even though the new IT-enabled process could not be implemented.

Sadly, few members of the top management team took the opportunity to signal or symbolically express concern for the suffering being experienced by organizational members, who described themselves as "dying here in the trenches." Finally, during the "traumatic" transition period, the president who had initiated the project retired and was replaced by a president who believed in growth rather than in downsizing through reengineering, resulting in discontinuity in leadership and in the strategic direction of the organization. This sudden change in focus was seen by TELECO's employees as a symbol suggesting that all their suffering had been in vain. Reflecting on the entire project, a process owner (VP) as well as a reengineering team member mentioned that, throughout the reengineering initiative, the top management team had not communicated a consistent message to the employees, and much of the confusion and lack of commitment in the organization were results of the management's contradicting signals and symbols.

The *failures* of TELECO's top management to (1) establish and communicate a vision clearly, (2) participate actively in the redesign and implementation phases, (3) empathize with reengineering team members or organizational members, (4) use consistent signals and symbols regarding the goals of the redesign to the reengineering team members, (5) show commitment to the reengineering plans by respecting the dependencies between the IS and HR plans, (6) maintain a continuity in the management team as well as the strategic direction of the organization, and (7) reflectively (not blindly) take advantage of the consultants' experience and wisdom all contributed to the failure of the BPR initiative. Based on a synthesis of the existing literature and our observations at TELECO regarding leadership, we propose the following diagnostic questions for organizations embarking on a radical change initiative.

- Do the members of the top management team have a *clear vision* for the organization after the radical change, or are they merely reacting to market forces by choosing the "easy path" of downsizing (using the rhetoric of BPR to legitimate their short-term easy fix)?
- Are the members of the top management *in touch with the human organization* that they manage or do they merely view their organization in terms of revenue, cost, or profitability *numbers*?
- Are the top-level managers willing to be *closely involved* in the formulation of the redesign and implementation plans, and thereafter be *committed to the plans*? Or are they inclined to delegate all the responsibilities to a team of middle managers and consultants, whose plans can be changed at their (i.e., the top managers') whims?
- Is there likely to be a *continuity/stability in the leadership* while the radical change initiative is in progress?
- Finally, should conditions necessitating the radical change initiative no longer hold true, does the top management team have *contingency plans* for easing the organization toward a different strategic direction?

## Communication

Communication is seen as a central organizational issue by a number of authors. Hammer and Stanton see the importance of communication or selling change "over and above all their other challenges" (1995, p. 136). They identify impediments to communication such as "false familiarity, disbelief, fear of layoffs" and propose "ten principles of reengineering communications":

1. Segment the audience
2. Use multiple channels
3. Use multiple voices
4. Be clear
5. Communicate, communicate, communicate
6. Honesty is the only policy
7. Use emotion, not just logic
8. Heal, console, encourage
9. Make the message tangible
10. Listen, listen, listen (Hammer and Stanton, 1995, p. 151)

Carr and Johansson (1995) also emphasize the importance of communication in BPR implementation in their list of 16 best practices. They state, "Communicate effectively to create a buy-in. Then communicate more" (1995, p. 31). On similar lines, Caron et al. advise BPR practitioners to communicate "truthfully, broadly and via multiple forums" (1994, p. 248). Davenport provides similar guidance when he states:

> a concerted effort must be made to communicate throughout the change program and to build commitment to the new design. . . . Communication and commitment building must occur at all levels and for all types of audiences . . . regular communication must be established between the executive and process innovation teams and those who will be affected by the new process. Sensitive issues, such as level and type of personnel reductions to result from the initiative, must be addressed honestly and openly. (1993, p. 191)

Problems in TELECO's communication strategy were apparent from the beginning of the initiative, and the guidelines regarding communication in the BPR literature were clearly not utilized in this initiative. The early stages of TELECO's reengineering initiative were shrouded in secrecy (due to confidentiality regarding the goals of the initiative and insider trading concerns), which resulted in the development of considerable ill feeling and mistrust among employees. There were few (if any) attempts to address concerns and fears of employees and thereby gain back their trust.

The use of offensive, rather than enabling, metaphors (Hirschheim and Newman 1991; Tillquist 2002) such as "quick hits" and "low-hanging fruit," some of which were introduced by consultants in the reengineering language (and their use not controlled by management), further widened the rift between the employees and those driving the reengineering initiative. During the implementation phase, there appeared to have been a genuine attempt made by some reengineering team members to get feedback regarding the redesigns from the other organizational members through "quick-look sessions." Unfortunately, participants of these sessions did not feel comfortable in sharing their honest views regarding the redesigns, perhaps due to fear of losing jobs or the lack of trust, or both. More communication was initiated later during implementation, with special information sessions conducted to explain "what the [new] jobs are going to entail, and how the process was supposed to work, and things like that." In addition, there were sessions where reengineering team members or "open" members of the management invited input from employees about the effects of the initiative and ways to smooth over some potential difficulties. Regretfully, hardly any action was taken to reflect that employees' inputs had been understood and valued. A marketing executive explained:

> I don't think there was a good feedback loop . . . they heard all the things . . . we're dying here in the trenches, things are going wrong and people are losing orders and everything is falling apart on us, things are not coming together like we need them to. And all the input went above or somewhere and we never heard anything . . . well, how are you fixing it, how [has] anything changed? I think everyone feels like they are dying and struggling . . . it's really hard on the morale, too.

To summarize, while there was some sharing of information after the initial phases of the reengineering, communication at TELECO was rarely directed toward building trust and mutual understanding. Communication was unilaterally initiated by the management/reengineering team members when they needed information or needed to share information; communication was discontinued when there was no such need, in their view. Based on our understanding of the literature as well as the events at TELECO, we propose the following diagnostic questions regarding communication for organizations undertaking a radical change initiative:

- Does the organization have *well thought-out plans* for communicating with the employees *throughout the life* of the initiative?
- Is the communication merely intended to *share information unidirectionally*, or is it to promote *mutual understanding* and *trust* between the management and the employees?
- Is there an *open communication* directed toward promoting mutual understanding among the reengineering team members and between the members of the top management and the reengineering team, or are there likely to be serious *distortions* in their communication due to power differences and conflicting self-interests?
- Finally, are the *metaphors in the organizational language* carefully controlled to ensure that they do not lead to the breakdown of communication and trust among the different stakeholder groups?

**IT Knowledge and Management**

Last, but certainly not the least, is the issue of an appropriate conceptualization of IT, adequate knowledge of IT, and the adoption of appropriate IT management principles.

Many authors appear to share the belief that IT is one of the key enablers of BPR (Davenport, 1993; Manganelli and Klein, 1994; Sethi and King, 1998). A number of authors have discussed the capabilities of IT and attempted to explain how reengineering team members can take advantage of IT in enabling more efficient and effective business processes. For example, Lucas and Baroudi (1994) provided a set of new organizational design variables enabled by IT pertaining primarily to the structure and to the work processes within organizations. Davenport (1993) categorized the different ways in which IT can change organizations as automational, informational, tracking, analytical, capturing, sharing and distributing intellectual assets, sequential, integrative, geographical, and disintermediation, and has also provided a description of a number of generic technologies useful in enabling new processes. Hammer and Champy (1993) argued for "inductive thinking" in harnessing the "disruptive power" of IT in order to break old rules that limit the potential of business processes. Grover et al. (1995) described how IT may be used to increase the functional coupling among elements of a process. Stoddard and Jarvenpaa (1995) highlighted the importance of IT infrastructure as an enabler if present or inhibitor if absent or deficient. A number of authors have also evaluated the advantages of using IT-based BPR tools (Kettinger et al., 1997; Sarker and Lee, 2006), and many have recommended their adoption by redesign teams (e.g., Davenport, 1993; Irani et al., 2000; Klein, 1998).

Examination of the TELECO situation in conjunction with the existing body of knowledge suggests that a number of IT-related issues at TELECO have not been prominently addressed in the BPR literature. This seems somewhat ironic, given the prominence of IS researchers/practitioners in the BPR community and the widely acknowledged importance of IT in enabling and implementing BPR (Land, 1996). One of the main problems during redesign at TELECO was that the redesigners did not have an adequate understanding of the capabilities and limitations of process-enabling technologies, and there was no organizational mechanism in place for them to improve their understanding. This lack of understanding of IT, consequently, led to unrealistic process redesigns that relied on underspecified systems that were extremely complex. In some cases, infeasible BPR tools used in the redesign process also appeared to have had both positive and negative effects on the redesign effectiveness, and this observation is at odds with the existing literature that unequivocally portrays tools as having positive influence on redesign effectiveness. Moreover, the lack of awareness of active and emergent characteristics of IT resulted in the BPR team not being at all prepared to deal with complications associated with BPR tools and with the nonperformance of IT applications. Outsourcing contracts with vague systems specifications were awarded preferentially to a "sister organization" and not managed carefully to ensure on-budget and on-time delivery. IT infrastructure was not adequately planned for and implemented to enable a smooth transition to the new systems. Finally, IS management and personnel appeared to have lacked the credibility to convince top management to respect the dependencies between the IS and HR strategies. Again, based on our observations at TELECO, we propose the following diagnostic questions addressing the IT knowledge and management issue:

- Is there a sufficient level of understanding among the reengineering team members regarding the *capabilities and limitations of a broad range of process-enabling IT* options?
- Is there some understanding among the redesigners/management regarding the *circumstances and the extent of use of computerized BPR tools* (for flowcharting, simulation, project manage-

ment, etc.) that is actually helpful in creating effective process redesigns? Have the redesigners/management entertained the possibility that *IT applications/tools may have unintended or unanticipated "revenge" effects* (Markus and Robey, 2004)? Or have they considered that the likelihood that the tools to *enact active roles* of a "manipulator" or a "traitor" rather than the presumed passive roles (Askenas and Westelius, 2000; Hanseth and Braa, 1998)?

- Is there an appreciation among the reengineering team members as well as the organization's top management of the *complexities, lead times,* and *costs* associated with the development and implementation of IT required to enable the redesigned processes?
- Are there *formal or informal organizational mechanisms* in place that can enable redesigners to educate themselves in areas (both functional and technological) where they may be deficient?
- Do formal organizational *procedures and standards* exist *with respect to outsourcing* of systems development and managing vendor contracts, and are they followed during the initiative?
- Does the organization possess the *necessary IT infrastructure* for the smooth adoption of the new systems?
- Is there *alignment between the overall organizational strategy-in-use with respect to BPR and the IT strategy-in-use* and between *the IT strategy-in-use and the strategies-in-use of other functional areas* (e.g., HR)? Does *IS management have the credibility* to advise or convince top management regarding the need to align the efforts of different functions toward the achievement of organizational goals?

In conclusion, we reiterate that managing a BPR initiative is extremely complex and difficult, and there is (and can be) no guaranteed path to success (Galliers and Baets, 1998). Although BPR may no longer be the hottest topic in management (Jones, 1994), and the rhetoric associated with BPR may appear less pompous and less self-assured today, the underlying notion of IT-enabled BPC (e.g., Grover and Kettinger, 2000) continues to enjoy significant popularity and relevance, whether as part of radical organizational transformation with or without downsizing, quality programs, enterprise resource planning (ERP) implementation, or e-commerce implementation. An in-depth understanding of the organizational experiences, such as those at TELECO, can help in anticipating problems and initiating action to mitigate or avoid them. We believe that this paper makes two significant contributions in this regard. First, it sensitizes readers to issues that can prove to be critical to the outcome of a BPR initiative, and this sensitivity is likely to help readers recognize problems arising from those issues in their own contexts and take timely action. Second, the in-depth documentation of events at TELECO provides the BPR and IS communities with an opportunity to revisit, reevaluate, relearn, and reconsolidate knowledge regarding BPR and IT management. We have attempted to consolidate the knowledge on three key issues in the form of questions that organizations can use to examine their preparedness for undertaking BPR. While the diagnostic questions proposed are neither comprehensive nor universally applicable, they provide a useful set of pointers for organizations seeking to avert a disaster in their IT-enabled radical change initiatives similar to the one experienced at TELECO.

## ACKNOWLEDGMENTS

This is an updated version of an article previously published as S. Sarker and A.S. Lee, IT-enabled organizational transformation: A case study of BPR failure at TELECO, *Journal of Strategic Information Systems,* 8, 1 (1999), 83–103. Revised and expanded with permission from Elsevier B.V.

## NOTES

1. We use redesigner, process redesigner, and reengineering team member interchangeably in this case.

2. Cells representing most critical and lowest cost projects, moderately critical and lowest cost projects, and most critical and moderate cost projects.

## REFERENCES

Askenas, L., and Westelius, A. 2000. Five roles of an information system: A social constructivist approach to analyzing the use of ERP systems. In W.J. Orlikowski, S. Ang, P. Weill, and H.C. Krcmar (eds.), *Proceedings of the Twenty-First International Conference on Information Systems*. Atlanta: Association for Information Systems, pp. 426–433.

Caron, J.R.; Jarvenpaa, S.L.; and Stoddard, D.B. 1994. Business reengineering at CIGNA Corporation: Experiences and lessons from the first five years. *MIS Quarterly*, 18, 3, 233–250.

Carr, D.K., and Johansson, H.J. 1995. *Best Practices in Reengineering: What Works and What Doesn't in the Reengineering Process*. New York: McGraw-Hill.

Davenport, T.H. 1993. *Process Innovation: Reengineering Work Through Information Technology*. Boston: Harvard Business School Press.

Galliers, R.D., and Baets, W.R.J. 1998. *Information Technology and Organizational Transformation: Innovation for the 21st Century Organization*. Chichester, UK: Wiley.

Grover, V., and Kettinger, W.J. 2000. Business process change: A reflective view of theory, practice, and implications. In R.W. Zmud (ed.), *Framing the Domains of IT Management*. Cincinnati, OH: Pinnaflex, pp. 147–172.

Grover, V.; Teng, J.T.C.; and Fiedler, K. 1995. Technological and organizational enablers of business process reengineering. In V. Grover and W.J. Kettinger (eds.), *Business Process Change: Reengineering Concepts, Methods and Technologies*. Hershey, PA: Idea Group, pp. 16–33.

Hammer, M., and Champy, J. 1993. *Reengineering the Corporation*. New York: Free Press.

Hammer, M., and Stanton, S. 1995. *The Reengineering Revolution*. New York: HarperCollins.

Hanseth, O., and Braa, K. 1998. Technology as traitor: SAP infrastructures in global organization. In R. Hirschheim, M. Newman, and J.I. DeGross (eds.), *Proceedings of the Nineteenth International Conference on Information Systems*. Atlanta: Association for Information Systems, pp. 188–196.

Hirschheim, R., and Newman, M. 1991. Symbolism and information systems development: Myth, metaphor and magic. *Information Systems Research*, 2, 1, 29–62.

Irani, Z.; Hlupic, V.; Baldwin, L.P.; and Love, P. 2000. Re-engineering manufacturing process through simulation modeling. *Logistics Information Management*, 13, 1, 7–13.

Jones, M. 1994. Don't emancipate, exaggerate: Rhetoric, reality and reengineering. In R. Baskerville, S. Smithson, O. Ngwenyama, and J.I. DeGross (eds.), *Transforming Organizations with Information Technology*. Amsterdam: Elsevier Science, pp. 357–378.

Kettinger, W.J.; Teng, J.T.C.; and Guha, S. 1997. Business process change: A study of methodologies, techniques and tools. *MIS Quarterly*, 21, 1, 55–80.

Klein, M.M. 1998. Reengineering methodologies and tools: A prescription for enhancing success. In V. Sethi and W.R. King (eds.), *Organizational Transformation Through Business Process Reengineering*. Upper Saddle River, NJ: Prentice Hall, pp. 243–251.

Land, F. 1996. The new alchemist: How to transmute base organizations into corporations of gleaming gold. *Journal of Strategic Information Systems*, 5, 1, 7–17.

Lucas, H.C., and Baroudi, J. 1994. The role of information technology in organizational design. *Journal of Management Information Systems*, 10, 4 (Spring), 9–23.

Manganelli, R.L., and Klein, M.M. 1994. *The Reengineering Handbook: A Step-By-Step Guide to Business Transformation*. New York: AMACOM.

Markus, M.L., and Robey, D. 2004. Why stuff happens: Explaining the unintended consequences of using IT. In K.V. Andersen and M.T. Vendelø (eds.), *The Past and Future of Information Systems*. Oxford: Elsevier Butterworth-Heinemann, pp. 61–93.

Sarker, S., and Lee, A.S. 2002. Using a positivist case research methodology to test three competing practitioner theories-in-use of business process redesign. *Journal of the AIS*, 2, article 7, 1–72.

————. 2006. Does the use of computer-based BPC tools contribute to redesign effectiveness? Insights from a hermeneutic study. *IEEE Transactions on Engineering Management,* 53, 1, 130–145.

Sethi, V., and King, W.R. 1998. *Organizational Transformation Through Business Process Reengineering.* Upper Saddle River, NJ: Prentice Hall.

Stoddard, D.B., and Jarvenpaa, S.L. 1995. Business process redesign: Tactics for managing radical change. *Journal of Management Information Systems*, 12, 1 (Summer), 81–107.

Tillquist, J. 2000. Institutional bridging: How conceptions of IT-enabled change shape the planning process. *Journal of Management Information Systems*, 17, 2 (Fall), 115–152.

————. 2002. Rules of the game: Constructing norms of influence, subordination and constraint in IT planning. *Information & Organization,* 12, 1, 39–70.

# PART VI

# TRENDS AND CHALLENGES IN TRANSFORMING BUSINESS PROCESSES

# CHAPTER 13

# TRANSFORMING HUMAN RESOURCE PROCESSES THROUGH OUTSOURCING

## Enterprise Partnership at BAE Systems

LESLIE P. WILLCOCKS, MARY LACITY, AND DAVID FEENY

**Abstract:** *Senior executives continue to seek ways to transform back-office processes such as information technology (IT), human resource management, finance, and accounting. Can these functions be managed to simultaneously reduce costs and improve service? Historically, senior executives have used several models of transformation: do-it-yourself, management consultants, fee-for-service outsourcing, and even the occasional joint venture. Although these transformation models remain viable for various contexts, a more recent model has emerged that warrants attention—the enterprise partnership. With an enterprise partnership, the customer and supplier create a jointly owned enterprise that both services the customer investor as well as seeks external customers. The enterprise partnership model is illustrated through an in-depth case study of BAE Systems and Xchanging's partnership for human resource management, including underlying IT support. The chapter provides a framework and assesses the lessons for selecting and managing back-office transformations. Many lessons seem counterintuitive to previous research findings, including selecting a supplier with generic business competencies rather than domain-specific knowledge, selecting a culturally "incompatible" supplier, and delaying due diligence until after the deal is well under way.*

**Keywords:** *Business Transformation Models, Back Offices, Business Process Outsourcing, Supplier Relationships, Core Capabilities, Management Consultancy, Human Resource Management*

## INTRODUCTION

Given the global economic recession from 2001–4, senior executives have more than ever been seeking ways to radically reduce the costs and improve the service of back-office functions such as information technology (IT), human resource management, finance, and accounting. One way forward has been to outsource. According to some estimates, if business process outsourcing (BPO) was a $119.4 billion industry in 2001, it will be a $234 billion plus industry by the end of 2005. By our estimates, it is likely to grow worldwide by 10 percent a year between 2005 and 2010 (Lacity and Willcocks, 2006; Willcocks and Cullen, 2005). One trend has been to move from incremental improvements to a few processes, toward attempting organizational reformations in back-office functions. Bank of America provides an example. During the past decade, its growth was spawned by acquisitions, resulting in overstaffed, idiosyncratic, duplicate, and incompatible back offices. In the area of human resources (HR), the bank recognized significant savings could be achieved through centralization, standardization, and downsizing. Bank of America chose to transform the back office through a partnership with start-up company Exult.[1] Bank of America took equity stake in Exult in exchange for guaranteed cost savings and significant improvement in HR services, largely enabled by Exult's proprietary eHR platform (Cagle and Campbell, 2002). The deal, worth about $1.1 billion over 10 years, also provides Bank of America with shares in Exult's revenues from external customers. Exult has won significant contracts beyond Bank of America, including a $700 million deal with Prudential Financial and a $600 million deal with International Paper.

Theoretically, Bank of America could have done the transformation itself, thereby accruing all of the savings, or pursued other transformation models, such as management consultants or fee-for-service outsourcing. In this chapter, we provide a framework for evaluating five back-office transformation models—do-it-yourself, management consultants, fee-for-service outsourcing, joint ventures, and enterprise partnerships. While most senior executives are familiar with the first four transformation models, the enterprise partnership warrants particular attention because of its relative newness. With an enterprise partnership, the customer and supplier create a jointly owned enterprise that both services the customer investor as well as seeks external customers. However, this is not a traditional "joint venture" with equally shared risks and rewards. Rather, the supplier bears more risk and the primary purpose of the enterprise is to service the customer investor. The enterprise partnership addresses the lack of alignment in fee-for-service outsourcing while minimizing the customer risks of a joint venture.

Here we will illustrate the enterprise partnership model through an in-depth case study of BAE Systems (BAES) and Xchanging's partnership for human resource management, including underlying IT support. When outsourcing human resource management in 2001, BAES and Xchanging employed an *enterprise partnership model* in which the parties created a new business, called Xchanging HR Services (XHRS). BAES is both a customer and an investor in this new enterprise. After its first two years of operations, BAES had already received the following benefits:

- contractual cost savings delivered on baseline HR services,
- service improvement in many service areas,
- new Web-based technology capabilities rolled out to over 40,000 users,
- a new state-of-the art shared service center built and occupied,
- greater focus on strategic activities by retained BAES managers, and
- greater service focus of transferred BAES staff through retraining.

Of course, such transformation is never painless, and BAES and Xchanging learned many lessons along the way. This chapter analyses their experiences and provides:

- A framework for assessing back-office transformation models, including do-it-yourself, management consultancy, fee-for-service outsourcing, joint ventures, and enterprise partnership.
- A profile of the ideal customer for the enterprise partnership model.
- Lessons on back-office transformation that challenge common wisdom. For example, clients are advised to consider a supplier that may be culturally "incompatible" and a supplier with generic business competencies rather than domain-specific knowledge.

As will be shown, findings from this research counter findings from research on fee-for-service outsourcing carried out from the 1990s (see Cullen and Willcocks, 2003; Kern and Willcocks, 2001; Lacity and Willcocks, 2001). Previously, the research suggested: write complete, detailed contracts; carry out due diligence; do not trust the supplier (and be sure to retain core IT capability); ensure the supplier has cultural fit together with sector and domain knowledge and experience; and write short-term (three-to-five year) contracts because the technology changes so fast. We can see in the BAES case all of these prescriptions being contradicted to some degree. For customers and suppliers alike, these innovations create both new possibilities and also genuine challenges. For researchers, it is going to be particularly interesting to study over this decade how the enterprise partnership model plays out alongside other models of back-office transformation.

## BAE SYSTEMS: THE CUSTOMER CONTEXT

British Aerospace (BAe) was formed as a government-owned enterprise in 1978 from a series of independent companies in the UK aerospace industry. It brought together businesses that included military aircraft, commercial aircraft (through its shareholding in Airbus), Jetstream (commuter aircraft), Dynamics (missiles), and Royal Ordinance (weapons). Since its inception, BAe fostered the independence of its operating divisions. Business units had historically been in charge of their own profitability and support services, including IT and HR. The decentralized culture is required because each strategic business unit (SBU) operates under dramatically different production, marketing, and legal environments.

In the early 1990s, BAe was confronted with loss of sales due to the end of the cold war and economic recession. To improve profitability, BAe senior management focused on core competencies in aircraft, divested noncore divisions, refinanced the company, and outsourced some back-office functions such as IT. BAe reduced head count by 21,000 employees. As a result, profitability increased to £230 million[2] on £11 billion in sales in 1994. But from 1997 through 1999, BAe's sales growth stagnated. To expand their global markets, British Aerospace and GEC's Marconi Electronic Systems proposed a merger in January 1999, called BAE Systems. Investors were promised that the synergies from the merger would result in annual cost savings in excess of £275 million within three years of completion of the transaction. While BAES would continue to invest in their core capabilities in military aircraft, weapon systems, nuclear submarines, and large commercial aircraft, all support functions were mandated to deliver significant cost savings.

In the area of human resource management, BAE's Group HR Director, Terry Morgan, was charged with delivering a minimum of 15 percent cost savings with a stretch target of 40 percent on an estimated annual HR internal spend of £25 million while maintaining the same level of service. At that time in 1999, Group HR was actually a small department, focusing on senior pay and benefits, senior-level development, and organizational design. Nearly all of the HR head count of about 700 people were decentralized within the SBU. Within the SBUs, the decentralized HR people delivered transactional activities, such as payroll, benefits administration, recruiting, and training as well as professional services such as training design, industrial relations, and HR procurement (see Figure 13.1). Morgan believed the only way he could deliver the mandated cost savings was to centralize much of HR into shared services.

Morgan assembled a team to investigate the shared services concept, including people interviewed for this case (see Appendix 13.1 for a full list of interviewees):

- Chris Dickson, who was responsible for senior management pay and benefits in the HR head office, became one of the lead architects of shared services;

Figure 13.1 **BAE Systems's Vision for Transforming Human Resources**

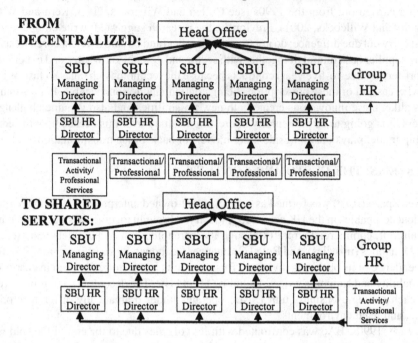

- Alan Bailey, a 20-year BAe veteran who had moved from engineering to project management to HR, became the team's project manager;
- David Bauernfeind, seconded from a financial controller role in BAe, analyzed the financial consequences of shared service options;
- Steve Hodgson, HR Director for BAe's Royal Ordnance business, was one of those who represented business unit interests in plans for shared HR services;
- Kim Reid, HR Director for the Customer Solutions and Support business group, was in a similar role as Hodgson.

According to Dickson, the team had in mind that 80 percent of HR was probably transactional activity and only 20 percent of HR was strategic or core. Thus the team proposed a design of HR shared services that entailed a significant centralization of HR head count and resources, leaving only HR directors and small HR teams in the SBUs.

## REJECTING TRADITIONAL TRANSFORMATION CHOICES

Initially, the HR team considered and rejected three possibilities for implementation of shared services: do it themselves, hire a management consultancy to help with the transition, or outsource HR entirely (see Table 13.1).

### Do It Themselves

The major benefit of doing it themselves was obviously that BAES would directly benefit from the savings without sharing them with a third party. For this reason, many business unit managers preferred this option over hiring outsiders:

Table 13.1

**BAE Systems's Assessment of Transformation Options**

| Pros | Cons |
|---|---|
| **Do It Yourself** | |
| • Realize all the cost benefits internally | • Senior management will not make technology investment required to implement shared service |
| • Most politically acceptable | • Internal resistance from business units to centralized services |
| | • Lack of empowerment and skills of internal HR to make the quantum changes required |
| **Management Consultancy** | |
| • Infusion of external energy and skills | • Large, expensive project that will likely cost escalate once consultancy is on-site |
| • Ability of outsiders to bypass internal political resistance | • Consultancy has no ultimate accountability or ownership of outcome |
| • Clear mandate from senior management that project will be done | • Lack of skills and knowledge transfer |
| | • Lack of sustainability |
| **Fee-for-Service Outsourcing** | |
| • Infusion of external energy and skills | • Customer and supplier incentives are misaligned |
| • Ability of outsiders to bypass internal political resistance | • Power asymmetries develop in favor of supplier |
| • Clear mandate from senior management that project will be done | |
| • One-time savings achieved up front | |
| • Supplier accountability for results | |
| • Escalating costs | |
| • Lack of sustainability | |
| **Enterprise Partnership** | |
| • Infusion of external energy and skills | • Start-up company, may subsequently go out of business |
| • Ability of outsiders to bypass internal political resistance | • Business model may be overly dependent on revenues from external customers that do not materialize |
| • Clear mandate from senior management that project will be done | |
| • One-time savings achieved up front and continued cost savings guaranteed for five years | |
| • Supplier accountability for results | |
| • Up-front technology investment made by supplier | |
| • Customer and supplier incentives aligned | |
| • Joint board of directors ensures customer participation and oversight | |

My initial feeling was, why the hell can't we do this ourselves? If we can do it ourselves, it might be a better proposition because we are not giving half of the savings away. (David Bauernfeind, previously BAe Divisional Financial Controller, now CFO of XHRS)

However, there were three major impediments to doing it themselves. First, the creation of shared services would require a significant investment in facilities and Web-based technology, known as eHR. Given senior management's penchant for cost cuts, as well as their preference for investing only in core businesses, the HR team knew a request for HR capital funding would probably be rejected. Second, because the business unit managers would resist giving up resource control, significant political resistance was anticipated. A project led by in-house back-office managers may be sabotaged. Third, senior management perceived that the internal HR staff lacked the power, enthusiasm, skills, and mentality to drive forth such a drastic change. This was not a reflection on the HR individuals, just recognition that most HR personnel historically were treated, and therefore behaved, as "nine-to-five" back-office staff. Clearly, an infusion of external energy, experience, and skills was needed.

## Management Consultancy

The HR team considered whether to hire an outside management consultancy to manage a one-time, big-bang implementation project. The benefits of this option were the necessary infusion of energy and skills and the ability of external managers to bypass internal politics by having a direct conduit to senior BAES management. Furthermore, by bringing in prestigious consultants, senior management would signal to the organization that they had committed to the project. But the HR team identified these major risks that they previously experienced with consultants: high costs, lack of accountability for and sustainability of results, and lack of skills transfer.

## Fee-for-Service Outsourcing

The HR team did not seriously consider a traditional, fee-for-service outsourcing option because of the perceived problems the model caused in prior supplier relationships. Although fee-for-service outsourcing had many benefits, such as an external infusion of energy and skills, the ability to bypass internal politics, the clear message that services would be centralized, up-front savings, and supplier accountability for results, there were at least three negative consequences: escalating costs due to unbridled demand, lack of sustainability of cost savings and service levels, and power asymmetries favoring the supplier. With some prior outsourcing deals, BAES found that once central control of the budget had gone, demand for services—and thus costs—ran amuck. For example, some managers within BAES complained that their IT costs were too high since they outsourced IT in 1994 to Computer Sciences Corp. (CSC). But much of the higher cost was attributable to that fact that BAES relied more heavily on IT in the design and manufacture of aircraft, a rationale that is often neglected when discussing IT cost escalation.

BAES management also feared the possible lack of sustainability with fee-for-service outsourcing. While BAES enjoyed an initial one-time, up-front savings with many of their outsourcing deals, over time, it found that some suppliers lacked incentives to sustain innovation, to improve service, or to share additional cost savings with BAES. Although lengthy contract negotiations up front were designed to prevent such deterioration, the fact remained that customer and supplier incentives were never adequately aligned with fee-for-service outsourcing. Supplier margins were based on squeezing as much profit as they could from baseline service definitions while encouraging significant contract additions from decentralized users. The final negative consequence BAES experienced with fee-for-service outsourcing was power asymmetries developing in favor of the supplier. It is difficult to award additions to a contract to an alternative supplier because technologies and services are highly integrated, thus suppliers can premium price add-ons.

These three negative consequences stem from the governance structure of fee-for-service outsourcing. With a fee-for-service outsourcing deal, every dollar from the customer's pocket is a dollar in the supplier's pocket. Because incentives are not aligned, the parties must take extreme efforts to protect their interests during lengthy contract negotiations. Moreover, global outsourcing contracts can literally occupy ten legal boxes. Such contracts are extremely difficult to understand, monitor, and enforce. In the midst of debating these three options in early 2000, a serendipitous fourth option emerged—the enterprise partnership.

## CHOOSING THE ENTERPRISE PARTNERSHIP

David Andrews, CEO and founder of the newly formed company, Xchanging, proposed that BAES and Xchanging should form a fifty-fifty jointly owned enterprise. The enterprise would be operated as an SBU within Xchanging, giving Xchanging the responsibility and accountability for implementation and subsequent operations. But both BAES and Xchanging would sit on the board of directors to ensure continued customer involvement and oversight. The enterprise would initially behave as a traditional outsourcer by transferring BAES HR assets and personnel to the enterprise, governed by a ten-year contract. The enterprise, in turn, would implement the shared services concept and deliver HR services back to BAES. But, in the long run, the enterprise would further leverage the HR assets and personnel to attract external HR customers, of which profits would be shared fifty-fifty with BAES. Andrews also promised the following:

- to transfer top talent to the enterprise to ensure the necessary infusion of experience, energy, and competency;
- to deliver guaranteed minimum cost savings for five years to BAES in the form of a rebate;
- to significantly invest in technology, worth $25 million, primarily to implement eHR; and
- to provide warrants in Xchanging, which could be very valuable if and when Xchanging went public.

In concept, an enterprise partnership offered significantly more benefits over the previous three options while mitigating their negative consequences. However, there was an obvious risk: as a start-up company, with no existing revenue stream, the possibility that Xchanging would experience financial difficulties in its first few years seemed very high. However, the HR team was impressed by Xchanging's executives and finances. Concerning executives, they concluded Xchanging's talent was world-class:

> Are these people winners or losers? You just couldn't form any view other than these people are going to be winners. (David Bauernfeind, previously BAe Divisional Financial Controller, now CFO of XHRS)

They knew that General Atlantic Partners had provided $60 million in venture capital to Xchanging. Clearly Xchanging had the cash to develop their business. The enterprise partnership was deemed the best model.

In June 2000, a letter of intent was signed. BAES retained HR strategy, executive recruitment and development, organizational design, and other strategic HR activities. The HR team had planned to transfer all transactional/professional HR activities to the partnership, but negotiations within BAES proved long and difficult. Divisional managers argued to de-scope the deal by retaining nearly 40 percent of the targeted 20 percent of HR staff. A final agreement was signed February 22, 2001, effective May 1, 2001.

## CONTRACT OVERVIEW

The BAES–Xchanging HR contract is worth at least £250 million and endures for ten years. From a BAES perspective, all cost savings would be shared 50/50 in line with the ownership structure. However, a proportion of these savings would be guaranteed with only Xchanging at risk. In the first year Xchanging would guarantee them x percent savings, with the percentage increasing to x plus 5 percent for the next four years. In May 2006, BAES and Xchanging will re-base the price using a cost-plus model for the remainder of the ten-year contract.

Much of the contract specifies how the parties will govern the enterprise, including the identification of three boards: the board of directors, the service review board, and the technology review board. The *board of directors* comprises both Xchanging executives as well as BAES HR executives and non-HR managing directors. Xchanging has a majority of the board to ensure operational control. The board of directors meets quarterly. The *service review board* is a committee, with equal membership, charged with ensuring excellent HR service by monitoring service delivery and quickly remedying service problems. A service problem escalated to the service review board requires an action plan to remedy the situation within a maximum three-month period. The service review board is given teeth through provision for price reductions as a result of poor performance. The ultimate sanction is the board's ability to oust the enterprise partnership CEO for continuing poor performance. The *technology review board,* also jointly populated by Xchanging and BAES, was created to ensure that Xchanging makes the promised $25 million investment. Other important aspects of the contract include:

- Xchanging is required to provide the "as-is" service, to be measured during the first six months of operation. The contract also requires Xchanging to improve on the baseline service to the upper quartile by the end of year five.
- Xchanging must make a $25 million investment, primarily in IT to realize eHR and physical facilities to house the centralized HR staff.
- 462 BAES people were identified for transfer, together with another 53 "positions vacant."

## IMPLEMENTING THE ENTERPRISE PARTNERSHIP: MAY 2001–DECEMBER 2002

During the May 2001–December 2002 period, Xchanging successfully transferred and reoriented BAES employees, defined and gained approval of 400 service levels, delivered Web-based eHR, reorganized the HR function to realize the shared services vision, built and occupied a new XHRS facility, and began redesigning service processes. Each of these activities is explained in more detail.

### Employee Reorientation

In May 2001, 462 BAES employees formally transferred into the enterprise partnership. The supplier celebrated their arrival with a major launch event. Richard Houghton, CEO of XHRS, discussed the exciting things employees would experience now that they were a profit center. Next, all of the transferred employees attended a three-day induction training. The training included personal presentations by all XHRS senior executives about the employees' new roles in developing XHRS. The training not only served to invigorate transfers but also to explain the realities of a commercial enterprise:

We started up by saying "these are the cost reduction commitments," I said "we'd have to double productivity in five years," I said "insofar as we can offset that through third-party revenues by effectively using spare capacity to deliver services to third parties we will, but that's what we are going to do." (Richard Houghton, CEO of XHRS)

## Defining Over 400 Service Levels

As promised in the contract, Xchanging created 400 service levels for eight service classes within the first six months of operation:

- reward and recognition,
- learning and development,
- resource management,
- employee documentation,
- HR information services,
- international resources,
- pension management,
- advisory and support service

The completed Service Definition was ratified by the service review board in October 2001. These service definitions became the basis for both customers and providers to measure performance. From the BAES perspective, the HR service improved quickly:

I do think that the service from a process, control point of view has improved extraordinarily. I think Xchanging really does have the right processes in place, they really know what they are doing on that. Some of the transformation that I have seen in some of the people that are in XHRS, especially the customer relationship managers, one or two of them, they never would have interacted with the business in the way that are doing now, they have become a lot more professional. They are a lot more understanding of what drives a business, understanding of cost base and how you actually get value out of a business, so that's been quite a nice surprise to see that happen and to see that happen so quickly. (Kim Reid, HR Director, BAES)

## Managing £80 Million in Indirect HR Spending

During the measurement exercise, BAES and Xchanging recognized that HR spent much more than the direct cost to BAES of £25 million per annum; HR was also the agent for no less than £80 million per annum of indirect procurement for items such as cars, health care, and nontechnical contract labor such as clerical staff and cleaners from an estimated 200 suppliers. BAES had begun to more closely manage this spending, but both parties saw huge opportunities for improvement by consolidating the buying power across BAES's SBUs and across Xchanging's other customers (which now included large clients such as Lloyd's of London for Policy Administration). Given the scale and scope of this HR procurement, BAES and Xchanging felt it needed the attention of a separate enterprise partnership. This led to the establishment of Xchanging Procurement Services in November 2001, a partnership deal worth £800 million over ten years.

**Delivering eHR**

Xchanging had committed to launch the first version of eHR, called "peopleportal," within six months of signing the contract. Xchanging's CEO believed this date was realistic because Xchanging Practice Director for Technology, Steve Bowen, already had a detailed technology blueprint based on reusable components. Xchanging first thought they would hire suppliers to build the design, but that quickly proved too expensive and too risky, because the suppliers would retain all the knowledge of the source code. Instead, Xchanging went on a recruiting rampage and quickly hired 19 full-time technology managers, architects, and specialists supplemented by six contract workers hired through mid-2002. As promised, Xchanging delivered the first version of people-portal on October 4, 2001. Its effects were profound:

> The peopleportal has been the first sign from within the business that something has changed, something has actually happened. . . . We had a lot of very good feedback, it was very good, the technology was great, it was Web-based, but we've had some very good feedback but we've also had people who just can't get the hang of using the technology. (Kim Reid, HR Director, BAES)

**Reorganizing into Shared Service Streams**

On January 1, 2002, XHRS was reorganized along centralized service streams (see Figure 13.1). To house these centralized teams, David Andrews built a state-of-the-art shared service facility for XHRS. The new building served to further boost employee morale and clearly signaled to BAES and the world that XHRS was truly a front-office HR business.

Overall, there are seven service stream heads and initially 40 service stream team leaders now in charge of cross-business services. Each service stream now operates as its own mini-business, and the service heads understand that they are responsible for further cost reductions and further streamlining. Most of the savings have come from downsizing staff. For example, recruitment, when consolidated, comprised 106 HR people, but Xchanging estimates that only 40 people will be required in the centralized location and only another 10 people will be required for local interviewing. In total, the 40 team leaders will be reduced to 22. The HR staff, already reduced to 411 by April 2002, will be reduced to 311 people by year-end 2002. The cost reductions have been accompanied by another round of town meetings to explain to the staff that "this is what we said we were going to do at the induction, and this is what we did do."

**Redesigning Business Processes**

Xchanging uses their own version of the Six Sigma methodology to redesign business processes. The senior leader peer-review process for BAES as a whole involved 640 people and serves as an example of a business process redesign. Traditionally, peer review involved an extremely inefficient process of an HR person sitting down with a senior leader to fill out paperwork. Instead, Xchanging redesigned the process based more on self-service and enabled interconnectivity for the process via the peopleportal:

> What would have happened before, 30 people would have happily expanded a task to fill three months and as it is now, eight people have been busy for a month—bang! Done. (Mike Margetts, Head of Implementation, XHRS)

**Transformation Complete**

Xchanging completed the HR transformation by the end of 2002, 20 months after start-up. Up to that point, the enterprise partnership had delivered on its promises:

- contractual cost savings delivered on baseline HR services,
- service quality improvement in many HR services,
- new eHR capabilities rolled out to over 40,000 BAES users,
- a new service center facility at Preston, UK, built and occupied,
- BAES HR focusing on more strategic HR decisions,
- staff transferred to the enterprise partnership trained and reoriented to "front-office" mindset.

The following year, the major challenge was realizing revenue growth by attracting external customers to XHRS and sustaining cost cuts and service improvements. On this last point, Xchanging was confident that sustainability would occur:

> My view is that it's all about people. It's probably just following straight from where we were. In the first 18 months, it is about a small group of people, many of whom have done it before on something similar, picking the right team and then giving those people the confidence and skills to be able to deliver. That is the first 18 months. After that, that group of people, with those skills and confidence, will do it for themselves; they won't need to be told, they will do it for themselves because they want the challenge. I'm absolutely convinced that is what will happen. (David Bauernfeind, previously BAe Divisional Financial Controller, now CFO of XHRS)

## FIVE BACK-OFFICE TRANSFORMATION MODELS: CHALLENGES

Let us step back from the case and look at the wider issue of back-office transformation. If the goal is to radically reduce costs and improve service, the practices to achieve this normally include centralization, standardization, reorientation of staff, and process redesign. In considering which back-office transformation model is best suited for a given organization, an organization needs to take into account the required resources and skills required to implement these practices, such as up-front investment in technology and physical facilities, proven management capability, and effective and strongly motivated staff. Furthermore, which transformation model will be politically feasible, given the stakeholders affected by these decisions, including senior management, business unit directors, process directors, process staff, and of course, the large body of users?

In the BAES case, agents within the company rejected three viable options for back-office transformation of HR—do-it-yourself, management consultants, and fee-for-service outsourcing—before selecting the enterprise partnership model. Much of the logic in their internal debates is certainly not specific to BAES. Tables 13.2 and 13.3 capture the potential benefits and risks of the transformation models as viewed by BAES and other customers we have studied. The tables are not intended to provide a deterministic set of variables but, rather, are designed to serve as templates to help structure debates on the relative merits of different transformation models.

Tables 13.2 and 13.3 include a fifth model to those discussed thus far—joint ventures. Although BAES did not consider a joint venture because it would involve too much of their own financial and resource investment, it is useful to establish the differences between an enterprise partnership

Table 13.2

**Major Benefits of Five Back-Office Transformation Approaches**

| Do It Yourself | Management Consultants | Fee-for-Service Outsourcing | Joint Venture | Enterprise Partnership |
|---|---|---|---|---|
| Realize all cost benefits internally | Infusion of external energy and capabilities | Infusion of external energy and capabilities | Infusion of external energy and capabilities | Infusion of external energy and capabilities |
| Easiest model to sell to internal organization | Ability of outsiders to bypass political resistance | Ability of outsiders to bypass political resistance | Ability of outsiders to bypass political resistance | Ability of outsiders to bypass political resistance |
| Under complete in-house control | Clear indication that management is committed to transformation | Clear indication that management is committed to transformation | Clear indication that management is committed to transformation | Clear indication that management is committed to transformation |
| | Most scalable solution among transformation approaches involving outsiders | Guaranteed cost and service improvements for predefined baseline services | Joint board of directors promotes customer participation and oversight | Guaranteed cost and service improvements for five years on both identified baseline services and discovered services |
| | | One-time savings achieved up front | Customer shares in any additional revenues obtained from external sales | Guaranteed cost-plus pricing on new services |
| | | Potential for up-front investment by supplier | | Up-front investment made by supplier |
| | | | | Joint board of directors, service review board, and technology review board promote customer participation and oversight |
| | | | | Customer shares in any additional revenues obtained from external sales |

Table 13.3

## Major Risks of Five Back-Office Transformation Approaches

| MAJOR RISKS | Do It Yourself | Management Consultants | Fee-for-service Outsourcing | Joint Venture | Enterprise Partnership |
|---|---|---|---|---|---|
| Senior management will not make the investment in a non-core area to complete the transformation | HIGH, must obtain internal funding for entire transformation | MED, must obtain consultant's fee | VARIES by how much investment is negotiated by parties | VARIES by how much investment is negotiated by parties | LOW, supplier makes most of the investment |
| Lack of empowerment or skills to complete transformation | HIGH, lack of empowerment and skills of internal staff to make the quantum changes required | LOW, supplier experts manage the transformation | MED, depending on how much expertise supplier devotes to contract (typically customer only has approval of supplier account manager) | LOW, customer and supplier select management team | LOW, customer and supplier select management team; supplier experts manage the transformation |
| Cost escalation due to unbridled demand, power asymmetries allowing the supplier to premium price add-ons, and discovery of previously hidden spend | LOW, demand restricted by amount of internal resources | HIGH, mostly from premium add-ons | HIGH, one of biggest risks realized among fee-for-service customers; all sources of cost escalation evident | MED/HIGH, one of biggest risks realized among JV customers but Joint Board of Directors helps to mediate power asymmetries | MED, cost savings on undiscovered spend guaranteed; Joint Board of Directors, Service Review Board, and Technology Review Board help bridle demand; add-ons are pre-priced at cost-plus percentage and monitored with open-book accounting |
| Internal resistance from business units to centralize back office to achieve cost cuts | HIGH, easy to sabotage projects led by back-office managers | MED, depending on whether momentum is lost once consultants have vacated | LOW, resources now owned by supplier | LOW, resources now owned by the venture | LOW, resources now owned by supplier |

*(continues)*

Table 13.3 (continued)

| MAJOR RISKS | Do It Yourself | Management Consultants | Fee-for-service Outsourcing | Joint Venture | Enterprise Partnership |
|---|---|---|---|---|---|
| Internal resistance from business units to standardize back office to achieve cost cuts | HIGH, easy to sabotage projects led by back-office managers | MED, depending on whether momentum is lost once consultants have vacated | MED, users can request customization, which supplier will gladly grant for additional price | MED/LOW, users can request customization for additional charge; but Joint Board of Directors should ensure customer oversight that requests are value-added | LOW, supplier can only meet P&L targets through standardization; all requests to customize must be approved by Service Review Board |
| Lack of sustainability of one-time results | MED, depending on whether new structures and processes become institutionalized | HIGH, consultants eventually vacate | HIGH, most customers complain that momentum wanes after 3 years | HIGH, most JVs in IT we studied do not guarantee sustained improvements but instead rely on nebulous notions of partnership | MED, structure of contracts guarantees cost savings and service improvements for at least 5 years |
| Supplier has no/little accountability or ownership of outcome | N/A | HIGH, time and materials contracts require little accountability | LOW, if service levels and penalties for non-performance are well-defined and measured | MED, service levels are frequently defined but penalties often are not | LOW, if service levels and penalties for non-performance are well-defined and measured |
| Supplier maintains key knowledge that is not transferred to customer | N/A | HIGH, suppliers vacate | MED, top talent may not remain on customer account | MED, top talent may not remain on customer account | LOW, transferees are fully trained in new culture, services, and processes |
| Customer and supplier incentives are not truly aligned | N/A | HIGHEST risk, but consequences are smaller due to project work | HIGH, every dollar from customer's pocket is a dollar in supplier's pocket | MED, conflicts can arise between maximizing venture's profits and minimizing customer investor's costs | MED, conflicts can arise between maximizing enterprise's profits and minimizing customer investor's costs |

| | | | | | |
|---|---|---|---|---|---|
| Inability of customer to manage long-term relationship with supplier | N/A | N/A | HIGH, one of the major problems experienced with this approach, relationship often deteriorates into us/them mentality. | MED, governance structure requires long-term joint customer and supplier participation, decision making, and problem solving. | MED, governance structure requires long-term joint customer and supplier participation, decision making, and problem solving. |
| Business model too dependent on revenues from external customers, which may not materialize | N/A | N/A | N/A | HIGH, particularly if venture is relying heavily on customer's idiosyncratic resources for competitiveness | HIGH, although partnership's resources are based on supplier's templated technology, it still does not guarantee competitiveness in the open market. |

and a joint venture. The first difference is the primary purpose for joining together. With a joint venture, the primary purpose is revenue generation through external sales to third parties. Essentially, the customer views their function as world-class and believes they can gain more revenues by selling to competitors than keeping the advantage to themselves. They seek a supplier to help with commercialization. With an enterprise partnership model, the main focus is delivering cost cuts and better services to the customer investor. A customer's back offices are certainly not yet world class, and they seek a supplier to help transform the function through better management, better IT systems, and better processes. External sales are merely a bonus.

The second difference between the models relates to risk. In a joint venture model, the customer and supplier share risks and rewards in proportion to their initial investments. But with the enterprise partnership model, the customer bears less risk than the supplier because the customer receives guaranteed rewards even if the supplier has to deliver the rewards at the expense of their own profitability.

If customers select a joint venture model, they need to be sure the venture can successfully compete in the open market. In the past, we have studied a number of joint ventures between customers and suppliers that failed because the venture was never able to attract external customers. The essential problem was that the new venture was not competitive. The assets, technology, and people transferred to the venture had created a company-specific "product." The estimated costs to transform to a generic and competitive level were ten times the initial value, an investment the customer was clearly not willing to make for an uncertain outcome. This issue has not been relevant to enterprise partnerships as instantiated by Xchanging and Exult because they developed technology with intent to commercialize, thus their eHR platforms are templated and modularized.

The other impediment to joint venture success is that when the venture becomes so preoccupied with providing service to the customer investor, they have no additional resources devoted to external sales. In instances where customers truly had a competitive offering, a spin-off was a more successful vehicle for creating a venture, such as General Motors' spin-off of EDS or American Airlines' spin-off of SABRE.

## LESSONS ON BACK-OFFICE TRANSFORMATION MODELS

In this section, we describe our preliminary lessons on the effectiveness of using an enterprise partnership as a vehicle for back-office transformation. In presenting these lessons, we warn readers that:

- Our lessons are based on only two and a half years of evidence from what is contracted to be a ten-year relationship. That having been said, subsequent evidence to mid-2005 shows that the enterprise partnership continues to be successful on the major metrics used to assess its progress and performance.
- The effectiveness of the enterprise partnership model is not an absolute assessment but rather an assessment vis-à-vis alternative transformation models; namely, do-it-yourself, management consulting, fee-for-service outsourcing, and joint ventures. Clearly, no model is perfect, and decision makers must weigh the benefits, costs, and risks of competing models.

Below, we classify the lessons into four types—profile, costs, innovation, and incentives.

**Profile**

*Lesson 1: The Enterprise Partnership May Be Best Suited for a Particular Size and Type of Back-Office Function*

We are cautious about prescribing ideal circumstances for any of the models, instead believing that organizations are in a much better position to make the final judgment after considering each model's major benefits and risks that best suit their own rich, organizational context. Nonetheless, evidence from this and three other enterprise partnership cases we studied suggests that the enterprise partnership model may work best for a customer with the following profile:

- The customer seeks substantial improvement in back-office performance in service quality as well as costs.
- The customer has a substantial back-office spend to make the deal large enough to attract a competent external supplier.
- The customer's back-office operations are highly decentralized, allowing the opportunity for significant cost reductions from centralization and standardization.
- The customer's back-office operations have not historically received high management attention, allowing the opportunity for significant cost savings and service improvement from better management.
- The customer's organization would resist centralizing and standardizing itself due to internal political resistance, unwillingness of senior management to make the required up-front investment, or lack of skills and experience of back-office staff to make the transformation.
- The customer sees the potential for sustainable, long-term development of a new business.

**Cost**

*Lesson 2: When Employing Any Transformation Model Involving Third-Party Suppliers, Be Sure to Manage User Demand to Reduce the Risk of Cost Escalation*

In outsourcing, clients naturally worry about the risk of cost escalation. As previously discussed, unbridled demand is a major source of cost escalation. The key is for customers to ensure that additional demand is valid—that is, users are demanding value-adding services that the customer deems worth more than the price.

Prior to the partnership model, demand at BAES was constrained by the number of HR staff in the SBUs. If a managing director in an SBU only wanted to hire a staff of 25 people, his or her unit could only demand enough HR services to occupy these 25 people. A decentralized user community of 40,000 can now demand HR resources:

> We are seeing some evidence of increased demand with Xchanging HR Services. It's the early days yet, but demand for service before XHRS was always restricted because as an HR Director, you only have the number of people that you could get your MD [managing director] to agree to, so that effectively capped it. Of course, we have taken that away now and people can demand ever more and more. (Steve Hodgson, previously HR Director, now Head of Resources for XHRS)

The solution for both the fee-for-service outsourcing and enterprise partnership models is a customer liaison role that collects, prioritizes, and approves service demands. The function of this role is to ensure that additional demand adds more value than the additional costs it triggers. Although a liaison/oversight role adds to the bureaucracy and thus slows down customer service, it is vital to prevent unreasonable cost escalation. BAES achieved this oversight role through their service review board. BAES also prevented the supplier from charging a premium price due to customer captivity by prepricing add-ons in the contract. Additions are priced on a cost plus percentage basis and monitored through open book accounting.

### Lesson 3: Transformation Models Involving Third-Party Suppliers Can Help Customers Proactively Manage Spending Previously Hidden in Decentralized Budgets

Another major source of "cost escalation" is that disaggregated spending becomes aggregated, often leading to uncomfortable surprises. In our study of over 100 fee-for-service outsourcing cases, we found that customers typically received unit cost reductions on their baseline services, but that visible overall costs rose because hidden spending became illuminated after outsourcing. The customer should welcome this illumination because it offers them the opportunity to finally manage the true spend.

Certainly, BAES can expect enormous benefit by consolidating the dispersed £80 million annual HR spend on miscellaneous items such as health care and clerical staff, now managed by a separate enterprise partnership called Xchanging Procurement Services. Within a year of operation, indirect procurement costs dropped by 12 percent, with more savings anticipated when existing procurement contacts expire and can be renegotiated.

But even removing the procurement spend from the equation, HR costs at BAES appear to have risen, as more hidden HR costs are found and transferred to XHRS, such as IT spend on HR systems and spend on temporary HR staff:

> The cost has increased quite substantially . . . in reality it probably isn't going up because of Xchanging. It just means that we need to probably transfer budget over that hasn't traditionally sat within the HR team. (Kim Reid, HR Director, BAES)

How enterprise partnerships deal with the phenomenon of hidden costs leads us to our next finding.

### Lesson 4: Delaying Due Diligence Until After the Contract Is in Effect Can Speed the Negotiation Process and More Fairly Distribute the Burden of Newly Discovered Costs

With most third-party relationships, the supplier typically verifies the customer's claims on baseline costs, services, and resources prior to signing a contract. This due diligence process ensures that the suppliers understand their commitments and can still generate a profit on those commitments. But due diligence slows down the negotiation process and almost never uncovers all the costs to which the supplier inadvertently commits:

> One thing in this business you cannot underestimate is, no matter how long from the outside in you try to do due diligence, you will always get it wrong. It's only when you actually go in there and start running it that you find out what's going on and the sooner you do that the better for everyone. (Richard Houghton, CEO, XHRS)

This immediately puts the customer and supplier in an adversarial position. The customer claims, "You are responsible for this, you contracted for this, it's not our fault you didn't do your homework." The supplier counters, "I am getting ripped off, I have to earn a reasonable profit, you hid these costs from us."

In contrast, the enterprise partnership model delays detailed due diligence until after the contract is signed. The customer and supplier do not need to verify all the costs beforehand because they do not contract a flat fee. Instead, the partners agree to provide a percentage of savings on the total costs transferred, including hidden costs as they become illuminated. Delaying the due diligence process under this model protects both the customer and supplier. Consider some of what Xchanging discovered after the contract was signed: an additional 15 percent of costs were uncovered, including 35 temporary HR staff, wrong salaries reported, and wrong pensions reported. At Xchanging, these costs were added to the baseline, and BAES will get their agreed-upon percentage of savings.

**Innovation**

*Lesson 5: The Enterprise Partnership Model Creates a Clash of Cultures, but Cultural Incompatibility May Be Just What Is Needed for Innovation*

In the more than 100 outsourcing cases we previously studied, customers nearly always sought a supplier with a similar culture to their own. For example, global hierarchical customers, such as DuPont, CIGNA, or General Motors, typically sought global hierarchical suppliers such as CSC, IBM, and EDS. But is this approach flawed? Certainly the BAES–Xchanging partnership challenges the conventional wisdom of cultural homogeneity. Nearly every person interviewed for this case—from both the customer and supplier sides—noted the cultural differences between BAES and Xchanging. BAES was systematically described as "risk averse," "detailed," and "cautious." This is precisely the culture BAES needs to ensure safety and quality in their core products such as aircraft, submarines, and weapons. But such a culture is not helpful if the task is trying to radically transform a back-office function such as HR.

In contrast, the Xchanging people have been consistently described as "aggressive," "winners," and "impressive." This culture is needed for a start-up company seeking to establish its reputation:

> What was obvious to me, the Xchanging people were part of a small company desperate to succeed, and that desire to succeed just didn't exist in the BAE SYSTEMS HR culture. (David Bauernfeind, previously BAe Divisional Financial Controller, now CFO of XHRS)

Xchanging's results-oriented culture was taught to the transferees through launch events, training sessions, videos, and town meetings. According to one transitioned employee, it paid off:

> If you left work at half-past six, you were having a late night at BAE. I mean, that is the BAE culture. I was in at ten to seven this morning and I'll be here at nine o'clock tonight and that is the Xchanging culture. The Xchanging guys I just could associate with very, very, very easily. From day one, I felt much, much more comfortable. The hard thing was it was a damned sight harder work, much more disciplined environment, much more focused environment. It still took me a little while to make that leap—probably two or three months.

Overall, BAES embraces the culture shock imputed on its transferees:

> Yes, as a business, Xchanging has placed a lot more pressure on the people in terms of responsiveness and acting in a service environment. We could never have gotten our people to do that because we couldn't have got the culture that would have taken, I don't think it would have happened. (Kim Reid, HR Director, BAES)

*Lesson 6: Selecting a Supplier with Generic Business Competencies Rather Than Domain-Specific Knowledge May Yield Better Results*

What fascinated us most about BAES's selection of Xchanging is that it ignored a number of "conventional wisdoms":

- Xchanging had no track record—BAES would be the first customer;
- Xchanging had no industry-specific knowledge—that is, no aerospace knowledge; and
- Xchanging had little domain-specific knowledge—that is, little human resource management expertise.

Nearly every fee-for-service outsourcer positions their core capabilities in the functions they are taking over. For example, EDS, IBM, and CSC claim core capabilities in managing IT. The big accounting firms claim their competencies in accounting and auditing. But Xchanging claims no preexisting competency in HR. Instead, Xchanging believes that the talent needed to transform back offices to front offices requires six powerful cross-functional, cross-industry competencies, which they group together in the Xcellence platform:

- service excellence,
- process improvement,
- people development,
- technology enablement,
- slick physical facilities,
- efficient third-party sourcing.

They then need to know when and how to deploy these six competencies through the seventh competency of implementation. Xchanging's enterprise partnership model absorbs the domain-specific knowledge—in this case HR knowledge—through employee transfers. Some executives from BAES actually saw this lack of HR knowledge as a plus:

> I always say the best HR people are people who haven't been in the HR function all their lives. You need a different view. So the Xchanging team, although they are not HR professionals, it works probably better that they are not because if they go in understanding all the pitfalls that there may be, then they'll never make any changes, so sometimes it is better. (Kim Reid, HR Director, BAES)

**Incentives**

*Lesson 7: Consider Letting the Supplier Clean Up Your Mess*

This is an extremely controversial finding and is indeed counter to our prior findings. Certainly in our studies on fee-for-service outsourcing, we warned customers to grab the low-hanging fruit so that they may accrue all of the savings themselves. In the BAES context, simple arithmetic shows that they only receive \$0.50 on every dollar Xchanging delivers in savings. In actuality, BAES had made strides in reducing some cost areas, such as indirect procurement, but the reality is that they needed significant investment in facilities, technology, training, and process redesign before head count could be downsized. The impediments of do it themselves in order to pocket all of the savings were just too immense. Indeed, during the decision process, BAES decided to invite a counter bid from another supplier to compete with Xchanging. The main difference between the two suppliers was their proposed handling of transferred employees. Xchanging proposed to accept all of the existing HR personnel BAES identified for transfer. In contrast, the alternative bidder proposed using their existing service center staff, with very few BAES transfers. Xchanging's proposal was an easier political sell to the unionized HR staff because the chances for continued employment were greater with Xchanging.

Thus, an organization must weigh the pros and cons of allowing the supplier to clean up the mess (thereby forfeiting a percentage of savings) against the up-front investment and political challenges of doing it themselves (thereby accruing all the savings).

*Lesson 8: The Enterprise Partnership Model Aligns Incentives Better Than Other Transformation Models*

In terms of alignment, the enterprise partnership model is clearly superior to traditional outsourcing. The fifty-fifty shared profits and the joint board of directors ensure that the parties both participate and make mutually beneficial decisions:

> It's brilliant because you have rules like the board of directors have to turn up for meetings. Could I get the sponsors to turn up for meetings on my previous outsourcing deals? Well, maybe, but it was hard work. When you have a board meeting, you have to be there. You have certain duties as board members: you have to act in the best interests of the enterprise, not your individual company. That is a big mind-set change. (David Andrews, CEO of Xchanging)

And while joint ventures also have a board of directors to align incentives, the enterprise partnership also includes joint boards for service and technology investment. Together, these governance mechanisms foster a strong sense of mutual responsibility and accountability. The customer certainly agrees that the enterprise partnership more closely aligns the parties:

> So if it was a traditional customer/supplier relationship, you would get the instance that the customer would blame the supplier for not delivering a service. For me, the partnership means that the accountability for delivering the service into the business is mine. I have to make sure that it delivers a seamless service so that myself and my other HR directors in this business will not say "the reason this went wrong was because Xchanging did this." If something goes wrong it's because we did it. It's very much a partner-type relationship. (Kim Reid, HR Director, BAES)

However, a caveat is warranted here.

*Lesson 9: Beware That the Enterprise Partnership Model Does Not Perfectly Align Incentives*

In the past, the joint governance between customers and suppliers we studied led to a managerial schizophrenia. Because the enterprise's primary customer is also an owner, the customer has two competing goals: to maximize cost-efficient service delivery from the enterprise and to maximize the revenue of the enterprise. How can the customer do both? Furthermore, if the same executives sit on the board of directors of the customer company and the enterprise company, which hat should they wear? Should they be pushing for more services at a reduced cost, thereby squeezing as much as they can from the enterprise? Or should they push for generating more revenues, which distract the enterprise from their needs?

Although this schizophrenia has not thus far been a big issue at BAES, it does exist:

> I guess one of the concerns from people in the business, if Xchanging goes out and wins more third-party business, is that going to affect the service? The concern within the business will always be if that happens will the level of service drop. With all the measures that are in place, I would find it would be difficult, you would spot the service dropping immediately and the contractual measures would be there to actually reign that back. (Kim Reid, HR Director, BAES)

*Lesson 10: Make the Economics of the Enterprise Partnership Model Work for Both Parties Without an Overreliance on Third-Party Revenues*

BAES learned this lesson and will receive the guaranteed cost savings over a five-year period regardless of whether Xchanging can attract external customers to the venture. This has proved a sensible move, because Xchanging was too busy servicing BAES to attract external customers during the first year and has attracted no major customers since:

> The business development in year one at this stage was almost zero because the focus was let's get our act together in delivering this to BAE Systems first before we all turn salesmen and go out and start selling ourselves. (Alan Bailey, previously with BAES, now Head of New Business Development for XHRS)

But the customer should not be too tough on the supplier, because if the supplier cannot earn a profit on the deal, the customer's service invariably deteriorates. Thus, the lesson also extends to the suppliers: make sure the supplier can earn a profit on the deal even if they cannot attract external customers.

In the case of Xchanging and BAES, the CEO of XHRS reports that Xchanging made a modest profit during the first year of operation and was on target to make a decent profit margin for 2002:

> We thought we could take at least half the costs out over a five-year period. The cost savings come from restructuring through to centralized delivery, through deployment of the peopleportal, so on and so forth. (Richard Houghton, CEO, XHRS)

Indeed, Xchanging executives note that they would have to work hard not to generate a profit because the savings from centralization, standardization, and downsizing were so significant:

> The reality if I just look at it in XHRS is we have to really work hard not to make this business work. It is pretty easy to make this business make money, the hard bit is the time scale

and the growth. So you concentrate resources and you put their management in place, you remove the weak people over time and you put in good technology. You really have to work to not make that add up to a significantly better position than you were in before. (David Bauernfeind, previously BAe Divisional Financial Controller, now CFO of XHRS)

Thus, Xchanging can earn a profit even if XHRS never attracts another customer.

## CONCLUSION

During the past 14 years, we have studied the benefits and risks of major transformation models, including do-it-yourself, management consultants, fee-for-service outsourcing, and joint ventures. As organizational experiences and learning accumulate, models evolve and new models emerge. We believe that the enterprise partnership is a sufficiently different transformation model to warrant attention among academics and practitioners alike. Our more detailed study of BPO suppliers shows an increasing move on their part toward building the capabilities we identified in the BAES–Xchanging enterprise partnership (Feeny et al., 2005). Meanwhile Xchanging's other enterprise partnerships have been relatively successful, with a new one signed in late 2004 for running the Frankfurt Stock Exchange back-office processes. Although we have focused on the model's obvious strengths, there are clear risks involved, such as the inability to sustain improvements over the long haul and the inability to profitably attract external customers. Certainly, many customer/IT supplier joint ventures have failed in the past, including joint ventures between Delta Airlines and AT&T, Xerox and EDS, and Swiss Bank and Perot Systems. What is new with the enterprise partnerships as implemented by Xchanging and Exult is the technology models. Both suppliers designed and developed Web-enabled software for one-to-many delivery and there is a clear demand in the market for business process outsourcing. But because the enterprise partnership model is new and as yet unproven in the long term, it is vital that we continue to trace the progress of the enterprise partnership's early adopters such as BAES, Lloyd's of London, British Petroleum, and Bank of America. Such customers will face significant challenges ahead, such as keeping their service fresh and sustaining cost reductions as more of the enterprise partnership's resources are focused on obtaining external customers.

## APPENDIX 13.1 RESEARCH METHODOLOGY

This case study is based on 14 interviews with BAE Systems and Xchanging employees and secondary data including internal practice manuals, organizational charts, budgets, presentations, and performance assessments. The interviews were conducted in person and were tape-recorded and transcribed. Each interview was conducted by two researchers and lasted one to two hours. The interviews covered representatives of the major stakeholders in the change, albeit at managerial level. The transcriptions were analyzed by two researchers, and an interpretation was developed that was also reviewed by the third researcher. It can therefore be seen that triangulation of sources and interpreters was applied in this research process.

| Name | Role in Xchanging | Role in Enterprise Partnership | Previous Role at BAES |
|------|-------------------|-------------------------------|------------------------|
| Chris Dickson | | BAE SYSTEMS Enterprise Relationship Director; customer | |
| Kim Reid | | BAE SYSTEMS HR Director; customer | |
| David Bauernfeind | | CFO | Finance |
| Alan Bailey | People Practice Director | New Business Development | Head of HR Shares Services Implementation |
| Richard Houghton | Managing Director, HR Services | CEO | |
| Steve Hodgson | | Head of Resources | SBU HR Director |
| Byrony Moore | Service Practice Director | Head of Service | |
| Mike Margetts | Implementation Practice Director | Head of Implementation | |
| David Andrews | Founder and CEO | | |
| John Bramley | Board of Directors | | |
| Paul Ruggier | Process Practice Director | | |
| Andrew Chadwick | Environment Practice Director | | |
| Steve Bowen | Technology Practice Director | | |
| John Attenborough | People Practice Director | | |

## ACKNOWLEDGMENTS

This chapter is developed from an earlier version published as M. Lacity, L. Willcocks, and D. Feeny, Transforming a back-office function: Lessons from BAE Systems' experiences with enterprise partnership, *MISQ Executive*, 2, 2 (2003), 86–103. Expanded and revised with permission from the Regents of the University of Minnesota.

## NOTES

1. Exult was purchased by Hewitt in 2003 for $690 million.
2. Using the June 4, 2007, exchange rate £230 million = $458 million.

## REFERENCES

Cagle, M.L., and Campbell, K. 2002. Taking HR from cost center to revenue generator at Bank of America. Paper presented at the 2002 Outsourcing World Summit, Lake Buena Vista, FL, February 19.
Cullen, S., and Willcocks, L. 2003. *Intelligent IT Outsourcing: Eight Building Blocks to Success.* Oxford: Butterworth.

Feeny, D.; Lacity, M.; and Willcocks, L. 2005. Taking the measure of outsourcing providers. *Sloan Management Review,* 46, 3 (April), 41–48.

Kern, T., and Willcocks, L. 2001. *The Relationship Advantage: Information Technology, Sourcing and Management.* Oxford: Oxford University Press.

Lacity, M., and Willcocks, L. 2001. *Global IT Outsourcing: Search for Business Advantage.* Chichester, UK: Wiley.

Lacity, M., and Willcocks, L. (eds.). 2006. *Global Sourcing of IT and Business Services.* London: Palgrave.

Lacity, M.; Feeny, D.; and Willcocks, L. 2003. Transforming indirect procurement spend: The story of BAE SYSTEMS and Xchanging's enterprise partnership. Working Paper, Oxford Institute of Information Management, Templeton College, Oxford University.

CHAPTER 14

# PROBLEMS IN THE TRANSFER OF REENGINEERING EFFORTS

## An Illustrative Case

SUE NEWELL, LINDA EDELMAN, HARRY SCARBROUGH, JACKY SWAN, AND MIKE BRESNEN

*Abstract: Process reengineering can lead to dramatic improvements in a service and, as such, can be seen to facilitate organizational transformation. It is sometimes assumed that once a process has been reengineered in one context, it can be transferred as a "best practice" to other contexts and thus facilitate transformation without the heavy burden of the reengineering effort. This chapter challenges this logic. We argue that reengineering, by definition, involves breaking down professional/functional boundaries so that a process can be looked at holistically rather than from a departmental perspective. This will only occur when there are significant shifts in ideology and power relations that allow the sharing and integration of knowledge across disparate groups. Such shifts in relations are unlikely to occur without fostering interaction that encourages discussion and dialogue across the various professional/functional communities that will need to change their practices. These power-knowledge shifts, therefore, need to occur in each context if reengineering is actually going to produce organizational transformation. Hence, we conclude that the sharing of relational knowledge that can help to foster this interaction is likely to be as useful as the sharing of the "best practices." A case study of the reengineering of a cataract diagnosis and treatment process is used to illustrate the argument.*

*Keywords: Business Process Reengineering, Knowledge Transfer, Organizational Transformation, Best Practice, Knowledge and Power, Case Study Research*

## INTRODUCTION

Transformational organizational change achieved through the redesign of business processes has been a mantra since the 1990s (Hammer and Champy, 1993). Although some empirical research has demonstrated that, in many cases, the change was not as extensive or radical as anticipated (Benders and Van Veen, 2001; Knights and Wilmott, 2000; McNulty and Ferlie, 2004), it is nevertheless the case that some organizations or sections within an organization do manage to radically redesign their business processes and achieve dramatic improvements in performance—for example, in terms of cost, quality, or service. In many cases, the business processes thus transformed are relevant to other organizations or to other sections within an organization. These transformed processes are often relabeled as "best practices" on the assumption that they can be transferred to other contexts where they are relevant to effect similar, albeit less painful, organizational transformation (Camp, 1989). That is, once it is clear that a particular business process is performed in a clearly superior way in one organization or one section of an organization, the process in this superior organization can be defined and this knowledge can be transferred to other organizations so that these other organizations can be similarly transformed. In this way, transformations can be achieved by using proven business process designs rather than having to reengineer processes starting with a blank sheet of paper (Dence, 1995). This is, after all, the logic of many information technology (IT) systems, such as an enterprise system, which are marketed as embedding "best" business processes into the software design.

These ideas about process reengineering transformation and "best practice" transfer have diffused to the British public sector (Department of Health, 1997). Thus, in the past ten years, there has been an effort to explore new ways of delivering health care through various types of process redesign (Locock, 2000). There has also been an increase in the publication of performance indicators, which are provided to stimulate the opportunity for "best practice" benchmarking and transfer (Jones, 2001).

Here, we explore an attempt to reengineer a particular organizational process within a Hospital Trust that is part of the UK National Health Service (NHS) and then to transfer this redesigned process more broadly across the NHS. Our case study demonstrates that the reengineering effort was very successful, leading to transformational change in the delivery of the particular service within the organization under consideration. However, the transfer of this new "best practice" was not effective. We explore why this was the case by drawing upon literature that examines organizational knowledge and learning. Specifically, we suggest that, at least in situations where the newly reengineered process is highly complex, so that those involved have only a limited understanding of the entire process and, where the process is divided among groups of interdependent professionals, the effective transfer of "best practices" cannot occur independently of the transformational change process. This is because, as we demonstrate, the process of knowledge generation (to support business process reengineering [BPR]) and knowledge transfer (to support the diffusion of "best practices") are mutually dependent. In order to overcome these problems, we suggest that, for the effective transfer of "best practices," as much emphasis should be placed on disseminating information that describes the process of achieving transformational process reengineering as on disseminating information of the new "best practice" per se.

The paper begins with discussion of BPR and why a knowledge perspective is useful in understanding process reengineering, organizational transformation, and "best practice" transfer. The next section describes the methodology used in the reported study. A case description and analysis follows in the subsequent sections. In the final discussion and conclusion section, the theoretical and practical implications of the analysis are drawn together.

## BUSINESS PROCESS REENGINEERING AND THE IMPORTANCE OF KNOWLEDGE

The ideas in Hammer and Champy's (1993) book outlining how organizations can achieve transformational change through reengineering their key business processes diffused widely, and many organizations have undertaken some kind of process reengineering (Denison, 1997). It is important to begin with an analysis of the core elements of their BPR proposition, which are related to process reengineering and organizational transformation.

First, in terms of process reengineering, the essential idea is that organizations should structure their activities around business processes rather than business functions or professional departments

(Denison, 1997). This is because most business processes cut across business functions, so that tasks associated with the process are handed off from one department to the next until the process has been completed. The handoff between functions is often where delays and breakdowns in the process occur. This is because each department has its own unique "thought world" (Dougherty, 1992) and set of priorities so that misunderstandings occur and bottlenecks are created. The idea behind reengineering is to redesign the key business processes so that there is a coherent focus on the overall process rather than allowing each department to do its "bit" of the process as it sees fit and in total isolation from what goes before or after. Information and reward systems can then be designed that support this process in an integrated way; data will not need to be input each time the activities associated with a process are handed over to the next department in the chain because the system is an integrated one. Moreover, rewards will be aligned so that those involved see the need to support the total business process rather than just their piece of it. The focus, therefore, is on process rather than function, and the idea is to break down the functional/professional boundaries that typically impede the smooth flow of business activities.

Second, in terms of organizational transformation, the idea is that these process redesign changes can lead to dramatic improvements in organizational performance. This transformation occurs because process orientation demands a change in the dominant ideologies, cultural systems of meanings, and power relations within the organization (Pettigrew, 1987). Ferlie et al. (1996) provide a useful model for assessing organizational transformation related to professional work, which is the focus of this chapter. They focus on both behavior and attitude change. Their six indicators of organizational transformation include multiple and interrelated changes across the system, the creation of new organizational forms, changes below the system level (affecting individuals and groups), changes in the services provided and the mode of delivery of these services, the reconfiguration of power relations, and the development of a new culture. They argue that all six indicators must be present for a change to be described as transformational.

Achieving such change is extremely difficult, requiring high levels of interactivity across stakeholders who are involved in the specific process being redesigned. This is because different stakeholders, representing different professional communities, will have access to different knowledge and information about the process so that, for the process to be redesigned, this knowledge must be shared and new knowledge created about how the practice can be radically altered. Thus, for process redesign that transforms an organization, it is not simply the availability of new knowledge that will create radical improvements in a practice but, rather, the ability to *integrate* knowledge across an increasingly distributed array of professional groups and organizations (Owen-Smith et al., 2002; Powell et al., 1996). As opposed to mere "knowledge sharing" (Grant, 1996), *knowledge integration* means that knowledge drawn from different domains is combined and deployed for achieving specific radical change outcomes. This concept builds on and extends Okhuysen and Eisenhardt's (2002) definition that understands knowledge integration as a process whereby individuals combine their information to create new knowledge. We next turn to a discussion of the literature on organizational knowledge, because this literature provides the theoretical framework we use for understanding the challenges involved in sharing and integrating knowledge needed for business process transformation in our case study. Moreover, our perspective on knowledge also helps us to understand the problems associated with transferring "best practice" design in this case, as we will discuss later.

## MANAGING ORGANIZATIONAL KNOWLEDGE

In this paper we use a knowledge-focused perspective (see, e.g., Newell et al., 2000) to consider what is involved in process redesign as well as to understand what limits the transfer of the process redesign (the new "best practice") to other contexts. We view knowledge as an integral aspect of the overall activity system of the organization (Blackler, 1995). Knowledge is neither a "resource" that can simply be transferred (Barney, 1991) nor is it "embedded" in organizational processes (Winter, 1987; 1995). Rather, from this perspective, knowledge is seen to emerge as people interact recurrently in the context of established routines and procedures. Therefore, when firm members participate in an organizational process, they have the potential to simultaneously create and extend the firm's knowledge (Spender, 1996). This implies a social constructivist view of knowledge, whereby all human knowledge is developed, transmitted, and maintained in social situations (Berger and Luckmann, 1966).

Looking more specifically at knowledge and practice, both Nelson (1991) and Tsoukas (1996) see firms as hierarchies of routines, where most organizational knowledge is tacit and resides not only in the minds of individuals but also in teams sharing common experiences. Each individual has only a partial view of what constitutes a particular organizational routine or process. In other words, "cognition, observed in everyday practice, is distributed—stretched over, not divided among—mind, body, activity and culturally organized settings" (Lave and Wenger, 1991). Knowledge of a particular organizational process, here considered in terms of the diagnosis and treatment of cataracts, does not therefore form a complete and coherent body of knowledge that can be precisely documented or even articulated by a single individual. Rather, it is a form of knowing that exists only through interaction among various collective actors (Gherardi and Nicolini, 2000).

Importantly, this suggests that to change a particular process, collective knowledge of that process has to first be generated through interaction and communication. Cook and Brown (1999) describe the course of collective knowledge creation as a "generative dance" because communication within a group does not simply add knowledge to each individual's knowledge. More importantly, communication and exchange within a group or a team can also evoke novel associations, connections, and hunches such that new meanings and insights are generated. In other words, communication not only affords the exchange of knowledge but also the generation of collective knowledge and new ways of using knowledge. From the knowledge-focused perspective, the redesign of a business process and the diffusion of a new "best practice" are considered knowledge generation and dissemination activities, whereby widely distributed knowledge is integrated through a process of negotiation and sense making (Weick, 1995). In this paper, we explore this process of knowledge generation in the context of a process reengineering effort and the subsequent transfer of this knowledge, packaged as a new "best practice," through a detailed examination of an NHS project team that was attempting to develop and disseminate an improved practice for diagnosing and treating cataracts.

## METHODS

The research discussed in this chapter is part of a larger project that examined a process reengineering effort and subsequent attempts at "best practice" transfer in five different industrial/technology sectors within the United Kingdom. For this study, a qualitative, grounded theory methodology was used (Strauss and Corbin, 1994). This method is especially suited to the current research and has been widely used in research on organizational change in professional settings, including health care (e.g., Radwin, 1998). Qualitative methods, such as case studies, allow the researcher to explore the phenomenon of interest in its natural setting and are particularly appropriate when the boundaries between the phenomenon and its context are not clearly evident (Yin, 1989). Given the closely coupled relationship between replication and firm processes, case studies are ideally suited to examine the linkage between knowledge generation to support process reengineering and knowledge transfer of "best practice" and the context in which this occurs (Spender, 1996). In this chapter, we utilize only one of the cases from this study, because we are interested in exploring the process reengineering and transfer efforts in some considerable depth.

We began our investigation with an introductory meeting with a senior hospital administrator. Although this administrator had a general familiarity with our interest in "best practice" transfer, it was necessary for us to acquaint him with the particulars of this inquiry and to help him identify an appropriate process improvement project for us to investigate. It was quickly determined that the fast-track cataract project was the most suitable project for us to investigate because it was an established project with some already identifiable outcomes. Most important, the outcomes of the cataract project—what could be described as the new "best practice"—clearly had the potential to be transferred to other NHS trusts within the United Kingdom.

We next met with the cataract project manager. It was at this meeting that we learned the details of the project as well as the names and contact information of the project members. We also collected archival project documentation, including project process charts as well as sets of minutes from previous project meetings. Subsequent to this meeting, we met with numerous members of the project team. In total, over a four-month period, we interviewed nine individuals—eight members of the cataract project team and one project manager, who was working on a project similar to the focal cataract project.

While the interviews varied in length from a half hour to over two hours, on average, each interview lasted for approximately one hour and fifteen minutes. Before each interview, interviewees were sent a letter describing the objectives of the research project and outlining the subject of the interview. Respondents were initially asked to describe their role in the overall cataract project, then to discuss the process of knowledge creation and transfer first within the project team and then between other teams and other organizations, if applicable. The role of technology as an aid to transfer was also examined. At each interview, numerous open-ended questions were asked to encourage respondents to relate stories of how knowledge was shared, created, and transferred within and across the organization.

All interviews followed a predesigned interview protocol. The protocol included questions about the facilitators and barriers to knowledge generation during the process reengineering effort and subsequent "best practice" transfer attempt. Questions in the interview protocol were developed based on an extensive review of the knowledge management and process reengineering/change management literatures.

As is typical in inductive studies, writing the case study was an iterative process in which the data were constantly revisited. To aid in data consistency, the interview data were initially coded using a coding scheme developed by the research team. However, the emergent categories discussed below—bringing together key individuals, social networks, and templates—were the result of an iterative process between the collected data and existing theory. Within each category, if inconsistencies occurred among the data that were collected from different sources, third-party sources were consulted for clarification. Triangulation across the different sources of primary and archival data revealed a high level of data consistency.

After the case study was completed, the data were reanalyzed to develop the conceptual insights presented in this paper. Although there were no preconceived hypotheses at the outset of the inquiry, patterns emerged from the data reflecting the mutual dependence between knowledge generation and transfer. These will be discussed further below.

## CASE DESCRIPTION: MIDLANDS HOSPITAL NHS TRUST

Midlands NHS Trust Hospital is one of a large number of trusts that together make up the National Health System of the United Kingdom. As mentioned in the Introduction, the NHS has been under intense government pressure to improve efficiency. One of the areas targeted by the NHS as in need of change is the cataract diagnosis and treatment procedure. Cataract surgery, which is a 20-minute procedure, represents 96 percent of the ophthalmology workload. In most NHS trusts, as was the case at the Midlands NHS Trust Hospital before the process improvement project, cataract diagnosis and treatment involve a patient in a number of visits to various specialists. Typically, patients begin at the optometrist because they believe that deteriorating eyesight suggests they need new glasses/contact lenses. However, the optometrist diagnoses that the problem is actually cataracts and then refers the patient to his or her general practitioner (GP). After a visit to the local GP who, not being an eye specialist generally relies on the diagnosis of the optometrist, the patient is forwarded to the hospital consultant for further examination. The patient then goes on a waiting list and is eventually called for a brief meeting with the consultant, who usually confirms the optometrist's diagnosis and, in a separate appointment, meets with the hospital nurse for a physical examination. Only when all of these visits are complete will the patient get in the queue for obtaining a date for cataract surgery. In many trusts, the lead time for cataract surgery is over 12 months. After surgery, another visit to the consultant is scheduled to check on the patient and then the patient is referred back to the optometrist for a new pair of glasses. Therefore, it takes patients at least six visits and often well over a year to have a routine, 20-minute, outpatient surgical procedure.

Given the complexity and long drawn-out nature of the existing process, a new reengineered cataract diagnostic and treatment process was seen as potentially beneficial. To facilitate that change, a designated member of the hospital's transformation team was assigned to help change the process. The transformation team is a set of eight individuals who are charged with reengineering hospital processes within this particular Midlands Trust. The transformation team member gathered a team of eye experts from the hospital and the community to discuss ways in which to cut surgery lead times and improve patient satisfaction. Members of the cataract team included the head nurse in the eye unit, a hospital administrator, GPs, a set of optometrists from the local community, and a surgical consultant who was instrumental in championing the need for change and in leading the reengineering effort. Team meetings were held in the evening to facilitate attendance and were led by the transformation team member. Minutes, flowcharts, and other necessary documentation for the process were produced by the transformation team member and distributed to all team members after each meeting. In total, approximately five project team meetings were held over a six-month period.

A number of substantive changes to the existing process were made. Nonessential visits to the GP, the consultant, and the nurse were eliminated. Instead, optometrists were empowered to decide if a patient needed cataract surgery. In doing so, they were required to fill out a detailed form that provided the consultant with specific information about the nature and severity of the cataract. They also called the hospital to book a time for the patient's surgery. For these additional responsibilities, the optometrists are given some extra training and receive a small amount of compensation from the trust.

The preliminary preoperative physical was replaced with a self-diagnostic questionnaire that each patient was required to fill out and return to the hospital before surgery. Nurses telephoned each patient before surgery to check the patient's details and to answer any questions. Postoperative appointments with the consultant were also replaced with follow-up telephone calls.

The new cataract procedure resulted in dramatic efficiency gains. Lead times were radically reduced from over 12 months to six to eight weeks. In addition, operating room (OR) utilization rates improved due to the addition of an administrator whose sole responsibility was scheduling. Finally, and most important, according to follow-up phone conversations with cataract project patients, patient satisfaction improved dramatically. The new reengineering cataract process can, therefore, clearly be seen as a new "best practice" that transformed the Midlands Trust's ability to deliver this service. However, attempts to transfer this "best practice" to other NHS trusts have not been successful. We will consider the reasons for this in the following analysis.

## CASE ANALYSIS

Our findings from this study indicate the overwhelming importance of social relations in generating knowledge, which can lead to the transformation of organizational processes. Reengineering the cataract diagnostic and treatment process involved building meaning out of often conflicting and confusing data. This was only possible through bringing together a number of individuals with different knowledge and understanding, who were willing to share their largely tacit knowledge in order to generate new knowledge. Here a crucial aspect of this "new" knowledge was a holistic overview and understanding of the cataract diagnostic and treatment process as it existed at the beginning of the reengineering effort. This was the essential first step in the successful reengineering of the process. This holistic knowledge of the cataract process did not exist before the formation of the project team and thus had to be generated through interaction and negotiation. In particular, this case study highlights the importance of bringing together key individuals, the use of social networks to bring new ideas into the reengineering effort, and the use of templates, which, in this case, served as tangible outcomes of the project. In the final part of the analysis, we consider how far the newly developed diagnosis and treatment process could be transferred to other contexts where it may be applicable.

### Bringing Together Key Individuals

Individuals from the different professional groups involved in cataract treatment were invited to attend the reengineering meetings. Each of these individuals was committed to seeing a new, streamlined cataract diagnostic and treatment process implemented. It is clear that the change in the cataract diagnostic and treatment process would not have occurred if there had not been a significant number from each of the professional groups who were keen and eager to get involved. All of those actively involved in the process wanted to enact change:

> From the beginning it seemed to be a relatively smooth process and that is probably because the people around the table were all of the same mind, they wanted it to work. (Project team member)

This involvement was driven by a perception that change would be beneficial to each group involved in the cataract diagnosis and treatment process. The optometrists benefited in that they were provided with an enhanced sense of professionalism and decision-making authority that was commensurate with their training and experience. In addition, they now had the opportunity to build stronger relationships with their customers by providing diagnostic services. The optometrists were also given a small amount of additional compensation for their increased role in this new process. The incentive for the GP was a reduction in their already large patient load as well as a reduction in their administrative paperwork. Under the new system, the GP is kept informed of which patient is going for surgery, but there is no longer a need for a special visit to the doctor. The consultants and the nurses also benefited from a reduced patient load, thereby freeing them up to focus on nonroutine cases. Midlands Hospital benefited from increased theatre utilization and increased patient satisfaction. Finally, the patient benefited from obtaining the same quality of care with a major reduction in wait-time to surgery as well as with much less inconvenience because now he or she did not have to make multiple visits to the different professionals involved.

With all of the benefits inherent in this change, it is important to note that there was substantial resistance from some individuals and groups. For example, the transformation team member recounted the story of an optometrist with a large local practice, who initially refused to participate in the newly designed cataract process. As luck would have it, the transformation team member happened to need a new pair of glasses and decided to visit the reluctant optometrist. The transformation team member touted the benefits of this new cataract diagnostic and treatment process throughout her eye exam. By the time her glasses were ready, the optometrist had reconsidered his position and decided to participate in the project.

Bringing together individuals from different professional backgrounds was necessary such that each group could understand and appreciate the skills and capabilities of other groups. Without this collective activity, the knowledge and understanding of the different groups would have remained unconnected and isolated, and preconceived notions of the limits of the professional competence of others would not have been challenged. Indeed, this remained an issue for some who had not been directly involved in the project team. For example, certain consultants in Midlands Hospital still assumed that optometrists could not properly diagnose cataracts and continued to want to see all patients to make the diagnosis:

> There are a lot of other departments where people express reservations about the skills of optometrists who will be referring patients to them and they are not prepared to go down that route [i.e., the new cataract process] because of that. (Project member)

However, through bringing together these different individuals, there was an opportunity to challenge and break down many of the existing professional barriers, at least among those who were willing to get involved: "We had never really got together before and that built great bridges" (Project member).

While bringing together individuals from different professional domains was important in the knowledge generation process, wider social networks were also crucial in terms of learning from the experience of others.

## Social Networks

One way in which new knowledge was brought into the project team was through the use of personal contacts. Similar to Granovetter's (1973) weak ties argument, the project team and, in particular, the nursing staff used their knowledge of developments at other local trusts as a source of information when making decisions about the new cataract diagnostic and treatment process. As there was no prototype for the new cataract process to follow, different trusts were called on to provide information about components of the proposed change.

For example, one of the most contentious changes in the new cataract process was the change in the role of the consultant's secretary. Under the old model, each secretary was assigned to one consultant and that secretary was charged with the responsibility for all OR scheduling for that surgeon. Under the new process, all OR scheduling was handled through one administrative assistant, and secretaries were reallocated to more than one consultant.

The secretaries, who insisted that they were far too busy to be assigned to more than one consultant, were extremely resistant to this change.

> They saw the waiting list management as a big part of their role. They felt that we were undermining their role by taking this away . . . taking away their patient contact. . . . We were just turning them into audio typists. (Project member)

To address their concerns, one of the nurses on the project used her personal contacts with a manager at another trust to arrange for the secretaries to go and visit their counterparts who, at this other location, were assigned to more than one consultant. Through this visit, the secretaries were able to see, firsthand, how their workloads would be reallocated, which helped to legitimate the new process. However, it must be stressed that this did not automatically lead to acceptance of the changed role. Resistance from the secretaries continued even after the changes had been implemented and the new OR scheduling administrator appointed. For example, initially, the new administrator in charge of OR scheduling was not provided with the OR schedules from the individual consultants' secretaries and, therefore, she was unable to perform her role. However, when it became clear that this was not going to be acceptable, the secretaries revised their strategy and all sent in their schedules together so that the new administrator was overwhelmed by the workload—"they were wanting her to sink" (Project member).

In this case, the social network enacted by the nurses on the project team was developed before the outset of the project. Other examples of networking during the cataract reengineering project involved contacting a particular trust that was pioneering in a particular area and, therefore, was known through various NHS communications. In this case, the pioneering trust was contacted, and a visit to their facilities was arranged. It is important to stress that the knowledge gained from these social networks was not simply imported into the design of the new cataract process. Rather, it was reinterpreted and blended with the collective knowledge that was developing within the project team.

## Templates

The new knowledge generated through the interactions between the project team members was used to reengineer the cataract diagnosis and treatment process. This included the design of some concrete deliverables or templates that were outputs from the project. For example, one of the deliverables of the cataract project team was the detailed diagnostic form that is currently used by participating optometrists. Another deliverable was the health form that is sent to all scheduled fast-track cataract surgery participants. Some components of the health form had been based on an existing form that was being used by another hospital project. However, this existing template was not simply reused in this new situation. Rather, each of the forms for the cataract project was developed through a series of iterations in which relevant users were contacted for input. Considerable negotiation and debate took place around the design of these templates, and there were several versions developed and tested in the process of finding the form that best met the needs of all individuals involved. The existing templates that were considered from other hospitals were used as examples during this process of template construction. They were not simply reused as is, but instead were blended with input from the team members to create new project-specific outputs. The creation of these output documents represented important milestones for the project participants. They provided the team members with a feeling of accomplishment, which helped to sustain their enthusiasm for the change process. In this way, the participative process of creating the templates was critical to the success of the newly designed cataract fast-track process.

### "Best Practice" Knowledge Transfer?

Once developed, these forms and a description of the new practice were available to other NHS trusts looking to improve their cataract diagnosis and treatment process. The Midlands project team disseminated information about their new cataract diagnosis and treatment practice at a range of NHS conferences and workshops as well as through personal communications with colleagues working in other hospital trusts across the United Kingdom where the new practice would be relevant. However, when others heard or read about the new "best practice," they dismissed it as unworkable in their context. For example, one hospital rejected Midlands Hospital's new process idea because it was seen as "too radical":

> We had some interest from one of the ophthalmologists [from another region] who wanted to start a similar project, so we sent them our paperwork and documentation. We had some interesting discussion and feedback from people who didn't like the idea. (Project member)

There are a number of reasons why the new "best practice" could not be transferred and used in other hospitals. One reason was that making changes to the existing process takes considerable time and effort. Given current workloads, this outlay of time may not have been feasible:

> In many cases consultants are keen to change things but feel that the clinical load is so great that they just get on and work to the best of their ability within the current system. It requires management facilitation to enable them to change. It is very difficult to just change on your own. (Project member)

In particular, the reengineering project at Midlands Hospital appeared to be successful because of the strong championing and leadership that was provided by the consultant involved. Where such a person does not exist, there is likely to be little impetus for change. All team members recognized the importance of the consultant to the change process.

In addition, the transformation team provided resources and expertise to facilitate the knowledge generation process. They successfully involved the various professional groups and convinced them of the need for change, so that these individuals were willing and able to learn from each other and realign their roles and responsibilities accordingly. In other contexts, these conditions are likely to be very different. Indeed, the existence of a dedicated transformation team at Midlands Hospital was somewhat unique, thereby making it a particularly conducive context for organizational change.

Together, these factors suggest that the Midlands Hospital Trust provided a "receptive context" for strategic change (Pettigrew et al., 1992). Leadership, resources, and motivation existed and provided a context conducive to the redesign of the cataract diagnostic and treatment process. In other trusts where this new "best practice" may be just as relevant, the context may be much less receptive. However, we argue that beyond this notion of context receptivity, there is a more fundamental reason "best practice" transfer did not occur. Specifically, our analysis of the learning process that was gone through by the cataract project team at the Midlands Hospital Trust leads us to conclude that knowledge of the new cataract diagnosis and treatment process could not readily transfer to other contexts because knowledge transfer does not occur independently of knowledge generation. This argument is developed below.

In other hospitals where the new diagnostic and treatment process could be relevant, the holistic knowledge of the existing process and of the skills and expertise of the various professionals involved would first need to be generated. For example, one of the optometrists who had been involved in the project from the outset explained how his changed role allowed him to diagnose and directly refer patients. However, he also explained that this process was not entirely straightforward and had been particularly difficult at the beginning of the pilot phase. He stated that, at times, he had needed to clarify issues with the consultant in order to ensure that a particular patient was actually suitable for the cataract operation. With many consultants, this would be difficult because they undervalued the knowledge of optometrists:

> When patients eventually find their way to hospital any comment that the optometrist has made that is relayed to the hospital staff is usually treated with contempt—"what do they know about it"—that sort of attitude. (Project member)

However, through working together on the project and sharing professional knowledge, the consultants involved had learned to respect and trust the competencies of optometrists. Moreover, the building of relationships, facilitated by membership in the project, meant that now an optometrist could telephone a consultant working at the hospital and directly ask his or her advice. The consultants were providing regular feedback to the optometrists, so that the optometrists could continue to learn how to make diagnoses that were acceptable to the consultants. Thus, an important outcome from involvement in the cataract project team had been the creation of a community of practice (Brown and Duguid, 1991), in which shared meaning was being continuously constructed through a process of narration and joint work. Essentially, through interactions that occurred during the process of redesigning the cataract practice, the landscape of social relations had been changed. However, in other NHS Trusts, in the absence of this holistic generation of knowledge and in the absence of changed relationships, the templates and new process orientation are likely to make little sense. In other words, it would not be possible to transfer the templates and knowledge of the new diagnostic and treatment process to other contexts where this knowledge generation process had not taken place, because barriers between the professional groups involved would still exist and there would not be the necessary unifying community of practice.

## DISCUSSION AND CONCLUSIONS

Before discussing the case, it is important to note that our findings are based on a single case study and, therefore, by definition, do not meet the criteria of credibility (a measure of the degree to which findings across cases fit the data) or transferability (the extent to which the findings can be replicated across cases) (Erlandson et al., 1993). Additional research, across multiple case studies, is needed in order to verify the tentative grounded theory developed in this paper (Eisenhardt, 1989; Glaser and Strauss, 1967). These limitations notwithstanding, our analysis suggests that this project team was successful in reengineering and producing a new "best practice" cataract diagnosis and treatment process. A single community of practice (Brown and Duguid, 1991) had been formed around the reengineered process. This community was superimposed on top of the existing multiple professional communities, allowing members from the different communities to work together with a single view of the cataract diagnostic and treatment process as opposed to their previous very divergent views (Dougherty, 1992). Before this community was formed, the process of diagnosing and treating cataracts had been a tortuous process, especially for the patient, who had to deal in turn with each of the professional groups involved. It was the patient, in other words, who had been forced to broker the dislocations in the process caused by the traditional professional/functional rather than business process focus. Through the reengineering effort, these professional boundaries had been broken down so that the process orientation was possible (Denison, 1997), which proved to be highly successful for all the stakeholders involved. Ultimately, the intention was to encourage an even smoother process through creating an integrated IT system so that the optometrist could complete the diagnostic form online. This would then automatically register the patient with a hospital appointment for the surgery, as well as inform the patient's GP that this had happened so that patient records could be updated. Thus, although the organizational changes had been essential to reengineer the process, IT would, in the future, facilitate this integrated process orientation even more (Hammer and Champy, 1993).

It is also possible to argue that the project had been successful in facilitating transformational organizational change using the six indicators suggested by Ferlie et al. (1996). Foremost, the service had become much more efficient, with a significant reduction in the number of visits the patient had to endure. The effective operation of the new cataract diagnosis and treatment process was only possible because of multiple, interrelated changes across the system, involving all stakeholders. For example, GPs had to remove themselves from the process, consultants had to agree to let the optometrists carry out diagnosis, optometrists had to agree to expand their roles to diagnosis even though the time this took was not fully compensated by the remuneration they received, nurses had to agree that patients were able to self-assess, and patients had to be willing to do this. These changes affected individuals and the professional groups they represented. Thus, the change had only been possible with a change in relations across the professional groups. What had been created was an emergent community of practice, with its own culture focusing on the total process rather than the independent pieces. Although this organizational form was not a formal structure, it did underpin a new governance process, with optometrists gaining diagnostic authority. This had only been possible because of the change in ideology and power relations within the organization (Pettigrew, 1987), with the optometrists gaining power because of increased respect from the other professional groups involved.

In many respects, this is an example of successful BPR, leading to organizational transformation in a professional service context. However, the case is also interesting because of the fact that the newly created "best practice" had failed to transfer to other contexts where it was potentially equally applicable. We argue that the key to understanding why transfer was not successful lies in understanding how this team was successful in reengineering the cataract process. As those involved in the project exchanged ideas and information, new meanings and insights were generated. In particular, through the process of interaction and deliberation, a holistic understanding of the diagnostic and treatment process was created, whereas before this project team was established, each professional group only had a partial view of what constituted the particular routine or business process (Shani et al., 2000; Tsoukas, 1996). In particular, through the exchange within the project team, all of the professional groups involved in the process started to recognize the value and underutilization of opticians' skills and expertise. Thus, micro-level shifts in the relative power of different professionals occurred through engaging in the project process. Indeed, these ideological and power shifts were the basis of the successful reengineering, as previously discussed.

However, the new business process could not be transferred to other hospital contexts where proposed recipients had not been through this shift in relations and therefore had not generated this holistic knowledge. They would not share the new reality about the process that had been generated at Midlands Hospital (Rowley, 2000). Existing professional boundaries and the concomitant distribution of knowing among those involved meant that the new cataract diagnostic and treatment process would be rejected as unworkable. Thus, within each new context, the various professionals needed to generate the collective knowledge that was the basis of the successful reengineering effort at Midlands Hospital.

In effect, knowledge of the process of the diagnosis and treatment of cataracts was sustained by the interaction of the various collective actors, and knowledge existed only through this social interaction (Gherardi and Nicolini, 2000). As Cook and Brown (1999) observe, it is groups, rather than individuals, that possess the "body of knowledge"—in this case, cataract diagnosis and treatment—and not everybody within a group possesses all that is contained within this body of knowledge. Knowledge of the routine had therefore to be generated through interaction and communication within the project team (Weick, 1995). Transferring knowledge of this new "best practice" to another situation in which those involved had not been through such a process of knowledge generation and its accompanying ideological and power shifts could not be, and was not, effective. In this "other" context, preexisting ideas about normal practice limited the absorptive capacity of those involved (Cohen and Leventhal, 1990). Absorptive capacity is a path-dependent process that is largely a function of pre-existing knowledge. Szulanski (1996) found that absorptive capacity was the biggest impediment to the internal transfer of knowledge. Szulanski's finding highlights our contention that any given work practice is culturally mediated and therefore is the outcome of a web of knowledge formed through social participation, material working conditions, and negotiated interpretations (Star, 1989; 1996). Thus, for consultants that have not been through the "conversion" that those in the case team have been through, their prior knowledge tells them that "opticians cannot accurately diagnose cataracts." Acceptance of a new work process that renders obsolete these taken-for-granted assumptions is unlikely (Orlikowski, 2000).

This does not mean that the templates and the description of the new "best practice" produced by Midlands Hospital will not be useful to those in other contexts. In understanding how they may be used, it is helpful to see the developed templates as boundary objects (Star, 1989). Boundary objects have interpretive flexibility (Hildreth, 2000). We should then expect that the templates designed at Midlands Hospital will be modified in each new context as those involved attempt to make sense of this explicit knowledge during their interactions. During these interactions, knowledge will be shared and blended with these existing templates in order to generate new knowledge in each new context. Thus, the knowledge embedded in the templates must undergo what Czarniawska and Joerges (1996) refer to as a process of traveling, whereby the knowledge must be legitimated in each new context.

Therefore, what is needed, we argue, is the production of project documentation that emphasizes the relational aspects of the project and demonstrates the way in which the situated knowledge produced in that project has been developed. If knowledge is going to be successfully transferred across contexts, it is arguably this relational knowledge that is at least as important as the "product" knowledge about the outcomes of the project—that is, knowledge about the "best practices." Relational knowledge could include, for example, information that highlighted who had been involved in the reengineering effort and what their contribution had been, what the sources of resistance had been, and how these had been overcome. Relational knowledge could also include information about how decisions and outcomes were arrived at, as well as knowledge about how to select team members, locate skills and interests, and build multidisciplinary groups and communities.

In summary, we argue that knowledge transfer (to support the diffusion of a newly identified "best practice") does not occur independently of knowledge generation (which is the necessary foundation for process reengineering). Rather, knowledge generation and its transfer are inexorably intertwined. In this case, knowledge transfer could only occur in conjunction with the generation of multidisciplinary/professional knowledge so that there was a more holistic understanding of the existing diagnostic and treatment process among the various expert professionals involved in the particular context. This knowledge generation allowed the various professionals to reconsider professional boundaries and so reengineer the process to create a new "best practice." Without this knowledge generation, the acceptance of the new knowledge, in this case, a new "best practice" for the diagnosis and treatment of cataracts, would be problematic or simply untenable. In other words, project learning leads to the generation of new knowledge, which facilitates the reengineering of work processes. However, "know-what" or "product" knowledge cannot simply be transferred to other locations because this "product" knowledge would not fit with taken-for-granted assumptions about existing practices in these other places. Rather, what can be transferred is knowledge about the means of building relationships that will encourage knowledge generation to support a reengineering effort, which, in turn, will facilitate the development of the "product" knowledge (a new "best practice") in each context of application. Relational knowledge can then be used so that the necessary knowledge generation occurs more smoothly in other contexts.

A conclusion from this inquiry is that it is rather simplistic to assume that reengineering efforts in one context can be relatively painlessly transferred as a "best practice" to other contexts—however successful this new practice may be in the place of origin. Reengineering, by definition, involves breaking down professional/functional boundaries so that a process can be looked at holistically rather than from a departmental perspective. This will only occur when there are significant shifts in ideology and power relations. Therefore, these shifts need to occur in each context if reengineering is actually going to produce organizational transformation. Such shifts in relations are unlikely to occur without fostering interaction that encourages discussion and dialogue across the various professional communities that will need to change their practices. Hence, we conclude that the sharing of relational knowledge that can help to foster this interaction is likely to be as useful as the sharing of the "best practices."

## ACKNOWLEDGMENTS

Funding and support for this project were generously provided by the Engineering and Physical Sciences Research Council (EPSRC). In part, this chapter expands on earlier work, Newell, S., Edelman, L., Scarbrough, H., Swan, J., and Bresnen, M. 2003. "Best practice" development and transfer in the NHS: The importance of process as well as product knowledge, *Health Services Management Research,* 16, 1–12. Expanded and revised with permission from *Health Services Management and Research* and RSM Press.

## REFERENCES

Barney, J.B. 1991. Firm resources and sustained competitive advantage. *Journal of Management,* 17, 1, 99–120.
Benders J., and Van Veen, K. 2001. What's in a fashion? Interpretative viability and management fashions. *Organization,* 8, 1, 33–53.
Berger, P.L., and Luckmann, T. 1966. *The Social Construction of Reality: A Treatise in the Sociology of Knowledge.* New York: Doubleday.
Blackler, F. 1995. Knowledge, knowledge work and organizations: An overview and interpretation. *Organization Studies,* 16, 6, 1021–1046.
Brown, J.S., and Duguid, P. 1991. Organizational learning and communities of practice: Towards a unified view of working, learning and innovation. *Organization Science,* 2, 1, 40–57.
Camp, R. 1989. *Benchmarking: The Search for Industry Best Practices That Lead to Superior Performance.* Milwaukee, WI: Quality Press.

Cohen, W.M., and Leventhal, D.A. 1990. Absorptive capacity: A new perspective on learning and innovation. *Administrative Science Quarterly,* 35, 128–152.

Cook, S.D.N., and Brown, J.S. 1999. Bridging epistemologies: The generative dance between organizational knowledge and organizational knowing. *Organization Science,* 190, 381–400.

Czarniawska, B., and Joerges, B. 1996. Travels of ideas. In B. Czarniawska and G. Seven (eds.), *Translating Organizational Change.* Berlin: De Gruyter, pp. 13–48.

Dence, R. 1995. Best practices in benchmarking. In J. Holloway, J. Lewis, and G. Mallory (eds.), *Performance Measurement and Evaluation.* London: Sage, pp. 124–152.

Denison, D. 1997. Towards a process-based theory of organizational design: Can organizations be designed around value-chains and networks? In J. Dutton (ed.), *Advances in Strategic Management,* vol. 14. Greenwich, CT: JAI Press, pp. 1–44.

Department of Health. 1997. The new NHS. White Paper, CM3807, Her Majesty's Stationary Office (MSO), London.

Dougherty, D. 1992. Interpretive barriers to successful product innovation in large firms. *Organization Science,* 3, 179–202.

Eisenhardt, K. 1989. Building theories from case study research. *Academy of Management Review,* 14, 532–555.

Erlandson, D.; Harris, E.; Skipper, B.; and Allen, S. 1993. *Doing Naturalistic Inquiry.* Newbury Park, CA: Sage.

Ferlie, E.; Firzgerald, L.; Wood, M.; and Hawkins, C. 2005. The nonspread of innovations: The mediating role of professionals. *Academy of Management Journal,* 48, 1, 117–134.

Gherardi, S., and Nicolini, D. 2000. The organizational learning of safety in communities of practice. *Journal of Management Inquiry,* 9, 1, 7–18.

Glaser, B.G., and Strauss, A.L. 1967. *The Discovery of Grounded Theory: Strategies for Qualitative Research.* Hawthorn, NY: De Gruyter.

Granovetter, M. 1973. The strength of weak ties. *American Journal of Sociology,* 78, 6, 1360–1380.

Grant, R. 1996. Prospering in a dynamically-competitive environment: Organizational capability as knowledge integration. *Organization Science,* 7, 375–387.

Hammer, M., and Champy, J. 1993. *Reengineering the Corporation: A Manifesto for Business Revolution.* New York: Harper Collins.

Hildreth, P. 2000. Communities of practice in the distributed international environment. *Journal of Knowledge Management,* 4, 1, 27–38.

Jones, C. 2001. Towards benchmarking in British acute hospitals. *Health Services Management Research,* 14, 2, 125–138.

Knights, D., and Wilmott, H. 2000. *The Reengineering Revolution: Critical Studies in Corporate Change.* London: Sage.

Lave, J., and Wegner, E. 1991. *Situated Learning: Legitimate Peripheral Participation.* Cambridge: Cambridge University Press.

Locock, L. 2000. Maps and journeys: Redesign in the NHS. University of Birmingham, Health Services Management Centre.

McNulty, T., and Ferlie, E. 2004. Process transformation: Limitations to radical organizational change within public sector organizations. *Organization Studies,* 25, 8, 1389–1412.

Nelson, R. 1991. Why do firms differ, and how does it matter? *Strategic Management Journal,* 12, 61–74.

Newell, S; Swan, J.; and Galliers, R. 2000. A knowledge-focused perspective on the diffusion and adoption of complex information technologies: The BPR example. *Information Systems Journal,* 10, 239–259.

Okhuysen, G., and Eisenhardt, K. 2002. Integrating knowledge in groups: How formal interventions enable flexibility. *Organization Science,* 13, 370–386.

Orlikowski, W. 2000. Using technology and constituting structures: A practice lens for studying technology in organizations. *Organization Science,* 11, 4, 404–428.

Owen-Smith, J.; Riccaboni, M.; Pammolli, F.; and Powell, W. 2002. A comparison of U.S. and European university–industry relations in the life sciences. *Management Science,* 48, 1, 24–43.

Pettigrew, A. 1987. Context and action in the transformation of the firm. *Journal of Management Studies,* 24, 649–670.

Pettigrew, A; Ferlie, E.; and McKee, L. 1992. *Shaping Strategic Change.* London: Sage.

Powell, W.; Koput, W.; and Smith-Doerr, L. 1996. Interorganizational collaboration and the locus of innovation: Networks of learning in biotechnology. *Administrative Science Quarterly,* 41, 1, 116–130.

Prusak, L. 1997. *Knowledge in Organizations.* Oxford: Butterworth-Heinemann.

Radwin, L. 1998. Empirically generated attributes of experience in nursing. *Journal of Advanced Nursing,* 27, 590–595.

Rowley, J. 2000. From learning organization to knowledge entrepreneur. *Journal of Knowledge Management,* 4, 1, 7–15.

Shani, A.B.; Sena, J.A.; and Stebbins, M.W. 2000. Knowledge work teams and groupware technology: Learning from Seagate's experience. *Journal of Knowledge Management,* 4, 2, 111–124.

Spender, J.-C. 1996. Making knowledge the basis for a dynamic theory of the firm. *Strategic Management Journal,* 17, 45–62.

Star, S.L. 1989. The structure of ill-structured solutions: Boundary objects and heterogeneous distributed problem-solving. *Distributed Artificial Intelligence,* 2, 37–54.

———. 1996. Working together: Symbolic interactionism, activity theory and information systems. In Y. Engestrom and D. Middleton (eds.), *Cognition and Communication at Work.* Cambridge: Cambridge University Press, pp. 296–318.

Strauss, A., and Corbin, J. 1994. Grounded theory methodology: An overview. In N. Denzin and Y. Loncoln (eds.), *Handbook of Qualitative Research.* Thousand Oaks, CA: Sage, pp. 273–285.

Szulanski, G. 1996. Exploring internal stickiness: Impediments to the transfer of best practices within the firm. *Strategic Management Journal,* 17, 27–43.

Tsoukas, H. 1996. The firm as a distributed knowledge system: A constructivist approach. *Strategic Management Journal,* 17, 11–25.

Weick, K.E. 1995. *Sensemaking in Organizations.* Thousand Oaks, CA: Sage.

Winter, S.G. 1987. Knowledge and competence as strategic assets. In D. Teece (ed.), *The Competitive Challenge.* Cambridge, MA: Ballinger, pp. 159–184.

Winter, S.G. 1995. Four Rs of profitability: Rents, resources, routines and replications. In C.A. Montgomery (ed.), *Resource-Based and Evolutionary Theories of the Firm: Towards a Synthesis.* Boston: Kluwer Academic Publishers, pp. 147–178.

Yin, R.K. 1989. *Case Study Research: Design and Methods.* Newbury Park, CA: Sage.

# CHAPTER 15

# PROCESS MANAGEMENT, TECHNOLOGICAL INNOVATION, AND ORGANIZATIONAL ADAPTATION

## MARY J. BENNER AND MICHAEL TUSHMAN

**Abstract:** *The promise of process management practices is that as organizations focus on variance reduction and increased process control, they will drive both speed and organizational efficiency. However, this promise also accentuates the dark side of process management. These practices will increasingly favor exploitative innovations at the expense of exploratory innovations. This inertia works to impede major change and transforms core competencies to core rigidities. Managers must exercise caution against considerable institutional pressures pushing process management activities. They need to adopt a more nuanced approach to creating organizations that can celebrate both variance reduction in the service of exploitation and variance creation in the service of exploration. This can be achieved by adopting an ambidextrous organizational design.*

**Keywords:** *Process Management, Innovation, Exploitation, Exploration, Organizational Adaptation, Ambidextrous Organization*

## INTRODUCTION

Process management, based on a view of an organization as a system of interlinked processes, involves concerted efforts to map, improve, and adhere to organizational processes. Initially, a central part of total quality management (TQM) programs in the 1980s, process management practices are now applied not only as part of quality-related initiatives in manufacturing operations but also to other organizational processes, such as those concerning the selection and development of technological innovations. Thus, process management activities have the potential to affect an organization's technological innovations.

More generally, research in organizational learning and evolution has suggested that increased routinization and coordination in an organization's activities may speed responsiveness in stable environments and also contribute to resistance to change, competency traps, and inadequate or inappropriate responses in changing environments (Cohen and Bacdayan, 1994; Levinthal, 1997a). The ability of a firm to compete over time is rooted not only in its focus on routinization and coordination of activities, central to process management techniques, but also in pursuing radical innovation simultaneously. Thus, a firm's dynamic capabilities are anchored in its ability to both exploit and explore; that is, a firm's ability to compete over time depends on its ability both to integrate and build on its current competencies while simultaneously developing fundamentally new capabilities (March, 1991; Teece et al., 1997).

In this chapter, we explore the impact of process management practices on innovation and organizational adaptation. We underscore that as these practices reduce variance in organizational routines and influence the selection of innovations, they enhance incremental innovation at the expense of exploratory innovation. We argue that widely adopted process management practices shift the balance of exploitation and exploration by focusing on efficiency, possibly at the expense of long-term adaptation. In other words, exploitation crowds out exploration in the context of process management activities.

The subsequent sections of the chapter are organized as follows. The next section describes the promise of process management practices, outlining the nature of these activities and their intended benefits. The third section discusses the reality of process management practices and the paradox they present to organizations in the pursuit of both exploitative and exploratory innovation, and in the choice of organizational adaptation mechanisms in both stable and turbulent environments. The fourth section offers some suggestions on how organizations can simultaneously pursue these inherently contradictory activities. In particular, we highlight an ambidextrous organizational design. The fifth section presents concluding remarks.

## THE PROMISE OF PROCESS MANAGEMENT PRACTICES

The process management view of organizations is as a system of interdependent processes that cross functions and link organizational activities rather than as just a collection of departments with separate functions and outputs (Dean and Bowen, 1994). Process management practices encompass three main areas—mapping, improving, and adhering to systems of improved processes. Mapping entails the recording of underlying processes, improving embraces the use of measures of process effectiveness and statistical methods to continually eliminate variation in processes and outputs, and adhering to systems of improved processes stresses ongoing conformance to the resulting mapped and improved processes. These three general practices are applied to processes across an organization.

Process management helps in rationalizing individual work processes and in streamlining the handoffs between processes (Garvin, 1995; Harry and Schroeder, 2000). Through adherence to mapped and improved processes, organizations can reap the benefits of improvement efforts as well as continue on a path of incremental improvements (Harrington and Mathers, 1997; Mukherjee et al., 1998). By streamlining the handoffs between activities, process management practices increase efficiency due to increased yields and less rework and waste as streamlined processes eliminate non-value-added activities. Generally, products resulting from improved processes are expected to better satisfy customers, leading to increased revenues and, ultimately, increased profits. Ideally, this is the promise or "bright" side of process management practices. However, in reality, there is also the "dark" side of process management practices as we shall see in the next section.

Notwithstanding the apparent dilemma, process management activities permeate both upstream activities, such as processes for selecting and developing technological innovations, and downstream activities, such as distribution, sales, and service. Indeed, the 9001 version of the ISO 9000 program involves processes for product design, development, and service (Harrington and Mathers, 1997), whereas Design for Six Sigma similarly promotes extending process control techniques into R&D, including product design and development activities (Harry and Schroeder, 2000).

## THE REALITY OF PROCESS MANAGEMENT

Process management practices, by design and intent, exploit existing capabilities. Although this favors exploitative innovation and organizational adaptation in stable environments, it may hamper exploratory innovation and adaptation in rapidly changing environments. Below, we discuss the realities of process management practices and the organizational puzzle they present.

### Process Management Effects on Exploitation and Exploration

The innovation process can be classified as either exploitation or exploration, each characterized by fundamentally different search modes. Exploitation involves local search that builds on a firm's existing technological capabilities, whereas exploration involves more distant search for new capabilities (March, 1991; Rosenkopf and Nerkar, 2001). While exploitative innovations involve improvements in existing components and architectures and build on the existing technological trajectory, exploratory innovations may involve a shift to a different technological trajectory (Christensen, 1997; Tushman and Anderson, 1986).

Process management activities can influence exploitative and exploratory innovation in organizations through two main mechanisms—through organizational learning and through their influence on the internal selection environment for innovation projects. Process management specifically prescribes a focus on incremental change in existing organizational routines, and its accompanying practices support this philosophy (Adler, 1993; Anderson et al., 1994). Adoption of process management initiatives favors a system of incremental learning as best practices are established and organizational activities are repeated in these standard processes.

Organizational learning research suggests that repetition of, and incremental improvement in, established practices results in both increased efficiency and proficiency in those activities (Levinthal and March, 1993; Levitt and March, 1988; March, 1991). Repetition through routines not only reduces the time to carry out the activity but also reduces the variance in performance of the routine, reflecting increased proficiency. Thus, as incremental learning associated with process management extends in an organization, the organization becomes not only more efficient in a set of practices but also increasingly reliable as the variation in its performance is reduced. This suggests that organizations will innovate more rapidly as they incrementally improve innovation processes, but the variance in the resulting innovation or new product development outcomes may be reduced.

The use of process management also provides an enabling structure that allows for more efficient horizontal coordination of activities toward a common organizational goal (cf. Adler and Borys, 1996). Tighter coupling occurs with the application of process management activities to intentionally streamline the system of organizational routines against the dual objectives of efficiency and quality. More specifically, tighter linkages emerge as efforts to improve downstream processes spur incremental changes in the outputs or handoffs from upstream, supplying processes. For example, focused efforts to improve manufacturing processes result in tweaking new product developments to better leverage downstream processes and spur continued measurable improvements in manufacturing efficiency and internal customer satisfaction. Such changes in the product development processes and outputs are themselves likely to be incremental, while at the same time, the handoffs between the product development and manufacturing processes become more efficient and streamlined.

Thus, while process management activities involve an explicit focus on continuous innovation and change, these practices increasingly trigger searches for solutions in the neighborhood of existing skills and knowledge and are likely to spur innovations that utilize existing or familiar knowledge. As a consequence, incremental innovation associated with process management reduces significant exploratory activity and learning outside the existing technological trajectory (Levinthal and March, 1993; March, 1991). The path-dependent nature of innovation suggests an even longer-lasting effect of process management practices. Past innovative activities play a role in future innovation by providing a firm with a knowledge base that allows it to absorb technological competence from external sources (Cohen and Levinthal, 1990; Levitt and March, 1988). Thus, an organization that lacks exploration in one period may be excluded from areas of future exploratory activity because it lacks the relevant knowledge base (Cohen and Levinthal, 1990; Teece et al., 1997). Because process management techniques reduce a firm's exploratory activities, its absorptive capacity will be stunted. Therefore, the firm is less likely to produce subsequent innovations that incorporate new technologies.

Process management techniques stabilize organizational routines and tighten the linkages between them, yet they make cross-boundary, cross-community linkages more difficult (Sitkin and Stickel, 1996). Organizations focused on incremental enhancements of current technology treat architectural innovation as merely incremental, fail to forge linkages across organizational boundaries, and, in turn, underperform (Christensen, 1997; Henderson and Clark, 1990; Lawless and Anderson, 1996; Tripsas, 1997). Although incremental innovation may, in some circumstances, actually accommodate architectural or modular innovations, adherence to standardized best practices ensures repetition of practices through these stable linkages within local domains, and an organization's ability to actually take advantage of subsystem and linking technologies is hampered. Increased proficiency with local search makes it unlikely that process management activities will produce innovations that significantly depart from the neighborhood of the organization's existing technological or market competencies.

Further, over time, process management shifts the balance between exploitation and exploration by affecting the selection of innovation projects. While the benefits of exploitation are certain, positive, and close in time, the returns to exploratory activities, if any, are distant and uncertain (Levinthal and March, 1993; March, 1991). The short-term certainty of exploitation crowds out exploratory learning and innovation by triggering a reduction in investments in experimentation (Levinthal and March, 1993). Thus, as the reach of process management activities extends further into research, R&D project selection activities, or product development, radical innovation projects increasingly give way to more certain, incremental activities (Henderson et al., 1998). As process intensity increases, even structures designed to produce radical innovations (e.g., heavyweight teams or independent units) increasingly will produce innovations close to past innovations (Brown and Duguid, 2000; Sitkin and Stickel, 1996; Tripsas and Gavetti, 2000). This is accentuated by organizational cultures focused on measures of incremental and continuous improvement, which squeeze out more distant innovations in favor of further improvements in the existing capabilities and skills defined by existing routines (Repenning and Sterman, 2002; Sørensen, 2002).

The above arguments are supported by our empirical results based on a 20-year longitudinal study of patenting activity and ISO 9000 quality program certifications in the paint and photography industries (Benner and Tushman, 2002). For both industries, we found that as firms increased their process management activity, on one hand, exploitative innovation increased, and the effect became continually stronger and more significant with increases in the proportion of prior knowledge used in patenting. On the other hand, our results indicate that increased ISO 9000 certifications were associated with a decrease in exploratory innovations. This negative result was particularly significant for the most variance-increasing forms of innovation. Increased process management was associated with a significant decline in the number of patents that were based entirely on knowledge new to the firm.

Furthermore, we found that increases in process management activity in a firm were associated with increases in exploitation's share of the total amount of innovation. Moreover, the effect was particularly strong for innovations that were very exploitative of previous firm knowledge. It appears that process management activities crowd out more exploratory, experimental forms of innovation. Increases in process management activities appear not only to increase exploitative patents but also trigger a shift toward more exploitative patents—that is, patents with a higher proportion of previously used knowledge. These effects exist even after controlling for fixed effects, such as age or size, year effects, R&D intensity over time, and increases in exploitation that occur over time and with age.

Our results also indicate that process management activities spur exploitation over and above the natural tendencies that unfold with age and size. These results suggest that it is not organizational age or size per se, but routinization that gives rise to increasingly exploitative behavior. Thus, our work highlights the importance of going beyond the proxy measures of age and size to pinpointing the specific organizational practices that are the roots of inertia.

These results suggest that the challenges firms face in maintaining exploration may be more difficult than previously suggested. Not only do organizations face a challenge in sustaining highly risky, distant search and exploration into new domains but it appears that they also face a challenge in sustaining moderately exploratory innovations—those that leverage existing organizational knowledge combined with some knowledge that is new to the firm. In addition, process management activities and the culture associated with exploitation appear to drive extremely local search and exploitation based almost entirely on familiar knowledge. It may be that the combination of learning and selection effects drives more incremental innovation and dramatically reduces the firm's ability to acquire new competencies.

While we found some consistency in the effects of process management activities on innovation outcomes, these effects may have different effects on other organizational outcomes. Even though the increase in exploitative innovations was consistent across industries, the subsequent effect of increased exploitation may have different implications for firm performance in these industries. In the photography industry, the dampening effect of process management on exploratory innovation may have implications for adaptation to subsequent transitions in technology. For example, troubles at Polaroid and Kodak in responding to the digital revolution in photography may be linked to organizational inertia rooted in their attempts to exploit film expertise (Tripsas and Gavetti, 2000).

In summary, while process management may enable rapid development of competence-enhancing innovations, it may also create innovation traps that restrict exploration. With its attendant bright and dark sides, process management, therefore, presents organizations with an innovation paradox.

## Process Management Effects on Organizational Adaptation

Process management activities, through their impact on organizational processes, heighten organizational inertia and dampen responsiveness to technological transitions. This has implications for organizational adaptation in stable and turbulent environments. Organizations with routines and procedures stabilized through process management activities are likely to do well in stable or predictable contexts, but not in turbulent or rapidly changing environments (Benner and Tushman, 2003).

During eras of incremental change, organizations that sustain incremental innovation will be more effective than those that initiate variance-increasing innovation (Abernathy and Utterback, 1978; Anderson and Tushman, 1990). This comes about because to take advantage of the effect of process management activities on incremental innovation, organizations have to nurture technological environments characterized by incremental refinements of an existing technological design. Tighter coordination and repetition of activities embedded in standardized best practices increase an organization's speed and efficiency. For example, streamlined linkages between processes for innovation and manufacturing allow for rapid screening and development of innovations that best leverage downstream manufacturing or distribution capabilities. Furthermore, as processes for identifying and addressing problems and opportunities in the environment are further refined and routinized by process management's influence, decision making and problem solving also become more efficient. Increasing organizational proficiency in recognizing and addressing recurring challenges leads to stable and increasingly efficient communication channels and information filters (Henderson and Clark, 1990; Tyre and Orlikowski, 1994). These stable patterns of communication and interaction lead to the development of norms, rules, and roles that further channel individual and group behavior into streamlined activities that carry out an organization's mission more efficiently (Nadler and Tushman, 1998). Over time, stable procedures and norms also drive increased demographic homogeneity within the organization, further speeding decision making and problem solving (Keck and Tushman, 1993; Williams and O'Reilly, 1998). These factors drive an increasingly tightly integrated organization focused on fast response to existing customer requirements.

However, in environments characterized by rapid innovation and change, an organization's ability to develop new technological capabilities rapidly becomes critical (Brown and Eisenhardt, 1997; Teece et al., 1997; Tushman and Anderson, 1986). Responding to environmental uncertainty and variation requires similar variety within the firm. However, the focus of process management activities on variation reduction restricts the development of alternatives for responding to environmental changes. The attendant delayed or inadequate responses to environmental turbulence affect organizational outcomes. In the evolution of the computer industry, for instance, IBM's relatively slow response to personal computers resulted in the successful entry of other less-powerful competitors. Similarly, slow or incompetent responses to environmental shifts prevented incumbents from retaining their leadership positions in the disk drive (Christensen and Bower, 1996), photolithographic equipment (Henderson and Clark, 1990), and watch (Glasmeier, 2000) industries, among others (Tushman and O'Reilly, 1997).

Further empirical results from the digital camera industry suggest that more extensive process management activities dampened a firm's ability to keep up with rapid technological change through new product introductions (Benner, forthcoming). These results were particularly strong for photography industry incumbents entering the new digital camera industry, suggesting that the incremental improvements in routines that enhanced their efficiency in film technology may have been inappropriate for responding to the rapid change in digital technology. Process management practices have also been positively associated with performance in the stable auto industry, but not in the more dynamic computer industry (Ittner and Larcker, 1997).

Although process management practices are aimed at helping organizations adapt, their possibly unintended effects on reducing variation or increasing inertia may impede adaptation to environmental shifts and increase the importance of selection processes in organizational outcomes. Rapid exploitation may be functional for organizations when environments are stable, but not when they are characterized by rapid change. Tighter linkages between organizational routines and a focus on incremental innovation help speed commercialization of innovations in stable or incrementally changing contexts. Yet such an innovation trajectory reduces technical variation and stunts a firm's ability to adapt in turbulent environments.

Thus, the same process management practices that help an organization learn and achieve efficiency more quickly can also impede an organization's adaptation to major technological transitions (Levinthal, 1991; 1997b). Over time, as these practices permeate an organization, radical change becomes difficult. Organizational momentum toward incremental changes in processes and products works to impede major change and consequently transforms core competencies into rigidities (Leonard-Barton, 1992). Such consequences of process management activities might reduce a firm's life chances in turbulent environments.

## REDRESSING PROCESS MANAGEMENT PARADOX: AN AMBIDEXTROUS ORGANIZATION

The apparent contradictions between exploitation and exploration and in organizational adaptation mechanisms in stable and turbulent environments present organizations with a paradox in pursuing process management practices. However, in order to survive in contemporary market environments characterized by rapid change, organizations need to address the question of how to balance these inherently conflicting activities and mechanisms. Otherwise, they will fall into traps that will hamper their ability to quickly adapt in changing market environments.

While there are varying points of view about how organizations could achieve the desired balance, we underscore the view of an ambidextrous or dual organizational form, which enables the organization to pursue contradicting innovation approaches or adaptation mechanisms simultaneously. An ambidextrous organizational design is composed of highly differentiated but weakly integrated subunits. While the exploratory units are small and decentralized, with loose cultures and processes, the exploitation units are larger and more centralized, with tight cultures and processes. Exploratory units succeed by experimenting—by frequently creating small wins and losses. Because process management tends to drive out experimentation, it must be prevented from migrating into exploratory units and processes. In contrast, exploitation units that succeed by reducing variability and maximizing efficiency and control are an ideal location for the tight coordination associated with process management efforts.

In an ambidextrous organizational design, these contrasting and inconsistent units must be physically and culturally separated from one another, have different measurement and incentives, and have distinct managerial teams (Bradach, 1997; Sutcliffe et al., 2000; Tushman and O'Reilly, 1997). For example, in Hewlett-Packard's Scanner Division, the more routine flatbed scanners had a completely different organizational architecture from the emerging consumer/knitting technology scanners. These distinct units were physically separated from one another and had their own management teams.

To leverage an ambidextrous organizational design, the highly differentiated but loosely coupled subsystems must be strategically integrated by the senior team. Such strategic linkage should be anchored with common aspiration levels and a senior team that both provides slack to the experimental subunits and holds the differentiated units to fundamentally different selection and search constraints (Levinthal and March, 1993; Rotemberg and Saloner, 2000). To be effective, ambidextrous senior teams must develop processes for establishing new, forward-looking cognitive models for exploration units while allowing backward-looking experiential learning to rapidly unfold for exploitation units (Gavetti and Levinthal, 2000). In other words, senior teams must develop techniques that permit them to be *consistently inconsistent* as they steer a balance between the need to be small and large, centralized and decentralized, and focused both on the short term and long term simultaneously (Gavetti and Levinthal, 2000; Weick, 1995).

In summary, although complex and politically difficult, an ambidextrous organizational form permits a firm with highly differentiated units to drive process management, with its associated variation reduction and control, as well as exploration and option creation. Experimental units provide variation from which the senior team can learn about and, in turn, bet on the future, even as the exploitation units build capabilities for short-term effectiveness. These internally inconsistent operating modes must be strategically linked by the senior team through their aspirations and actions and through a limited set of core values.

## CONCLUSION

This chapter explored the impact of process management practices on technological innovation and organizational adaptation. They can tip the balance toward incremental innovation in organizations through two main mechanisms—through incremental learning as process management activities are increasingly applied to an organization's routines and through their influence on the internal selection environment for innovation projects. Both of these mechanisms tend to favor exploitation at the expense of exploration, as organizations incrementally improve innovation processes and short-term, easy-to-measure efficiency improvements make vague, uncertain, difficult-to-quantify exploratory activities less attractive.

Furthermore, through their impact on organizational processes, process management activities increase organizational inertia and slow responsiveness to environmental changes. While this works fine in stable environments, in environments characterized by rapid innovation and change, an organization's ability to develop new technological capabilities rapidly becomes critical. The focus of process management activities on variation-reduction restricts the development of alternatives for responding to environmental changes, and delayed or inadequate responses to environmental turbulence ultimately affect organizational outcomes.

Organizations can resolve these contradictions by adopting ambidextrous organizational designs that enable them to pursue exploitation and exploration simultaneously. In an ambidextrous organization, exploration units succeed by experimenting while exploitation units succeed by reducing variability and maximizing efficiency and control. By being ambidextrous, organizations can develop processes for establishing new, forward-looking cognitive models for exploration units, while allowing backward-looking experiential learning to rapidly unfold for exploitation units.

## REFERENCES

Abernathy, W.J., and Utterback, J.M. 1978. Patterns of industrial innovation. *Technology Review,* 80, 7, 40–47.
Adler, P.S. 1993. Time-and-motion regained. *Harvard Business Review,* 71, 1, 97–108.
Adler, P.S., and Borys, B. 1996. Two types of bureaucracy: Enabling and coercive. *Administrative Science Quarterly,* 41 (March), 61–89.
Anderson, J.C.; Rungtusanatham, M.; and Schroeder, R.G. 1994. A theory of quality management underlying the Deming management method. *Academy of Management Review,* 19, 473–509.
Anderson, P., and Tushman, M.L. 1990. Technological discontinuities and dominant designs: A cyclical model of technological change. *Administrative Science Quarterly,* 35, 604–633.
Benner, M. Forthcoming. Dynamic or static capabilities? Process management practices and response to technological change. *Journal of Product Innovation Management.*
Benner, M., and Tushman, M. 2002. Process management and technological innovation: A longitudinal study of the photography and paint industries. *Administrative Science Quarterly,* 47, 4, 676–706.

————. 2003. Exploitation, exploration, and process management: The productivity dilemma revisited. *Academy of Management Review,* 28, 2, 238–256.

Bradach, J. 1997. Using the plural form in the management of restaurant chains. *Administrative Science Quarterly,* 42, 276–303.

Brown, J.S., and Duguid, P. 2000. *The Social Life of Information.* Boston: Harvard Business School Press.

Brown, S.L., and Eisenhardt, K.M. 1997. The art of continuous change: Linking complexity theory and time-paced evolution in relentlessly shifting organizations. *Administrative Science Quarterly,* 42, 1–34.

Christensen, C.M. 1997. *The Innovator's Dilemma: When New Technologies Cause Great Firms to Fail.* Boston: Harvard Business School Press.

Christensen, C.M., and Bower, J.L. 1996. Customer power, strategic investment, and the failure of leading firms. *Strategic Management Journal,* 17, 197–218.

Cohen, M.D., and Bacdayan, P. 1994. Organizational routines are stored as procedural memory: Evidence from a laboratory study. *Organization Science,* 5, 554–568.

Cohen, W.M., and Levinthal, D.A. 1990. Absorptive capacity: A new perspective on learning and innovation. *Administrative Science Quarterly,* 35, 128–152.

Dean, J.W., and Bowen, D.E. 1994. Management theory and total quality: Improving research and practice through theory development. *Academy of Management Review,* 19, 392–418.

Garvin, D.A. 1995. Leveraging processes for strategic advantage. *Harvard Business Review,* 73, 5, 77–90.

Gavetti, G., and Levinthal, D. 2000. Looking forward and looking backward: Cognitive and experiential search. *Administrative Science Quarterly,* 45, 113–137.

Glasmeier, A.K. 2000. *Manufacturing Time: Global Competition in the Watch Industry, 1795–2000.* New York/London: Guilford Press.

Harrington, H.J., and Mathers, D.D. 1997. *ISO 9000 and Beyond: From Compliance to Performance Improvement.* New York: McGraw-Hill.

Harry, M.J., and Schroeder, R. 2000. *Six Sigma: The Breakthrough Management Strategy Revolutionizing the World's Top Corporations.* New York: Currency.

Henderson, R.M. 1993. Underinvestment and incompetence as responses to radical innovation. *Rand Journal of Economics,* 24, 248–269.

Henderson, R.M., and Clark, K.B. 1990. Architectural innovation: The reconfiguration of existing product technologies and the failure of established firms. *Administrative Science Quarterly,* 35, 9–30.

Henderson, R.M.; Del Alamo, J.; Becker, T.; Lawton, J.; Moran, P.; and Shapiro, S. 1998. The perils of excellence: Barriers to effective process improvement in product-driven firms. *Production and Operations Quarterly,* 7, 1, 2–18.

Ittner, C.D., and Larcker, D. 1997. The performance effects of process management techniques. *Management Science,* 43, 522–534.

Keck, S., and Tushman, M. 1993. Environmental and organizational context and executive team structure. *Academy of Management Journal,* 36, 1314–1344.

Lawless, M.W., and Anderson, P.C. 1996. Generational technological change: Effects of innovation and local rivalry on performance. *Academy of Management Journal,* 39, 1185–1217.

Leonard-Barton, D. 1992. Core capabilities and core rigidities: A paradox in managing new product development. *Strategic Management Journal,* 14, 111–125.

Levinthal, D. 1991. Organizational adaptation and environmental selection—Interrelated processes of change. *Organization Science,* 2, 1, 140–145.

————. 1997a. Adaptation on rugged landscapes. *Management Science,* 43, 934–950.

————. 1997b. Three faces of organizational learning: Wisdom, inertia and discovery. In R. Garud, P. Nayyar, and Z. Shapira (eds.), *Technological Innovation: Oversights and Foresights.* Cambridge: Cambridge University Press, pp. 167–180.

Levinthal, D., and March, J.G. 1993. The myopia of learning. *Strategic Management Journal,* 14, 95–112.

Levitt, B., and March, J.G. 1988. Organizational learning. *Annual Review of Sociology,* 14, 319–340.

March, J. 1991. Exploration and exploitation in organizational learning. *Organization Science,* 2, 71–87.

Mukherjee, A.; Lapré, M.; and Van Wassenhove, L. 1998. Knowledge-driven quality improvement. *Management Science,* 44 (Supplement), S35–S49.

Nadler, D.A., and Tushman, M.L. 1998. *Competing by Design.* New York: Oxford University Press.

Repenning, N.P., and Sterman, J. 2002. Capability traps and self-confirming attribution errors in the dynamics of process improvement. *Administrative Science Quarterly,* 47, 265–295.

326    BENNER AND TUSHMAN

Rosenkopf, L., and Nerkar, A. 2001. Beyond local search: Boundary-spanning, exploration, and impact in the optical disc industry. *Strategic Management Journal,* 22, 287–306.

Rotemberg, J., and Saloner, G. 2000. Visionaries, managers and strategic direction. *Rand Journal of Economics,* 31, 693–716.

Sitkin, S., and Stickel, D. 1996. The road to hell: The dynamics of distrust in an era of quality. In R. Kramer and T. Tyler (eds.), *Trust in Organizations.* London: Sage, pp. 196–215.

Sørensen, J.B. 2002. The strength of corporate culture and the reliability of firm performance. *Administrative Science Quarterly,* 47, 70–91.

Sutcliffe, K.; Sitkin, S.; and Browning, L. 2000. Tailoring process management to situational requirements. In R. Cole and W. Scott (eds.), *The Quality Movement & Organization Theory.* London: Sage, pp. 315–330.

Teece, D.J.; Pisano, G.; and Shuen, A. 1997. Dynamic capabilities and strategic management. *Strategic Management Journal,* 18, 509–533.

Tripsas, M. 1997. Surviving radical technological change through dynamic capability. *Industrial and Corporate Change,* 6, 341–377.

Tripsas, M., and Gavetti, G. 2000. Capabilities, cognition, and inertia: Evidence from Digital Imaging. *Strategic Management Journal,* 21, 1147–1161.

Tushman, M.L., and Anderson, P. 1986. Technological discontinuities and organizational environments. *Administrative Science Quarterly,* 31, 439–465.

Tushman, M.L., and O'Reilly, C. 1997. *Winning Through Innovation.* Boston: Harvard Business School Press.

Tyre, M., and Orlikowski, W. 1994. Windows of opportunity: Temporal patterns of technological adaptation in organizations. *Organization Science,* 5, 98–109.

Weick, K. 1995. *Sensemaking in Organizations.* Thousand Oaks, CA: Sage.

Williams, K., and O'Reilly, C. 1998. Demography and diversity in organizations: A review of forty years of research. *Research in Organizational Behavior,* 20, 77–140.

# EDITORS AND CONTRIBUTORS

**Rainer Alt** is a professor of information systems, University of Leipzig, Germany. Prior to assuming his current position, Dr. Alt was a senior lecturer and project manager at the Institute of Information Management, University of St. Gallen, Switzerland. Before that he worked as a senior consultant for Roland Berger & Partners in Düsseldorf, Germany. He received his Ph.D. from the University of St. Gallen, Switzerland. He is coauthor of *Business Networking: Shaping Collaboration Between Enterprises* (Springer, 2001) and has published papers in *International Journal of Electronic Commerce* and *Journal of Supply Chain Management,* among others. At St. Gallen, he introduced the "networkability" concept to explain the development of IT-enabled business networks and to support management decision making on becoming and staying a networked enterprise.

**Mary J. Benner** is an assistant professor of management at the Wharton School, University of Pennsylvania. She received her Ph.D. in management from Columbia University and an MBA from Stanford University. Prior to receiving her Ph.D., Professor Benner held positions with Honeywell and Data Resources. She conducts research on the topics of technological innovation and change. Her current research focuses on how institutional pressures affect incumbent firm response to technological change, including the effects of process management practices on firm innovation and responsiveness. Her research has been published in *Academy of Management Review* and *Administrative Science Quarterly.*

**Mike Bresnen** is a professor of organizational behavior at the University of Leicester Management Centre. He holds a Ph.D. from the University of Nottingham. He previously worked at Warwick Business School, Cardiff Business School, and Loughborough University. He is coeditor of *Organisation* and a founding member of the Innovation, Knowledge and Organisational Networking research unit based at Warwick Business School, where he is also an associate fellow. He is the author of *Organising Construction* (Routledge, 1990) and has researched and published widely on the organization and management of the construction process, as well as on interorganizational relations, project management, leadership, and professionals. He is principal investigator on a number of recent EPSRC/ESRC projects investigating knowledge management and project-based learning in construction, manufacturing, and service sectors, as well as innovation in the biomedical field.

**Kevin Crowston** is an associate professor in the School of Information Studies at Syracuse University and director of the Ph.D. program. He joined the school in 1996. He received an A.B. (1984) in applied mathematics (computer science) from Harvard University and a Ph.D. (1991) in information technologies from the Sloan School of Management, Massachusetts Institute of Technology (MIT). Before moving to Syracuse, he was a founding member of the Collaboratory for Research on Electronic Work at the University of Michigan and of the Center for Coordination Science at MIT. His current research interests focus on new ways of organizing made possible by the use of information and communications technology. He approaches this issue in several ways: empirical studies of coordination-intensive processes in human organizations, theoretical characterizations of coordination problems and alternative methods for managing them, and design and empirical evaluation of new kinds of computer systems to support people working together.

**Nikunj Dalal** is a professor of management science and information systems in the William S. Spears School of Business at Oklahoma State University. He has previously consulted with an enterprise software company and has worked as a systems project manager. His research interests include enterprise systems, enterprise modeling, information systems philosophy, and Web perception. His research has appeared in *Communications of the ACM, European Journal of Information Systems, Decision Sciences, International Journal of Human-Computer Studies,* and other academic journals.

**Dursun Delen** is an assistant professor of management science and information systems in the William S. Spears School of Business at Oklahoma State University. His previous research has appeared in *Communications of the ACM, Computers in Industry, Computers and Operations Research, Intelligent Manufacturing Systems,* and *Artificial Intelligence in Medicine,* among others. His research interests include enterprise engineering, decision support systems, knowledge management, and data/text mining. Dr. Delen is a member of IIE, INFORMS, AIS, and ACM.

**Linda F. Edelman** is an assistant professor of strategic management at Bentley College. She received her DBA from Boston University. She is the author of five book chapters and over 20 scholarly articles. Her work has appeared in journals such as *Journal of Business Venturing, Journal of Small Business Management, Organization Studies, Management Learning,* and *British Journal of Management.* Her current research examines the resources, cognitive strategies, and networks of new ventures as well as the innovation strategies of project groups and teams. Prior to joining Bentley, she was a research fellow at the Warwick Business School.

**Omar A. El Sawy** is a professor of information systems in the Information and Operations Management Department at the Marshall School of Business. He is also director of research at the Center for Telecom Management (CTM) at USC, which is an industry-sponsored research and education center that focuses on the networked digital industry. Dr. El Sawy holds a Ph.D. from Stanford Business School, an MBA from the American University in Cairo, and a BSEE from Cairo University. His interests include redesigning electronic value chains, the design of vigilant information systems for turbulent dynamic environments, and knowledge management around business processes in fast-response contexts. Prior to joining USC in 1983, he worked as an engineer and manager for 12 years, first at NCR Corporation, and then as a manager of computer services at Stanford University. He has lectured, consulted, and carried out research in four continents, has been an information systems advisor to the United Nations Development Programme in Egypt, and a Fulbright scholar in Finland. Dr. El Sawy is the author of over 70 papers appearing in both information systems and management journals. He is the author of the book *Redesigning Enterprise Processes for e-Business.* He is a six-time winner of SIM's Paper Awards Competition.

**Varun Grover** is the William S. Lee (Duke Energy) Distinguished Professor of Information Systems at Clemson University. Prior to this, he was Business Partnership Foundation Fellow, Distinguished Researcher, and professor of IS at the University of South Carolina. Professor Grover has published extensively in the IS field, with over 150 publications in refereed journals. Five recent articles have ranked him first, second, or third in research productivity (among over 4,000 researchers) in the top IS journals (e.g., *Information Systems Research, Journal of Management Information Systems, MIS Quarterly*) in the past decade. His current areas of interest are creating IS value in organizations and business process change. Professor Grover has co-authored three books on business process change. He has received numerous awards for his research and teaching from USC, Clemson, DSI, Association for Information Systems, Anbar, and PriceWaterhouseCoopers. Currently, he serves as the senior editor of the *MIS Quarterly, Journal of the Association of Information Systems,* and *Database for Advances in Information Systems* and associate or advisory editor of many other journals including *Journal of Management Information Systems, International Journal of Electronic Commerce,* and *Journal of Business Process Management.*

**Mary Lacity** is a professor of information systems at the University of Missouri–St. Louis, a research affiliate at Templeton College, Oxford, and a Ph.D. faculty advisor at Washington University. Her research interests focus on IT management practices in the areas of sourcing, IT privatization, relationship management, and project management. She has given executive seminars worldwide and has served as an expert witness for the U.S. Congress. She was the recipient of the 2000 World Outsourcing Achievement Award sponsored by PricewaterhouseCoopers and Michael Corbett and Associates. She has written five books, including *Global IT Outsourcing: Search for Business Advantage* (Wiley, 2001; coauthor Leslie Willcocks) and *Information Systems Outsourcing: Myths, Metaphors, and Realities* (Wiley, 1993; coauthor Rudy Hirschheim). Her more than 60 publications have appeared in *Harvard Business Review, Sloan Management Review, MIS Quarterly, IEEE Computer, Communications of the ACM,* and many other academic and practitioner outlets. She is senior editor for *MIS Quarterly Executive* and U.S. editor of the *Journal of Information Technology.*

**Allen S. Lee** is a professor of information systems and associate dean for research and graduate studies in the School of Business at Virginia Commonwealth University. He earned his B.S., M.S., and Ph.D. from Cornell University, the University of California at Berkeley, and Massachusetts Institute of Technology, respectively. His articles, book chapters, editorials, and conference presentations have examined the use of research methods in the scientific study of information systems, including interpretive, positivist, qualitative, and case study methods. In December 2004, he retired from the *MIS Quarterly* editorial board after 15 years, during which time he served as associate editor, senior editor, and editor in chief. He has given research presentations in Australia, Canada, China, Denmark, Hong Kong SAR, the Netherlands, Singapore, Slovenia, South Africa, Sweden, the United Kingdom, and throughout the United States.

**Ann Majchrzak** is a professor of information systems at the Marshall School of Business, University of Southern California. She earned her Ph.D. in social psychology from UCLA in 1980. Professor Majchrzak's research interest is in the organizational effects and design of computer-automated work environments. Her recent publications have appeared in *Management Science, MIS Quarterly, Information Systems Research,* and *Harvard Business Review.* Some of her recent awards include *MIS Quarterly* Paper of the Year, Best Paper Award for the Academy of Management Organizational Communication and Information Systems Division, and Society for Information Management First Place Paper Competition.

**M. Lynne Markus** is the John W. Poduska, Sr. Professor of Information Management at the McCallum Graduate School of Business, Bentley College. She holds a B.S. in industrial engineering from the University of Pittsburgh and a Ph.D. in organizational behavior from Case Western

Reserve University. Professor Markus conducts research on enterprise and interenterprise systems, knowledge management, and IT-enabled organization change. She is the author/coauthor of five books and numerous articles in journals such as *MIS Quarterly, Information Systems Research, Journal of Management Information Systems, Organization Science,* and *Management Science.* She was named Fellow of the Association for Information Systems in 2004.

**Anne P. Massey** is the Dean's Research Professor and Lilly Faculty Fellow of Information Systems in the Kelley School of Business at Indiana University. She received her Ph.D. in decision sciences and engineering systems from Rensselaer Polytechnic Institute. Prior to receiving her Ph.D., she held positions with General Electric and IBM. Dr. Massey has conducted research on knowledge management, computer-mediated communication, technology adoption and implementation, business process transformation, and related topics. Her research has been published in *Decision Sciences, MIS Quarterly, Journal of Management Information Systems, Academy of Management Journal,* and *IEEE Transactions on Engineering Management,* among others. She is a member of the Institute for Electrical and Electronics Engineers (IEEE), Association for Information Systems, the Academy of Management, and Decision Sciences Institute.

**Mitzi M. Montoya-Weiss** is a professor of marketing and innovation management at North Carolina State University in Raleigh. She holds a Ph.D. in marketing and a B.S. in general engineering from Michigan State University. Dr. Montoya-Weiss has held positions or consulted with IBM, Allied Signal (Bendix Heavy Vehicle Systems), ABB, Menasha Paperboard, and Fusion Ventures LLP. She has published in the *Academy of Management Journal, Marketing Science, Management Science, Journal of Product Innovation Management, Journal of International Marketing, IEEE Transactions on Engineering Management,* and *European Journal of Marketing,* among others. Her research interests include product design optimization, new product development process management, and the use of advanced information technologies in marketing and new product development.

**Nuno Melão** is an assistant professor at the Catholic University of Portugal, where he teaches information systems, operations management, and management science courses to both graduate and postgraduate students. He received his M.S. and Ph.D. in management science from Lancaster University. His research interests focus on business process management, business process transformation, business process modeling and simulation, and e-business processes. His papers have appeared in the *Information Systems Journal, Journal of the Operational Research Society, International Journal of Management and Decision Making,* and *European Journal of Operational Research.* Dr. Melão is coexecutive editor of *International Journal of Simulation and Process Modelling* and serves on the editorial boards of the *International Journal of e-Business Research* and *International Journal of Business Process Integration and Management.*

**Sue Newell** is the Cammarata Professor of Management at Bentley College, a visiting professor at Royal Holloway, University of London, and an associate fellow at Warwick Business School. She graduated with first-class honors in psychology from Cardiff University, where she completed her Ph.D. She previously worked at Nottingham Trent, Birmingham, Aston, and Warwick universities. Dr. Newell was a founding member of IKON (the Innovation, Knowledge and Organizational Networks Research Centre), and she continues to research in this area. Other research interests include business and information technology and discrimination policies and practices. She has published extensively in a number of books and journals.

**Mark E. Nissen** is Assistant Secretary of Defense Chair Professor of Command & Control, and professor of information science and management at the Naval Postgraduate School. His research focuses on dynamic knowledge and organization for competitive advantage. He views work, technology, and organization as an integrated design problem, and has concentrated recently on the phenomenology of knowledge flows, culminating in his second book, entitled *Harnessing Knowledge Dynamics: Principled Organizational Knowing & Learning* (IRM Press, 2006). Dr. Nissen's extensive publications span information systems, project management, organization studies, knowledge management, counterterrorism, and related fields. In 2000, he received the Menneken Faculty Award for Excellence in Scientific Research, the top research award available to faculty at the Naval Postgraduate School. In 2001, he received a prestigious Young Investigator Grant Award from the Office of Naval Research for work on knowledge-flow theory. In 2002–3, he was visiting professor at Stanford, integrating knowledge-flow theory into agent-based tools for computational modeling. In 2004, he established the Center for Edge Power for multi-university, multidisciplinary research on what the military terms command & control. Before his information systems doctoral work at the University of Southern California (Ph.D., in 1996), he acquired over a dozen years' management experience in the aerospace and electronics industries.

**Tony O'Driscoll** serves as a professor of the practice at North Carolina State University's College of Management. He is credited with advancing both Nortel's and IBM's strategic thought leadership in formal and informal learning. Dr. O'Driscoll's research projects include the application of peer to peer technology to improve information sharing among workers and an examination of Massively Multiplayer Online Role Playing environments to study leadership in the enterprise of the future. He is a fellow with the American Society for Training and Development (ASTD), and he is a member of the editorial board for *Human Resources Development Quarterly*. Dr. O'Driscoll has contributed to science via publications in journals such as *Journal of Management Information Systems, MIS Quarterly, Performance Improvement Quarterly,* and *Journal of Product and Innovation Management.*

**Michael Pidd** is a professor of management science and an associate dean (research) at the Lancaster University Management School in the United Kingdom. He is author and editor of four books published by John Wiley: *Computer Simulation in Management Science* (5th ed.), *Tools for Thinking: Modelling in Management Science* (2d ed.), *Computer Modelling for Discrete Simulation,* and *Systems Modelling: Theory and Practice.* He is a past president of the Operational Research Society and was awarded its President's Medal for a paper on computer simulation. As part of the UK's Advanced Institute of Management Research, he has just completed a research fellowship examining the use of performance measurement in public services. His current research interests include modeling, discrete simulation, and performance measurement.

**Suprateek Sarker** is an associate professor of information systems and International Business Institute interim director at Washington State University, Pullman. He has served as visiting faculty at Copenhagen Business School, Denmark, Helsinki School of Economics, Finland, Cesar-Ritz University Center, Switzerland, and National Economics University, Vietnam. He received his Ph.D. from the University of Cincinnati. Dr. Sarker's research primarily utilizes qualitative methodologies to study IT-enabled organization change, systems implementation, global IS management, and virtual and mobile collaboration. His research has been published or is forthcoming in outlets such as *Journal of the AIS, Journal of Management Information Systems, IEEE Transactions on Engineering Management, European Journal of Information Systems, IEEE Transactions on*

*Professional Communication, Information & Management, Data Base, Journal of Strategic Information Systems, Information Resources Management Journal, Communications of the ACM, Communications of the AIS,* and ICIS.

**Joseph Sarkis** is a professor of operations and environmental management in the Graduate School of Management at Clark University. He earned his Ph.D. from the University of Buffalo. He has published widely on topics such as management of technology, operations management, corporate environmental management, and enterprise engineering. He is a member of numerous professional organizations and serves on a variety of journal editorial boards.

**Harry Scarbrough** is a professor at Warwick Business School, director of the ESRC (Economic and Social Research Council) program on the Evolution of Business Knowledge (www.ebkresearch. org), and cofounder of the Knowledge and Innovation Network (KIN) (www.ki-network.org). His Ph.D. work was carried out at the Technology Policy Unit, Aston University. His subsequent research on knowledge and learning in organizations has been published in a number of books and articles in the management and organization studies fields.

**R.P. Sundarraj** is an associate professor of information systems at the University of Waterloo. He obtained his B.S. in electrical engineering from the University of Madras, India, and his M.S. and Ph.D. in management and computer sciences from the University of Tennessee, Knoxville. Professor Sundarraj's teaching and research encompass the development of methodologies for the efficient design and management of emerging information systems, as well as the use of massively parallel computing for solving large-scale problems. He has published in various national and international journals such as *Mathematical Programming, IEEE Transactions on Power Systems, ACM Transactions on Mathematical Software,* and *European Journal of Operational Research.* In addition, he has provided e-commerce solutions for marketing and inventory-management problems arising in Fortune 100 companies.

**Jacky Swan** is a professor of organizational behavior at Warwick Business School, University of Warwick. She completed her Ph.D. in psychology at Cardiff. She is a founding member of IKON—a research center in innovation knowledge and organizational networks—and conducts her research in related areas. Her current interests are in linking innovation and networking to processes of managing knowledge across different industry sectors and national contexts. She has been responsible for a number of UK Research Council projects in innovation and is currently working on projects investigating managing knowledge in project-based environments and the evolution of biomedical knowledge for interactive innovation in the United Kingdom and United States. She has published widely, including articles in *Organization Studies, Organization, Human Relations,* and the coauthored book, *Managing Knowledge Work* (Palgrave, 2002). She is a senior editor for *Organization Studies.*

**Michael Tushman** is the Paul R. Lawrence, MBA Class of 1942 Professor of Business Administration at the Graduate School of Business, Harvard University. He received his Ph.D. from the Sloan School of Management at MIT and was previously the Phillip Hettleman Professor of Business at the Graduate School of Business, Columbia University. Professor Tushman's research focuses on the relations between technological change, executive leadership, and organization adaptation. He has published numerous articles in many top journals, including *Administrative Science Quarterly, Management Science,* and *Academy of Management Journal,* and has also published several books on innovation, change, and organization design. He is a fellow of the Academy of Management and has received distinguished scholar awards in both the Technology and Innovation Management and Organization Management and Theory divisions of the Academy of Management.

**Ping Wang** is on the faculty of the University of Maryland at College Park. He received his Ph.D. from UCLA Anderson School of Management. His current research addresses how information technology innovations shape and are shaped by entrepreneurship, organizations, and institutions.

**Leslie Willcocks** is a professor of technology work and globalization at the London School of Economics. He is also an associate fellow at Templeton College, Oxford, an associate professor at the University of Melbourne, and a visiting professor at two other universities. He holds a Ph.D. in information systems from the University of Cambridge. For the past 14 years he has been editor in chief of *Journal of Information Technology*. He is coauthor of 24 books and has published over 150 papers in journals such as *Harvard Business Review, Sloan Management Review, California Management Review, MIS Quarterly, MISQ Executive,* and *Journal of Management Studies.* In February 2001, he won the PriceWaterhouseCoopers/Michael Corbett and Associates World Outsourcing Achievement Award for his contribution to this field. He is a regular keynote speaker at international practitioner and academic conferences, has extensive consulting experience, and is regularly retained as an adviser by major corporations and government institutions. His latest book, with Mary Lacity, is *Global Sourcing of Business and IT Services* (Palgrave, 2006).

# SERIES EDITOR

**Vladimir Zwass** is the University Distinguished Professor of Computer Science and Management Information Systems at Fairleigh Dickinson University. He holds a Ph.D. in Computer Science from Columbia University. Professor Zwass is the Founding Editor-in-Chief of the *Journal of Management Information Systems,* one of the three top-ranked journals in the field of Information Systems; the journal has celebrated 20 years in publication. He is also the Founding Editor-in-Chief of the *International Journal of Electronic Commerce,* ranked as the top journal in its field. More recently, Dr. Zwass has been the Founding Editor-in-Chief of the monograph series *Advances in Management Information Systems,* whose objective is to codify the knowledge and research methods in the field. Dr. Zwass is the author of six books and several book chapters, including entries in the *Encyclopaedia Britannica,* as well as of a number of papers in various journals and conference proceedings. He has received several grants, consulted for a number of major corporations, and is a frequent speaker to national and international audiences. He is a former member of the Professional Staff of the International Atomic Energy Agency in Vienna, Austria.

# INDEX